Thank you for picking up volume 17! Most of the coloring I do is digital, but I've also dabbled in analog. Conclusion? Analog is more fun.

KOHEI HORIKOSHI

MY HERO ACADEMIA

17

SHONEN JUMP Manga Edition

STORY & ART KOHEI HORIKOSHI

TRANSLATION & ENGLISH ADAPTATION **Caleb Cook**
TOUCH-UP ART & LETTERING **John Hunt**
DESIGNER **Julian [JR] Robinson**
SHONEN JUMP SERIES EDITOR **John Bae**
GRAPHIC NOVEL EDITOR **Mike Montesa**

BOKU NO HERO ACADEMIA © 2014 by Kohei Horikoshi
All rights reserved.
First published in Japan in 2014 by SHUEISHA Inc., Tokyo.
English translation rights arranged by SHUEISHA Inc.

The stories, characters and incidents mentioned in this publication are entirely fictional.

Printed in the U.S.A.

Published by VIZ Media, LLC
P.O. Box 77010
San Francisco, CA 94107

10 9 8 7 6 5 4 3 2 1
First printing, February 2019

PARENTAL ADVISORY
MY HERO ACADEMIA is rated T for Teen
and is recommended for ages 13 and up.
This volume contains fantasy violence.

MY HERO ACADEMIA

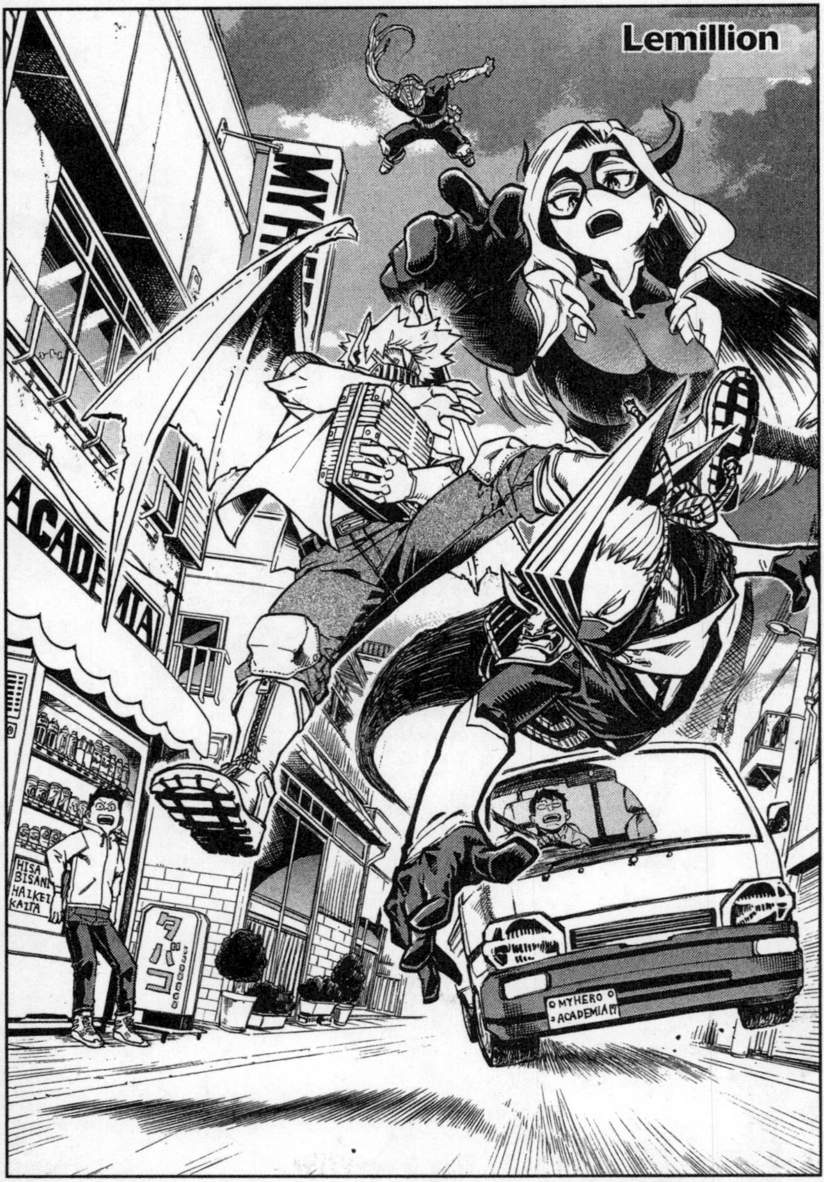
Lemillion
ACADEMIA
HISA BISANI HAIKEI KAITA
MYHERO ACADEMIA 17

KOHEI HORIKOSHI

SHONENJUMP MANGA

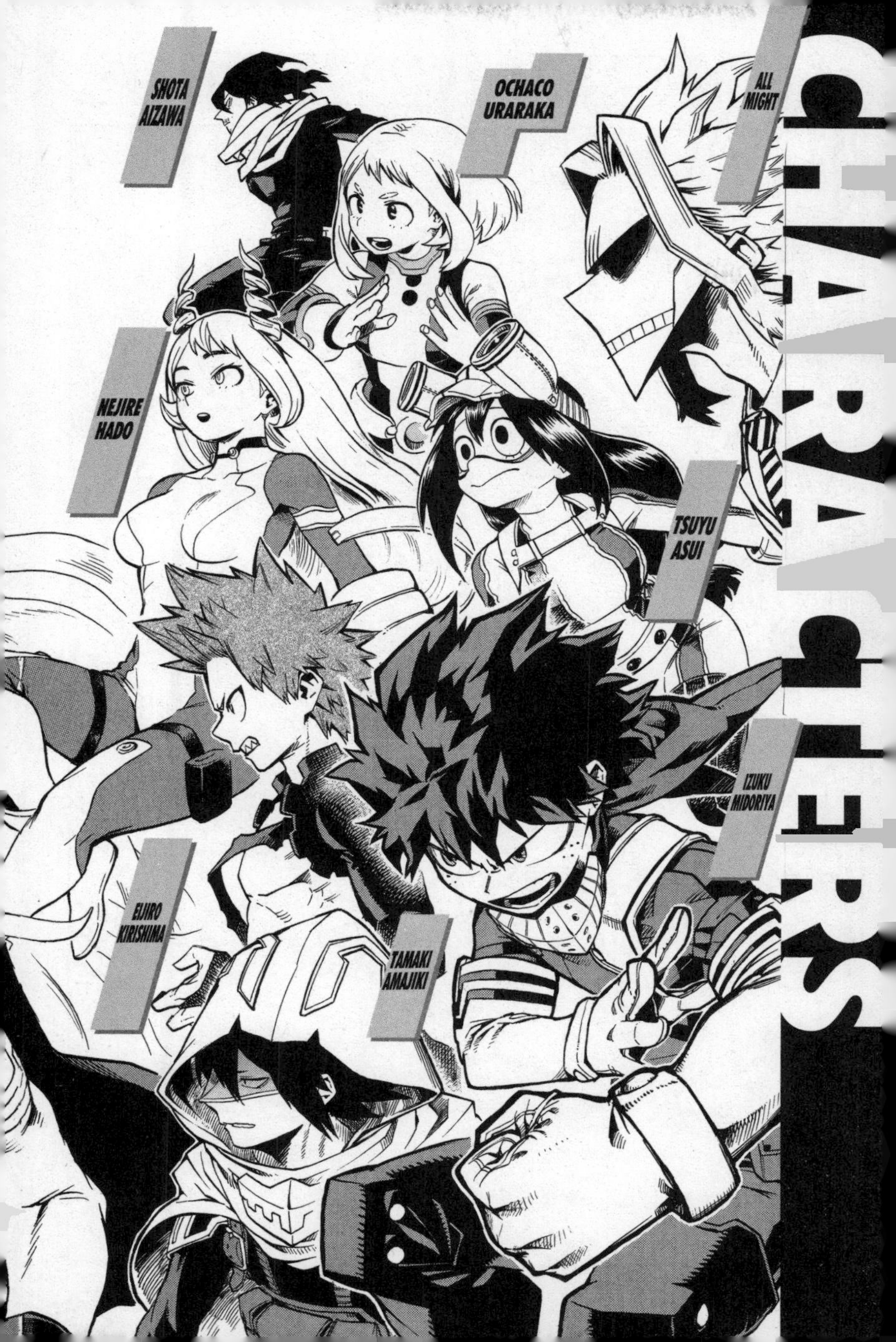
CHARACTERS
ALL MIGHT
OCHACO URARAKA
SHOTA AIZAWA
TSUYU ASUI
NEJIRE HADO
IZUKU MIDORIYA
TAMAKI AMAJIKI
EIJIRO KIRISHIMA

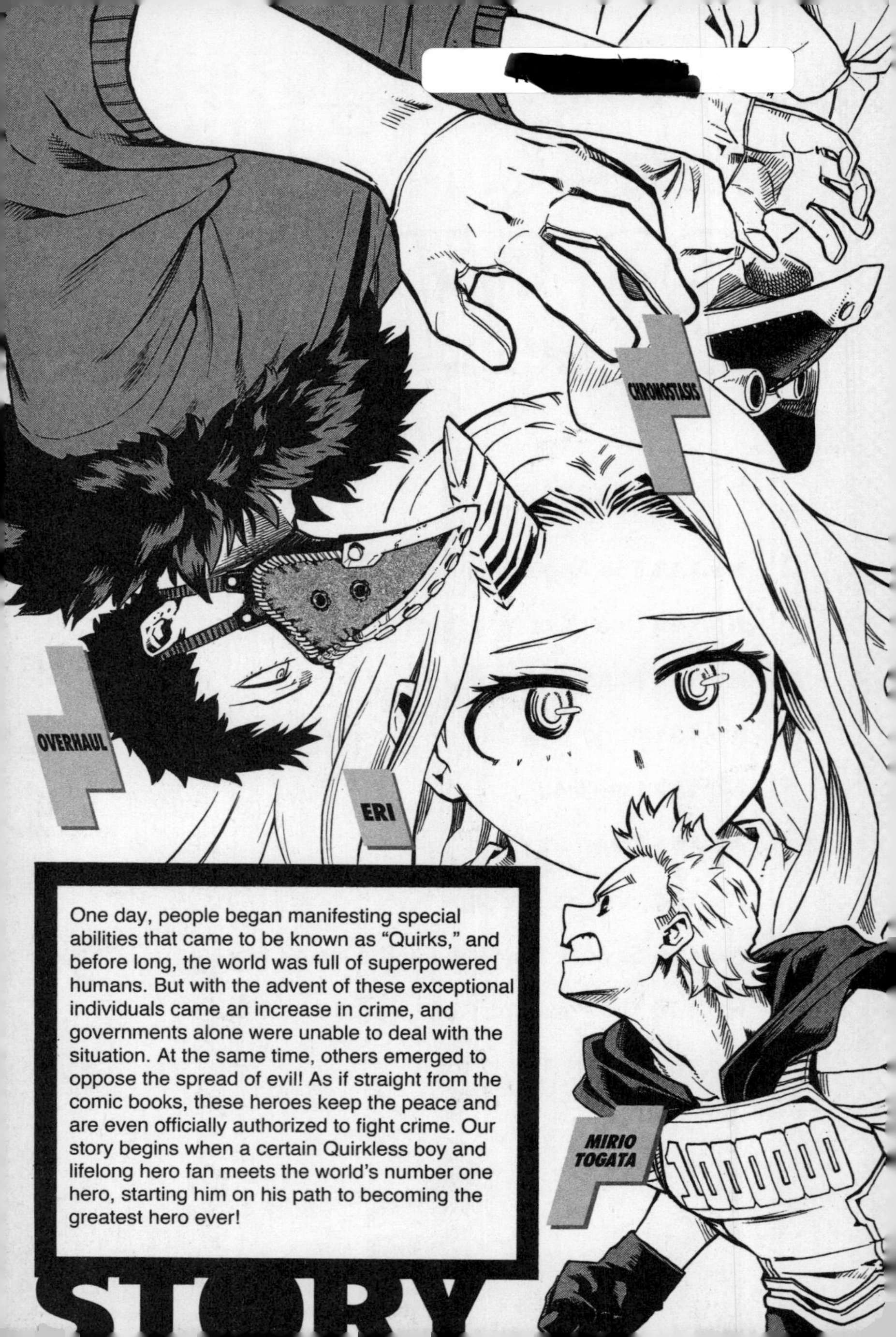
[redacted]
CHRONOSTASIS
OVERHAUL
ERI
MIRIO TOGATA
1000000

STORY

One day, people began manifesting special abilities that came to be known as "Quirks," and before long, the world was full of superpowered humans. But with the advent of these exceptional individuals came an increase in crime, and governments alone were unable to deal with the situation. At the same time, others emerged to oppose the spread of evil! As if straight from the comic books, these heroes keep the peace and are even officially authorized to fight crime. Our story begins when a certain Quirkless boy and lifelong hero fan meets the world's number one hero, starting him on his path to becoming the greatest hero ever!

Vol. 17

MY HERO ACADEMIA

CONTENTS

Lemillion

EXCITED
EXCITED
EXCITED

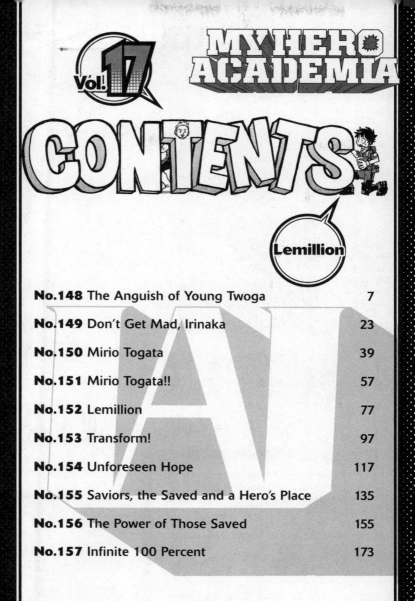

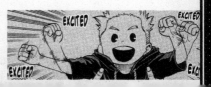

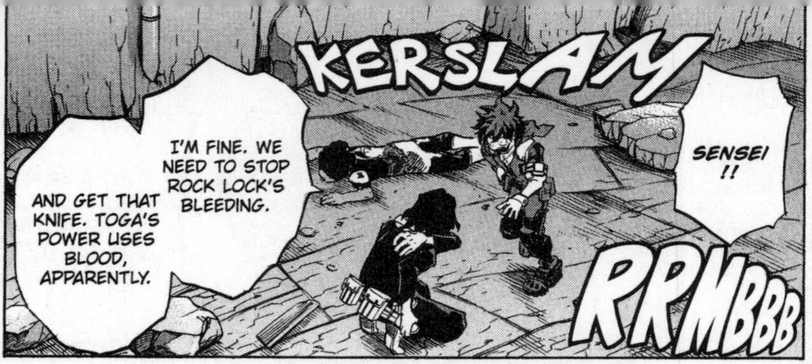
SENSEI !!
KERSLAM
RRMBBB
I'M FINE. WE NEED TO STOP ROCK LOCK'S BLEEDING.
AND GET THAT KNIFE. TOGA'S POWER USES BLOOD, APPARENTLY.

No. 148 - The Anguish of Young Twoga

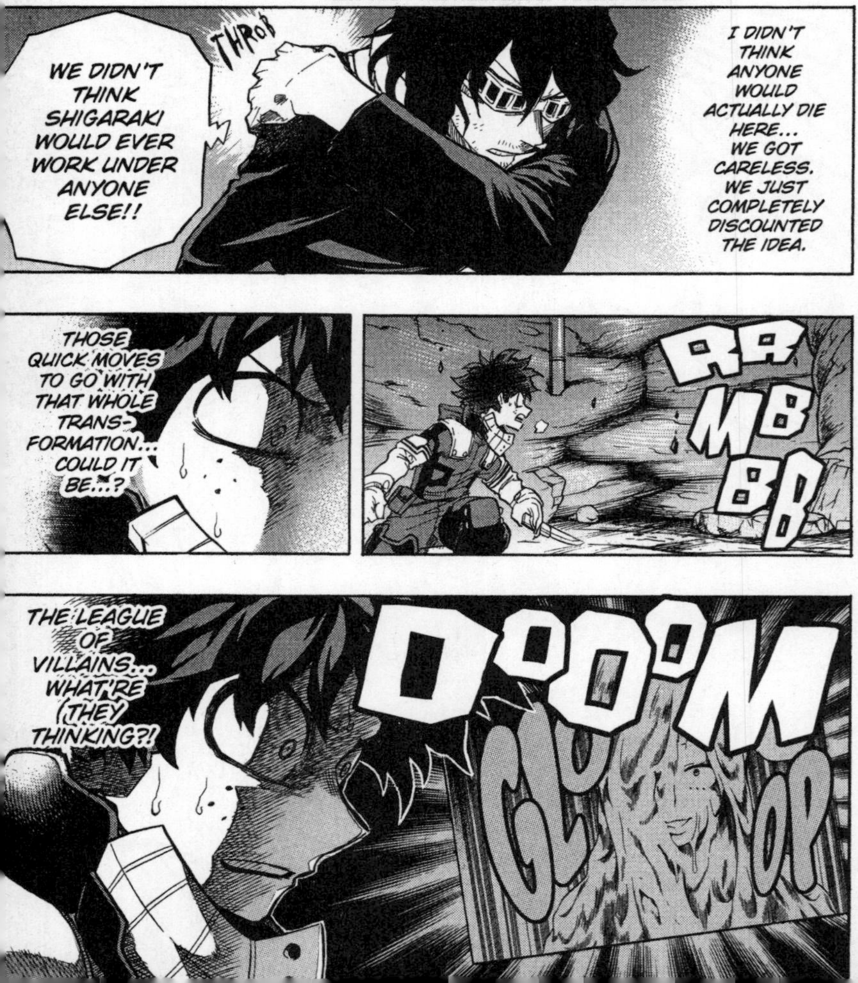
I DIDN'T THINK ANYONE WOULD ACTUALLY DIE HERE... WE GOT CARELESS. WE JUST COMPLETELY DISCOUNTED THE IDEA.
THROB
WE DIDN'T THINK SHIGARAKI WOULD EVER WORK UNDER ANYONE ELSE!!
RRMBBB
THOSE QUICK MOVES TO GO WITH THAT WHOLE TRANS-FORMATION... COULD IT BE...?
DOOOM
GLOOP
THE LEAGUE OF VILLAINS... WHAT'RE THEY THINKING?!

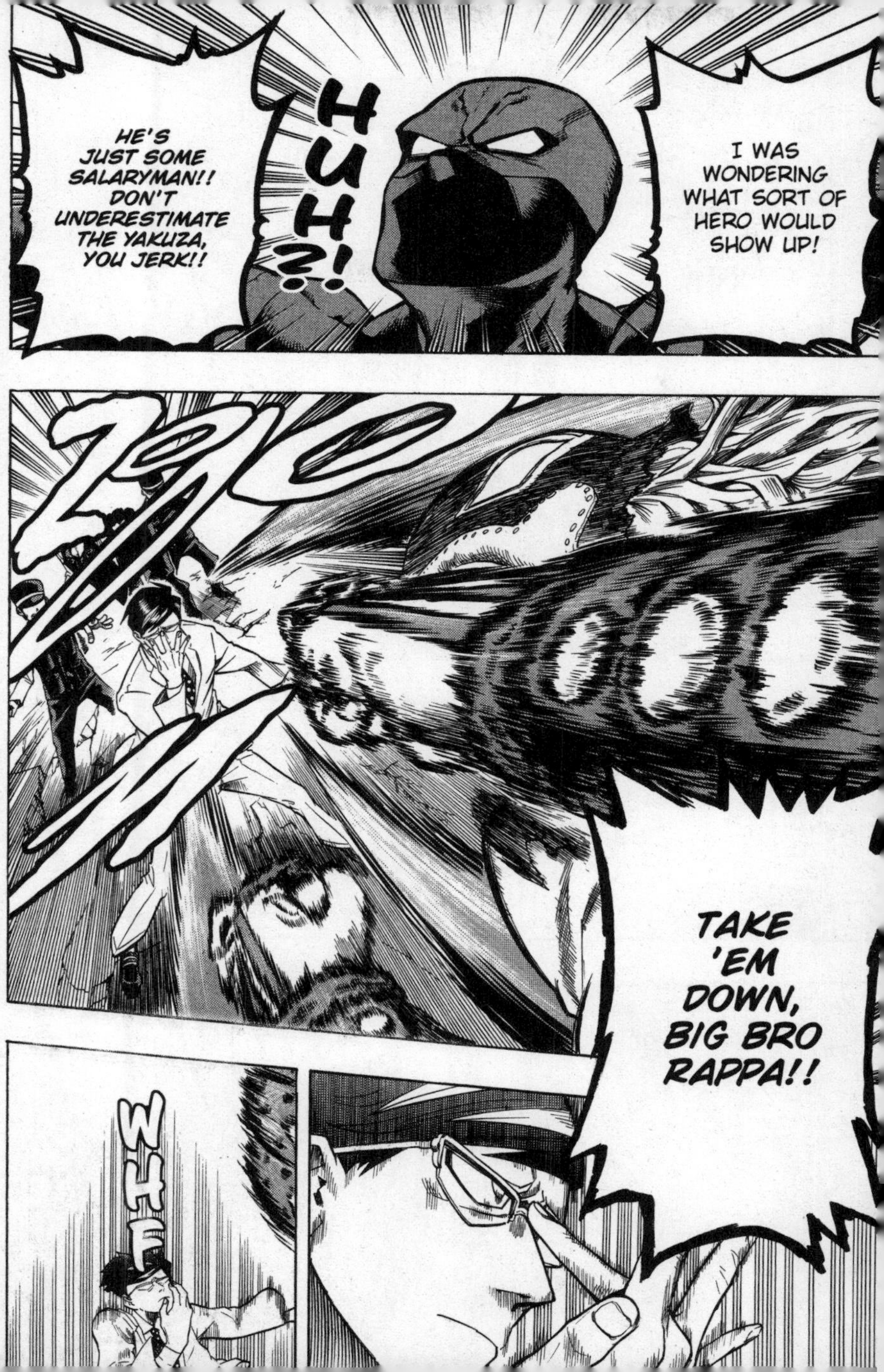
I WAS WONDERING WHAT SORT OF HERO WOULD SHOW UP!
HUH?!
HE'S JUST SOME SALARYMAN!! DON'T UNDERESTIMATE THE YAKUZA, YOU JERK!!
TAKE 'EM DOWN, BIG BRO RAPPA!!
WHF

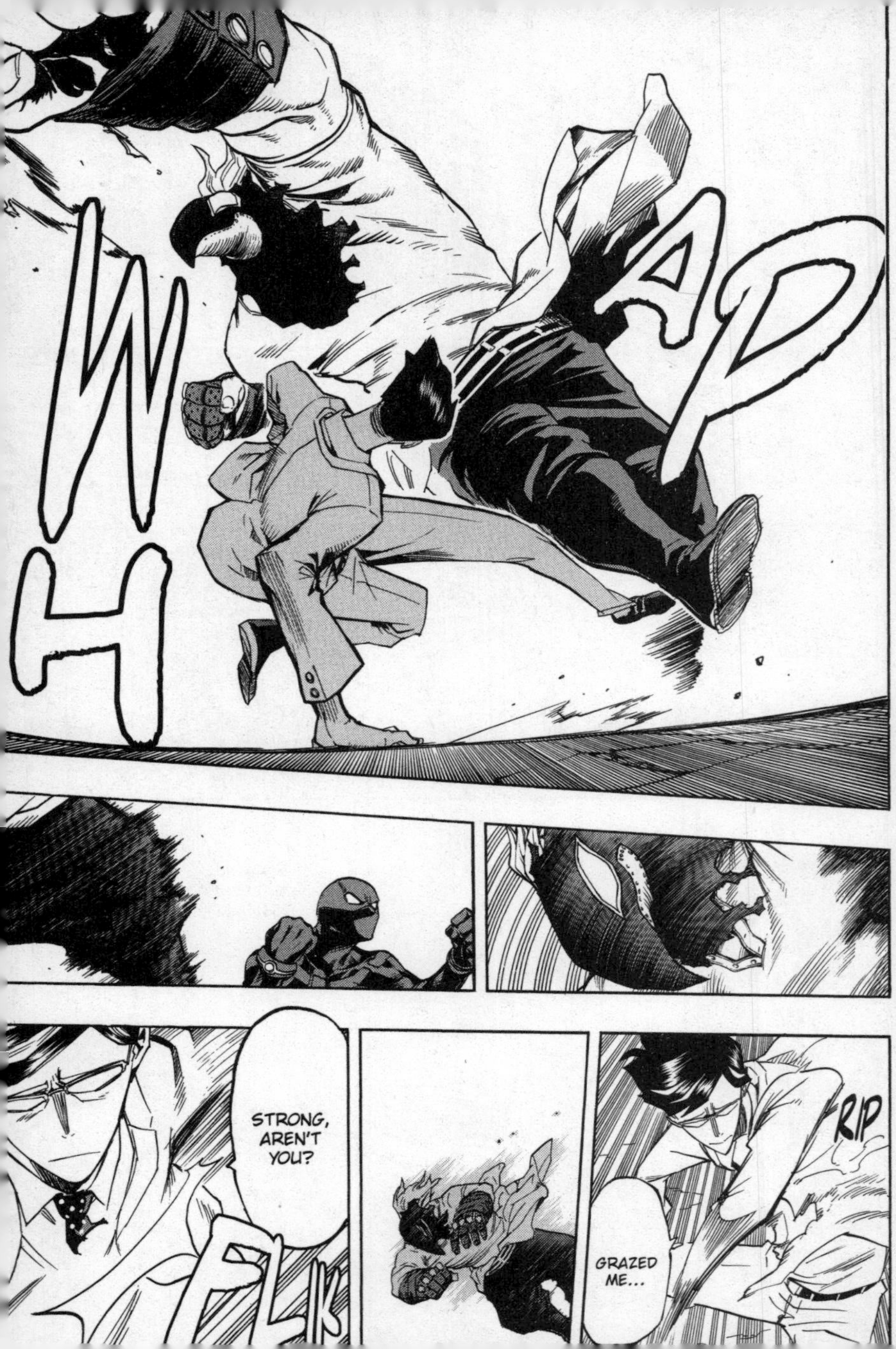
WHAP
RIP
GRAZED ME...
STRONG, AREN'T YOU?
FLK

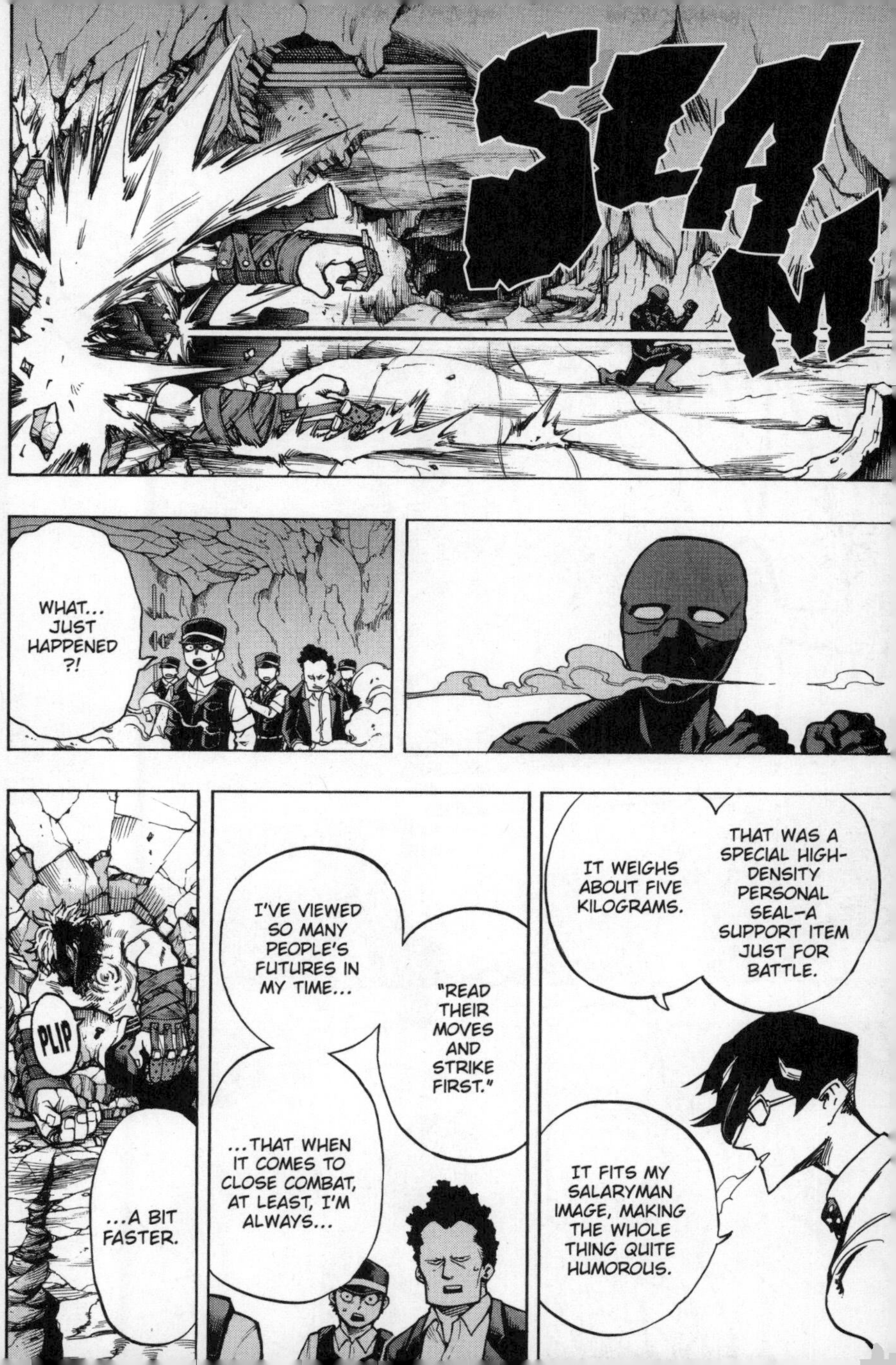
SLAM
WHAT... JUST HAPPENED ?!
THAT WAS A SPECIAL HIGH-DENSITY PERSONAL SEAL—A SUPPORT ITEM JUST FOR BATTLE.
IT WEIGHS ABOUT FIVE KILOGRAMS.
IT FITS MY SALARYMAN IMAGE, MAKING THE WHOLE THING QUITE HUMOROUS.
I'VE VIEWED SO MANY PEOPLE'S FUTURES IN MY TIME...
"READ THEIR MOVES AND STRIKE FIRST."
...THAT WHEN IT COMES TO CLOSE COMBAT, AT LEAST, I'M ALWAYS...
PLIP
...A BIT FASTER.

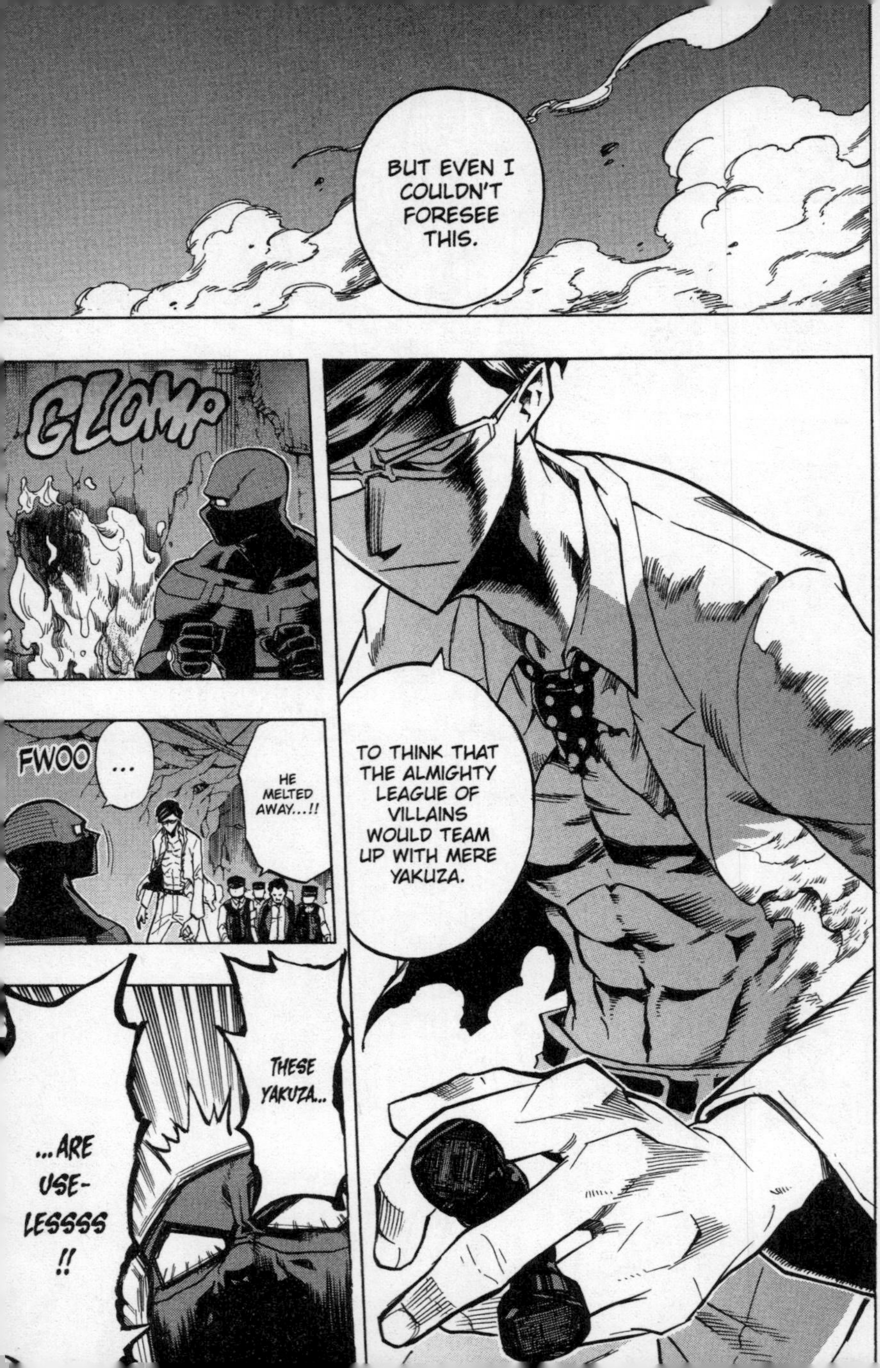
BUT EVEN I COULDN'T FORESEE THIS.
TO THINK THAT THE ALMIGHTY LEAGUE OF VILLAINS WOULD TEAM UP WITH MERE YAKUZA.
GLOMP
HE MELTED AWAY...!!
...
FWOO
THESE YAKUZA...
...ARE USE-LESSSS!!

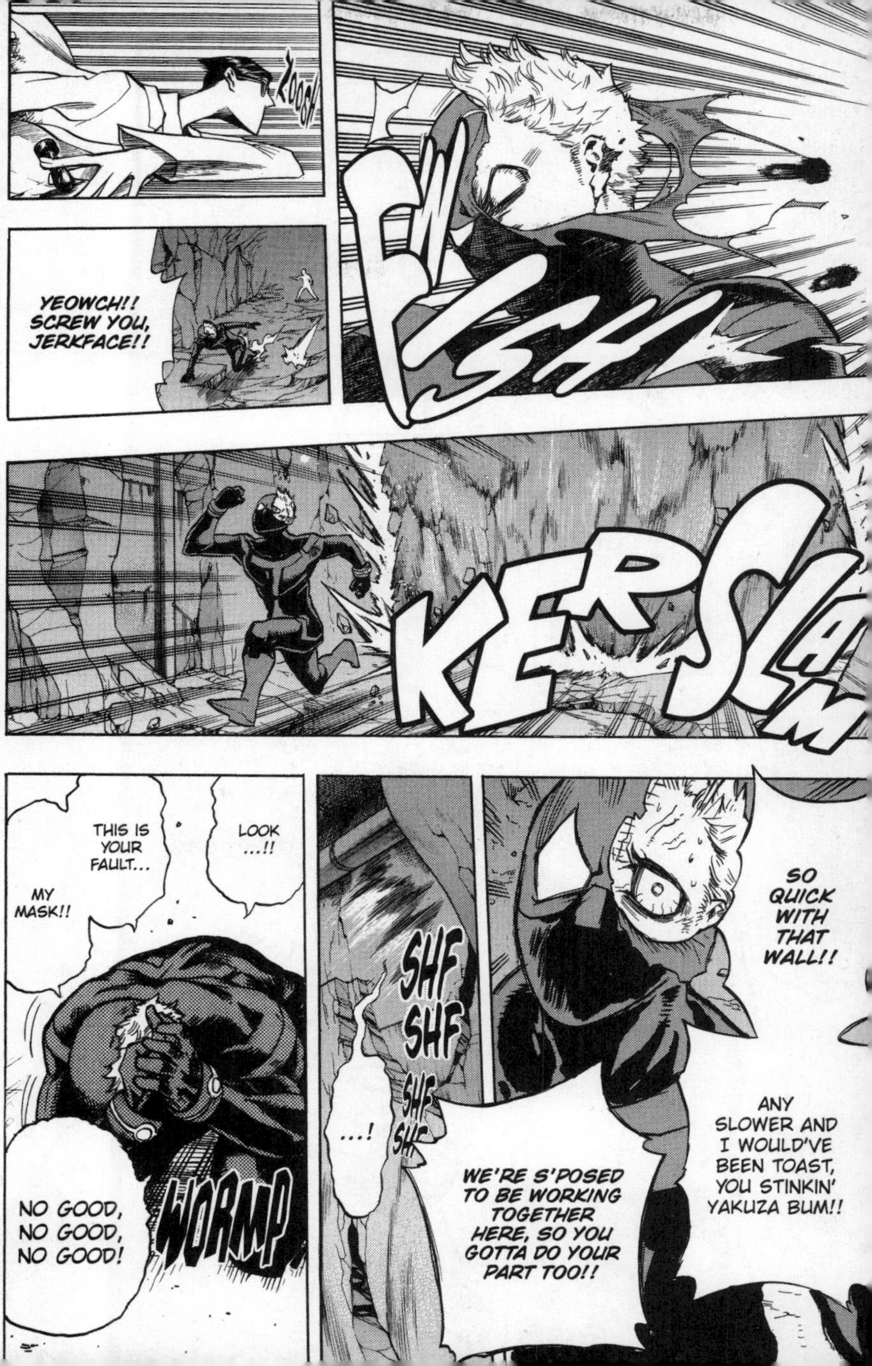
FWISH
ZOOSH
YEOWCH!! SCREW YOU, JERKFACE!!
KERSLAM
SO QUICK WITH THAT WALL!!
ANY SLOWER AND I WOULD'VE BEEN TOAST, YOU STINKIN' YAKUZA BUM!!
WE'RE S'POSED TO BE WORKING TOGETHER HERE, SO YOU GOTTA DO YOUR PART TOO!!
SHF SHF SHF SHF
...!
LOOK ...!!
THIS IS YOUR FAULT...
MY MASK!!
WORMP
NO GOOD, NO GOOD, NO GOOD!

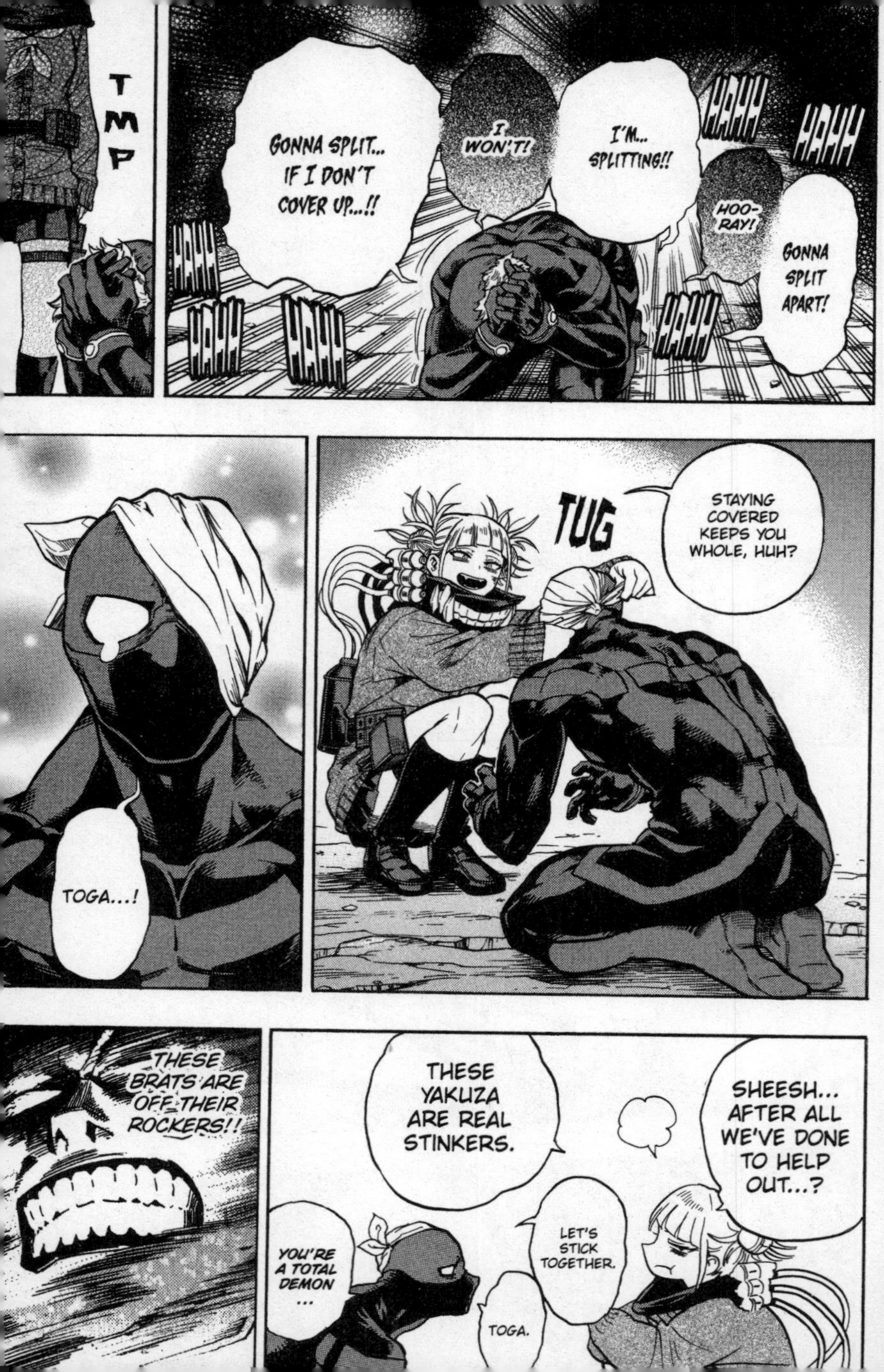
HAAH
HAAH
GONNA SPLIT APART!
HOO-RAY!
I'M... SPLITTING!!
I WON'T!
GONNA SPLIT... IF I DON'T COVER UP...!!
HAAH
HAAH
HAAH
HAAH
TMP
STAYING COVERED KEEPS YOU WHOLE, HUH?
TUG
TOGA...!
SHEESH... AFTER ALL WE'VE DONE TO HELP OUT...?
THESE YAKUZA ARE REAL STINKERS.
LET'S STICK TOGETHER.
TOGA.
YOU'RE A TOTAL DEMON ...
THESE BRATS ARE OFF THEIR ROCKERS!!

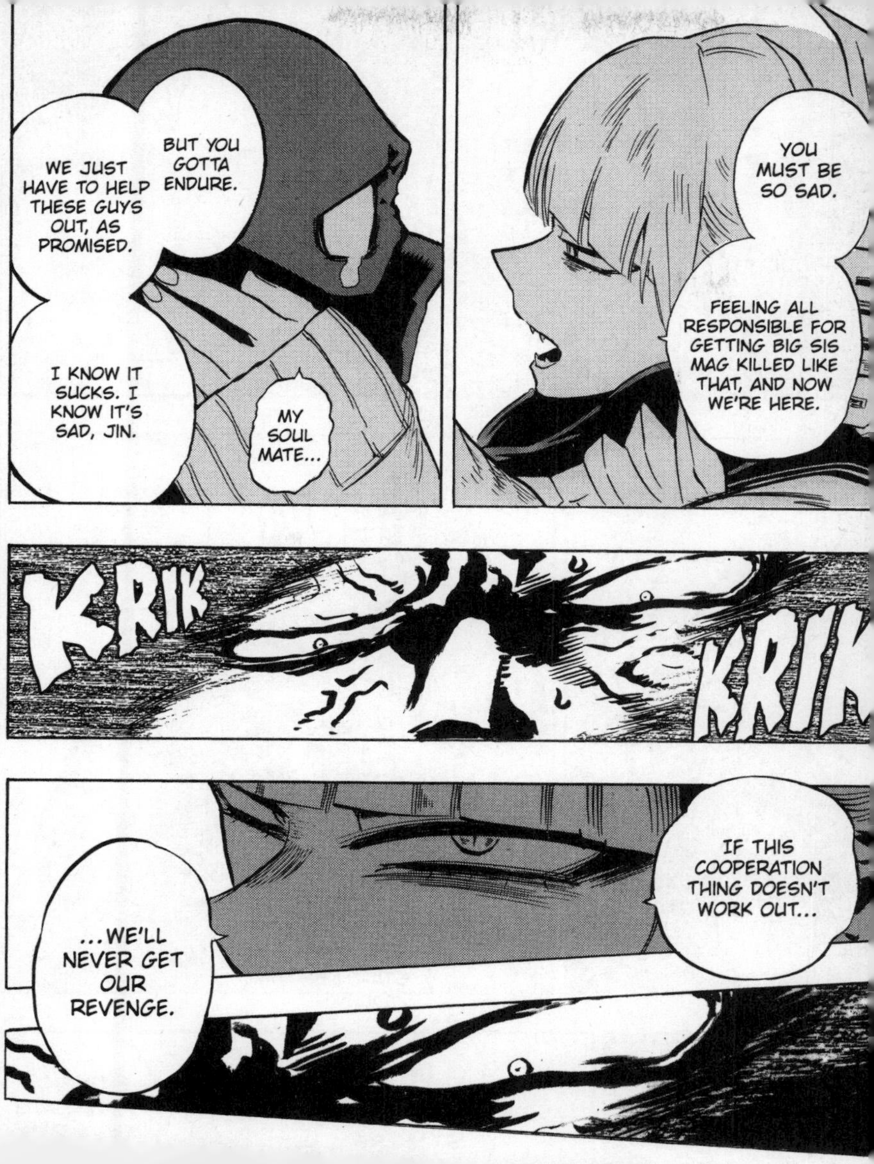
YOU MUST BE SO SAD.
FEELING ALL RESPONSIBLE FOR GETTING BIG SIS MAG KILLED LIKE THAT, AND NOW WE'RE HERE.
BUT YOU GOTTA ENDURE.
WE JUST HAVE TO HELP THESE GUYS OUT, AS PROMISED.
MY SOUL MATE...
I KNOW IT SUCKS. I KNOW IT'S SAD, JIN.
KRIK
KRIK
IF THIS COOPERATION THING DOESN'T WORK OUT...
...WE'LL NEVER GET OUR REVENGE.

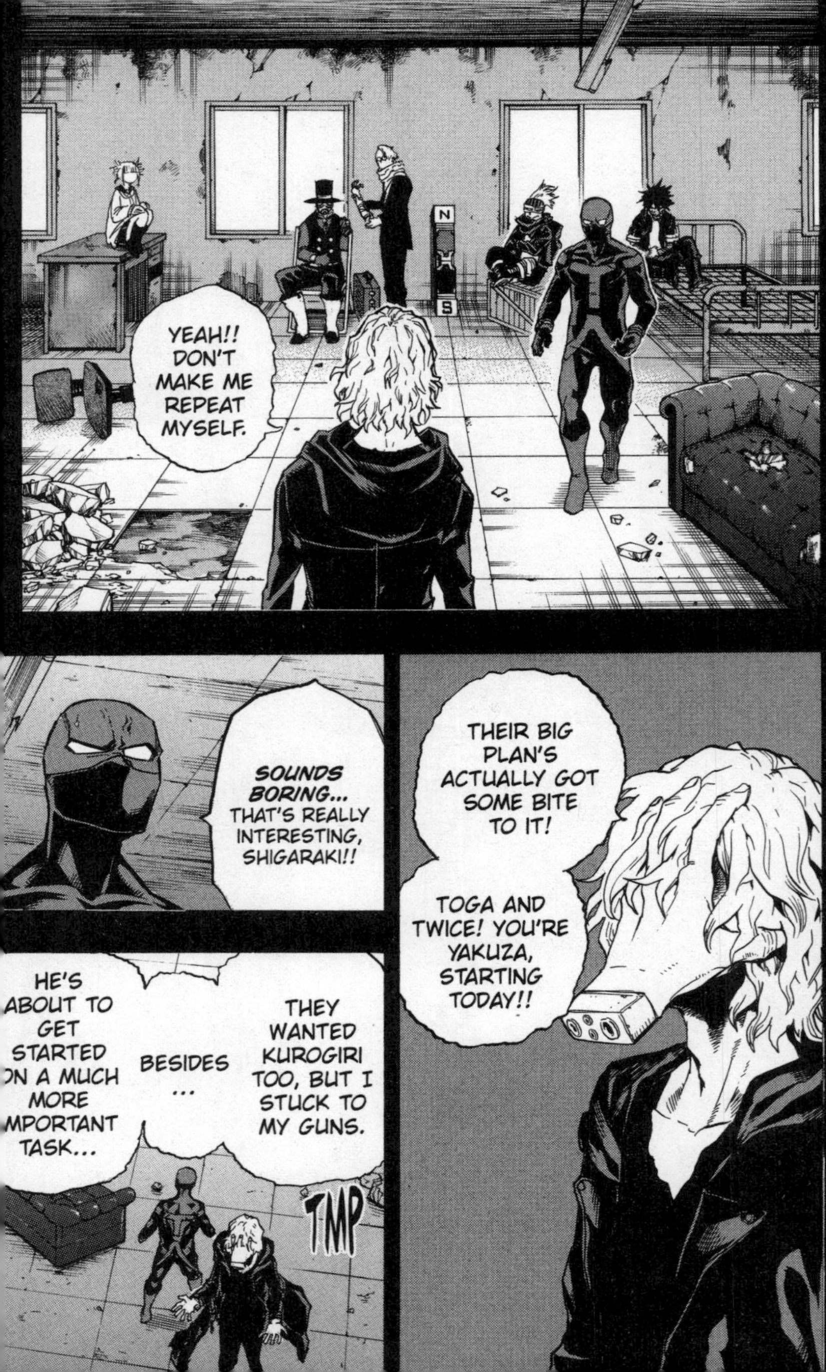
YEAH!! DON'T MAKE ME REPEAT MYSELF.
THEIR BIG PLAN'S ACTUALLY GOT SOME BITE TO IT!
TOGA AND TWICE! YOU'RE YAKUZA, STARTING TODAY!!
SOUNDS BORING... THAT'S REALLY INTERESTING, SHIGARAKI!!
THEY WANTED KUROGIRI TOO, BUT I STUCK TO MY GUNS.
BESIDES ...
HE'S ABOUT TO GET STARTED ON A MUCH MORE IMPORTANT TASK...
TMP

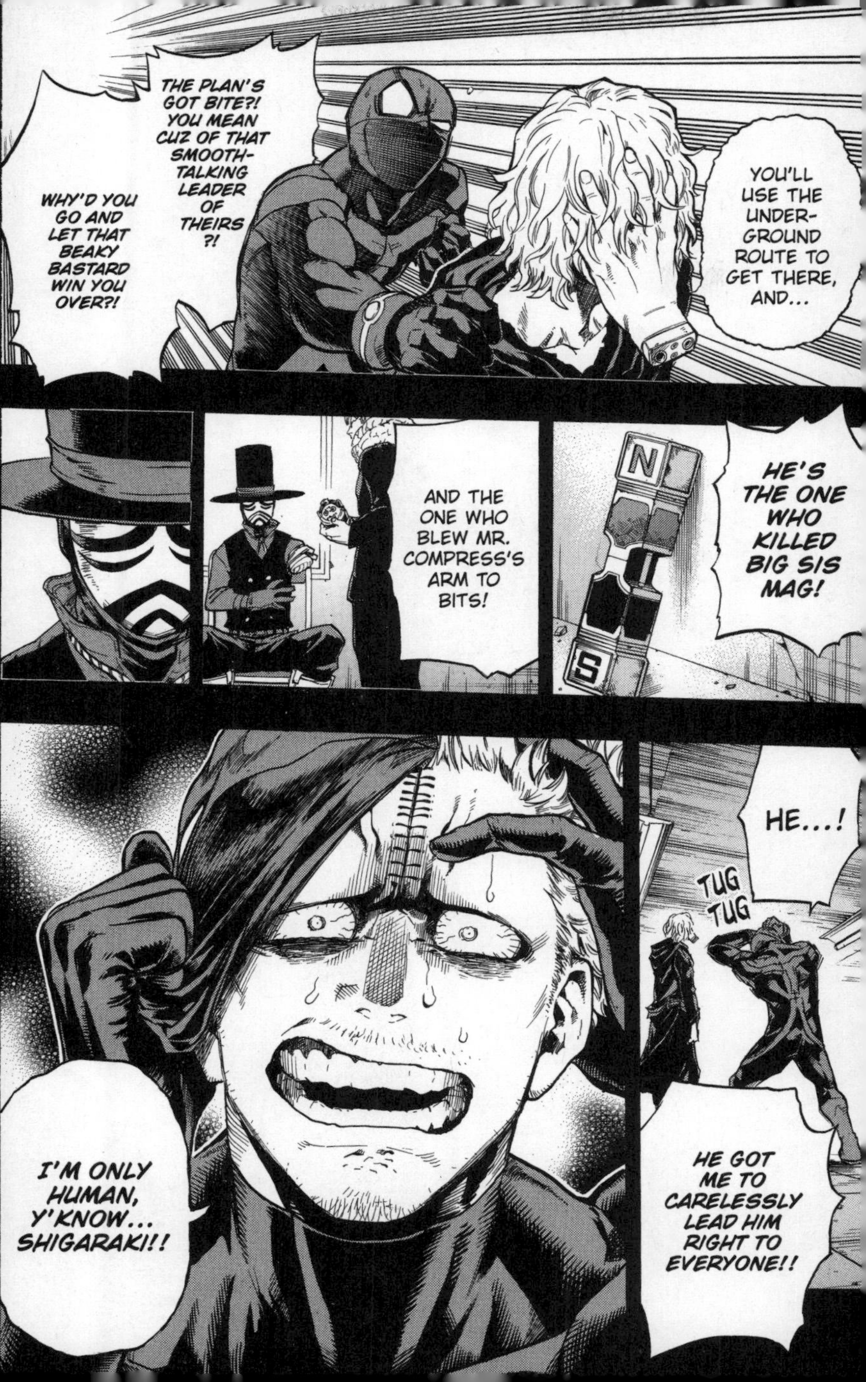
YOU'LL USE THE UNDERGROUND ROUTE TO GET THERE, AND...
THE PLAN'S GOT BITE?! YOU MEAN CUZ OF THAT SMOOTH-TALKING LEADER OF THEIRS?!
WHY'D YOU GO AND LET THAT BEAKY BASTARD WIN YOU OVER?!
HE'S THE ONE WHO KILLED BIG SIS MAG!
AND THE ONE WHO BLEW MR. COMPRESS'S ARM TO BITS!
HE...!
TUG TUG
HE GOT ME TO CARELESSLY LEAD HIM RIGHT TO EVERYONE!!
I'M ONLY HUMAN, Y'KNOW... SHIGARAKI!!

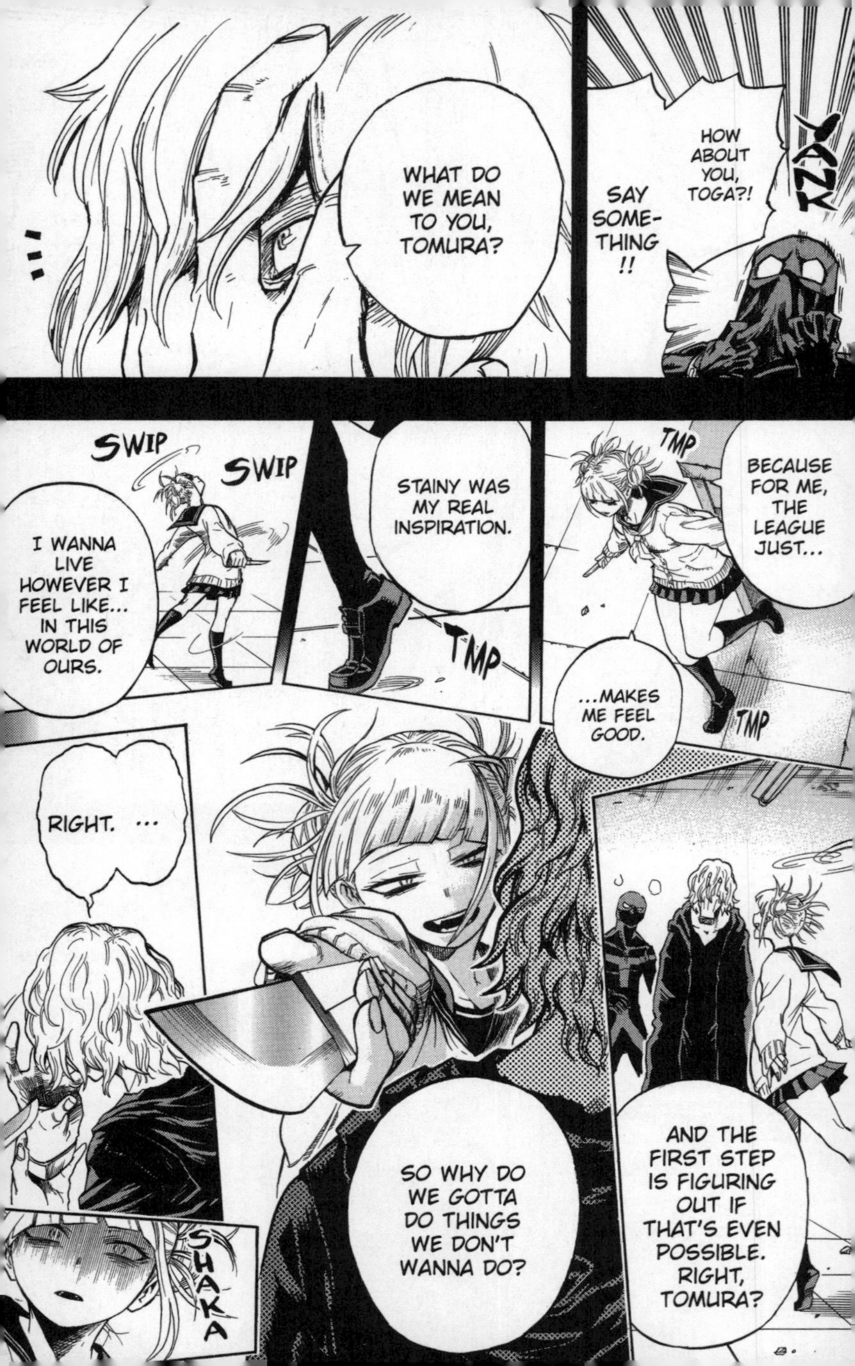
YANK
HOW ABOUT YOU, TOGA?!
SAY SOME-THING!!
WHAT DO WE MEAN TO YOU, TOMURA?
...
TMP
BECAUSE FOR ME, THE LEAGUE JUST...
...MAKES ME FEEL GOOD.
TMP
STAINY WAS MY REAL INSPIRATION.
TMP
SWIP
SWIP
I WANNA LIVE HOWEVER I FEEL LIKE... IN THIS WORLD OF OURS.
AND THE FIRST STEP IS FIGURING OUT IF THAT'S EVEN POSSIBLE. RIGHT, TOMURA?
SO WHY DO WE GOTTA DO THINGS WE DON'T WANNA DO?
RIGHT. ...
SHAKA

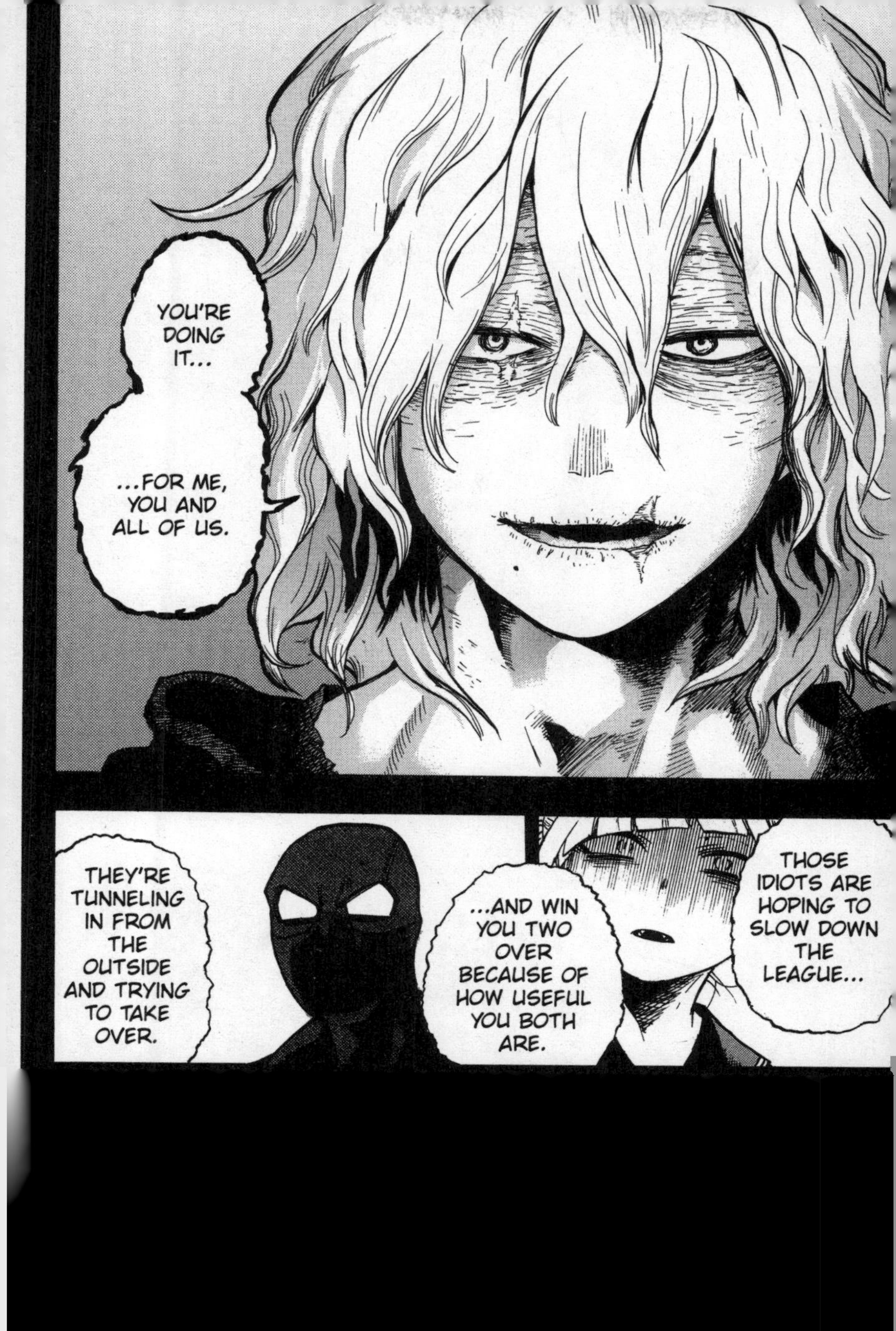
YOU'RE DOING IT...
...FOR ME, YOU AND ALL OF US.
THOSE IDIOTS ARE HOPING TO SLOW DOWN THE LEAGUE...
...AND WIN YOU TWO OVER BECAUSE OF HOW USEFUL YOU BOTH ARE.
THEY'RE TUNNELING IN FROM THE OUTSIDE AND TRYING TO TAKE OVER.

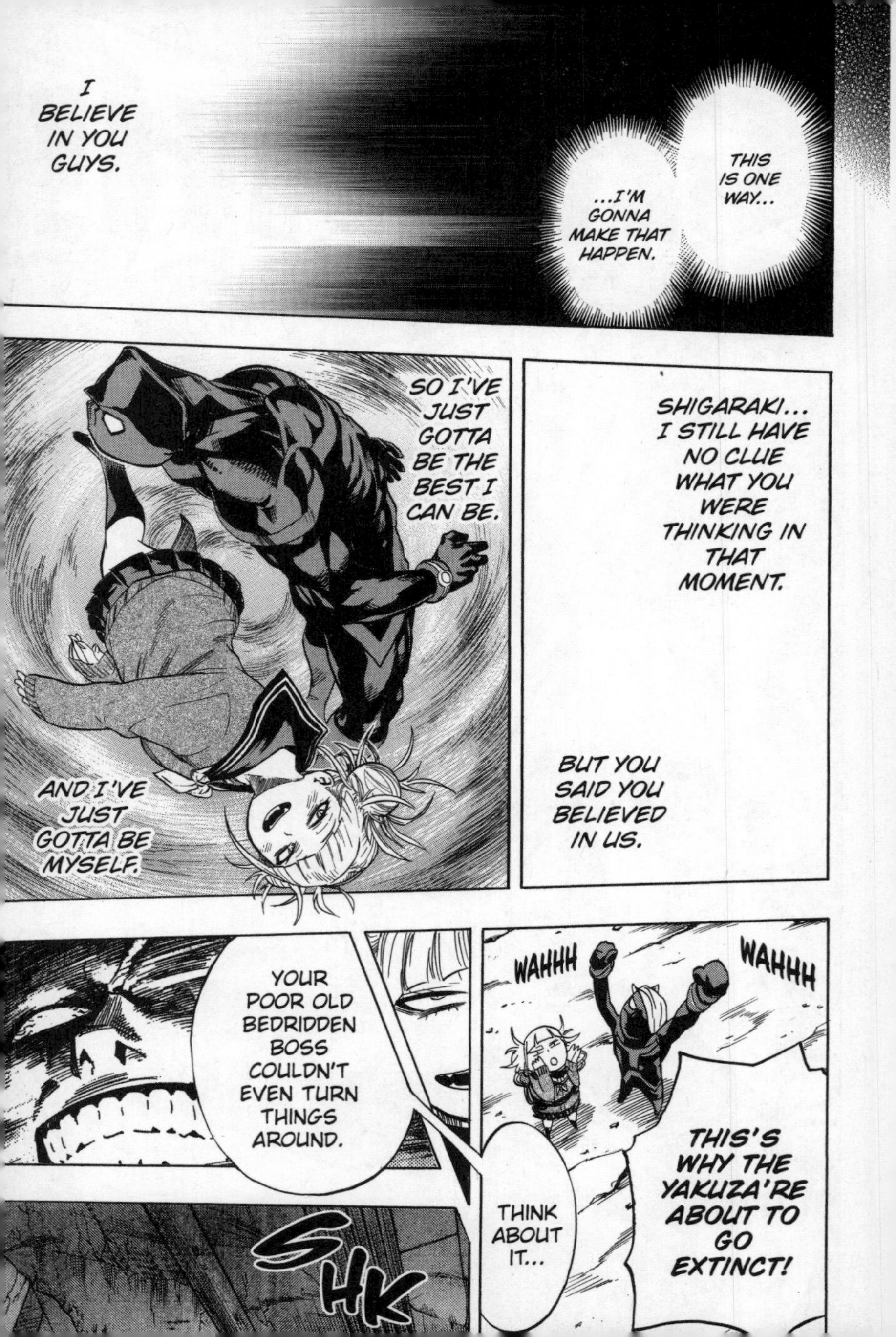
THIS IS ONE WAY...
...I'M GONNA MAKE THAT HAPPEN.
I BELIEVE IN YOU GUYS.
SHIGARAKI... I STILL HAVE NO CLUE WHAT YOU WERE THINKING IN THAT MOMENT.
BUT YOU SAID YOU BELIEVED IN US.
SO I'VE JUST GOTTA BE THE BEST I CAN BE.
AND I'VE JUST GOTTA BE MYSELF.
WAHHH
WAHHH
THIS'S WHY THE YAKUZA'RE ABOUT TO GO EXTINCT!
THINK ABOUT IT...
YOUR POOR OLD BEDRIDDEN BOSS COULDN'T EVEN TURN THINGS AROUND.
SHK

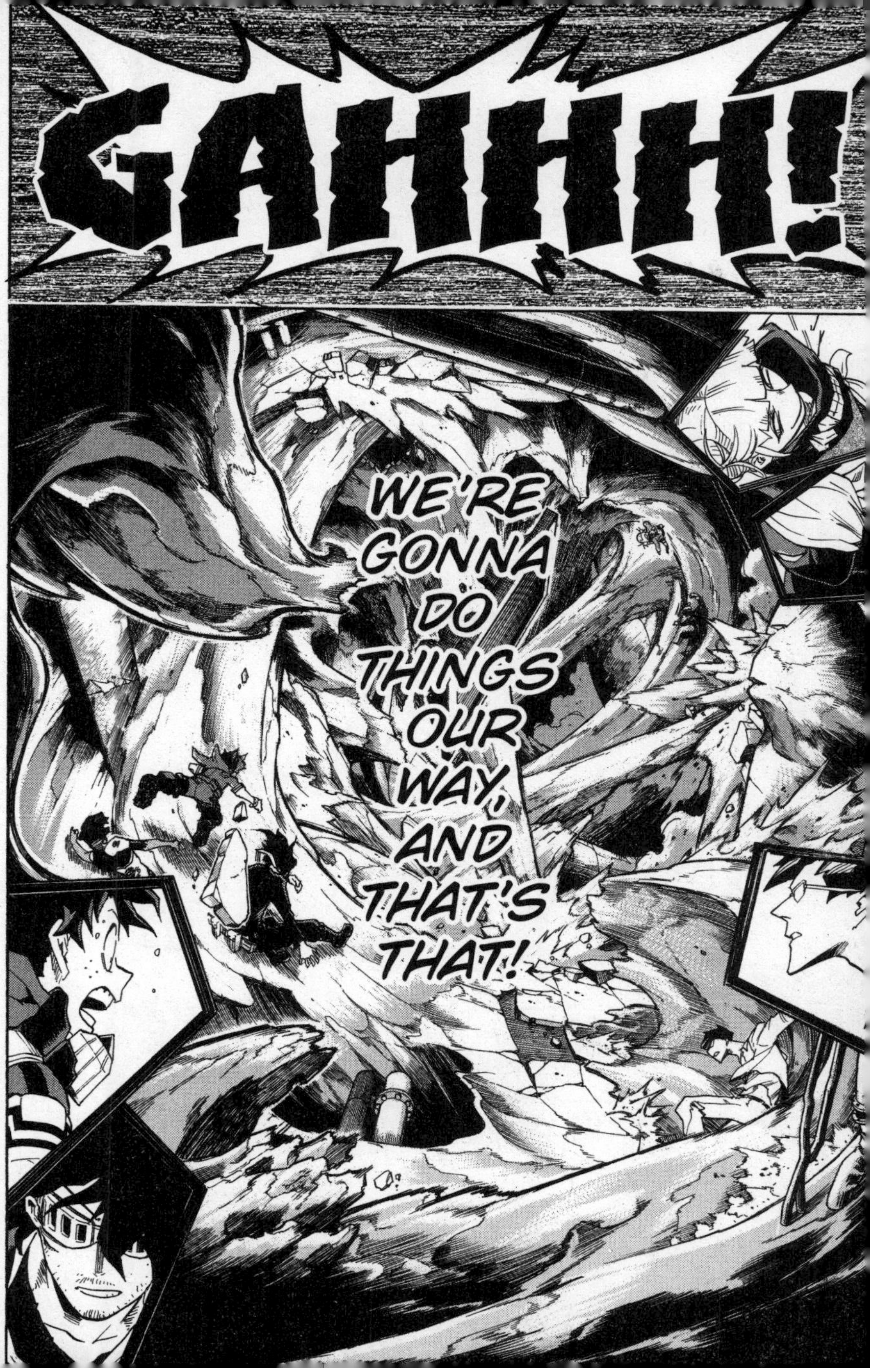
GAHHH!!
WE'RE GONNA DO THINGS OUR WAY, AND THAT'S THAT!

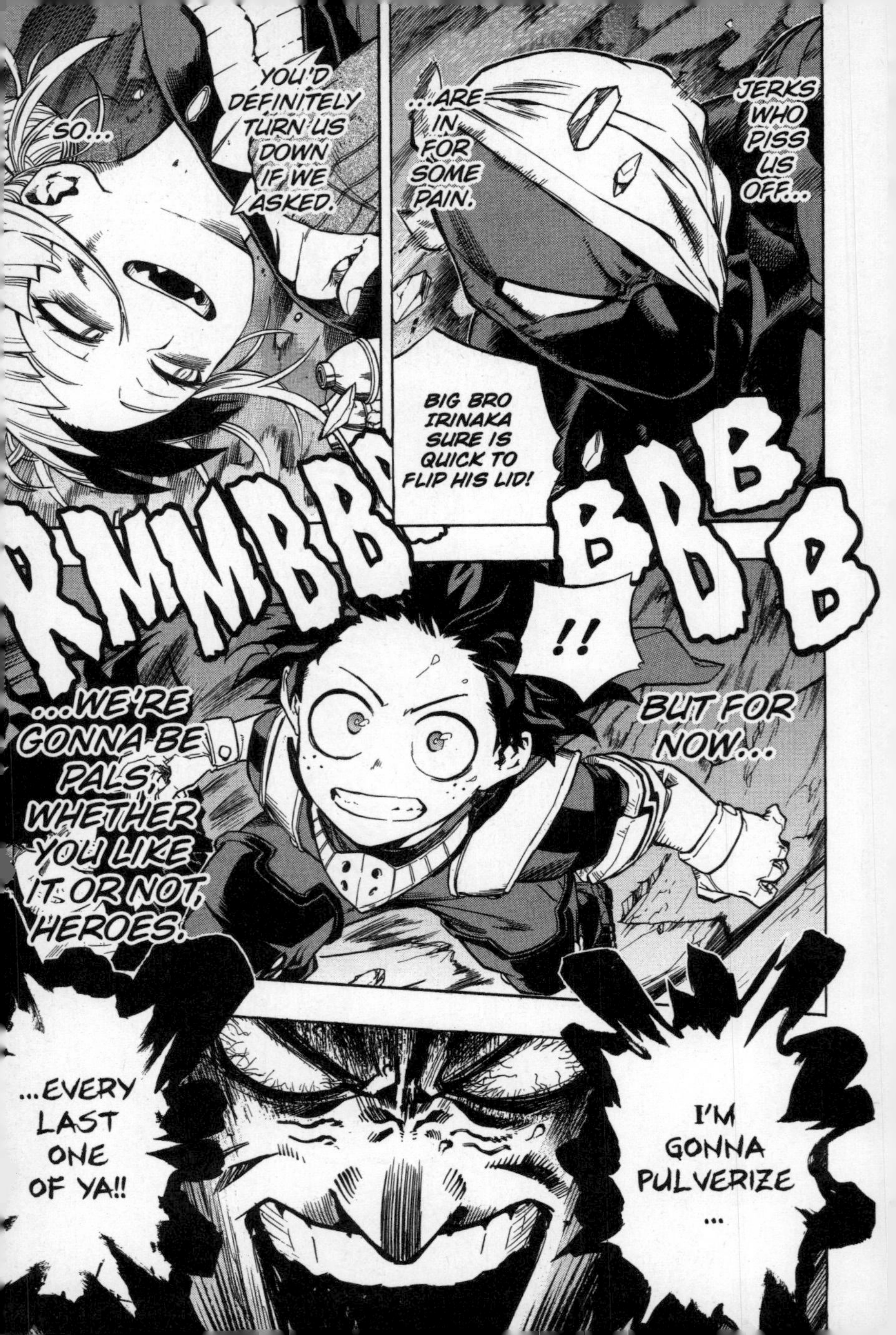
JERKS WHO PISS US OFF...
...ARE IN FOR SOME PAIN.
BIG BRO IRINAKA SURE IS QUICK TO FLIP HIS LID!
SO...
YOU'D DEFINITELY TURN US DOWN IF WE ASKED.
RMMBBBBBB
!!
BUT FOR NOW...
...WE'RE GONNA BE PALS, WHETHER YOU LIKE IT OR NOT, HEROES.
I'M GONNA PULVERIZE...
...EVERY LAST ONE OF YA!!

REJECTED VERSION OF THE IMAGE TO THE LEFT

(WHY REJECTED? THEY WERE HAVING TOO MUCH FUN HERE.)

BUT I PICKED IT UP OFF THE CUTTING ROOM FLOOR AND CLEANED IT UP.

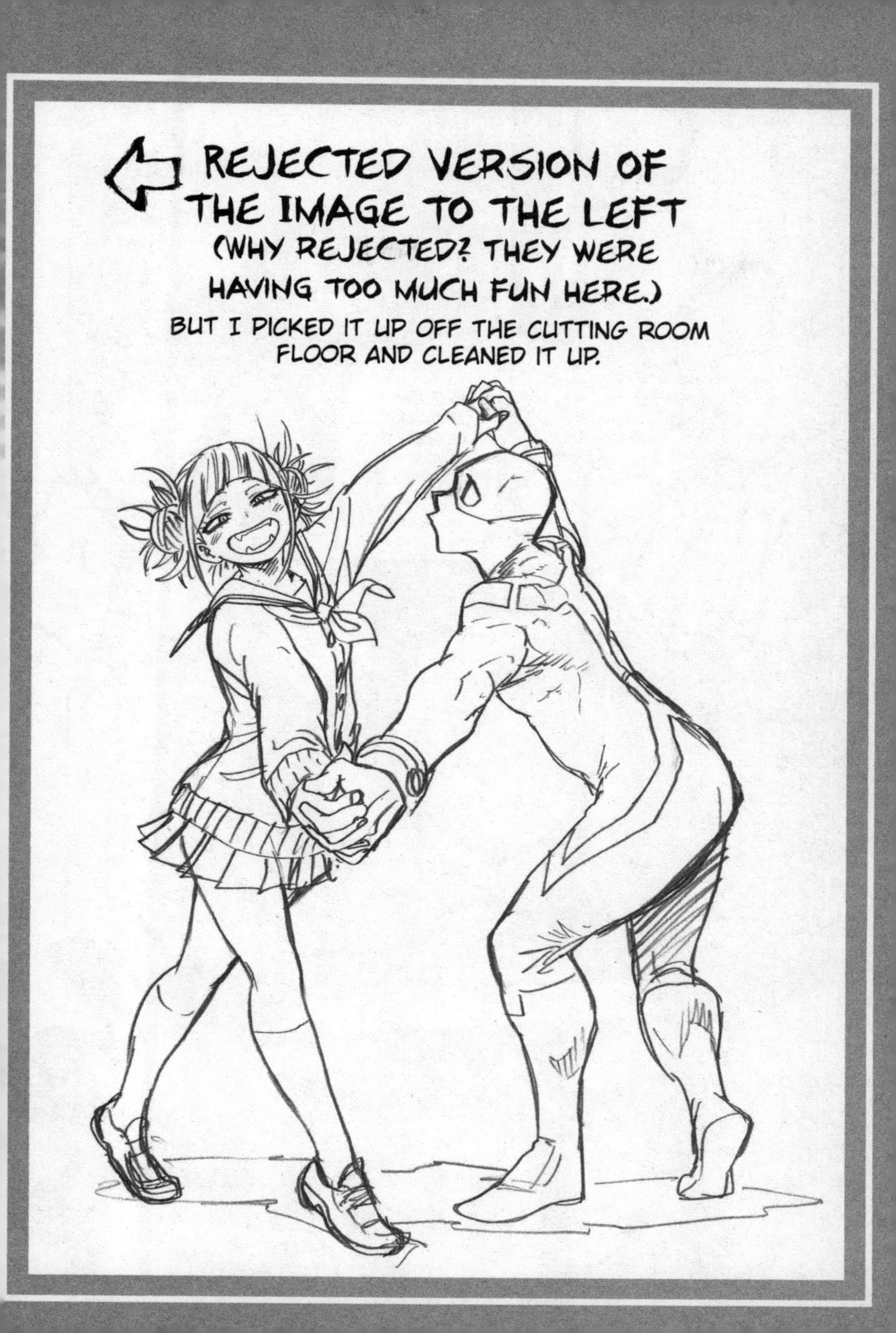

MY HERO ACADEMIA

No. 149 - Don't Get Mad, Irinaka

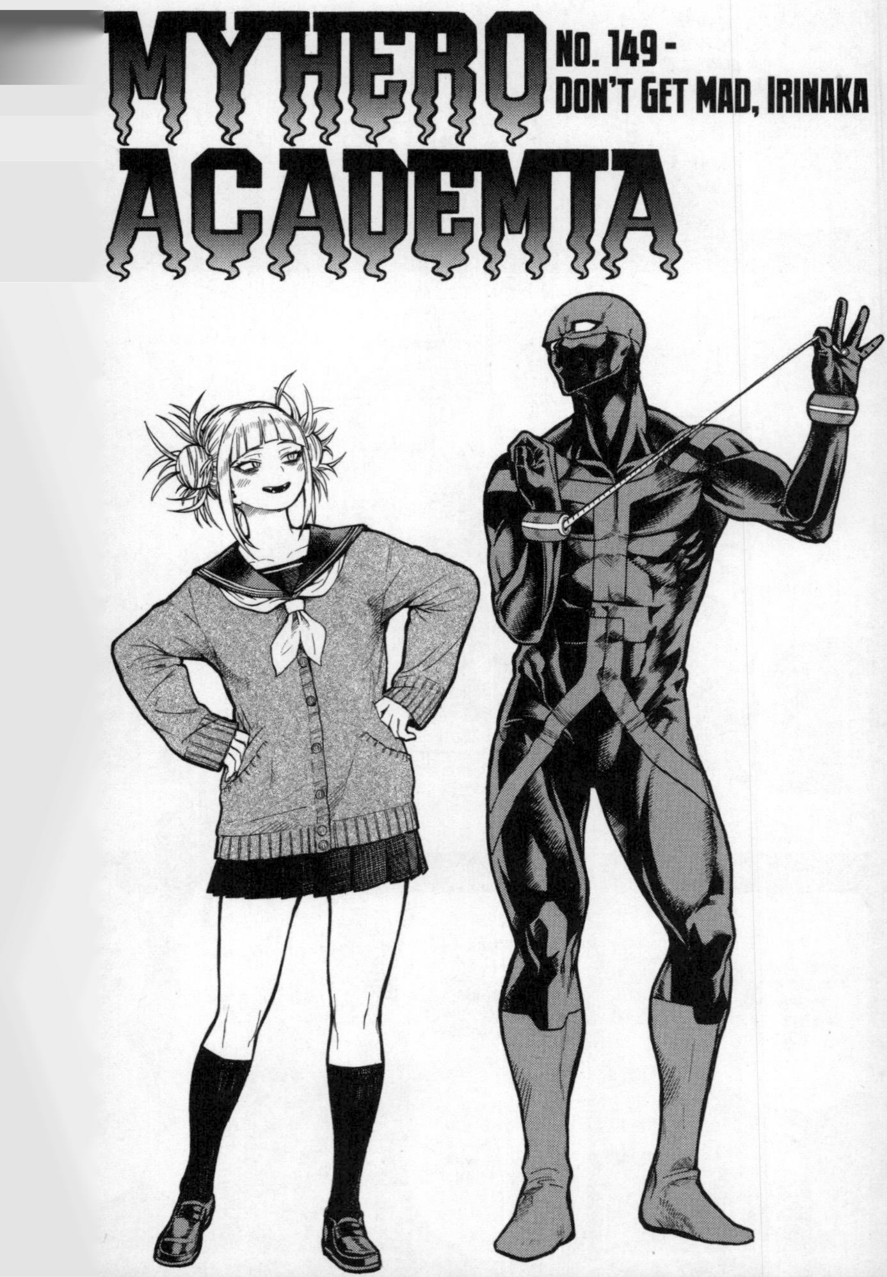

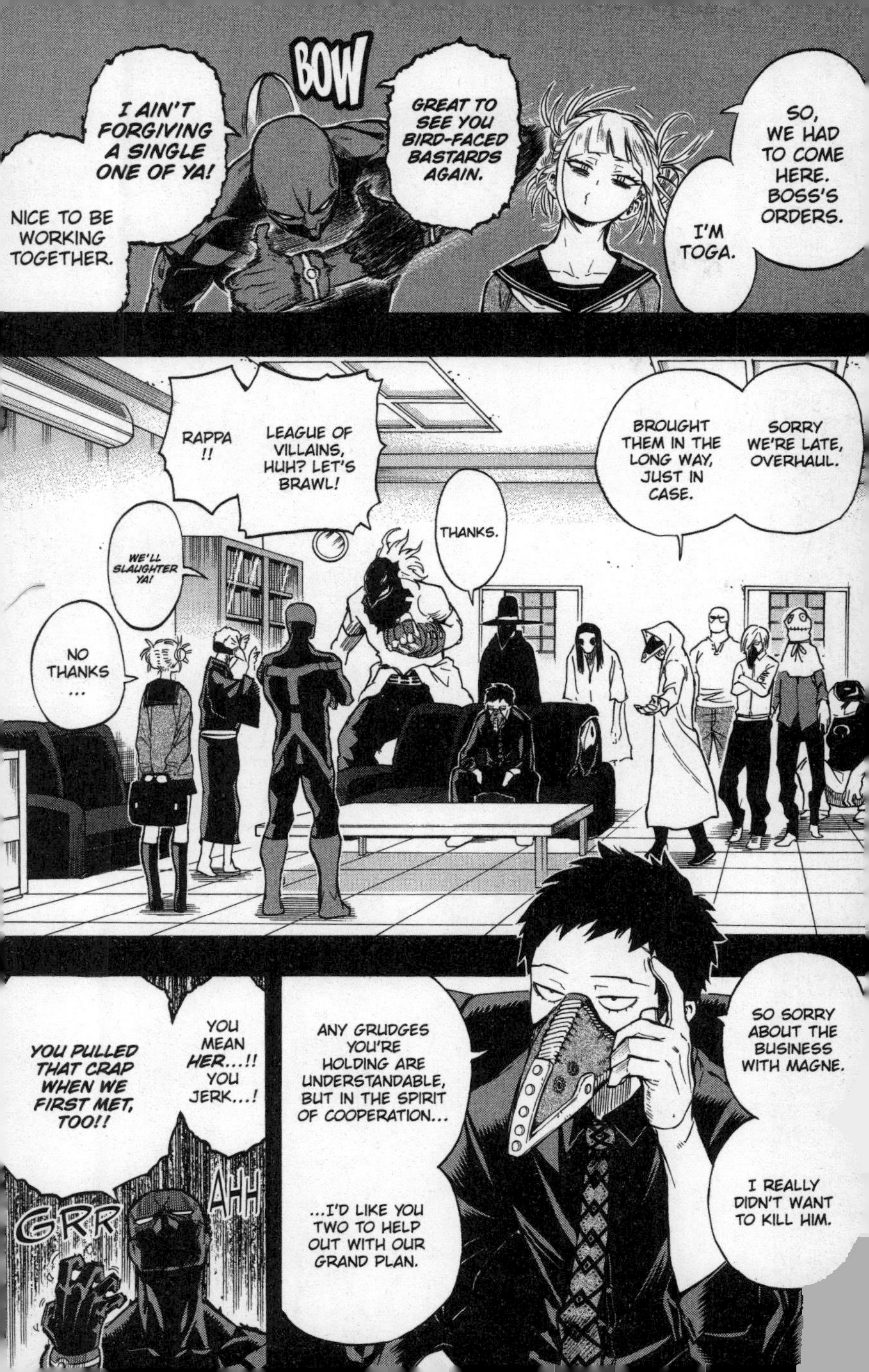

SO, WE HAD TO COME HERE. BOSS'S ORDERS.
I'M TOGA.
GREAT TO SEE YOU BIRD-FACED BASTARDS AGAIN.
BOW
I AIN'T FORGIVING A SINGLE ONE OF YA!
NICE TO BE WORKING TOGETHER.
SORRY WE'RE LATE, OVERHAUL.
BROUGHT THEM IN THE LONG WAY, JUST IN CASE.
THANKS.
LEAGUE OF VILLAINS, HUH? LET'S BRAWL!
RAPPA !!
WE'LL SLAUGHTER YA!
NO THANKS ...
SO SORRY ABOUT THE BUSINESS WITH MAGNE.
I REALLY DIDN'T WANT TO KILL HIM.
ANY GRUDGES YOU'RE HOLDING ARE UNDERSTANDABLE, BUT IN THE SPIRIT OF COOPERATION...
...I'D LIKE YOU TWO TO HELP OUT WITH OUR GRAND PLAN.
YOU MEAN HER...!! YOU JERK...!
YOU PULLED THAT CRAP WHEN WE FIRST MET, TOO!!
AHH
GRR

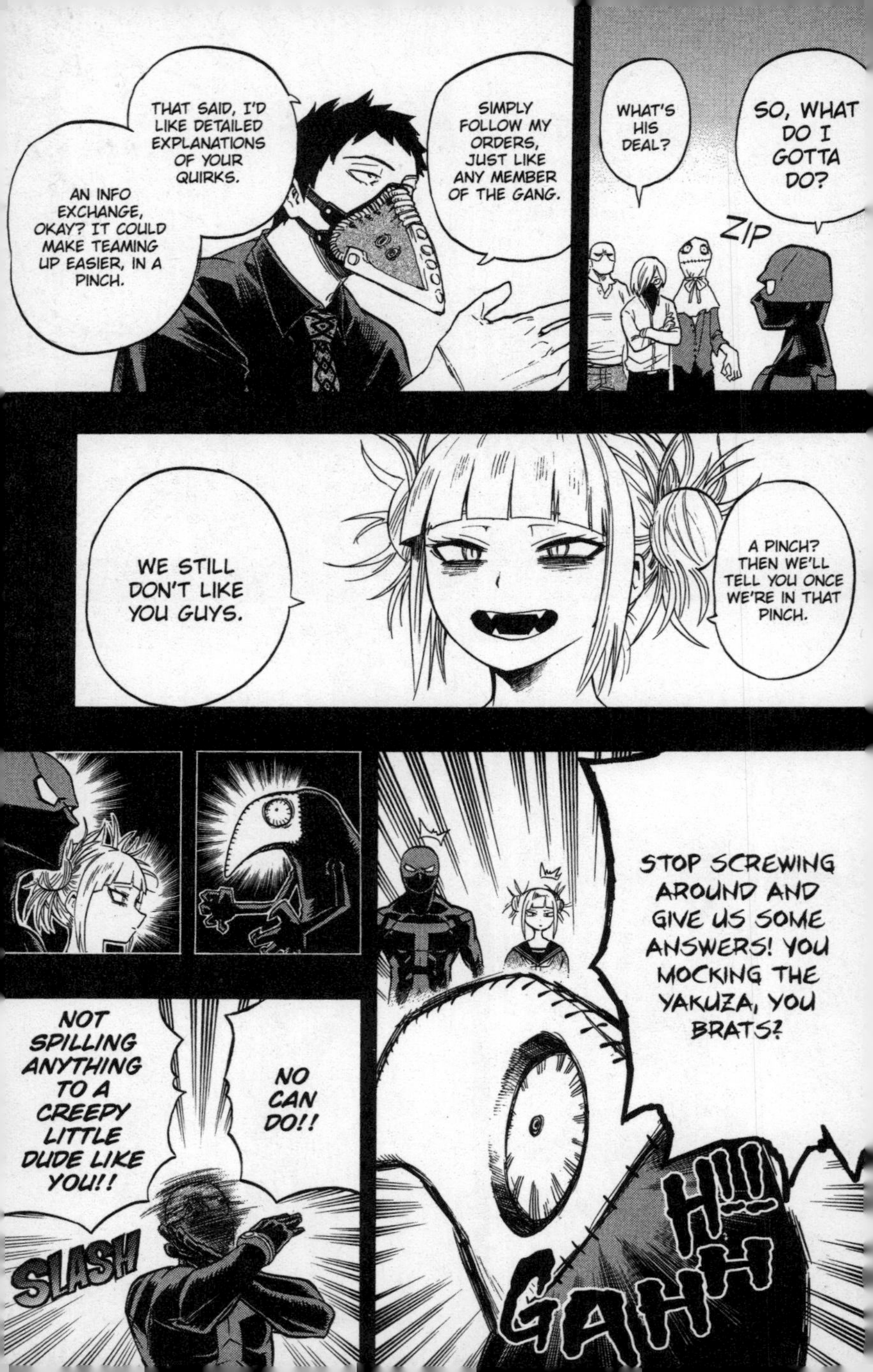
SO, WHAT DO I GOTTA DO?
WHAT'S HIS DEAL?
ZIP
SIMPLY FOLLOW MY ORDERS, JUST LIKE ANY MEMBER OF THE GANG.
THAT SAID, I'D LIKE DETAILED EXPLANATIONS OF YOUR QUIRKS.
AN INFO EXCHANGE, OKAY? IT COULD MAKE TEAMING UP EASIER, IN A PINCH.
A PINCH? THEN WE'LL TELL YOU ONCE WE'RE IN THAT PINCH.
WE STILL DON'T LIKE YOU GUYS.
STOP SCREWING AROUND AND GIVE US SOME ANSWERS! YOU MOCKING THE YAKUZA, YOU BRATS?
HI!!
GAHH
NO CAN DO!!
NOT SPILLING ANYTHING TO A CREEPY LITTLE DUDE LIKE YOU!!
SLASH

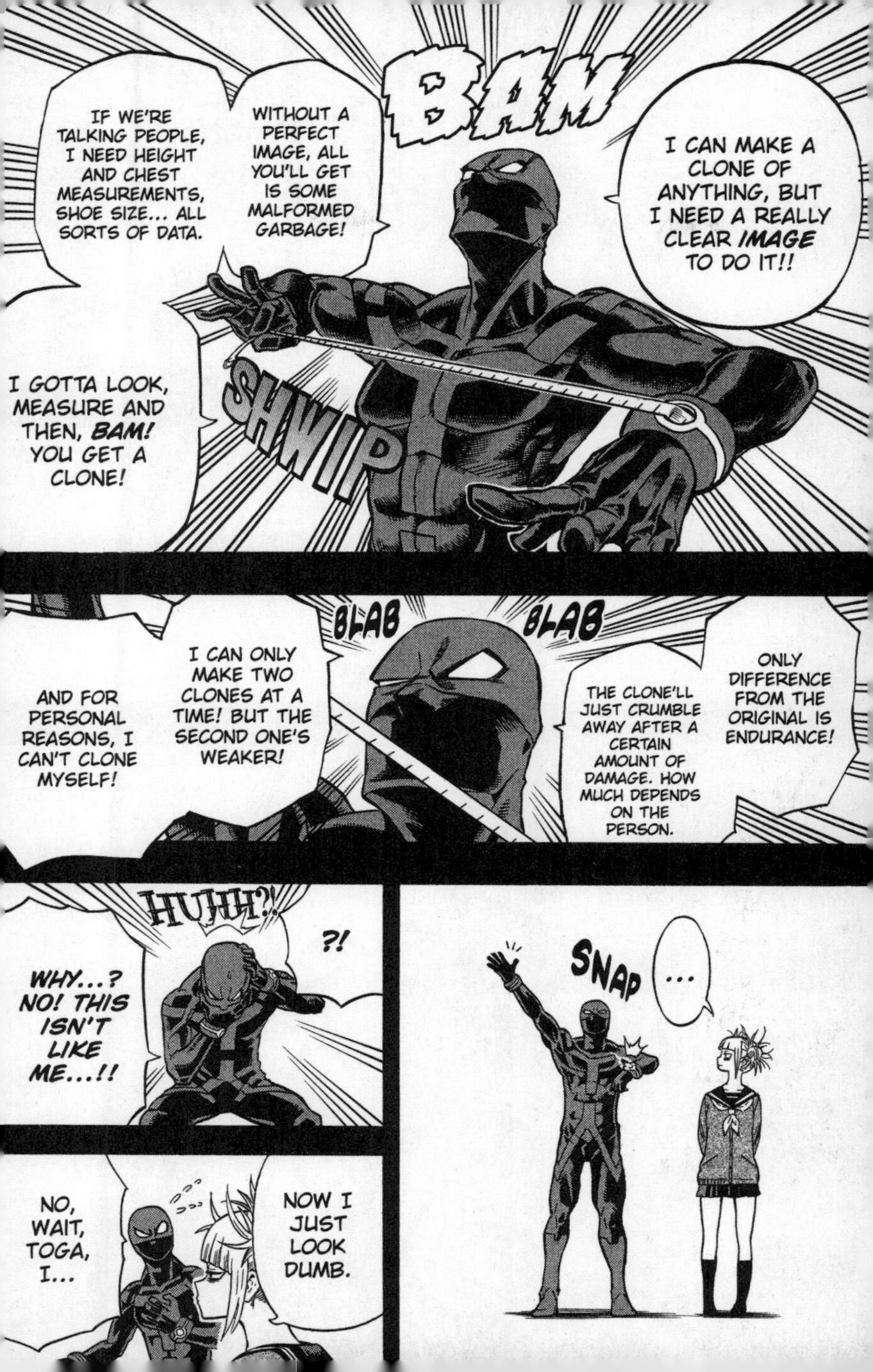
I CAN MAKE A CLONE OF ANYTHING, BUT I NEED A REALLY CLEAR *IMAGE* TO DO IT!!
BAM
WITHOUT A PERFECT IMAGE, ALL YOU'LL GET IS SOME MALFORMED GARBAGE!
IF WE'RE TALKING PEOPLE, I NEED HEIGHT AND CHEST MEASUREMENTS, SHOE SIZE... ALL SORTS OF DATA.
SHWIP
I GOTTA LOOK, MEASURE AND THEN, *BAM!* YOU GET A CLONE!
BLAB BLAB
ONLY DIFFERENCE FROM THE ORIGINAL IS ENDURANCE!
THE CLONE'LL JUST CRUMBLE AWAY AFTER A CERTAIN AMOUNT OF DAMAGE. HOW MUCH DEPENDS ON THE PERSON.
I CAN ONLY MAKE TWO CLONES AT A TIME! BUT THE SECOND ONE'S WEAKER!
AND FOR PERSONAL REASONS, I CAN'T CLONE MYSELF!
...
SNAP
HUHH?!
?!
WHY...? NO! THIS ISN'T LIKE ME...!!
NOW I JUST LOOK DUMB.
NO, WAIT, TOGA, I...

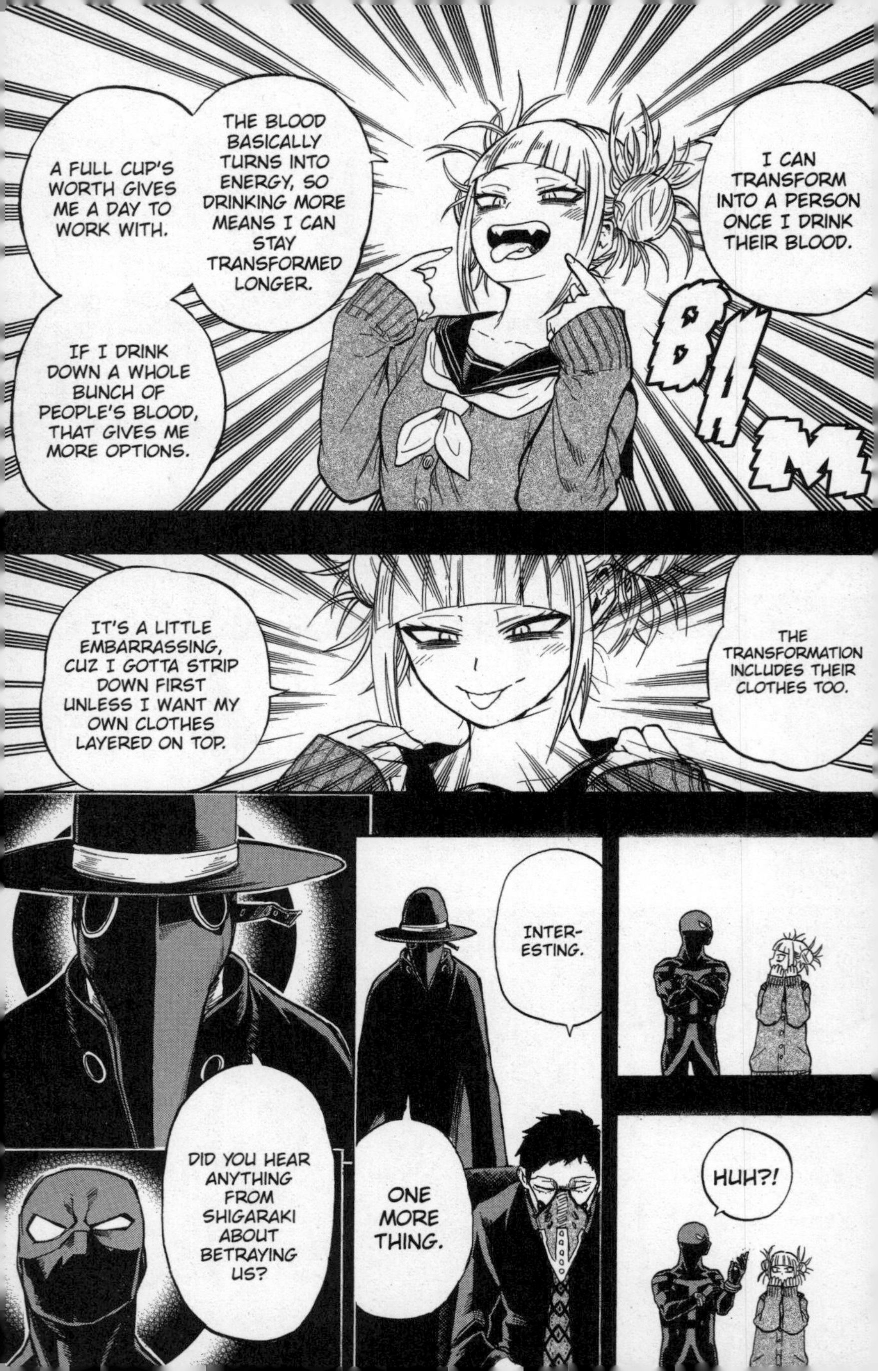
I CAN TRANSFORM INTO A PERSON ONCE I DRINK THEIR BLOOD.
BAM
THE BLOOD BASICALLY TURNS INTO ENERGY, SO DRINKING MORE MEANS I CAN STAY TRANSFORMED LONGER.
A FULL CUP'S WORTH GIVES ME A DAY TO WORK WITH.
IF I DRINK DOWN A WHOLE BUNCH OF PEOPLE'S BLOOD, THAT GIVES ME MORE OPTIONS.
THE TRANSFORMATION INCLUDES THEIR CLOTHES TOO.
IT'S A LITTLE EMBARRASSING, CUZ I GOTTA STRIP DOWN FIRST UNLESS I WANT MY OWN CLOTHES LAYERED ON TOP.
HUH?!
INTER-ESTING.
ONE MORE THING.
DID YOU HEAR ANYTHING FROM SHIGARAKI ABOUT BETRAYING US?

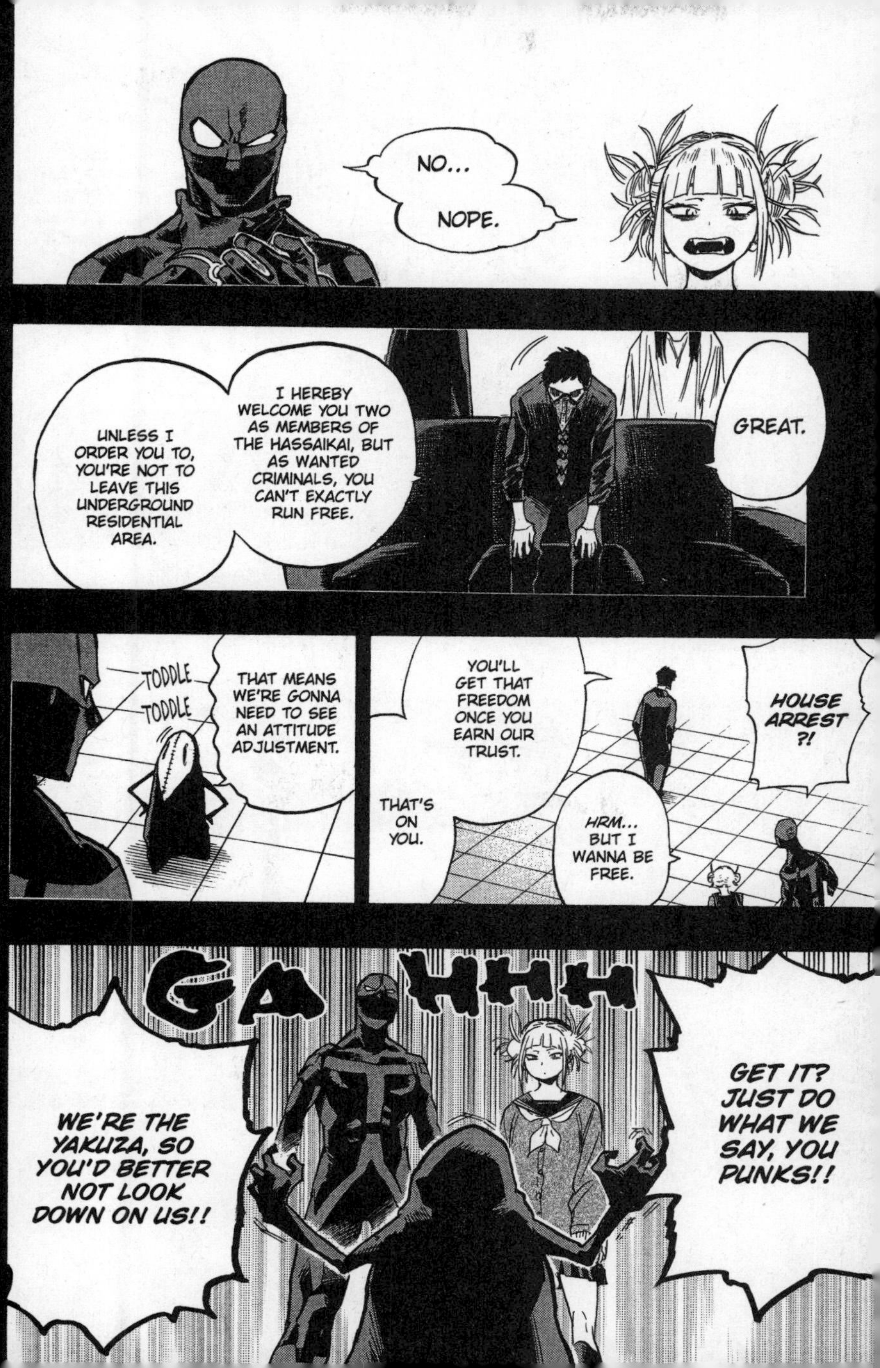
NO... NOPE.
GREAT.
I HEREBY WELCOME YOU TWO AS MEMBERS OF THE HASSAIKAI, BUT AS WANTED CRIMINALS, YOU CAN'T EXACTLY RUN FREE.
UNLESS I ORDER YOU TO, YOU'RE NOT TO LEAVE THIS UNDERGROUND RESIDENTIAL AREA.
HOUSE ARREST?!
YOU'LL GET THAT FREEDOM ONCE YOU EARN OUR TRUST.
HRM... BUT I WANNA BE FREE.
THAT'S ON YOU.
TODDLE TODDLE
THAT MEANS WE'RE GONNA NEED TO SEE AN ATTITUDE ADJUSTMENT.
GAHHH
GET IT? JUST DO WHAT WE SAY, YOU PUNKS!!
WE'RE THE YAKUZA, SO YOU'D BETTER NOT LOOK DOWN ON US!!

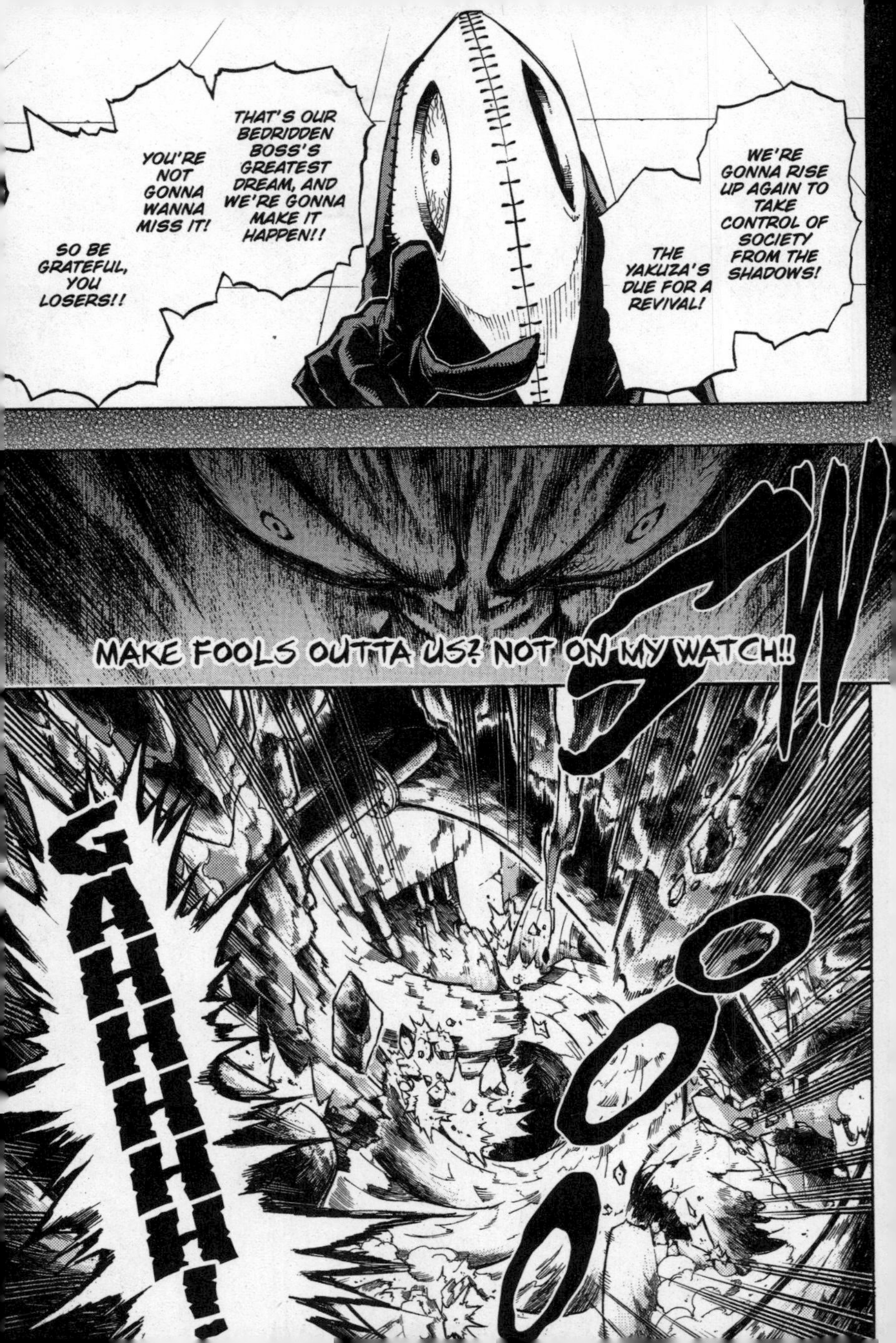
WE'RE GONNA RISE UP AGAIN TO TAKE CONTROL OF SOCIETY FROM THE SHADOWS!
THE YAKUZA'S DUE FOR A REVIVAL!
THAT'S OUR BEDRIDDEN BOSS'S GREATEST DREAM, AND WE'RE GONNA MAKE IT HAPPEN!!
YOU'RE NOT GONNA WANNA MISS IT!
SO BE GRATEFUL, YOU LOSERS!!
MAKE FOOLS OUTTA US? NOT ON MY WATCH!!

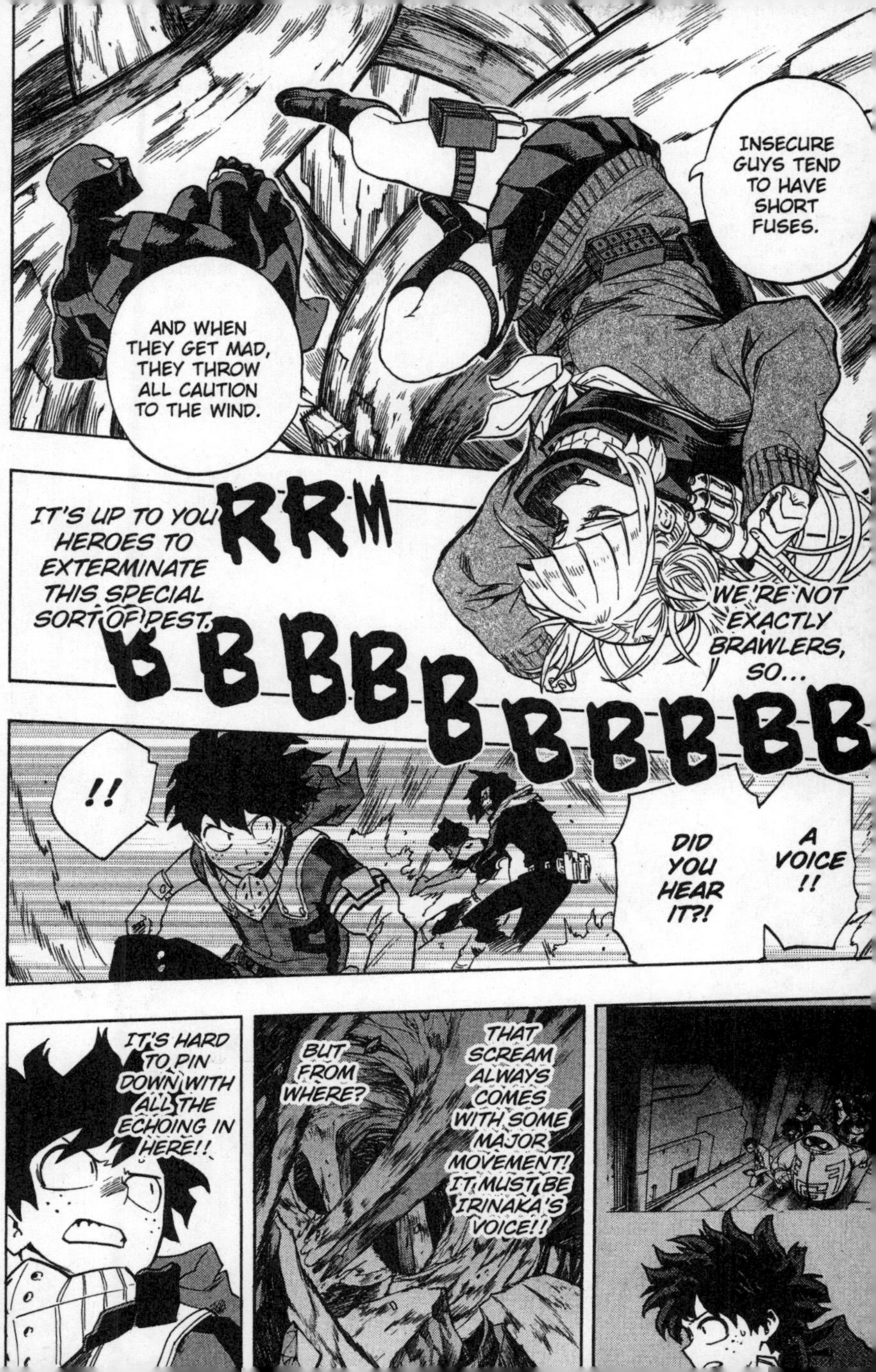
INSECURE GUYS TEND TO HAVE SHORT FUSES.
AND WHEN THEY GET MAD, THEY THROW ALL CAUTION TO THE WIND.
WE'RE NOT EXACTLY BRAWLERS, SO...
IT'S UP TO YOU HEROES TO EXTERMINATE THIS SPECIAL SORT OF PEST.
RRM
BBBBBBBBBBB
A VOICE!!
DID YOU HEAR IT?!
!!
THAT SCREAM ALWAYS COMES WITH SOME MAJOR MOVEMENT! IT MUST BE IRINAKA'S VOICE!!
BUT FROM WHERE?
IT'S HARD TO PIN DOWN WITH ALL THE ECHOING IN HERE!!

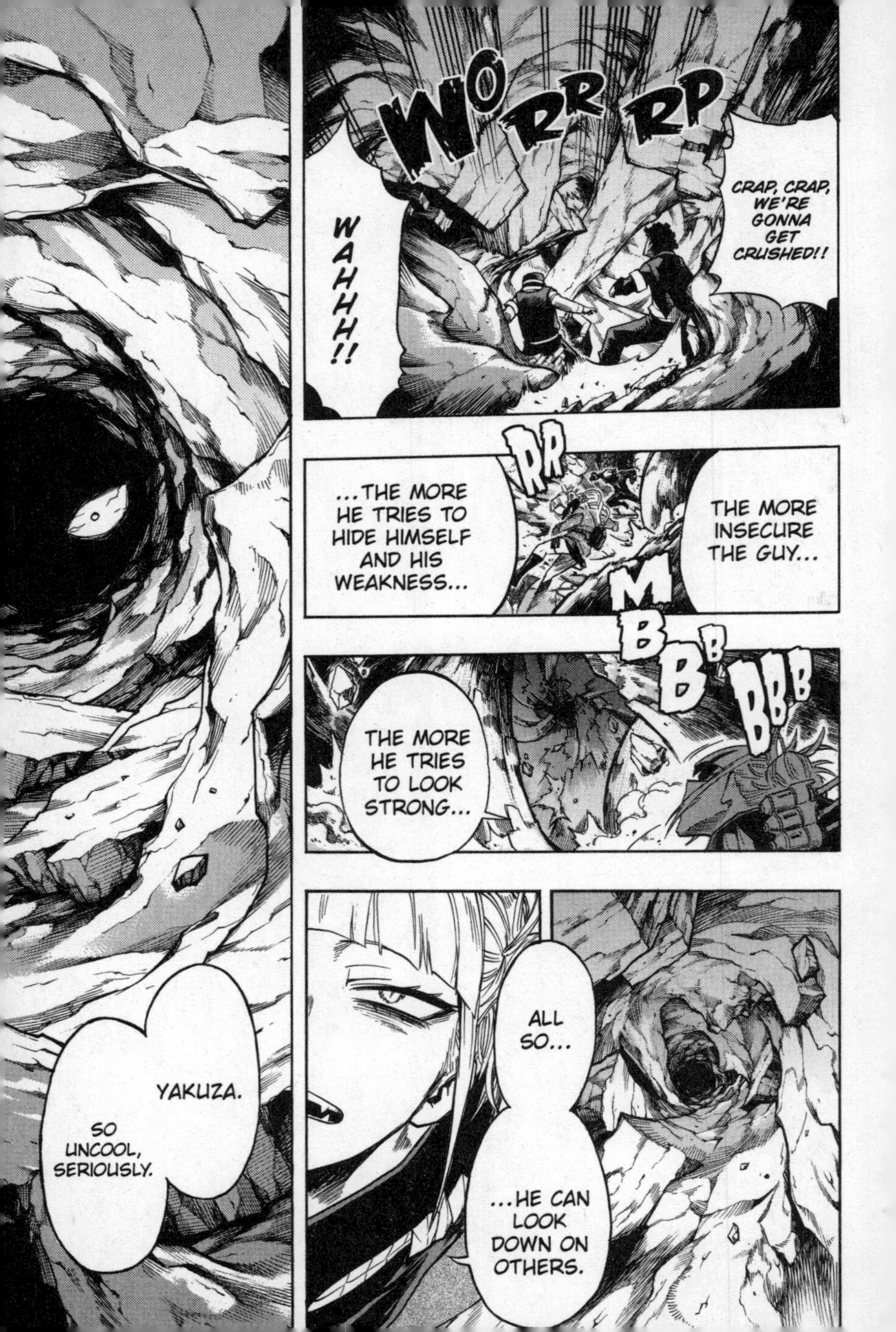
WORRRP
CRAP, CRAP, WE'RE GONNA GET CRUSHED!!
WAHHHH!!
THE MORE INSECURE THE GUY...
RR
...THE MORE HE TRIES TO HIDE HIMSELF AND HIS WEAKNESS...
MBBBBBB
THE MORE HE TRIES TO LOOK STRONG...
ALL SO...
...HE CAN LOOK DOWN ON OTHERS.
YAKUZA.
SO UNCOOL, SERIOUSLY.

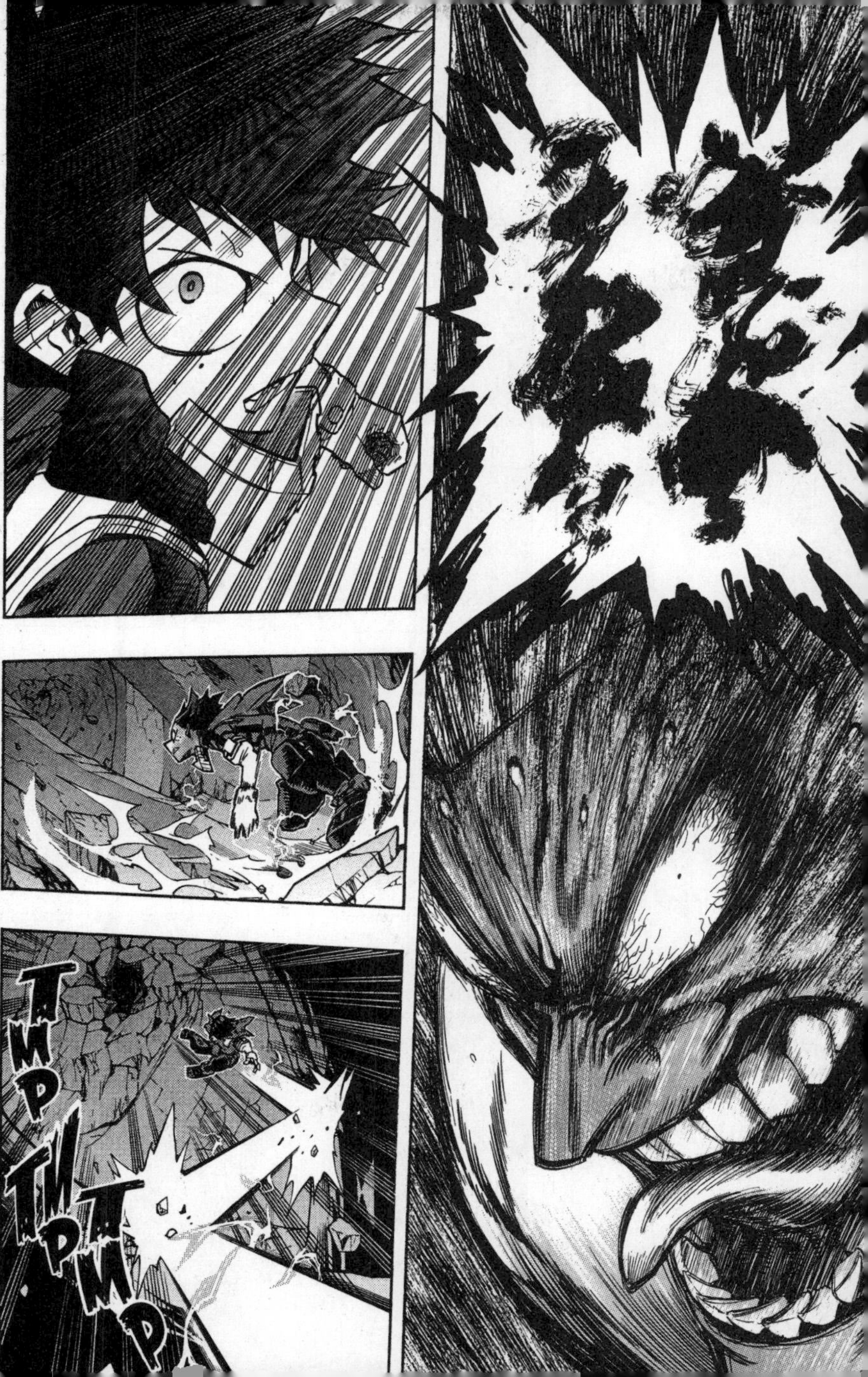
TMP
TMP
TMP

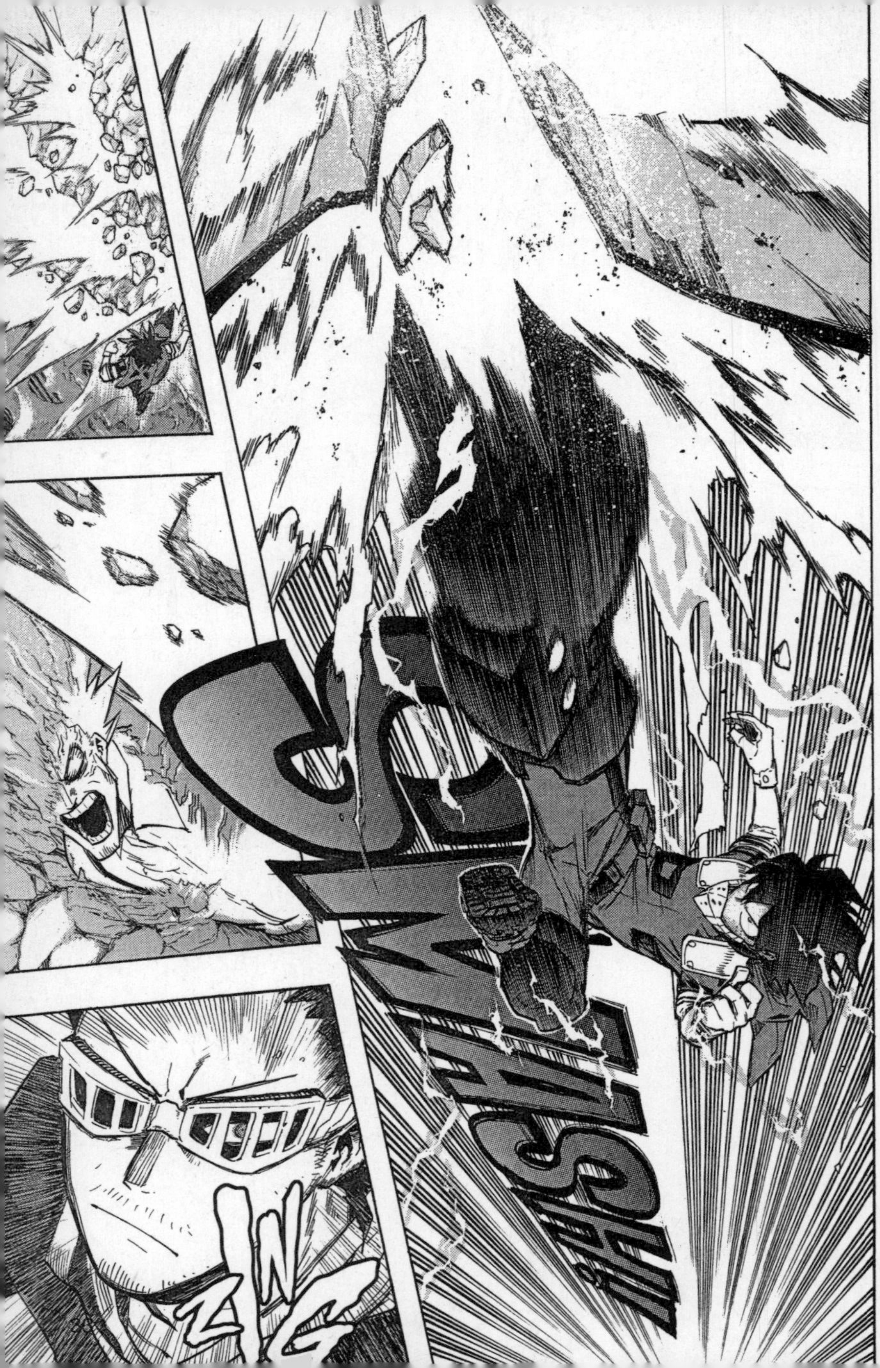
SWISH

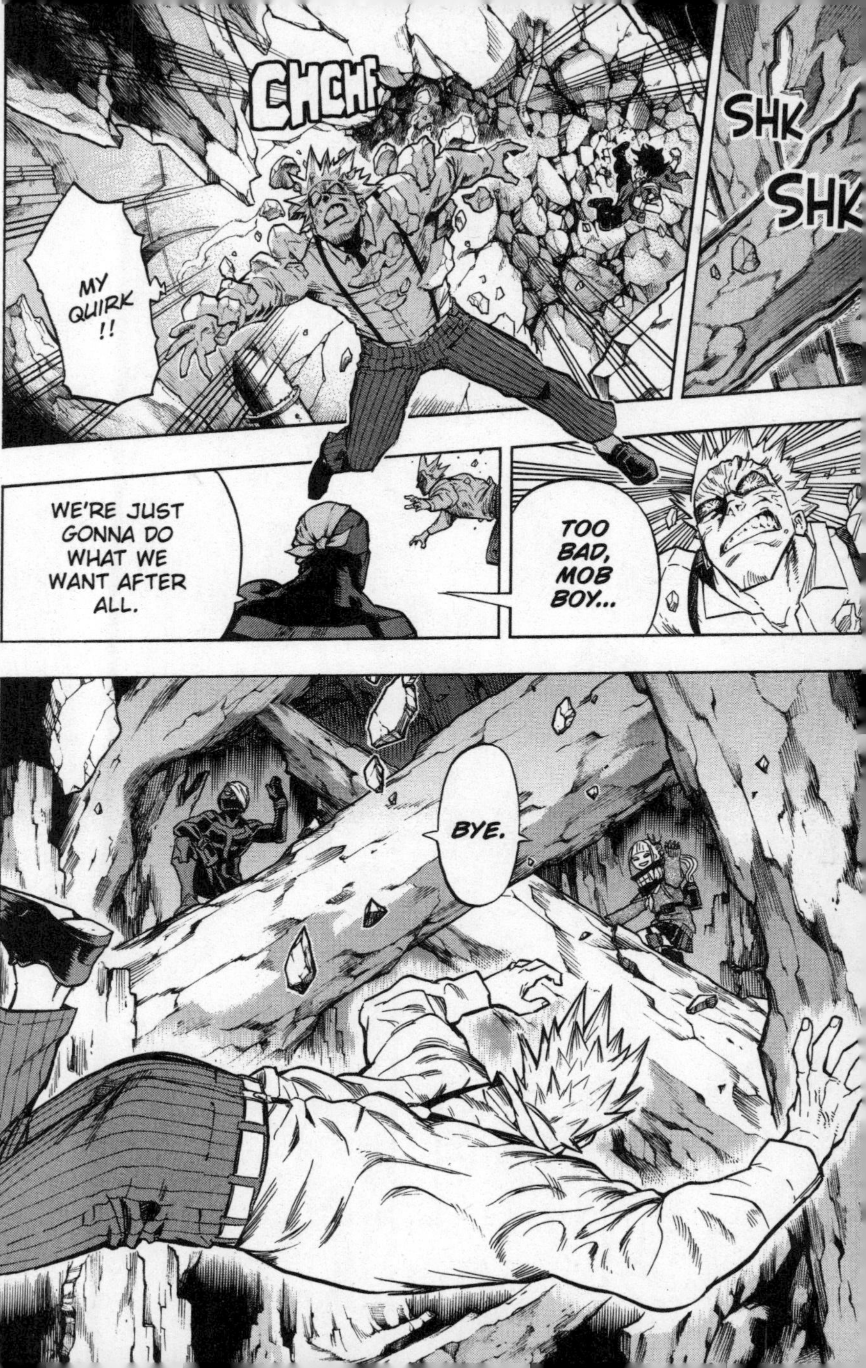
SHK
SHK
CHCHF
MY QUIRK !!
TOO BAD, MOB BOY...
WE'RE JUST GONNA DO WHAT WE WANT AFTER ALL.
BYE.

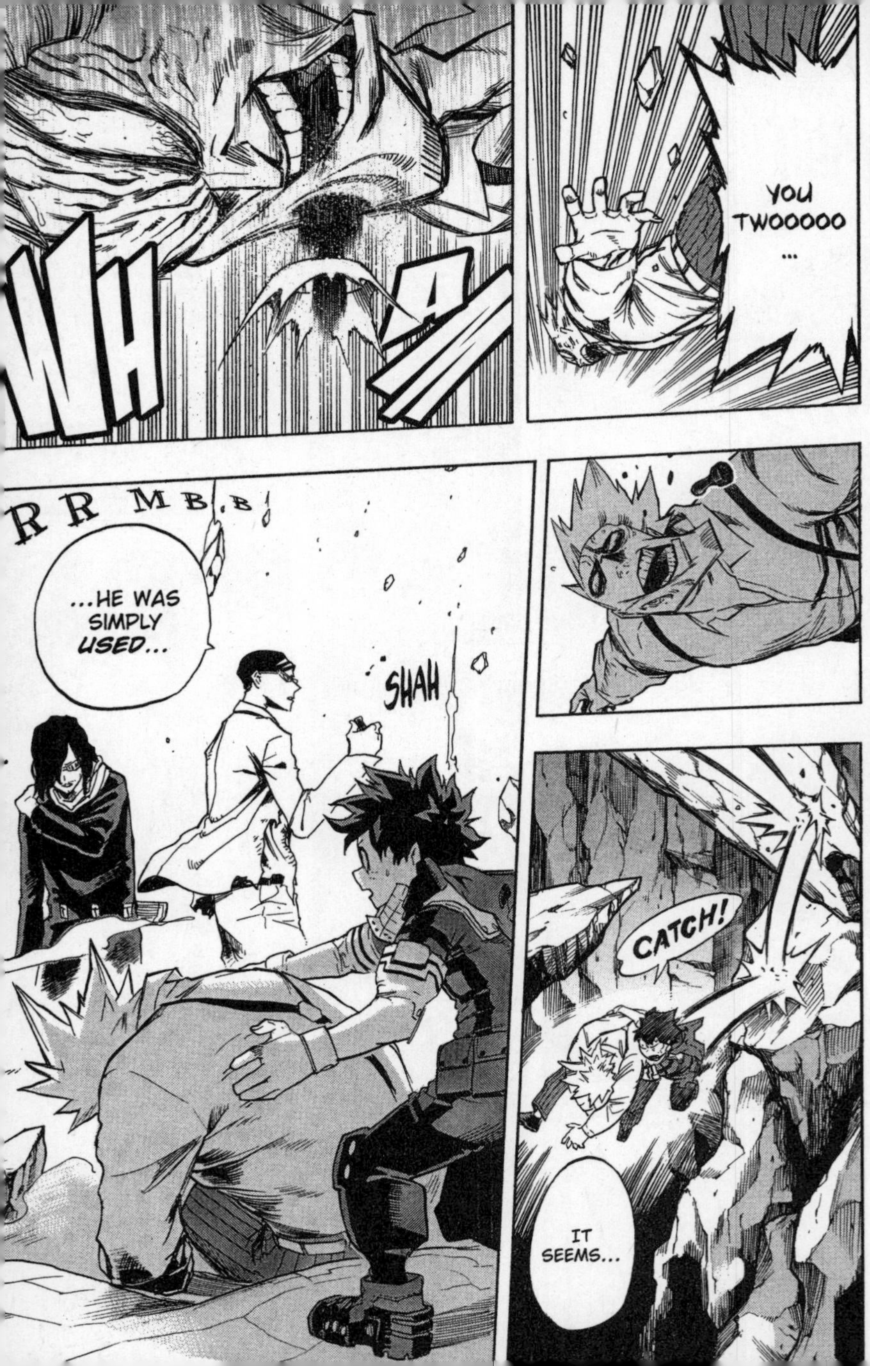
YOU TWOOOOO ...
WHA
CATCH!
IT SEEMS...
RR MB B
...HE WAS SIMPLY USED...
SHAH

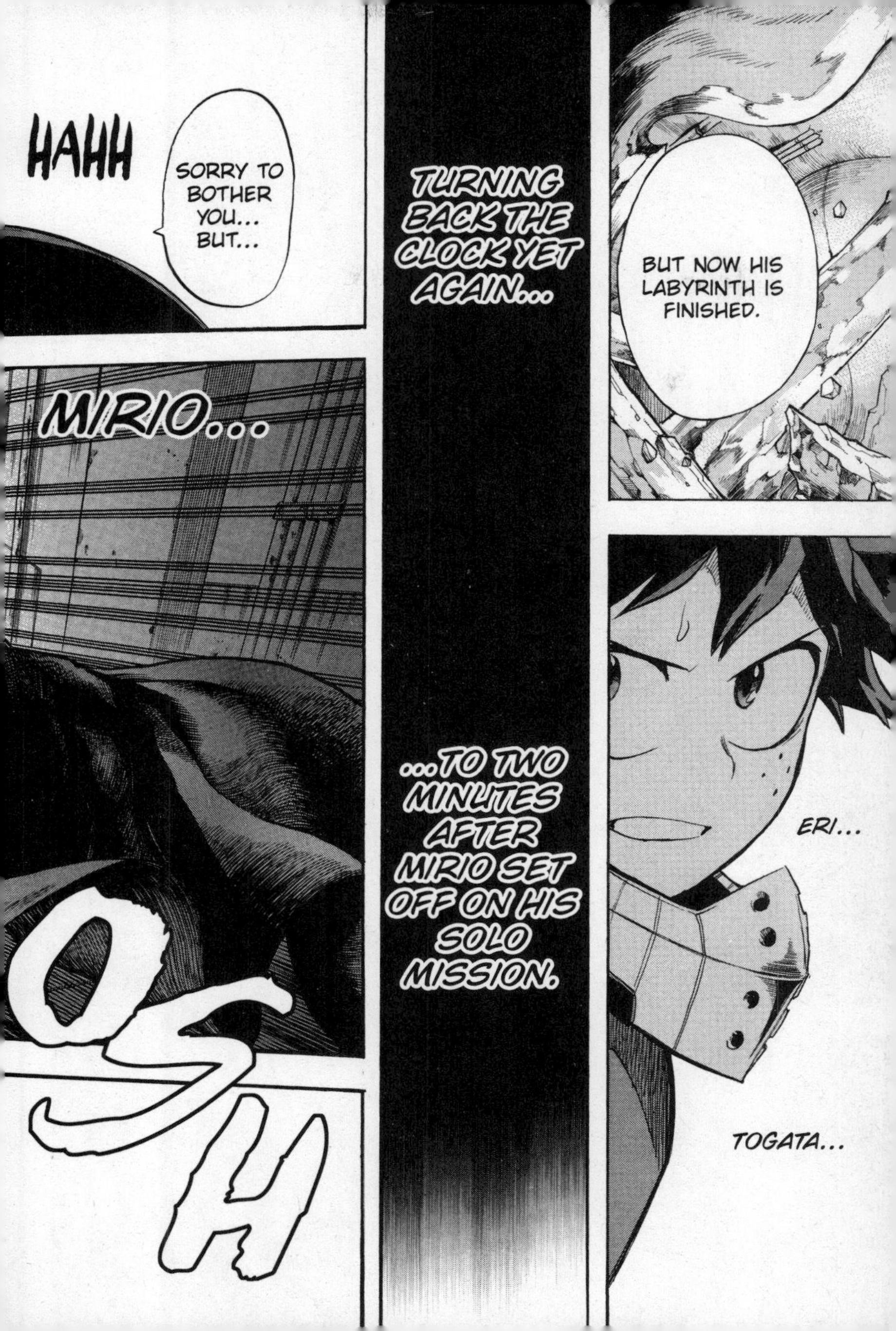
BUT NOW HIS LABYRINTH IS FINISHED.
ERI...
TOGATA...
TURNING BACK THE CLOCK YET AGAIN...
...TO TWO MINUTES AFTER MIRIO SET OFF ON HIS SOLO MISSION.
SORRY TO BOTHER YOU... BUT...
HAHH
MIRIO...
OSH

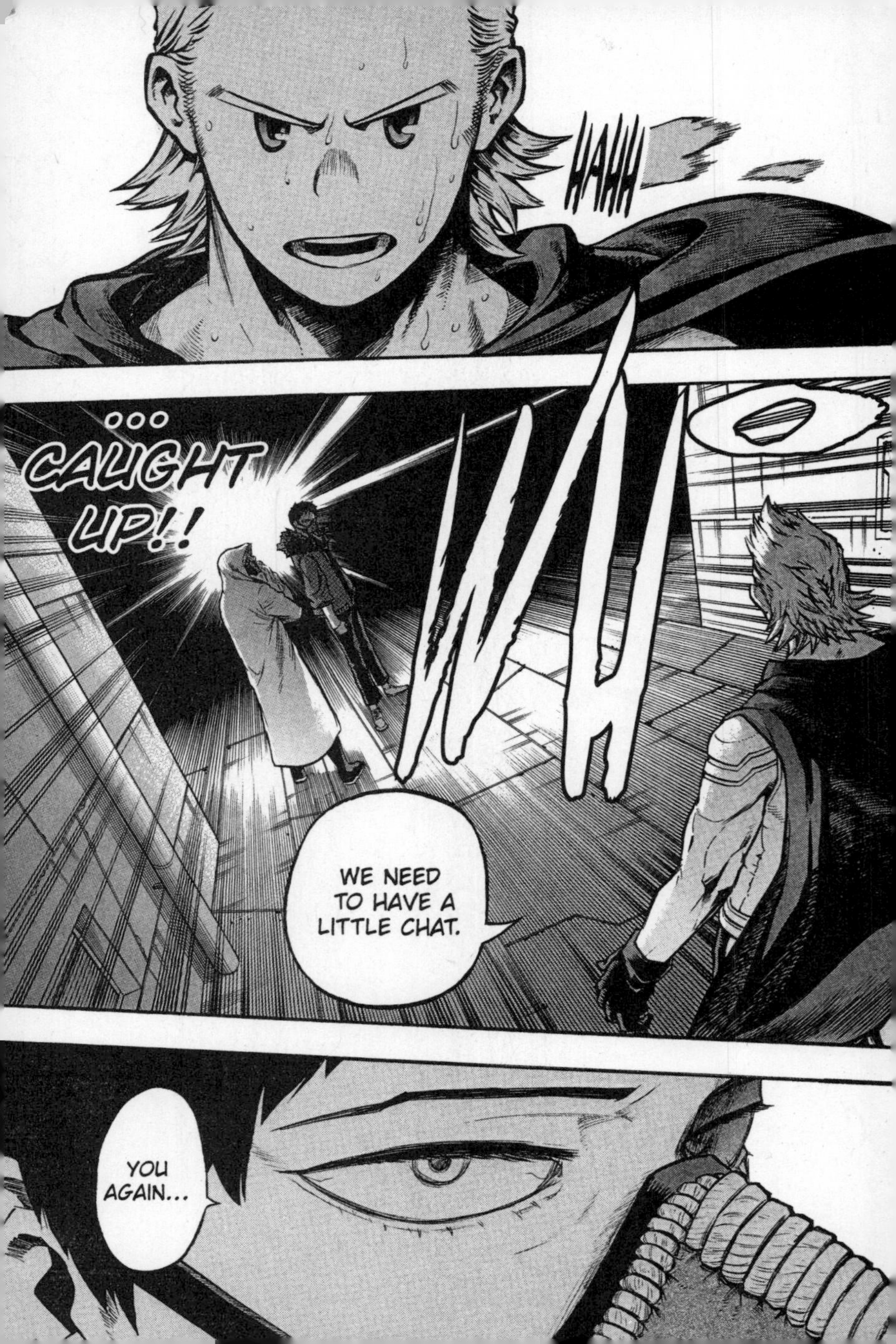
HAHH
WAH
...CAUGHT UP!!
WE NEED TO HAVE A LITTLE CHAT.
YOU AGAIN...

OVERHAUL SIDEBAR

With his Quirk, he could easily heal the scar Magne gave him, but the young boss made a conscious decision not to. By keeping it, it serves as a wordless, threatening reminder that both sides have been wronged. Overhaul's a nasty guy!

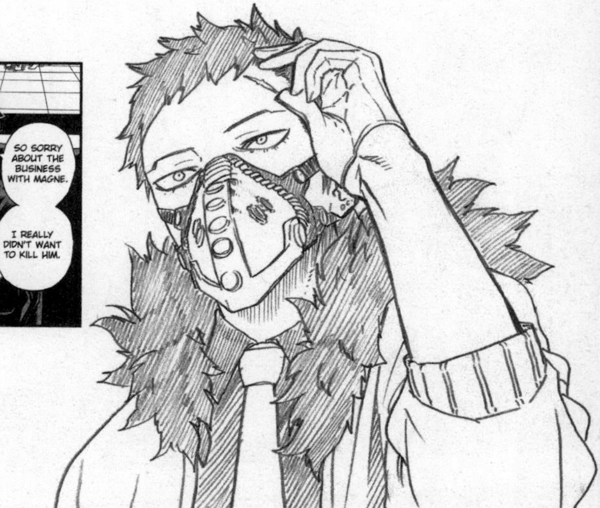

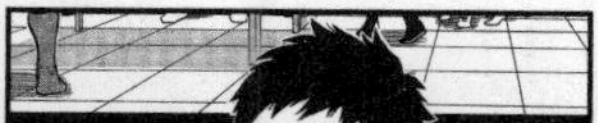
SO SORRY ABOUT THE BUSINESS WITH MAGNE.
I REALLY DIDN'T WANT TO KILL HIM.
ANY GRUDGES YOU'RE HOLDING ARE UNDERSTANDABLE, BUT IN THE SPIRIT OF COOPERATION...
...I'D LIKE YOU TWO TO HELP OUT WITH OUR GRAND PLAN.

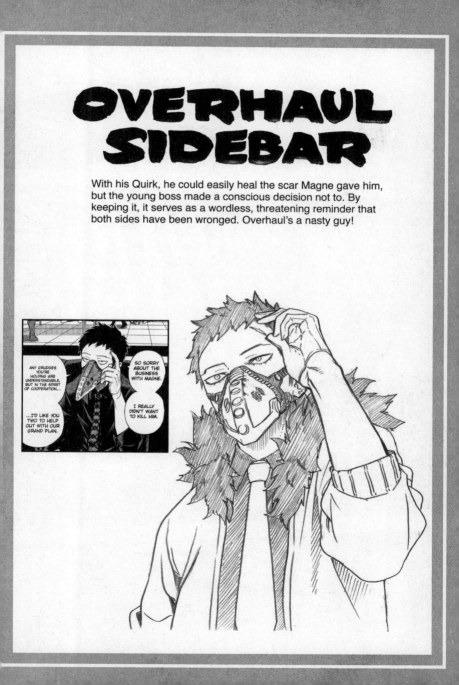

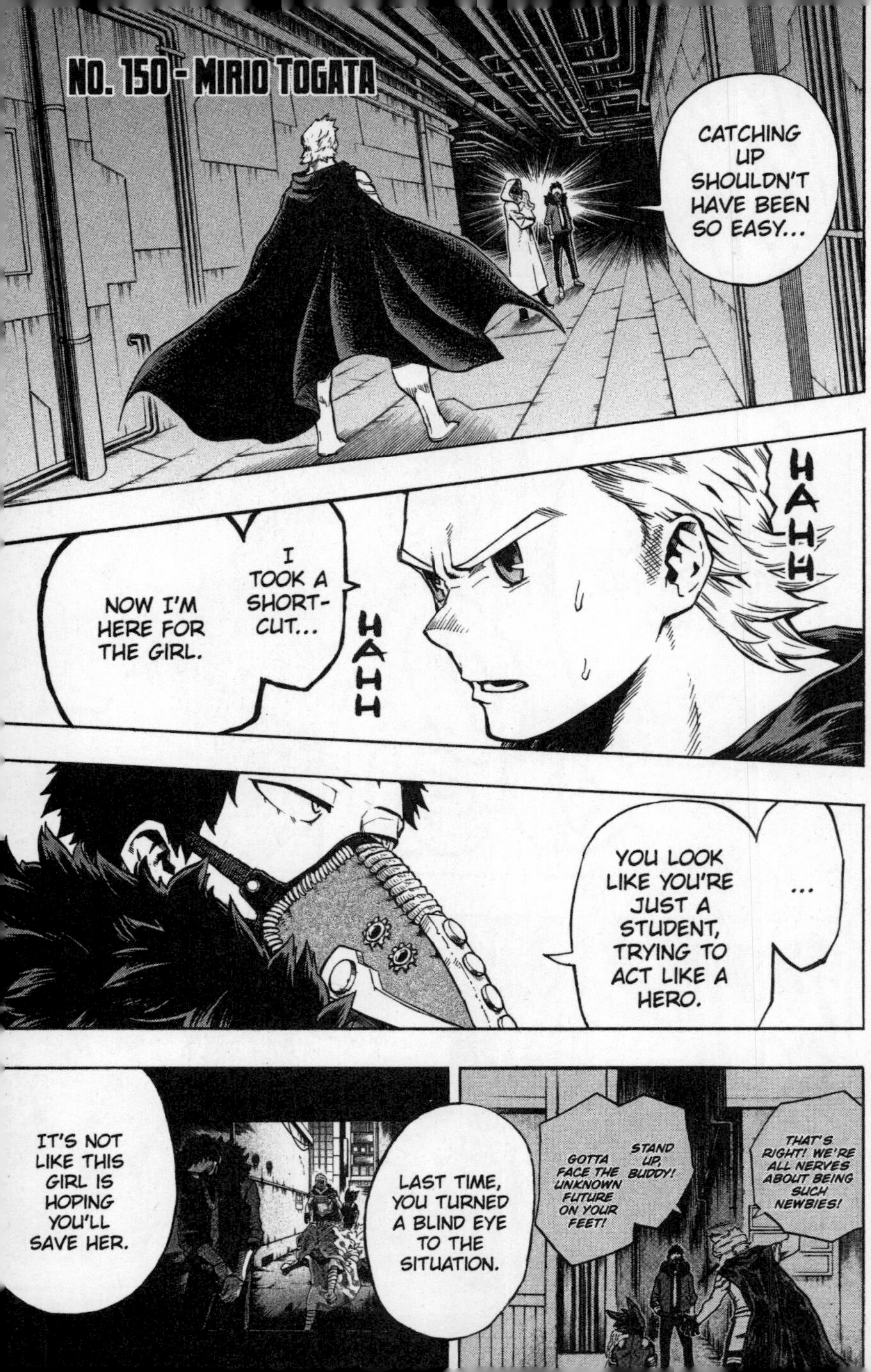
No. 150 - Mirio Togata
CATCHING UP SHOULDN'T HAVE BEEN SO EASY...
HAHH
I TOOK A SHORTCUT...
HAHH
NOW I'M HERE FOR THE GIRL.
...
YOU LOOK LIKE YOU'RE JUST A STUDENT, TRYING TO ACT LIKE A HERO.
THAT'S RIGHT! WE'RE ALL NERVES ABOUT BEING SUCH NEWBIES!
STAND UP, BUDDY!
GOTTA FACE THE UNKNOWN FUTURE ON YOUR FEET!
LAST TIME, YOU TURNED A BLIND EYE TO THE SITUATION.
IT'S NOT LIKE THIS GIRL IS HOPING YOU'LL SAVE HER.

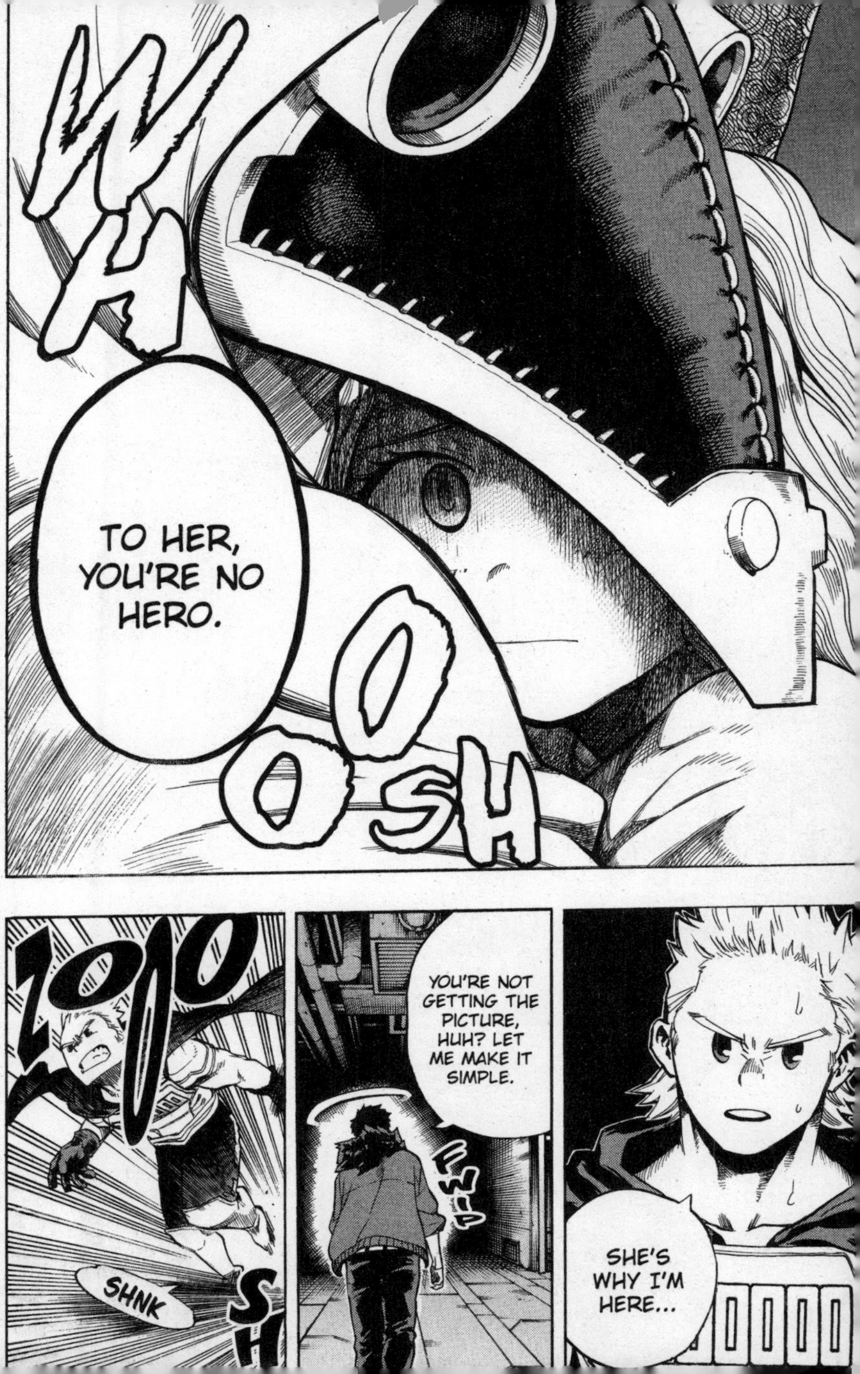
WHOOSH
TO HER, YOU'RE NO HERO.
SHE'S WHY I'M HERE...
YOU'RE NOT GETTING THE PICTURE, HUH? LET ME MAKE IT SIMPLE.
FWIP
ZOOO
SHNK
SH

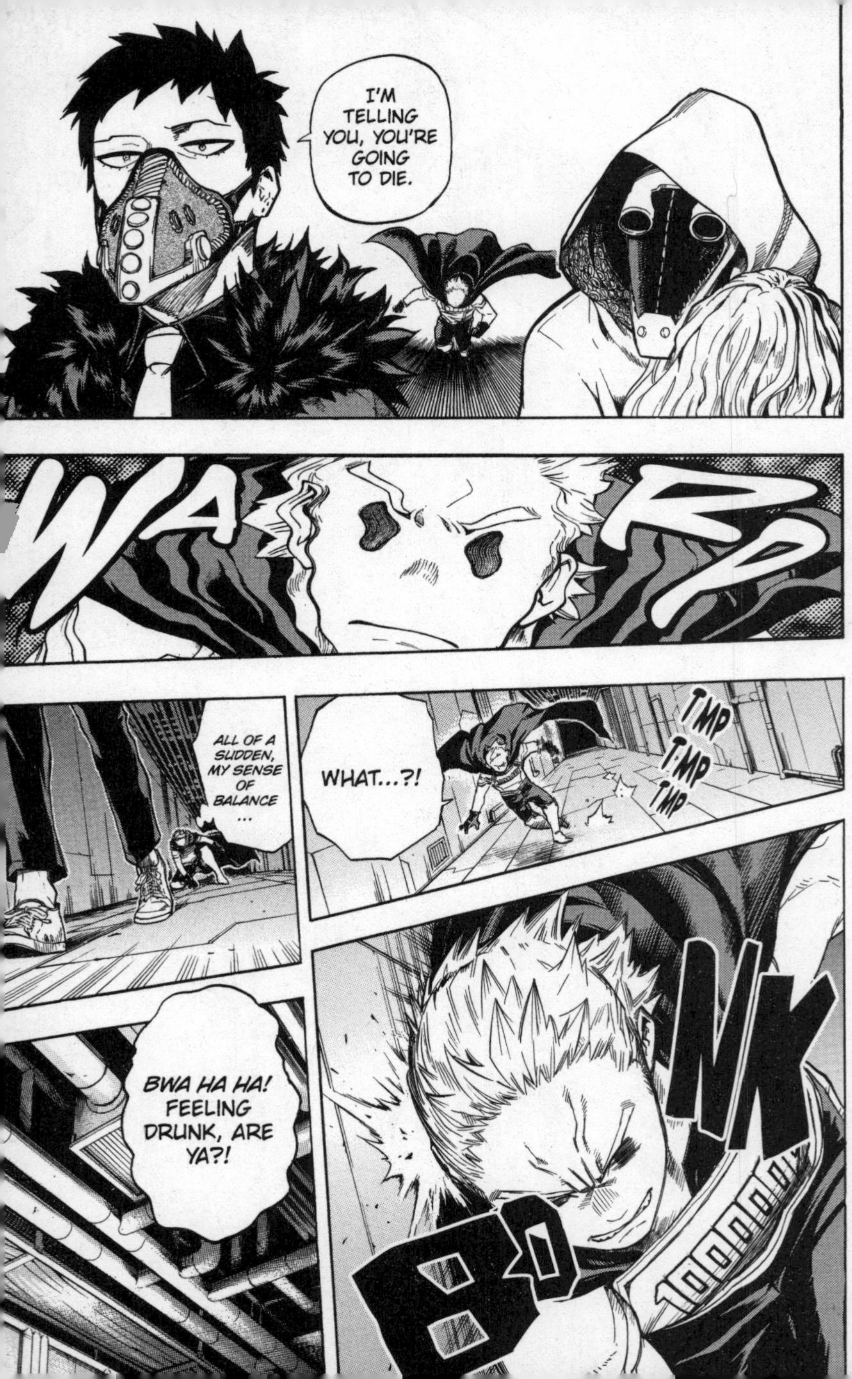
I'M TELLING YOU, YOU'RE GOING TO DIE.
WARP
TMP TMP TMP
WHAT...?!
ALL OF A SUDDEN, MY SENSE OF BALANCE ...
BONK
BWA HA HA! FEELING DRUNK, ARE YA?!

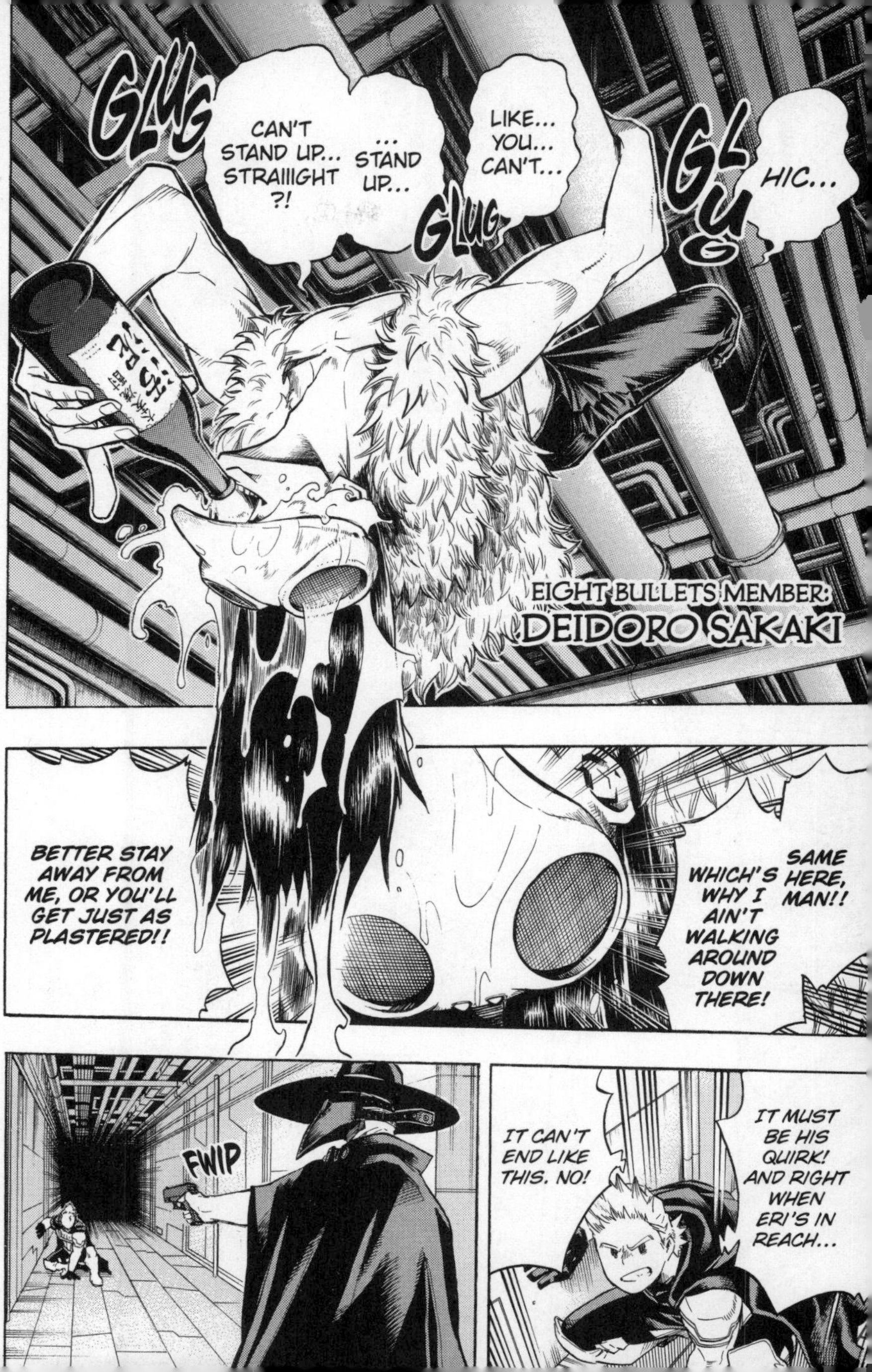
HIC...
GLUG
LIKE... YOU... CAN'T...
GLUG
... STAND UP...
CAN'T STAND UP... STRAIIIGHT ?!
GLUG
EIGHT BULLETS MEMBER: DEIDORO SAKAKI
SAME HERE, MAN!!
WHICH'S WHY I AIN'T WALKING AROUND DOWN THERE!
BETTER STAY AWAY FROM ME, OR YOU'LL GET JUST AS PLASTERED!!
IT MUST BE HIS QUIRK! AND RIGHT WHEN ERI'S IN REACH...
IT CAN'T END LIKE THIS. NO!
FWIP

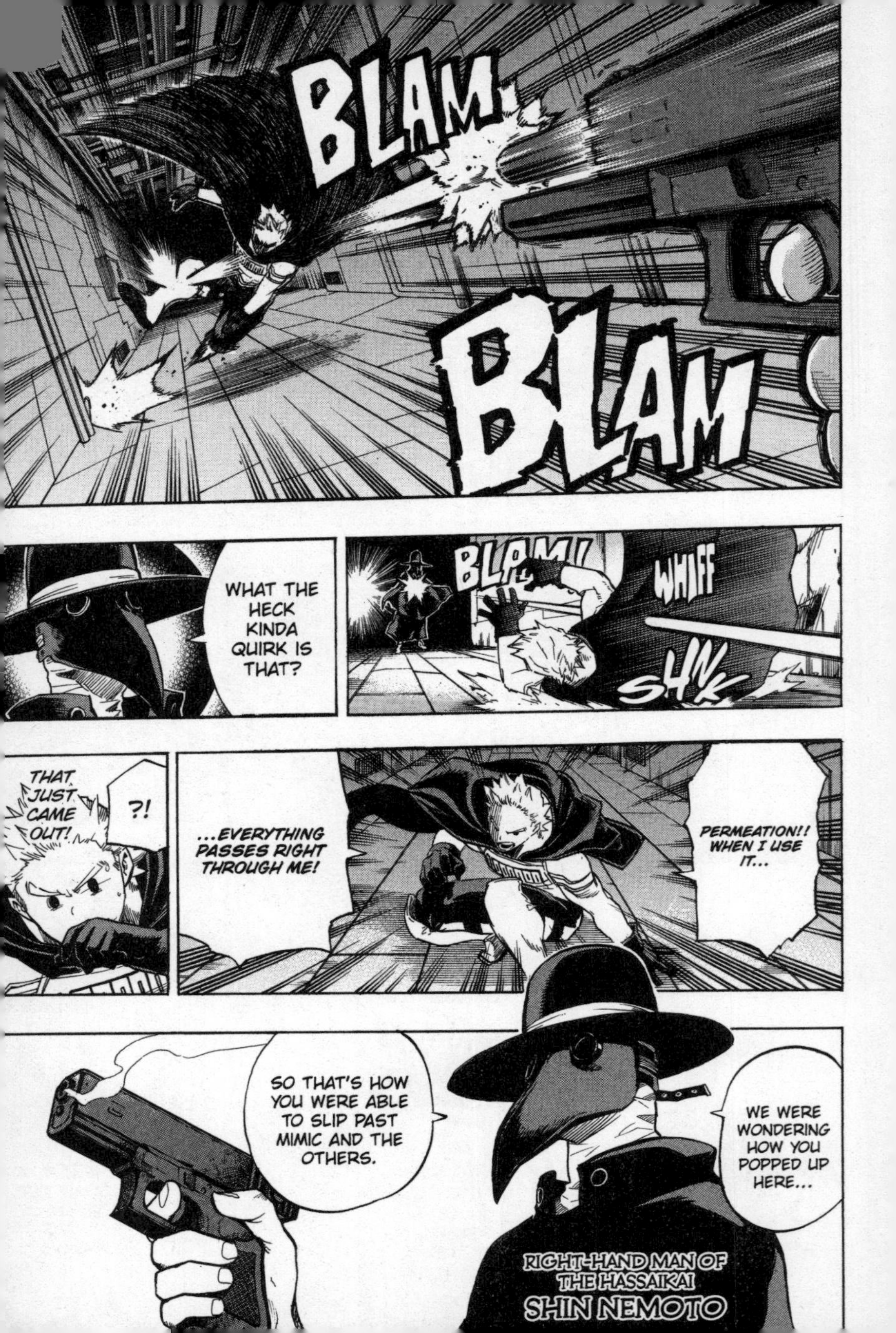
BLAM
BLAM
BLAM!
WHIFF
SHNK
WHAT THE HECK KINDA QUIRK IS THAT?
PERMEATION!! WHEN I USE IT...
...EVERYTHING PASSES RIGHT THROUGH ME!
?!
THAT JUST CAME OUT!
WE WERE WONDERING HOW YOU POPPED UP HERE...
SO THAT'S HOW YOU WERE ABLE TO SLIP PAST MIMIC AND THE OTHERS.
RIGHT-HAND MAN OF THE HASSAIKAI
SHIN NEMOTO

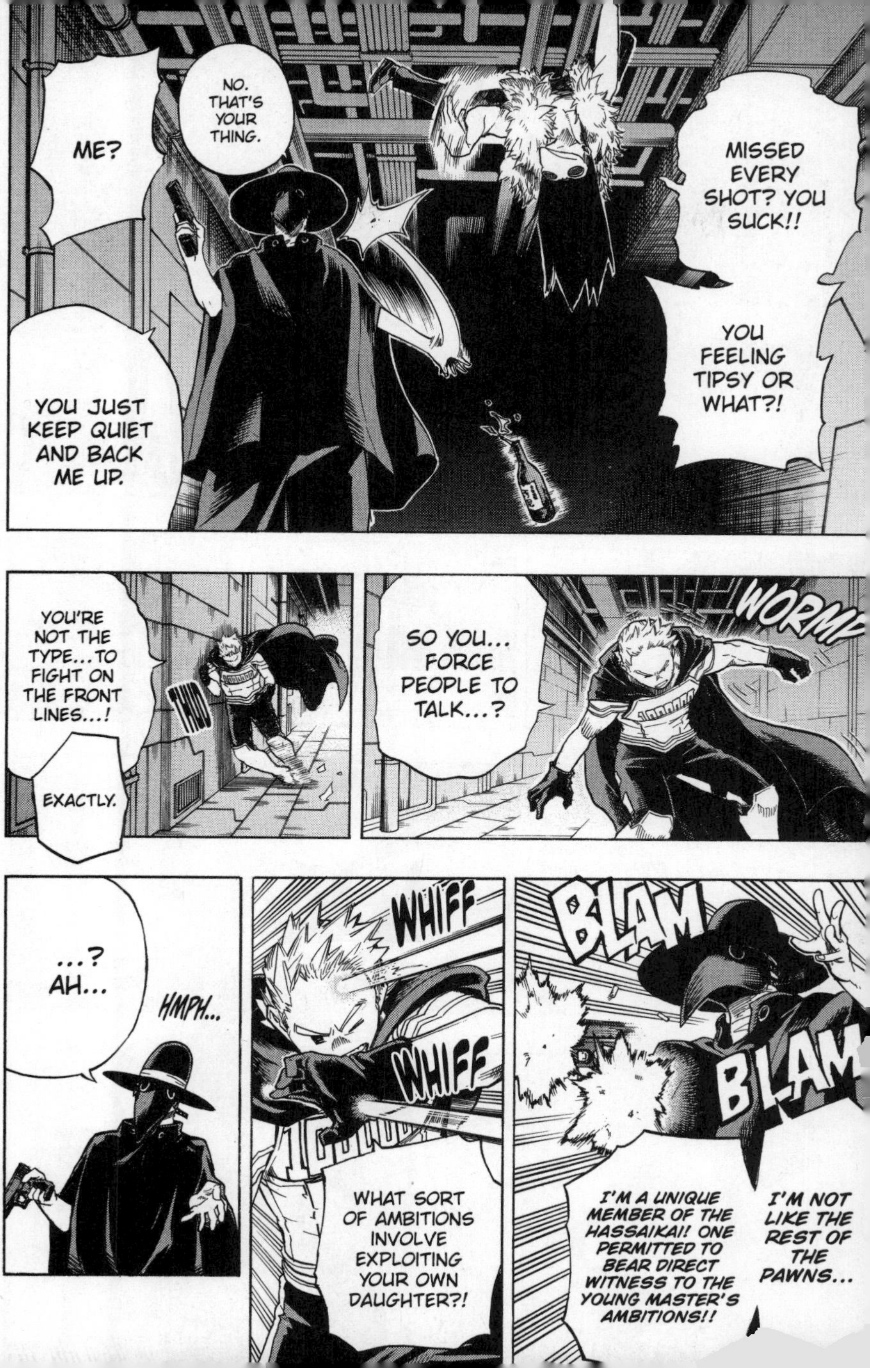
MISSED EVERY SHOT? YOU SUCK!!
YOU FEELING TIPSY OR WHAT?!
ME?
NO. THAT'S YOUR THING.
YOU JUST KEEP QUIET AND BACK ME UP.
WORMY
SO YOU... FORCE PEOPLE TO TALK...?
YOU'RE NOT THE TYPE...TO FIGHT ON THE FRONT LINES...!
THUD
EXACTLY.
BLAM
BLAM
I'M NOT LIKE THE REST OF THE PAWNS...
I'M A UNIQUE MEMBER OF THE HASSAIKAI! ONE PERMITTED TO BEAR DIRECT WITNESS TO THE YOUNG MASTER'S AMBITIONS!!
WHIFF
WHIFF
WHAT SORT OF AMBITIONS INVOLVE EXPLOITING YOUR OWN DAUGHTER?!
...? AH...
HMPH...

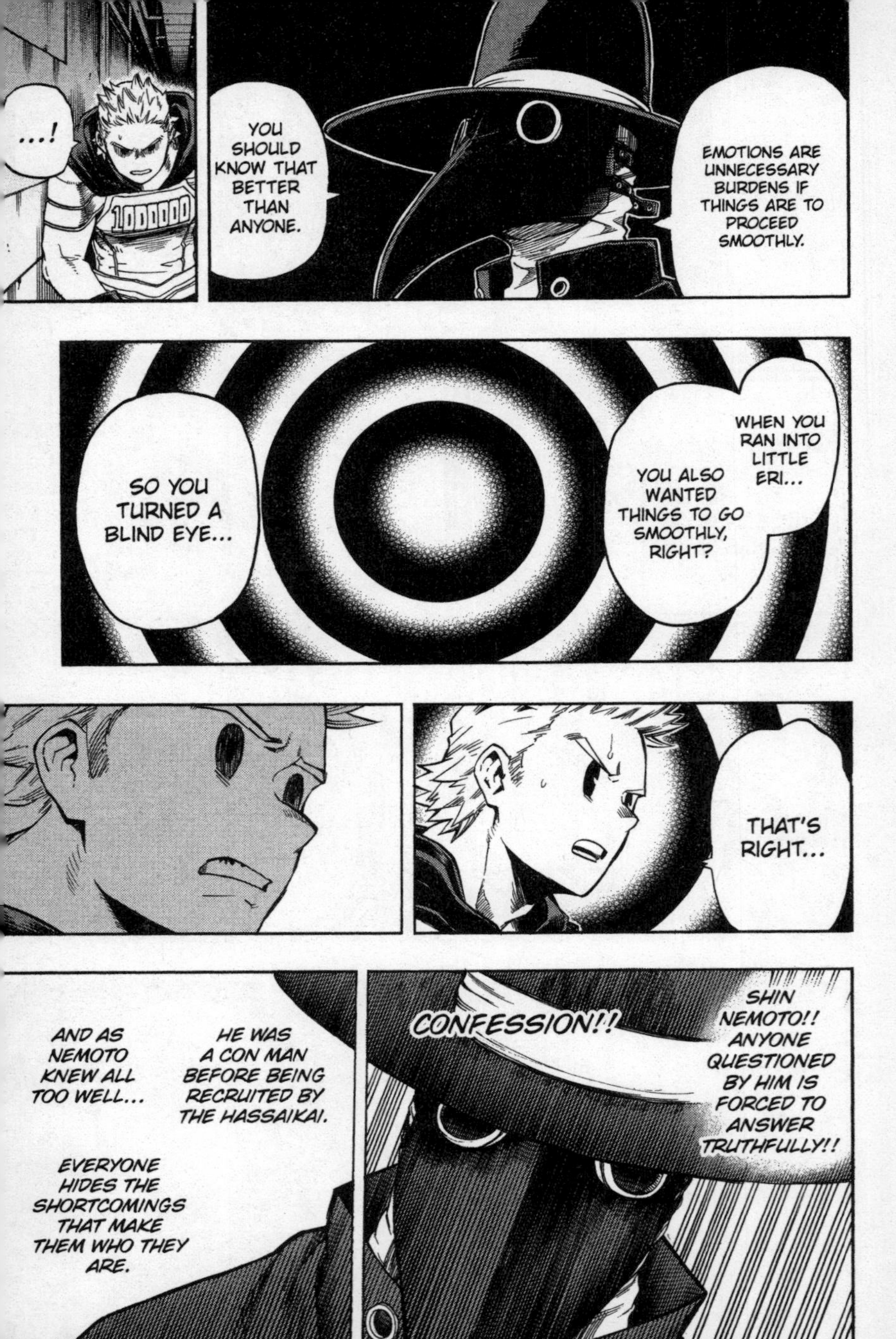

EMOTIONS ARE UNNECESSARY BURDENS IF THINGS ARE TO PROCEED SMOOTHLY.
YOU SHOULD KNOW THAT BETTER THAN ANYONE.
...!
1000000
WHEN YOU RAN INTO LITTLE ERI...
YOU ALSO WANTED THINGS TO GO SMOOTHLY, RIGHT?
SO YOU TURNED A BLIND EYE...
THAT'S RIGHT...
SHIN NEMOTO!! ANYONE QUESTIONED BY HIM IS FORCED TO ANSWER TRUTHFULLY!!
CONFESSION!!
HE WAS A CON MAN BEFORE BEING RECRUITED BY THE HASSAIKAI.
AND AS NEMOTO KNEW ALL TOO WELL...
EVERYONE HIDES THE SHORTCOMINGS THAT MAKE THEM WHO THEY ARE.

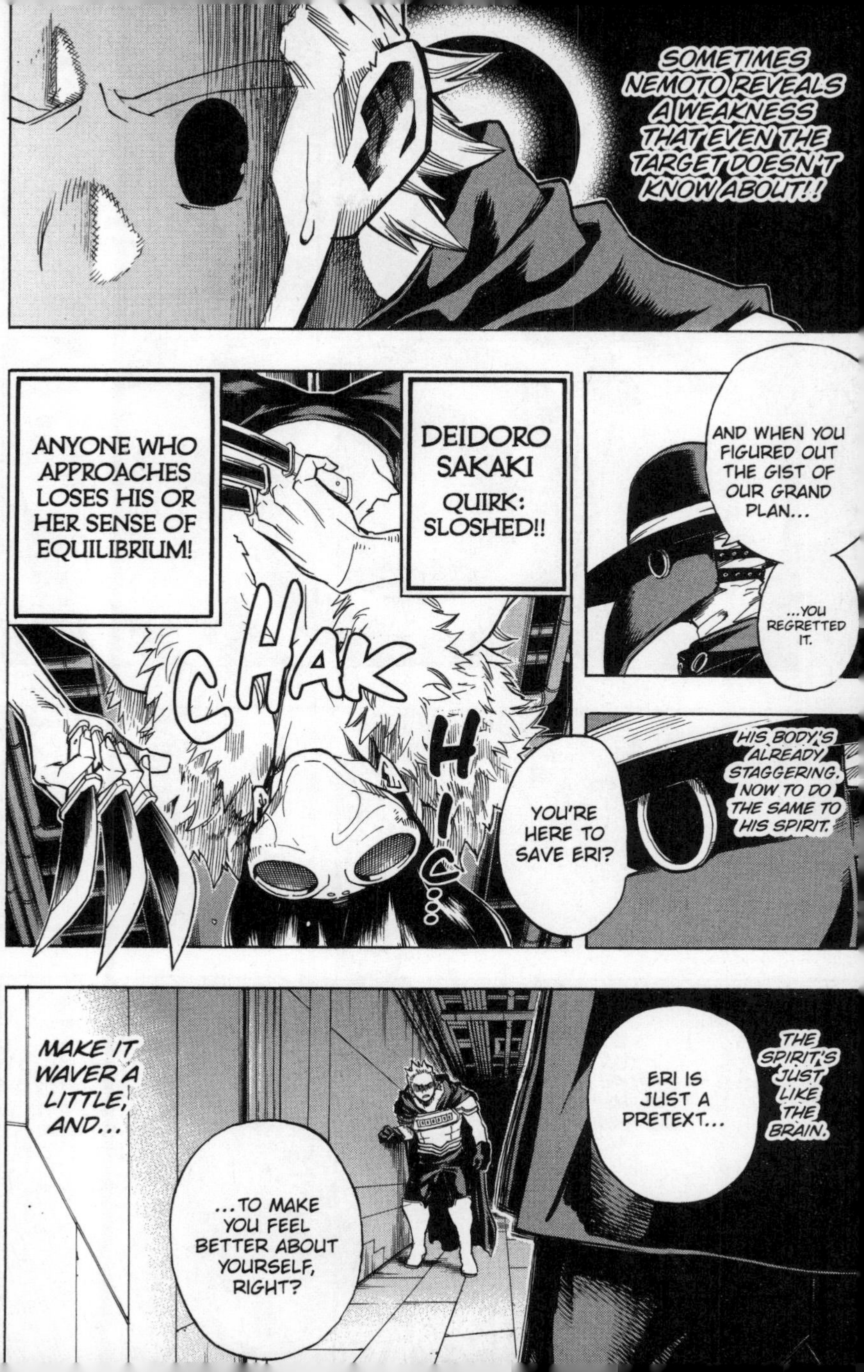
SOMETIMES NEMOTO REVEALS A WEAKNESS THAT EVEN THE TARGET DOESN'T KNOW ABOUT!!
AND WHEN YOU FIGURED OUT THE GIST OF OUR GRAND PLAN...
...YOU REGRETTED IT.
HIS BODY'S ALREADY STAGGERING. NOW TO DO THE SAME TO HIS SPIRIT.
YOU'RE HERE TO SAVE ERI?
DEIDORO SAKAKI QUIRK: SLOSHED!!
ANYONE WHO APPROACHES LOSES HIS OR HER SENSE OF EQUILIBRIUM!
CHAK
HIC...
THE SPIRIT'S JUST LIKE THE BRAIN.
ERI IS JUST A PRETEXT...
MAKE IT WAVER A LITTLE, AND...
...TO MAKE YOU FEEL BETTER ABOUT YOURSELF, RIGHT?

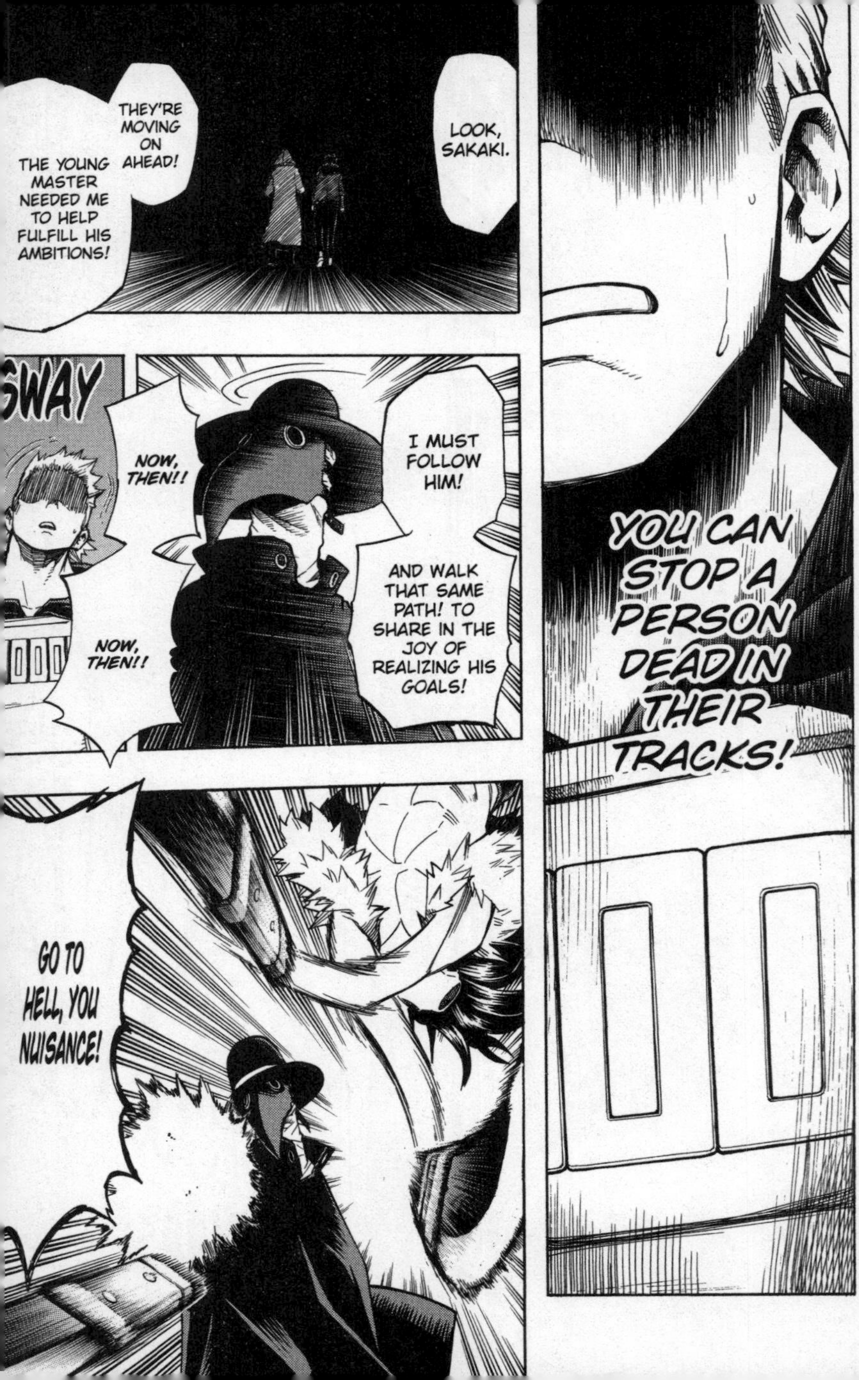
YOU CAN STOP A PERSON DEAD IN THEIR TRACKS!
LOOK, SAKAKI.
THEY'RE MOVING ON AHEAD!
THE YOUNG MASTER NEEDED ME TO HELP FULFILL HIS AMBITIONS!
I MUST FOLLOW HIM!
AND WALK THAT SAME PATH! TO SHARE IN THE JOY OF REALIZING HIS GOALS!
NOW, THEN!!
NOW, THEN!!
SWAY
GO TO HELL, YOU NUISANCE!

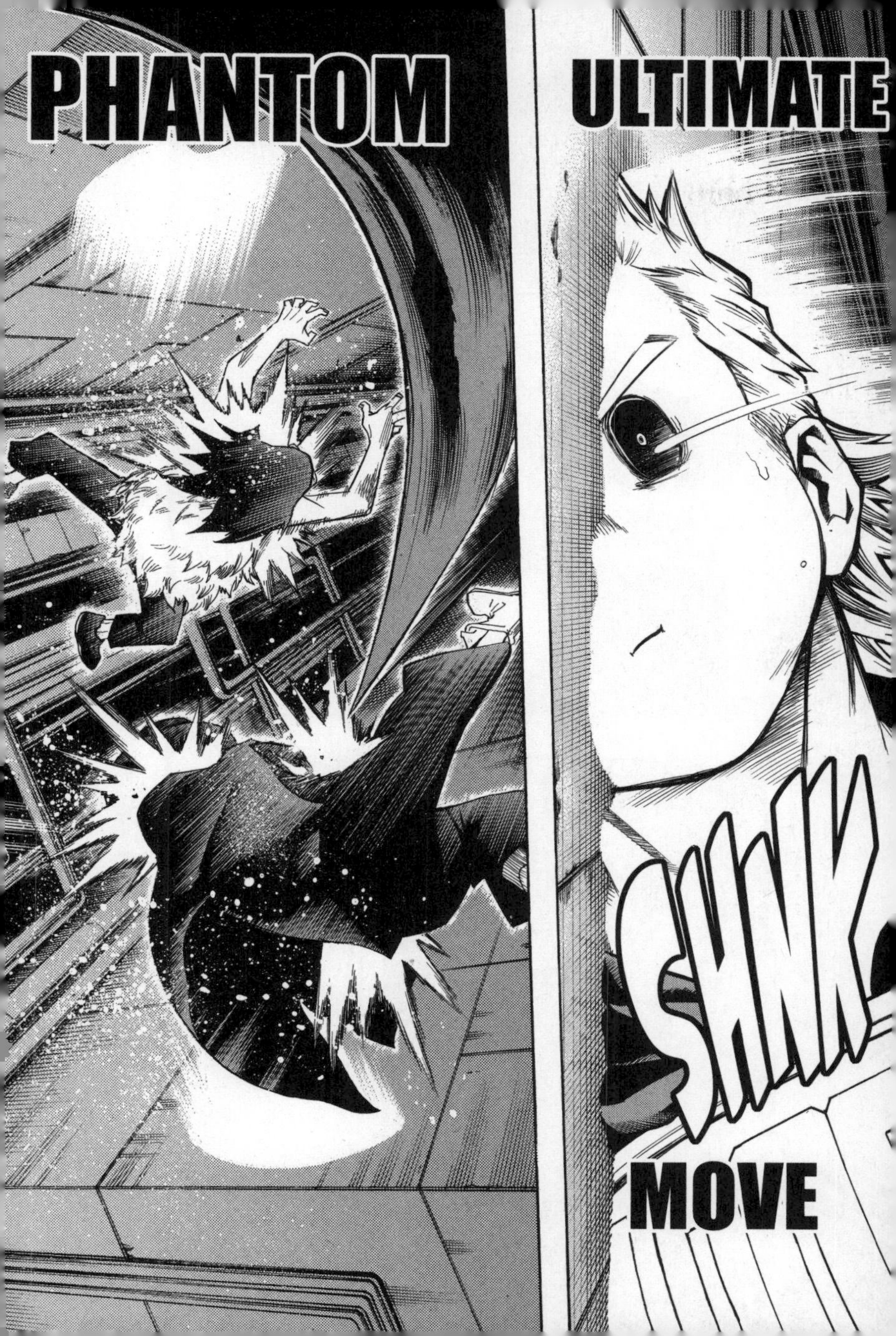
ULTIMATE
SHINK
MOVE
PHANTOM

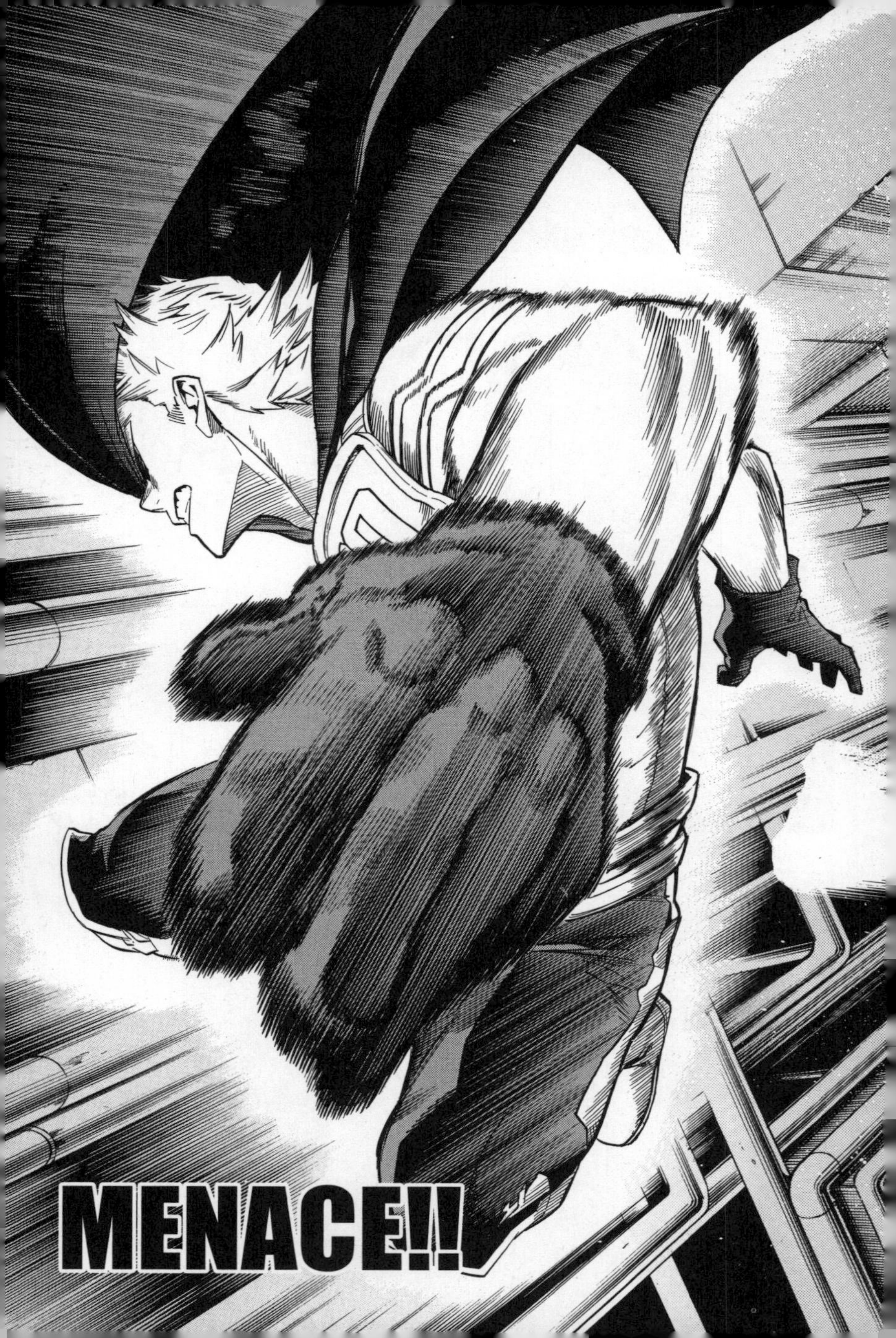
MENACE!!

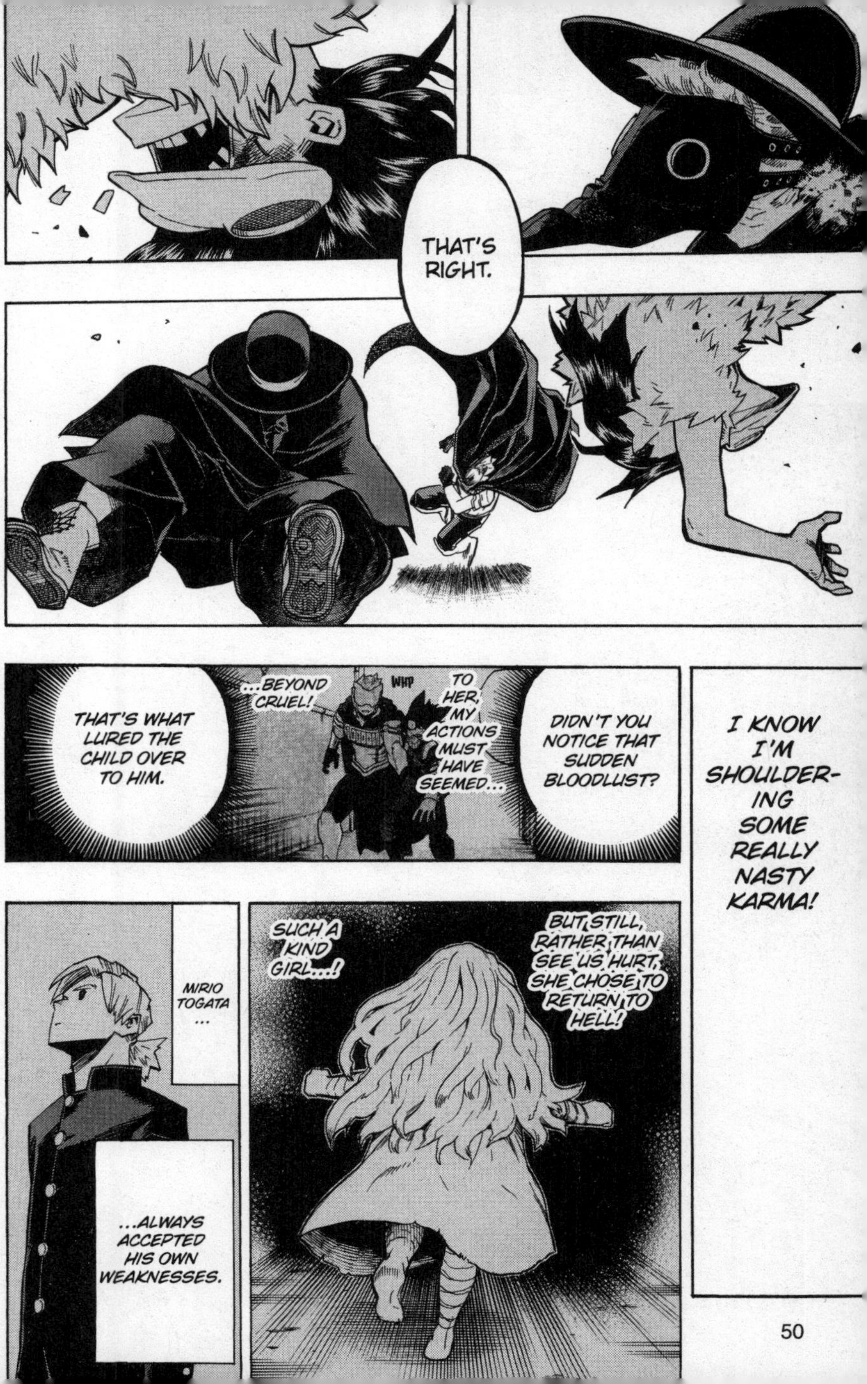
THAT'S RIGHT.
I KNOW I'M SHOULDER-ING SOME REALLY NASTY KARMA!
DIDN'T YOU NOTICE THAT SUDDEN BLOODLUST?
TO HER, MY ACTIONS MUST HAVE SEEMED...
WHP
...BEYOND CRUEL!
THAT'S WHAT LURED THE CHILD OVER TO HIM.
BUT STILL, RATHER THAN SEE US HURT, SHE CHOSE TO RETURN TO HELL!
SUCH A KIND GIRL...!
MIRIO TOGATA ...
...ALWAYS ACCEPTED HIS OWN WEAKNESSES.

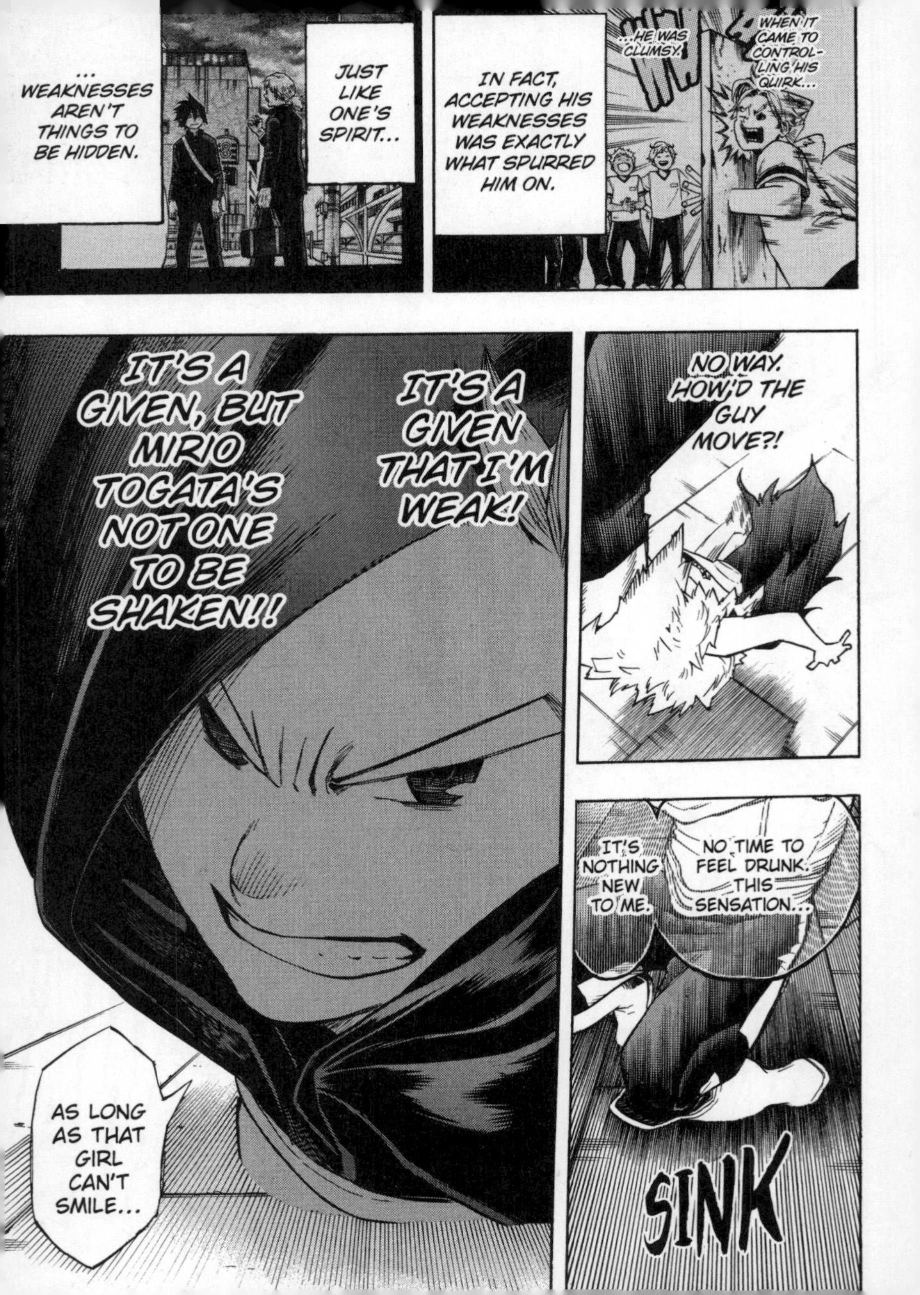
WHEN IT CAME TO CONTROL-LING HIS QUIRK...
...HE WAS CLUMSY.
IN FACT, ACCEPTING HIS WEAKNESSES WAS EXACTLY WHAT SPURRED HIM ON.
JUST LIKE ONE'S SPIRIT...
...WEAKNESSES AREN'T THINGS TO BE HIDDEN.
NO WAY. HOW'D THE GUY MOVE?!
NO TIME TO FEEL DRUNK. THIS SENSATION...
IT'S NOTHING NEW TO ME.
SINK
IT'S A GIVEN THAT I'M WEAK!
IT'S A GIVEN, BUT MIRIO TOGATA'S NOT ONE TO BE SHAKEN!!
AS LONG AS THAT GIRL CAN'T SMILE...

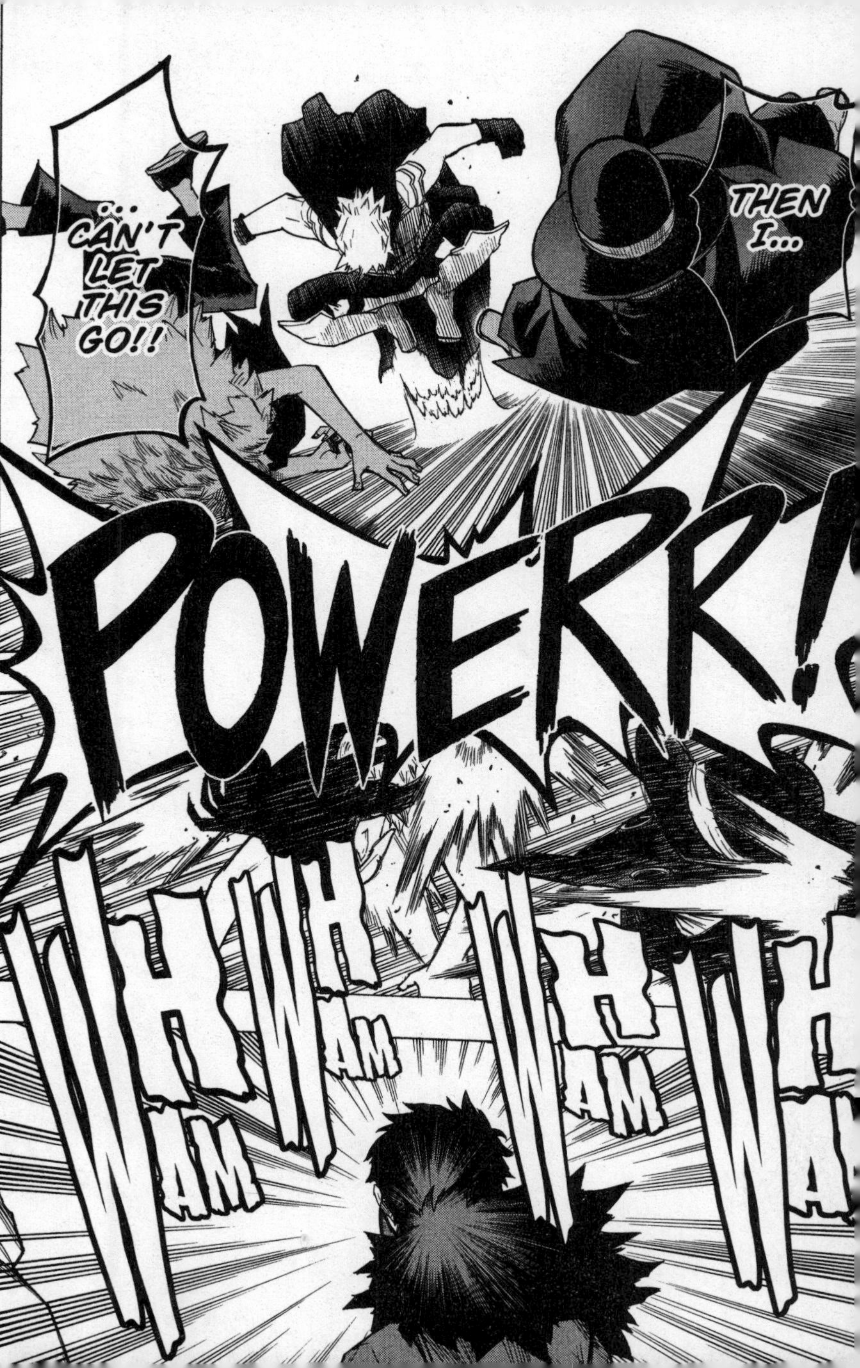
THEN I...
...CAN'T LET THIS GO!!
POWERR!!
WHAM
WHAM
WHAM

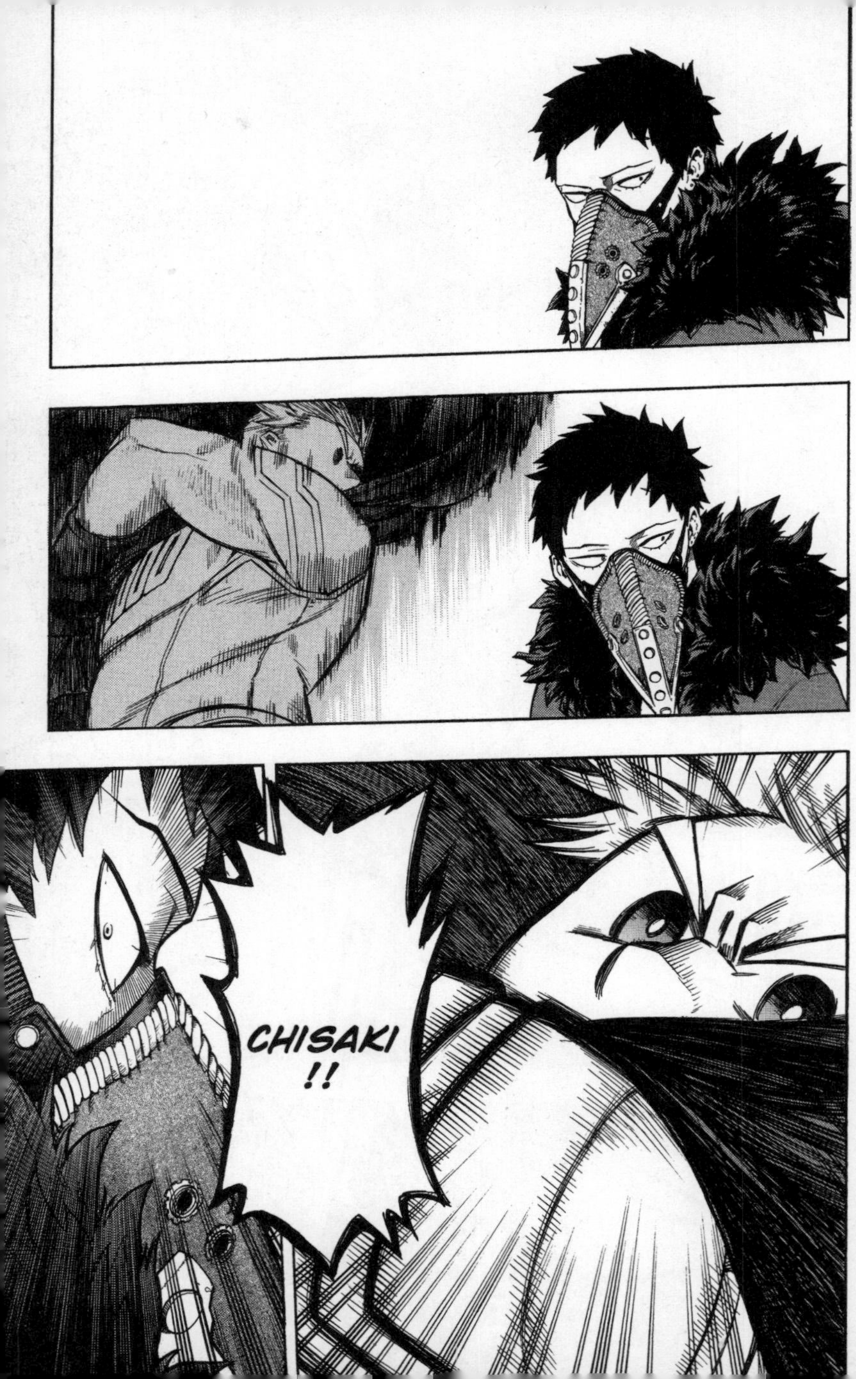
CHISAKI
!!

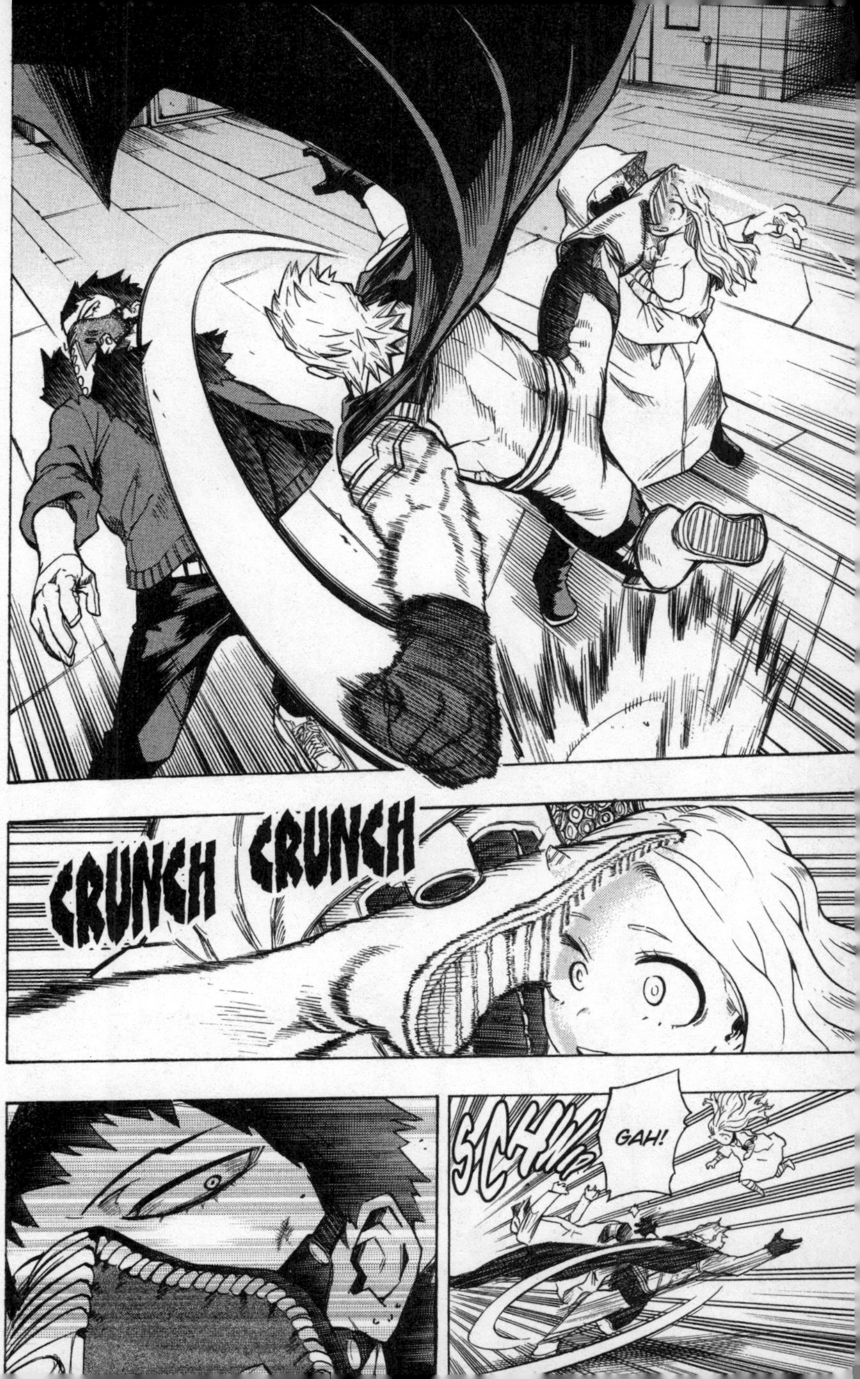
CRUNCH CRUNCH
GAH!
SCHLUK

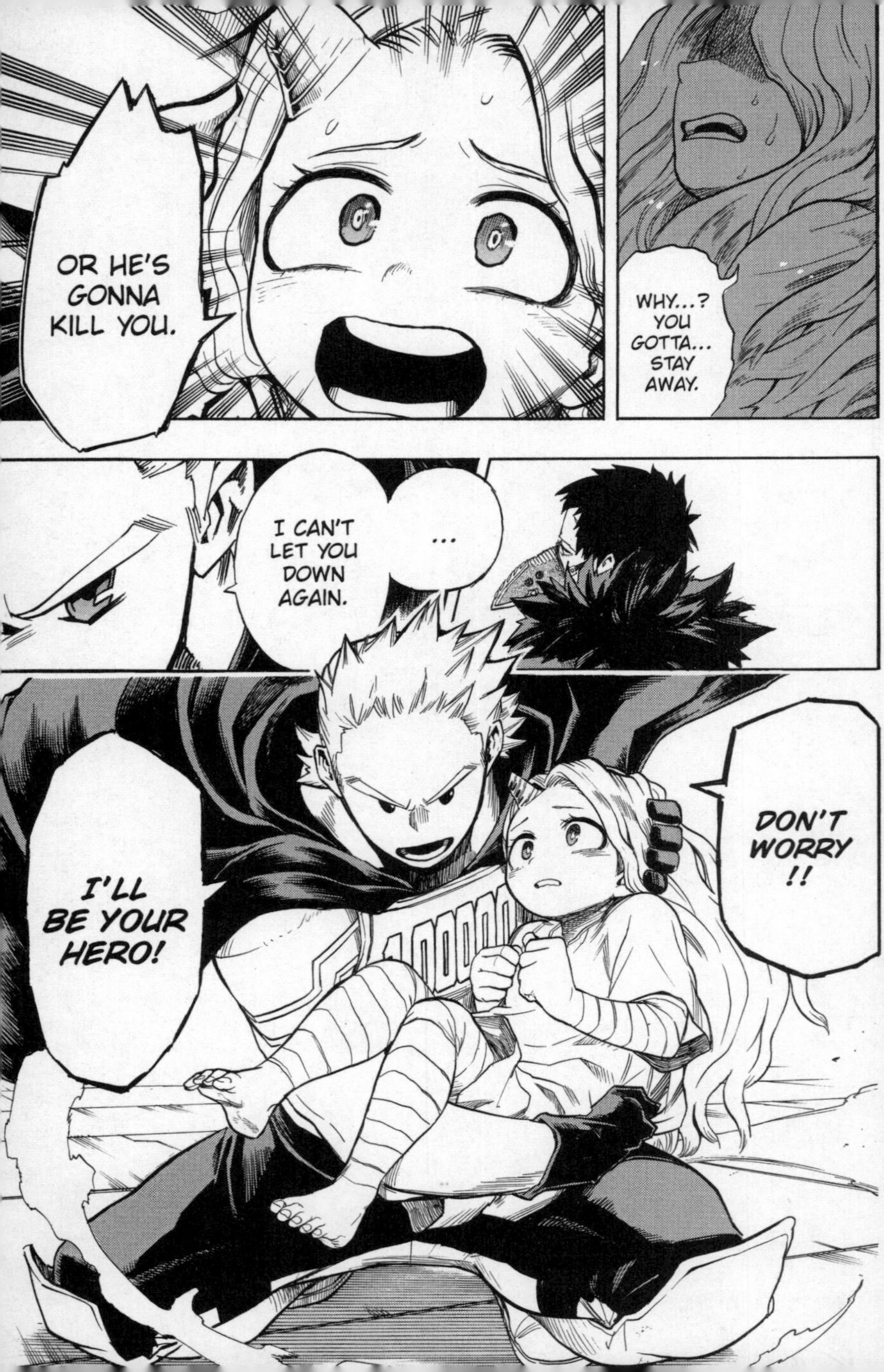
WHY...? YOU GOTTA... STAY AWAY.
OR HE'S GONNA KILL YOU.
...
I CAN'T LET YOU DOWN AGAIN.
DON'T WORRY!!
I'LL BE YOUR HERO!

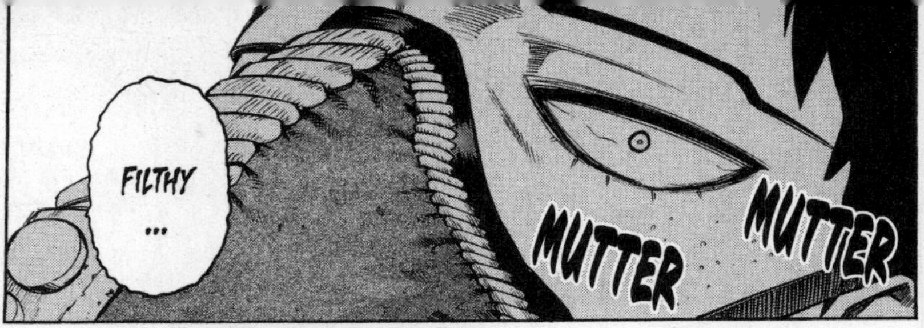
MUTTER
MUTTER
FILTHY ...

NO. 151 - MIRIO TOGATA!!

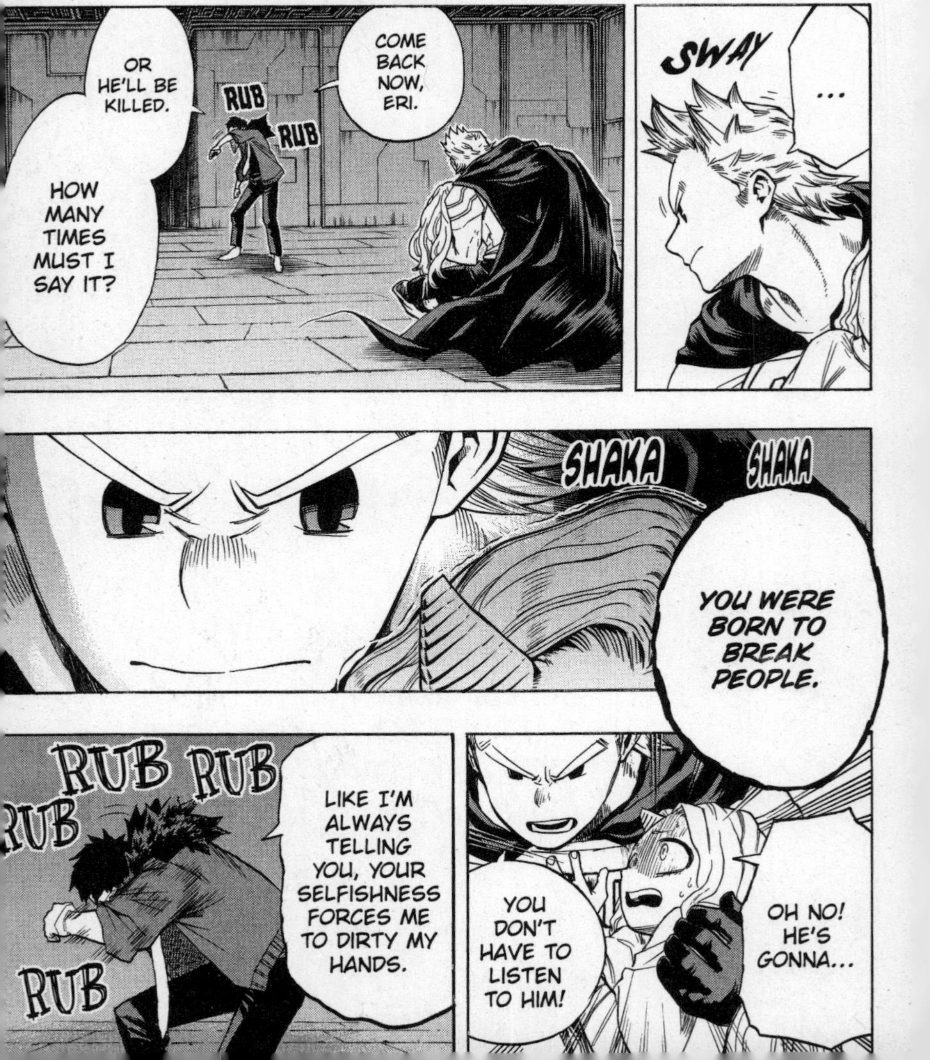
SWAY
...
COME BACK NOW, ERI.
OR HE'LL BE KILLED.
RUB
RUB
HOW MANY TIMES MUST I SAY IT?
SHAKA
SHAKA
YOU WERE BORN TO BREAK PEOPLE.
OH NO! HE'S GONNA...
YOU DON'T HAVE TO LISTEN TO HIM!
LIKE I'M ALWAYS TELLING YOU, YOUR SELFISHNESS FORCES ME TO DIRTY MY HANDS.
RUB RUB
RUB
RUB

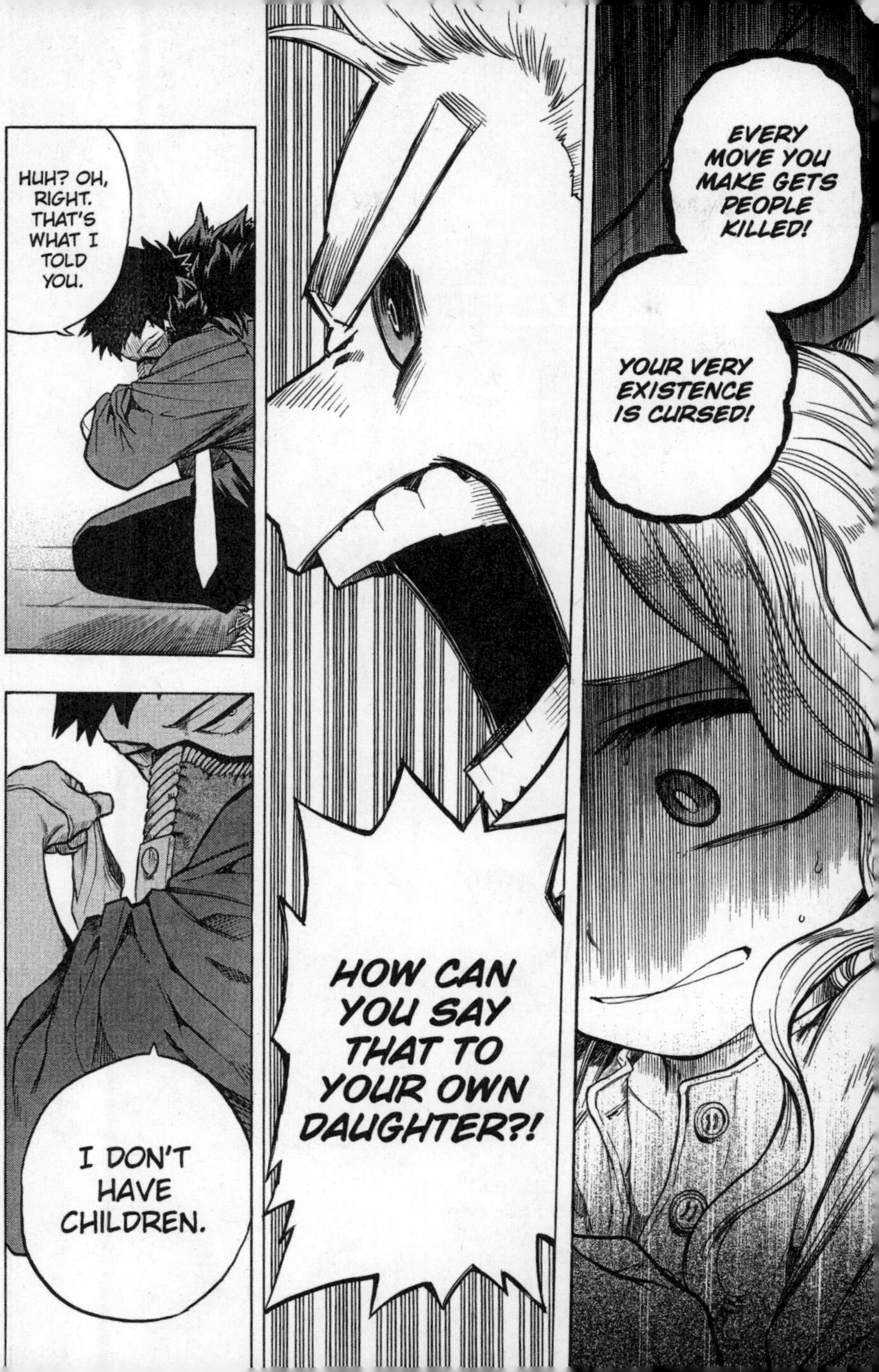

EVERY MOVE YOU MAKE GETS PEOPLE KILLED!
YOUR VERY EXISTENCE IS CURSED!
HOW CAN YOU SAY THAT TO YOUR OWN DAUGHTER?!
HUH? OH, RIGHT. THAT'S WHAT I TOLD YOU.
I DON'T HAVE CHILDREN.

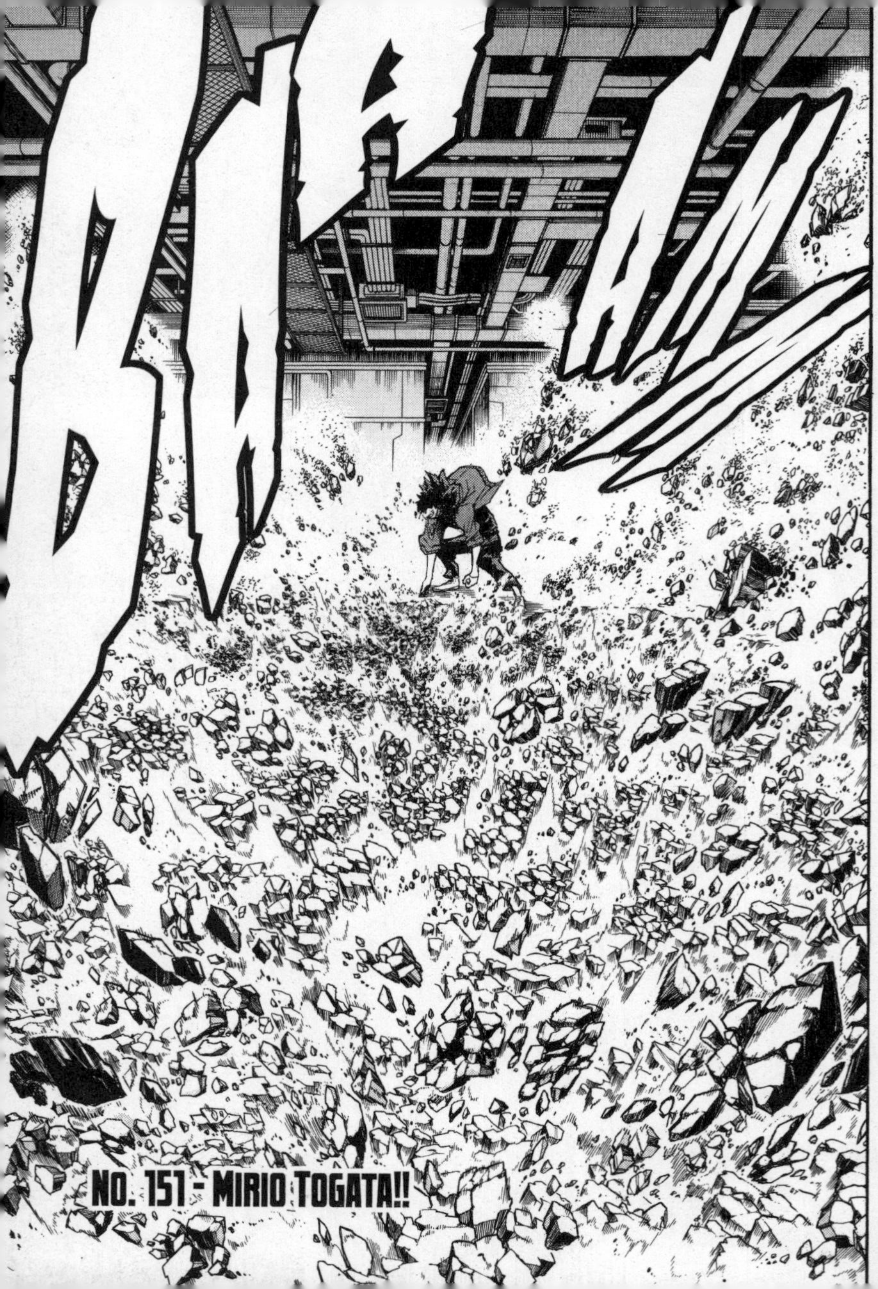
NO. 151 - MIRIO TOGATA!!

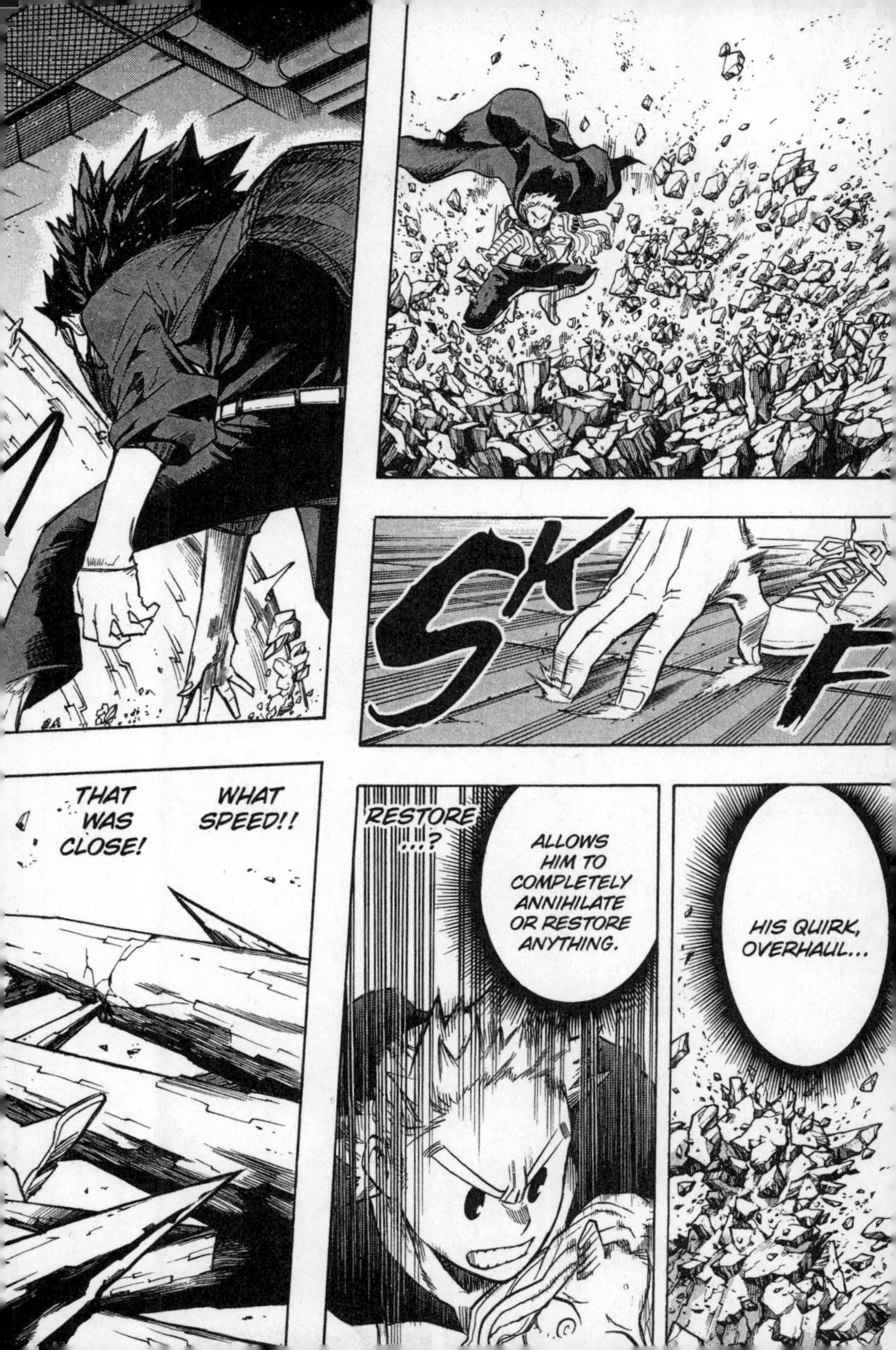
SK
F
HIS QUIRK, OVERHAUL...
ALLOWS HIM TO COMPLETELY ANNIHILATE OR RESTORE ANYTHING.
RESTORE ...?
WHAT SPEED!!
THAT WAS CLOSE!

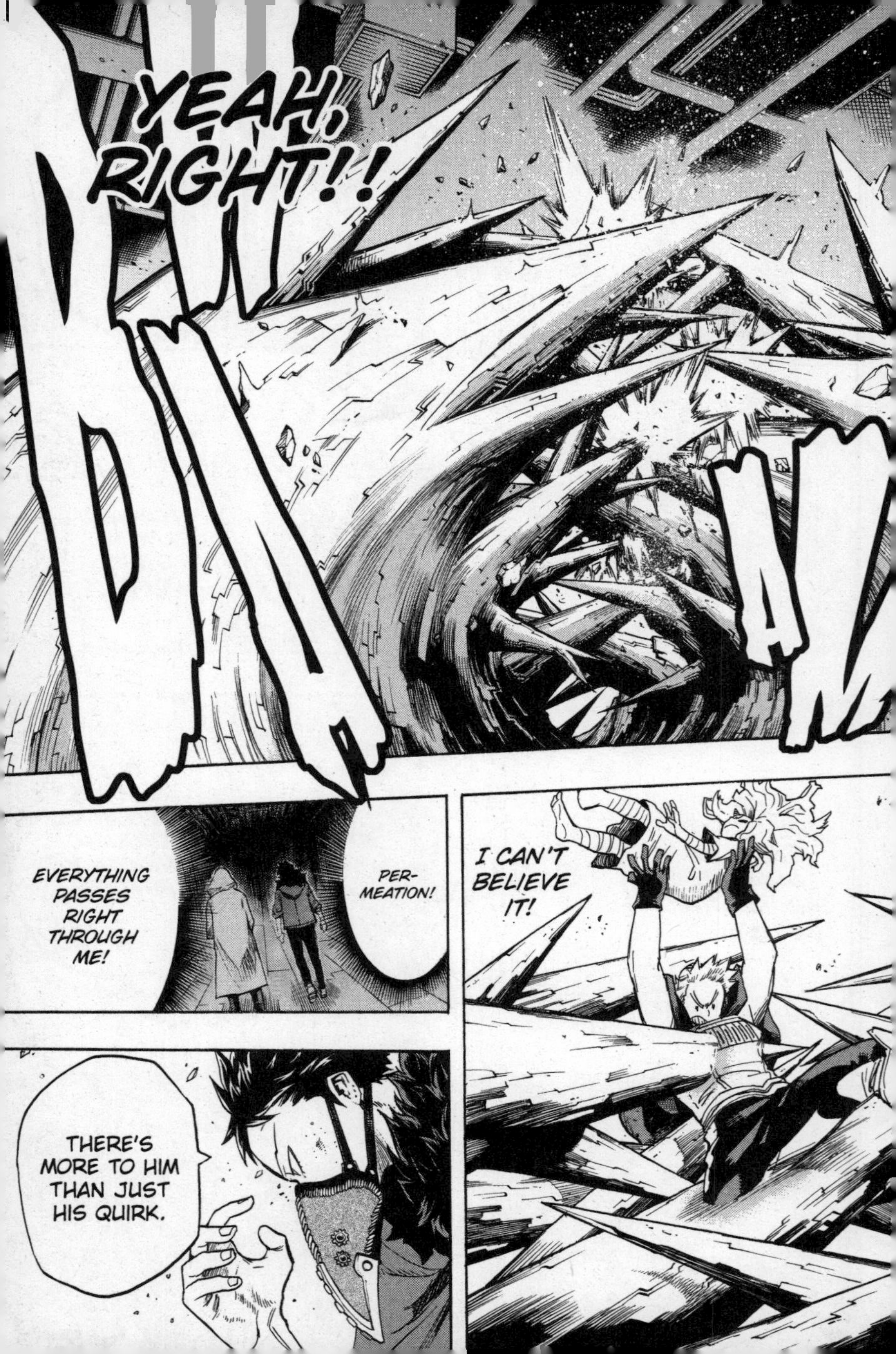
YEAH, RIGHT!!
I CAN'T BELIEVE IT!
PER-MEATION!
EVERYTHING PASSES RIGHT THROUGH ME!
THERE'S MORE TO HIM THAN JUST HIS QUIRK.

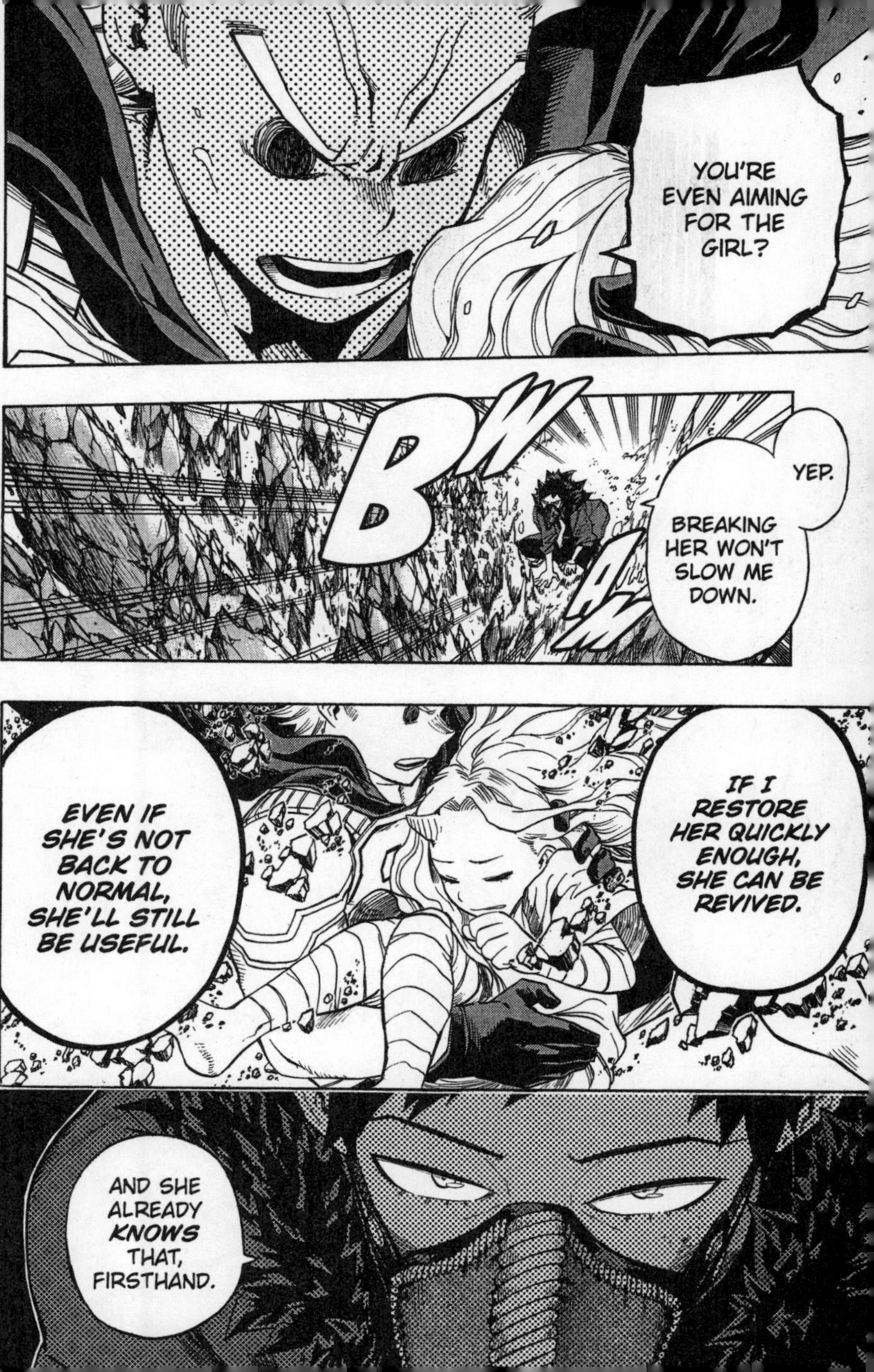
YOU'RE EVEN AIMING FOR THE GIRL?
YEP.
BREAKING HER WON'T SLOW ME DOWN.
IF I RESTORE HER QUICKLY ENOUGH, SHE CAN BE REVIVED.
EVEN IF SHE'S NOT BACK TO NORMAL, SHE'LL STILL BE USEFUL.
AND SHE ALREADY *KNOWS* THAT, FIRSTHAND.

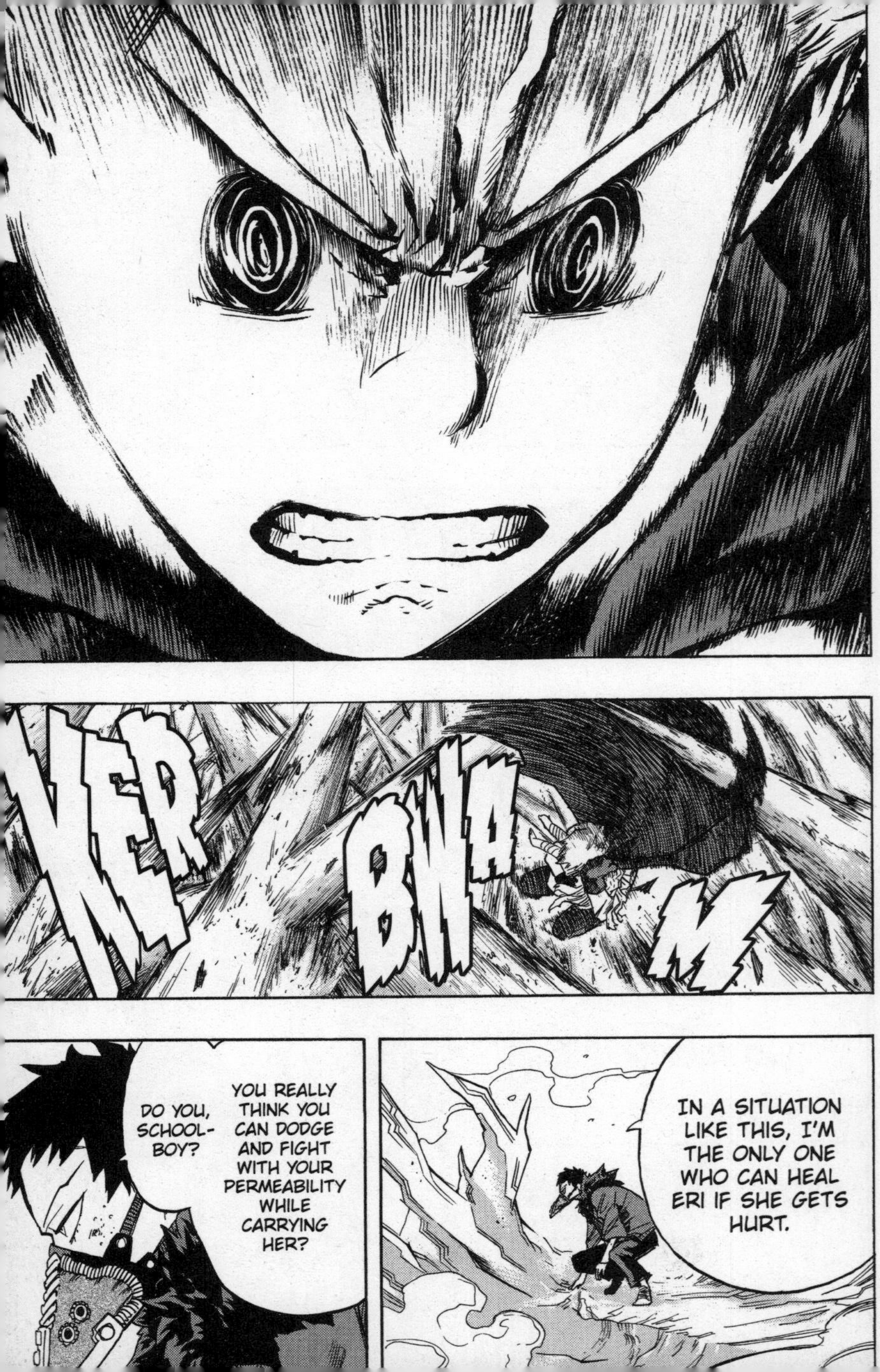
KER BWAM
IN A SITUATION LIKE THIS, I'M THE ONLY ONE WHO CAN HEAL ERI IF SHE GETS HURT.
YOU REALLY THINK YOU CAN DODGE AND FIGHT WITH YOUR PERMEABILITY WHILE CARRYING HER?
DO YOU, SCHOOL-BOY?

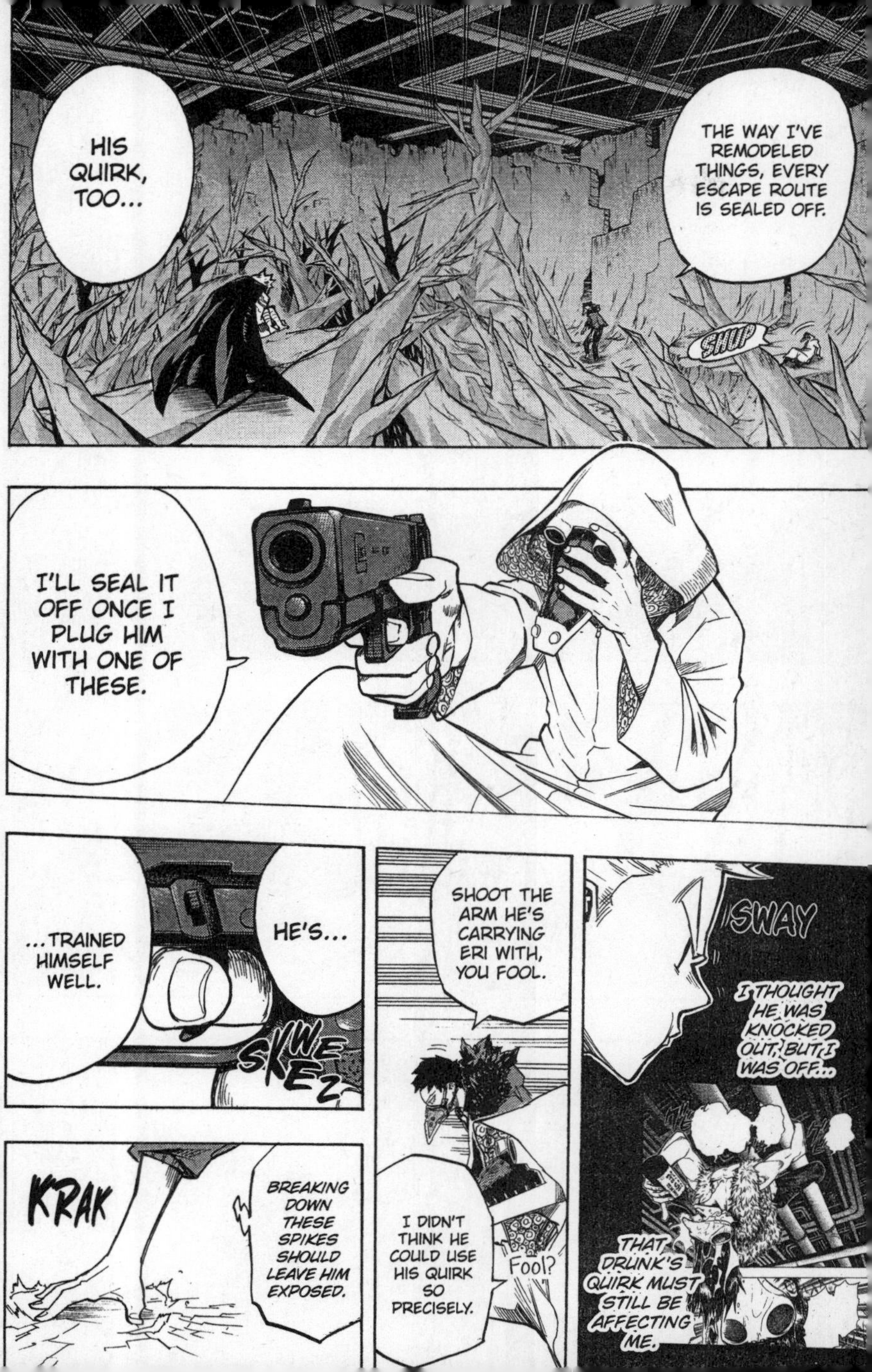
THE WAY I'VE REMODELED THINGS, EVERY ESCAPE ROUTE IS SEALED OFF.
SHOP
HIS QUIRK, TOO...
I'LL SEAL IT OFF ONCE I PLUG HIM WITH ONE OF THESE.
SWAY
I THOUGHT HE WAS KNOCKED OUT, BUT I WAS OFF...
THAT DRUNK'S QUIRK MUST STILL BE AFFECTING ME.
SHOOT THE ARM HE'S CARRYING ERI WITH, YOU FOOL.
I DIDN'T THINK HE COULD USE HIS QUIRK SO PRECISELY.
Fool?
HE'S...
...TRAINED HIMSELF WELL.
SKWEEZ
BREAKING DOWN THESE SPIKES SHOULD LEAVE HIM EXPOSED.
KRAK

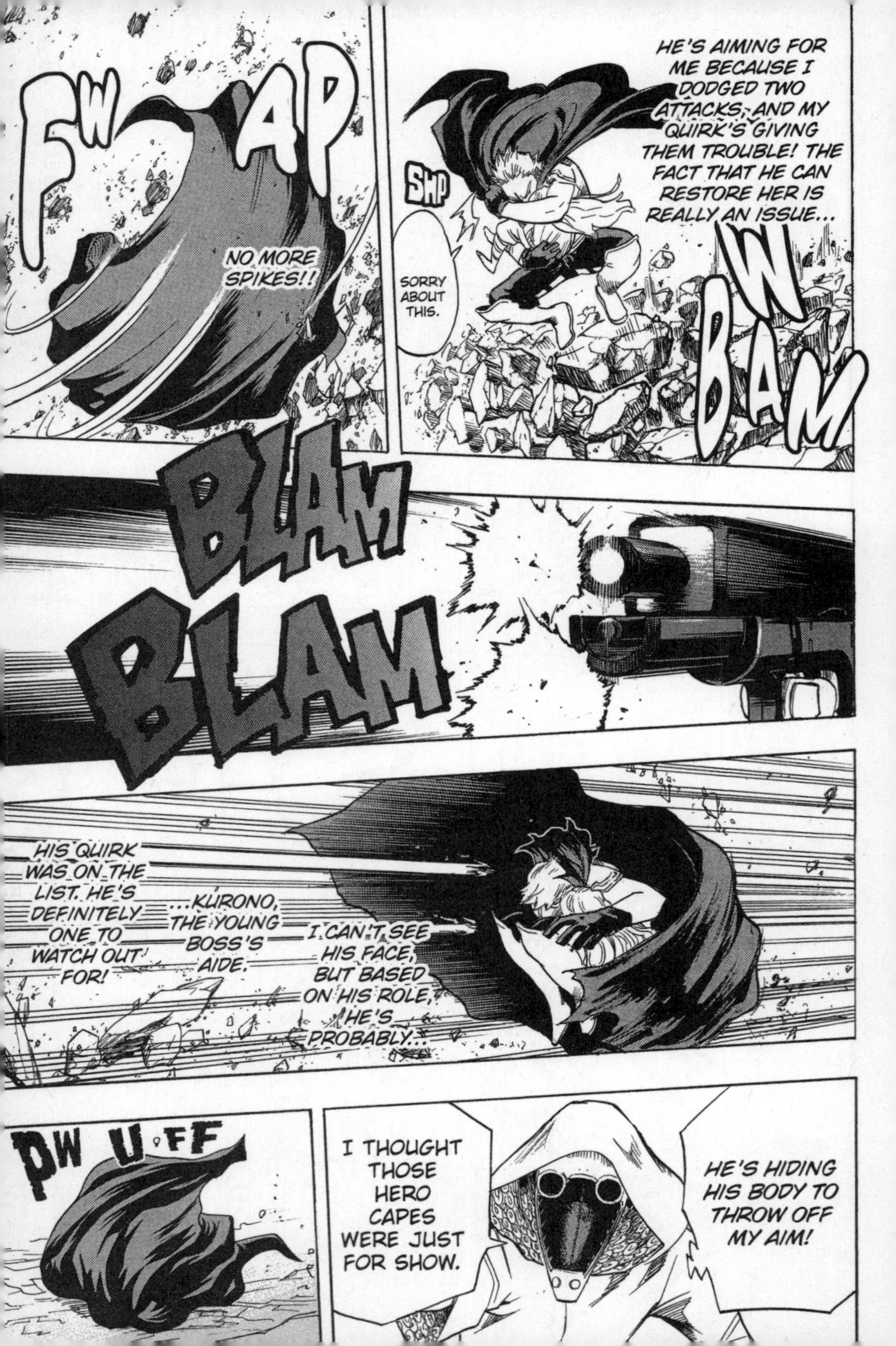
HE'S AIMING FOR ME BECAUSE I DODGED TWO ATTACKS, AND MY QUIRK'S GIVING THEM TROUBLE! THE FACT THAT HE CAN RESTORE HER IS REALLY AN ISSUE...
SHP
SORRY ABOUT THIS.
BWAM
FWAP
NO MORE SPIKES!!
BLAM
BLAM
I CAN'T SEE HIS FACE, BUT BASED ON HIS ROLE, HE'S PROBABLY...
...KURONO, THE YOUNG BOSS'S AIDE.
HIS QUIRK WAS ON THE LIST. HE'S DEFINITELY ONE TO WATCH OUT FOR!
HE'S HIDING HIS BODY TO THROW OFF MY AIM!
I THOUGHT THOSE HERO CAPES WERE JUST FOR SHOW.
PWUFF

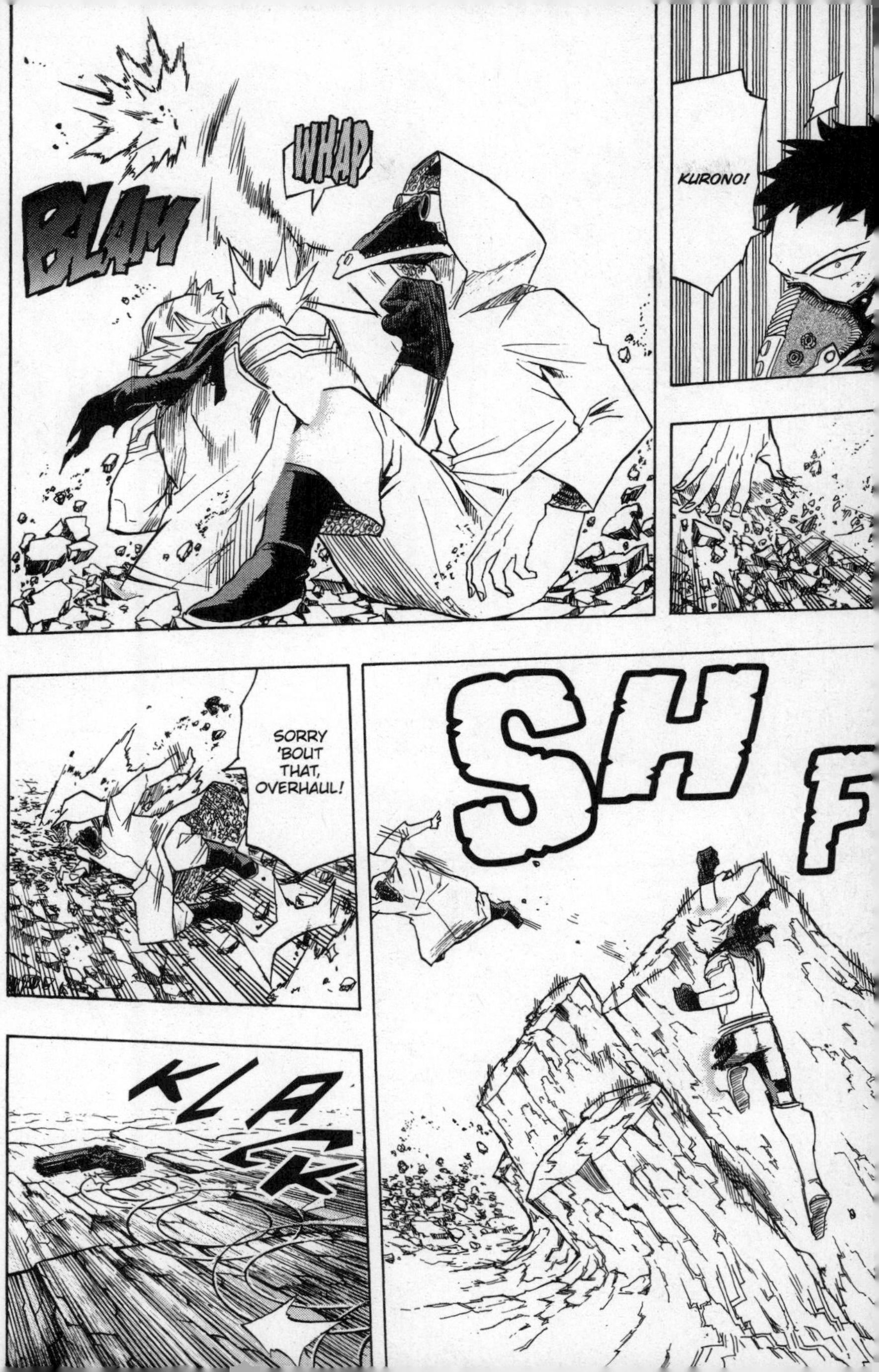
KURONO!
WHAP
BLAM
SH
F
SORRY 'BOUT THAT, OVERHAUL!
KLACK

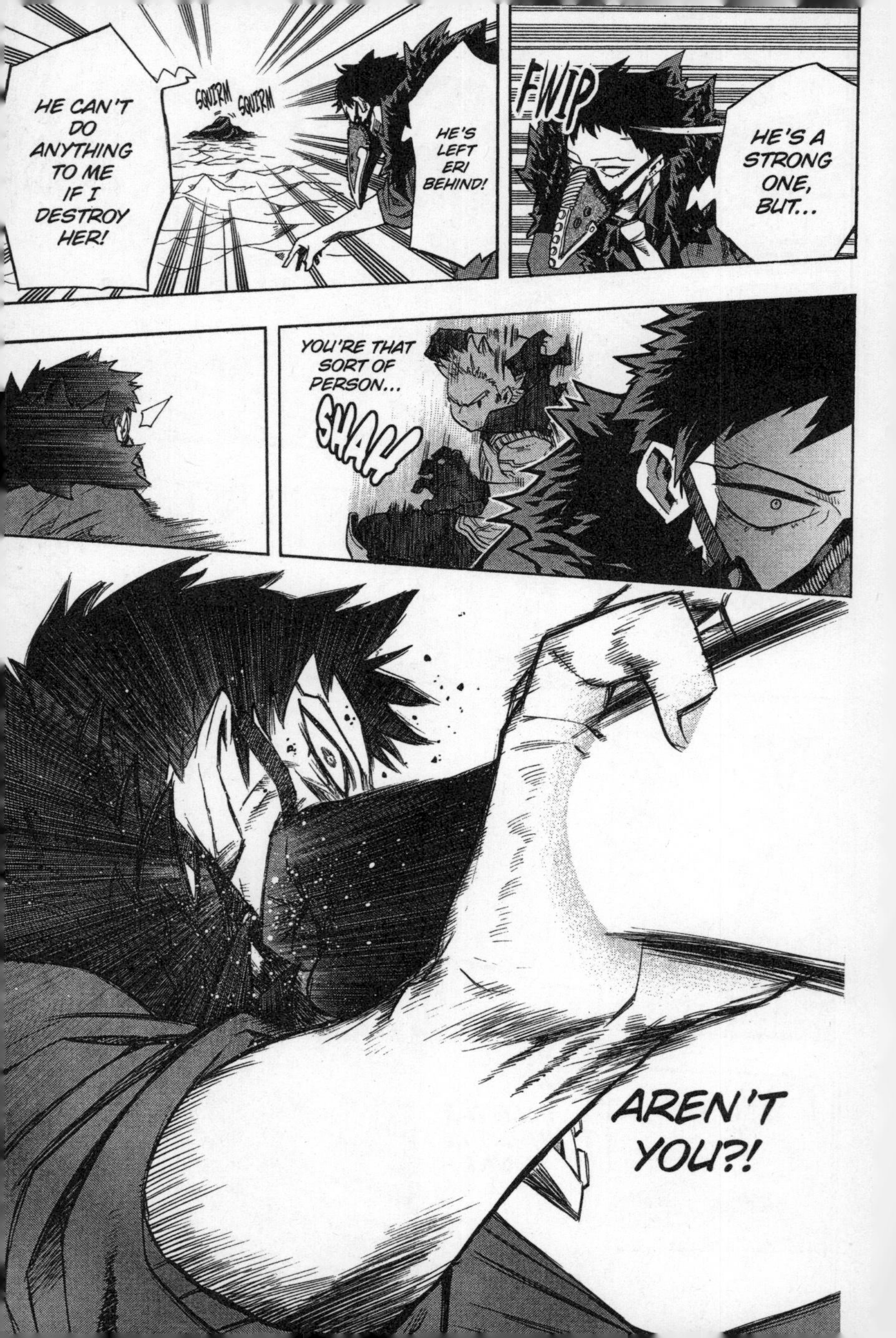

FWIP
HE'S A STRONG ONE, BUT...
HE'S LEFT ERI BEHIND!
SQUIRM SQUIRM
HE CAN'T DO ANYTHING TO ME IF I DESTROY HER!
YOU'RE THAT SORT OF PERSON...
SHAH
AREN'T YOU?!

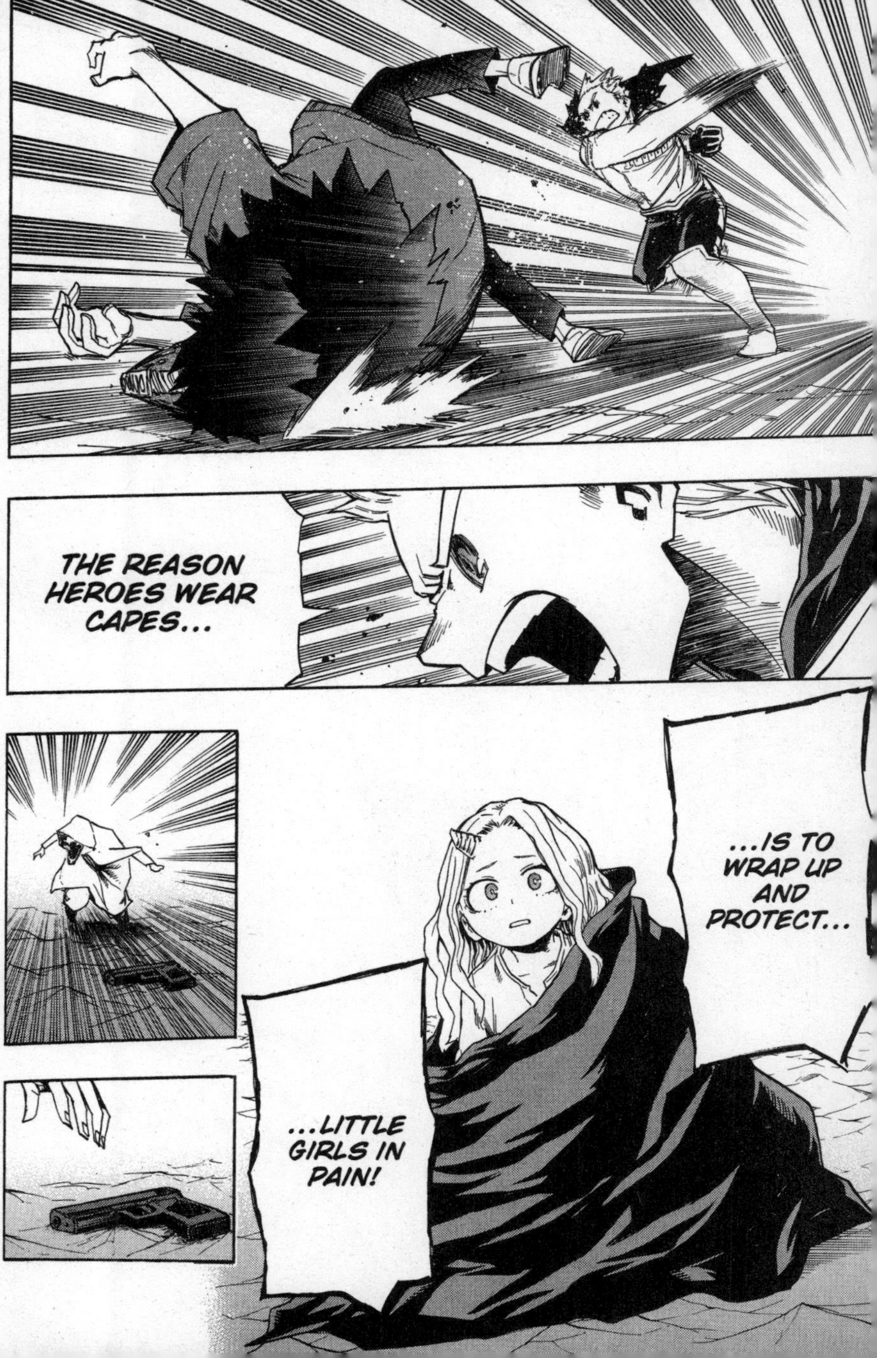
THE REASON HEROES WEAR CAPES...
...IS TO WRAP UP AND PROTECT...
...LITTLE GIRLS IN PAIN!

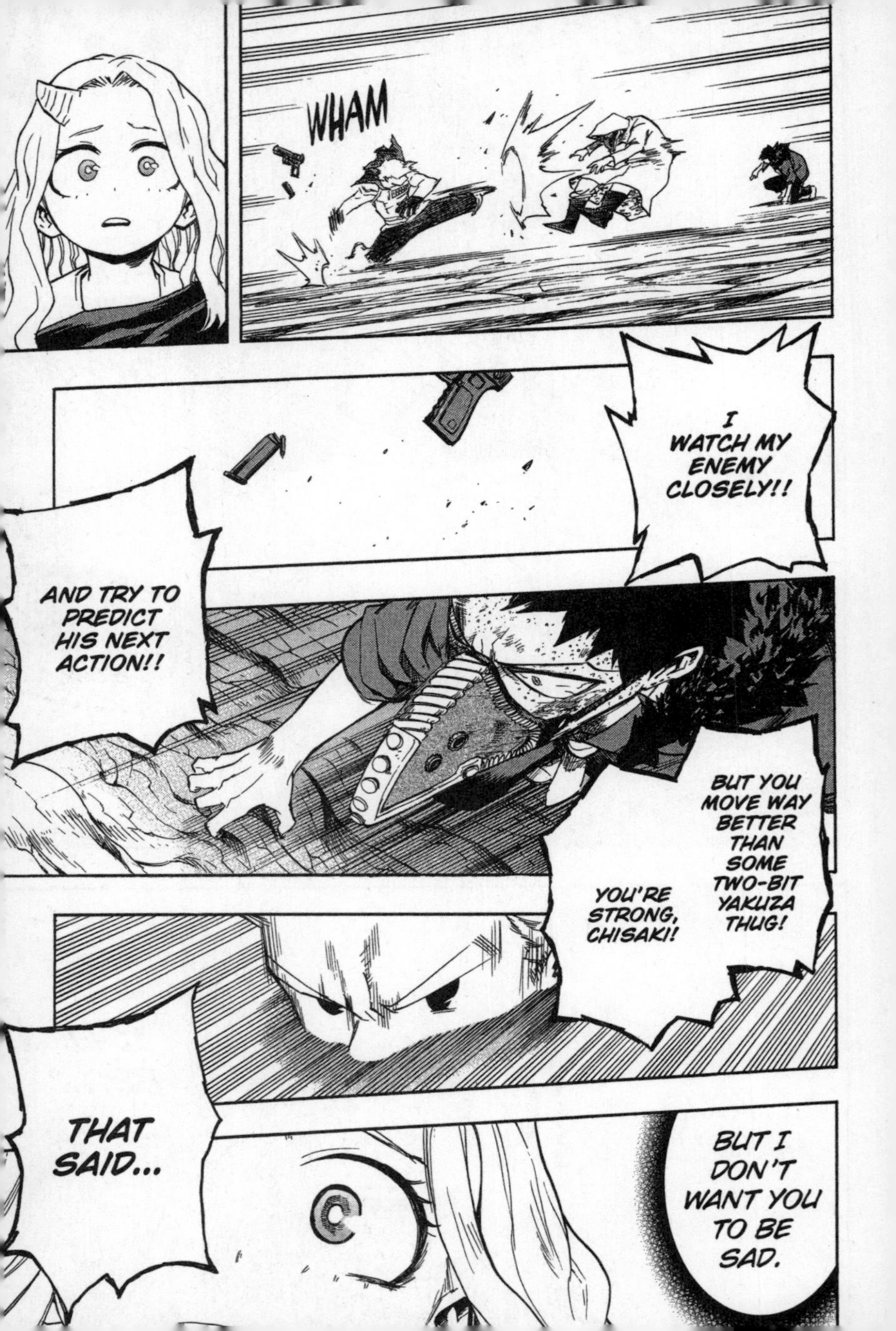

WHAM
I WATCH MY ENEMY CLOSELY!!
AND TRY TO PREDICT HIS NEXT ACTION!!
BUT YOU MOVE WAY BETTER THAN SOME TWO-BIT YAKUZA THUG!
YOU'RE STRONG, CHISAKI!
BUT I DON'T WANT YOU TO BE SAD.
THAT SAID...

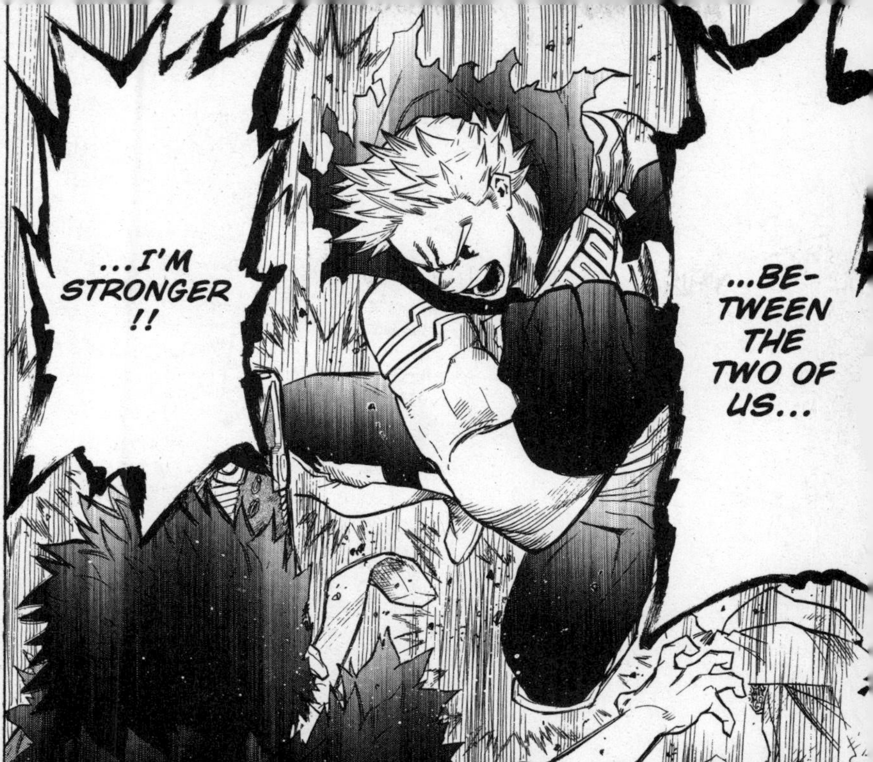
...BE-TWEEN THE TWO OF US...
...I'M STRONGER!!
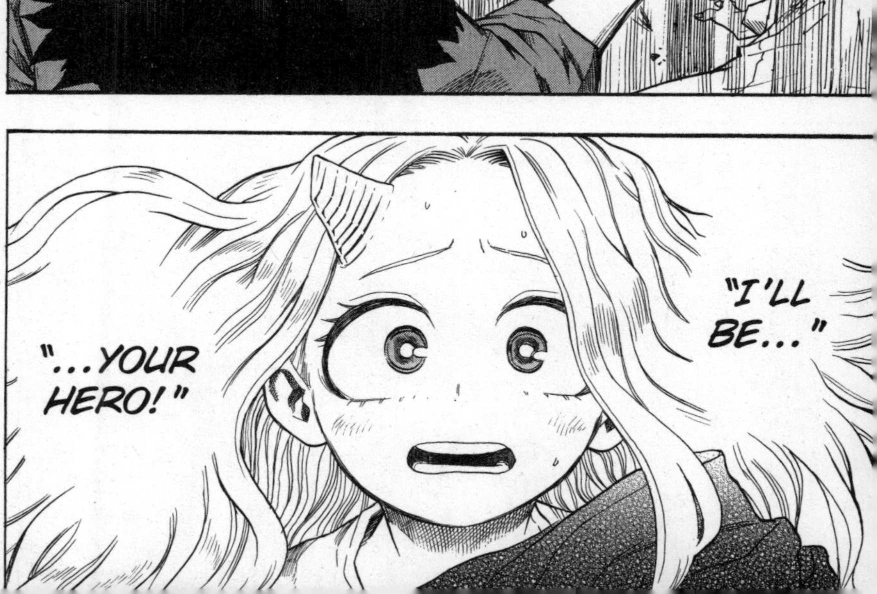
"I'LL BE..."
"...YOUR HERO!"

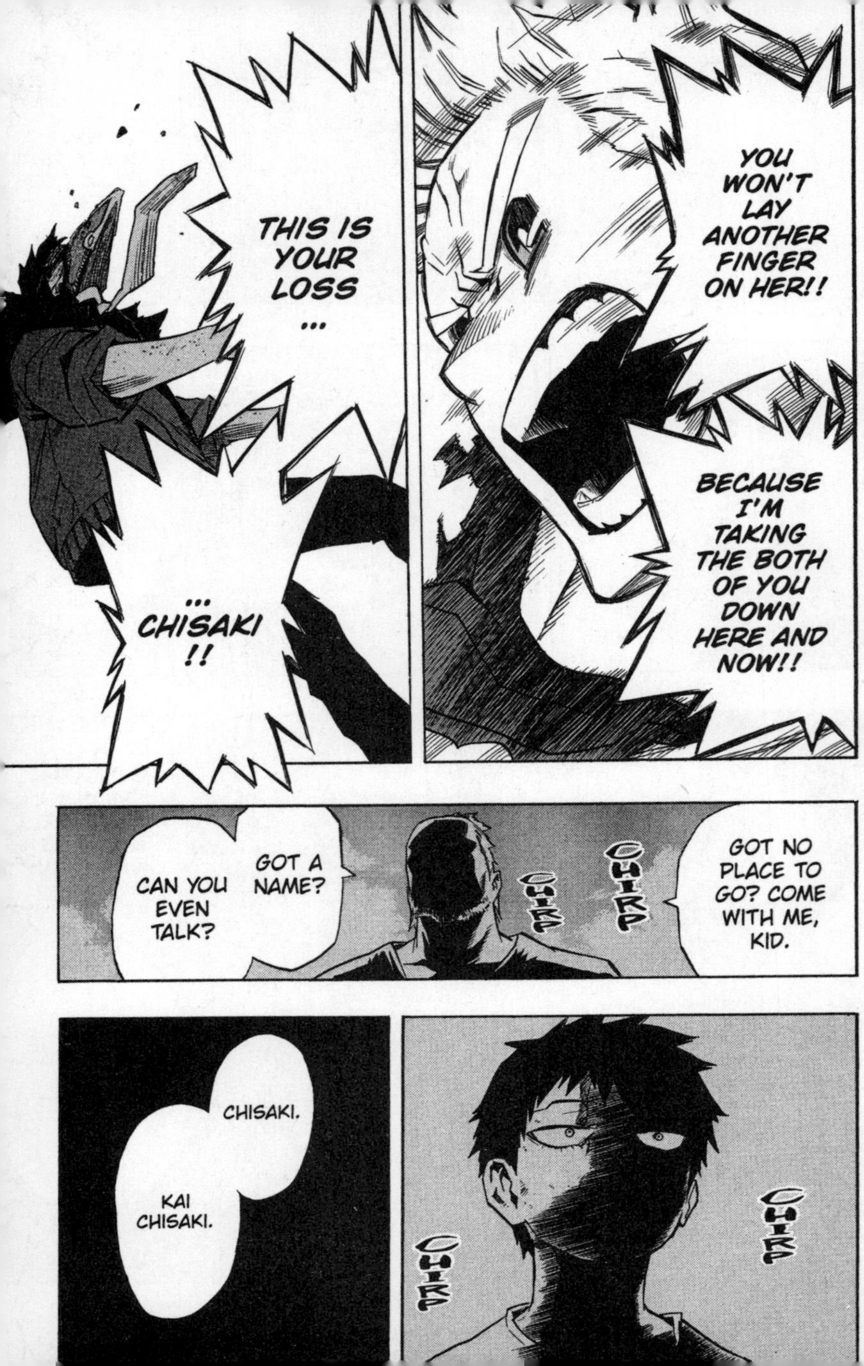
YOU WON'T LAY ANOTHER FINGER ON HER!!
BECAUSE I'M TAKING THE BOTH OF YOU DOWN HERE AND NOW!!
THIS IS YOUR LOSS ...
... CHISAKI !!
GOT NO PLACE TO GO? COME WITH ME, KID.
CHIRP
CHIRP
GOT A NAME?
CAN YOU EVEN TALK?
CHIRP
CHIRP
CHISAKI.
KAI CHISAKI.

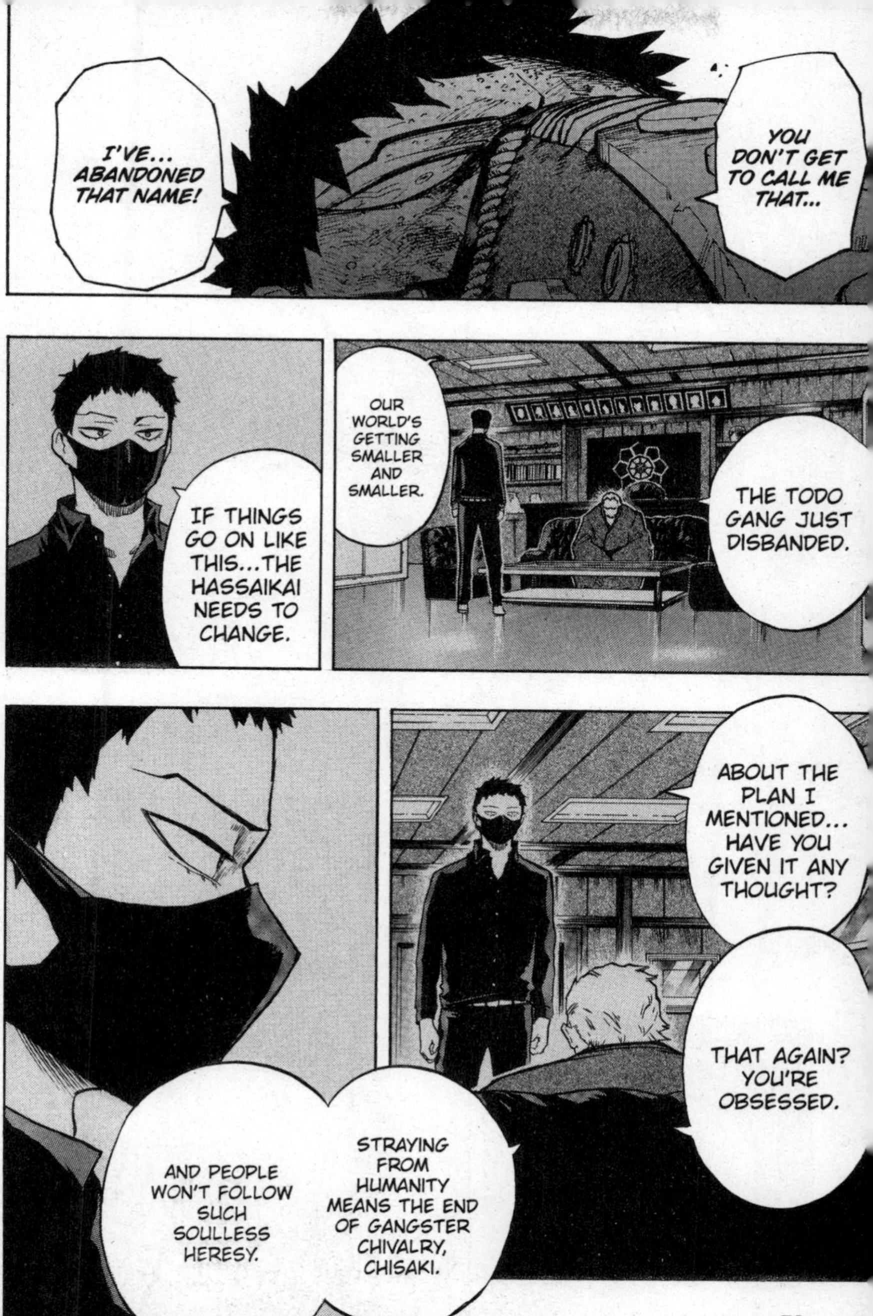
YOU DON'T GET TO CALL ME THAT...
I'VE... ABANDONED THAT NAME!
THE TODO GANG JUST DISBANDED.
OUR WORLD'S GETTING SMALLER AND SMALLER.
IF THINGS GO ON LIKE THIS...THE HASSAIKAI NEEDS TO CHANGE.
ABOUT THE PLAN I MENTIONED... HAVE YOU GIVEN IT ANY THOUGHT?
THAT AGAIN? YOU'RE OBSESSED.
STRAYING FROM HUMANITY MEANS THE END OF GANGSTER CHIVALRY, CHISAKI.
AND PEOPLE WON'T FOLLOW SUCH SOULLESS HERESY.

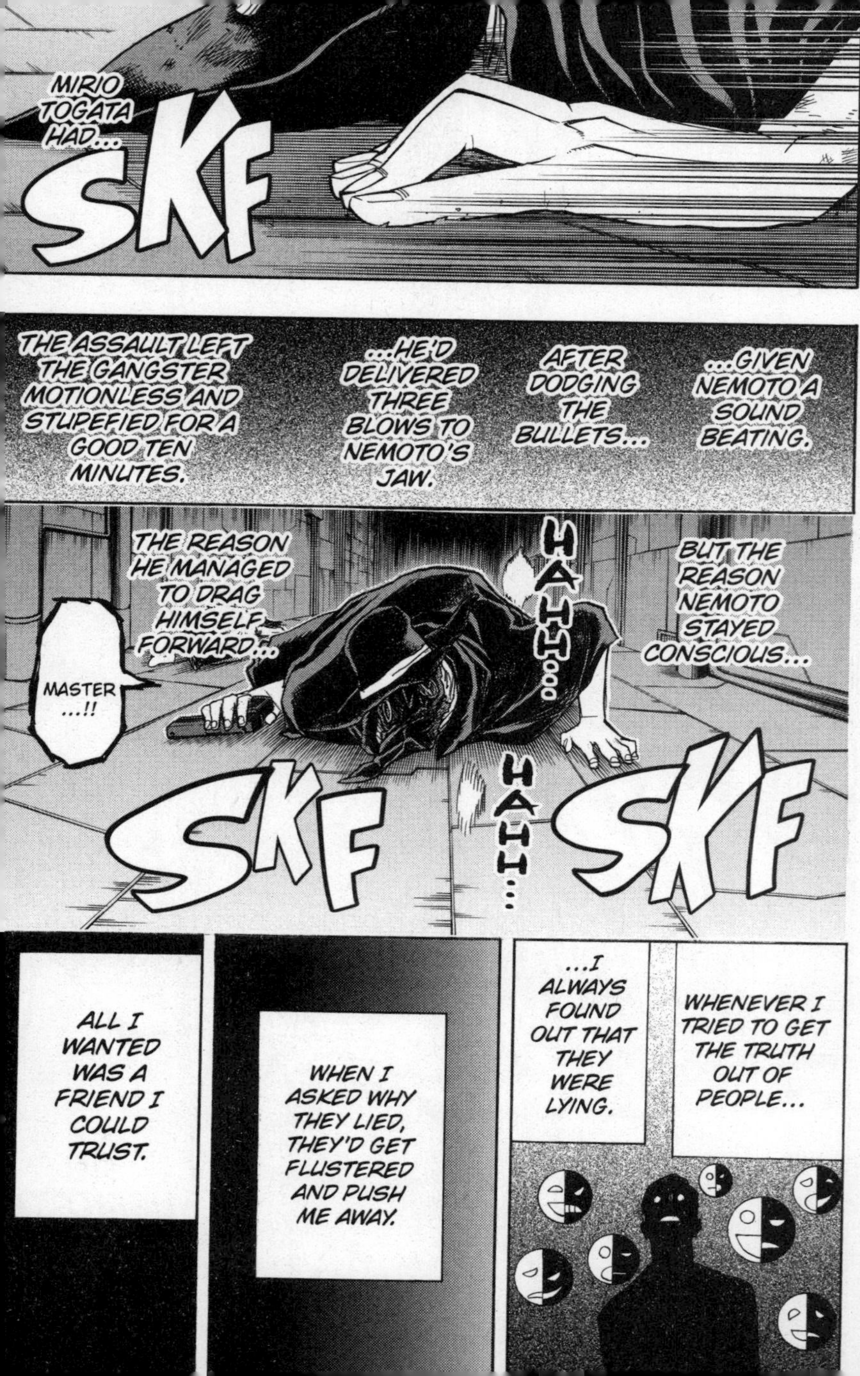
MIRIO TOGATA HAD...
SKF
...GIVEN NEMOTO A SOUND BEATING.
AFTER DODGING THE BULLETS...
...HE'D DELIVERED THREE BLOWS TO NEMOTO'S JAW.
THE ASSAULT LEFT THE GANGSTER MOTIONLESS AND STUPEFIED FOR A GOOD TEN MINUTES.
BUT THE REASON NEMOTO STAYED CONSCIOUS...
HAHH...
HAHH...
SKF
SKF
THE REASON HE MANAGED TO DRAG HIMSELF FORWARD...
MASTER ...!!
WHENEVER I TRIED TO GET THE TRUTH OUT OF PEOPLE...
...I ALWAYS FOUND OUT THAT THEY WERE LYING.
WHEN I ASKED WHY THEY LIED, THEY'D GET FLUSTERED AND PUSH ME AWAY.
ALL I WANTED WAS A FRIEND I COULD TRUST.

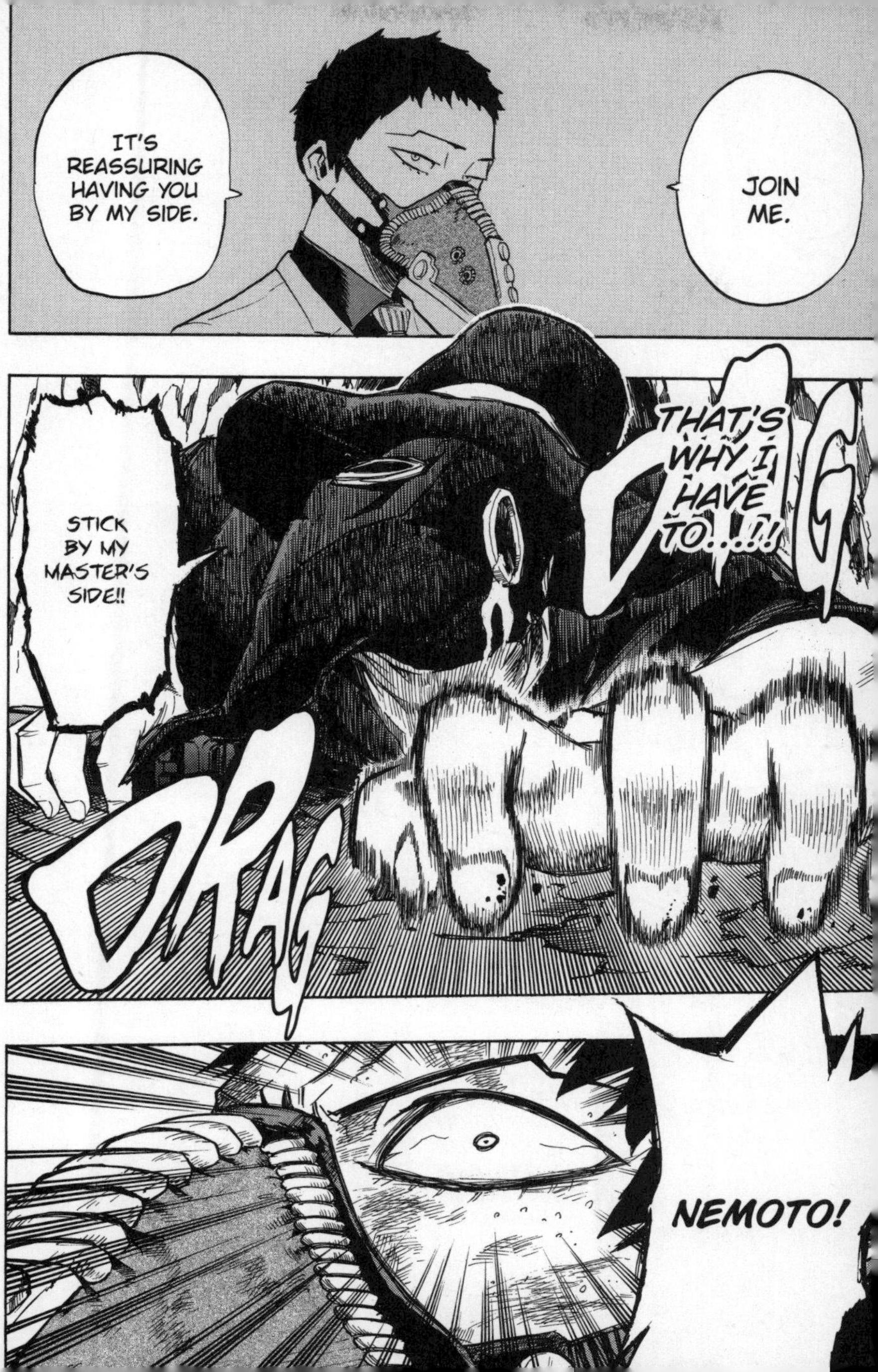
JOIN ME.
IT'S REASSURING HAVING YOU BY MY SIDE.
THAT'S WHY I HAVE TO...!!
STICK BY MY MASTER'S SIDE!!
DRAG
NEMOTO!

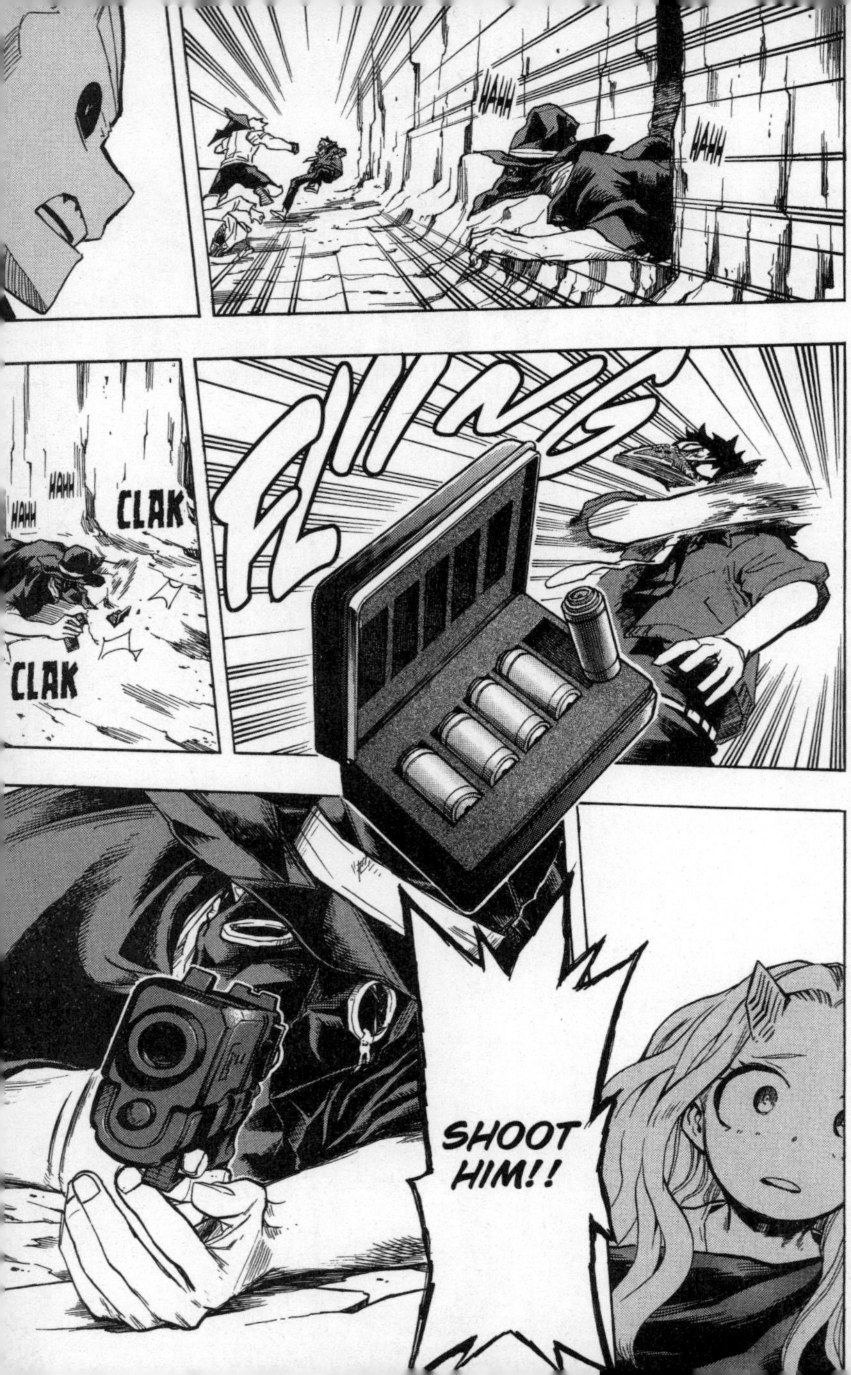
HAHH
HAHH
HAHH
HAHH
CLAK
CLAK
SHOOT HIM!!

THE FACES

DEIDORO SAKAKI »»

I'm particularly fond of his name.

Jealous of this guy, since I can't drink at all.

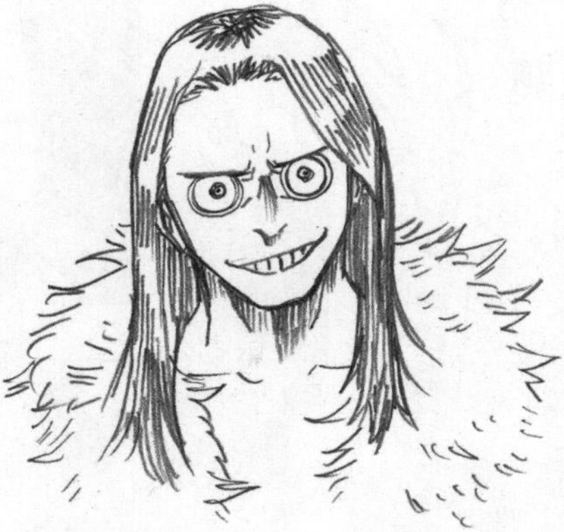

SHIN NEMOTO »»

I was planning to reveal his face, except that Overhaul ordered him to wear the mask, so he would never remove it in front of the boss. The character spoke to me, informing me of that.

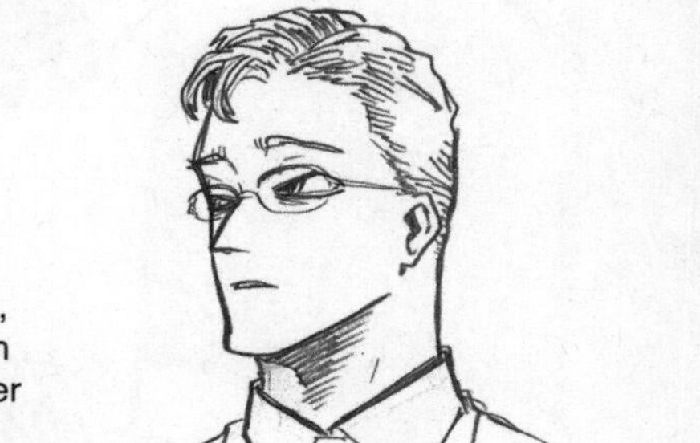

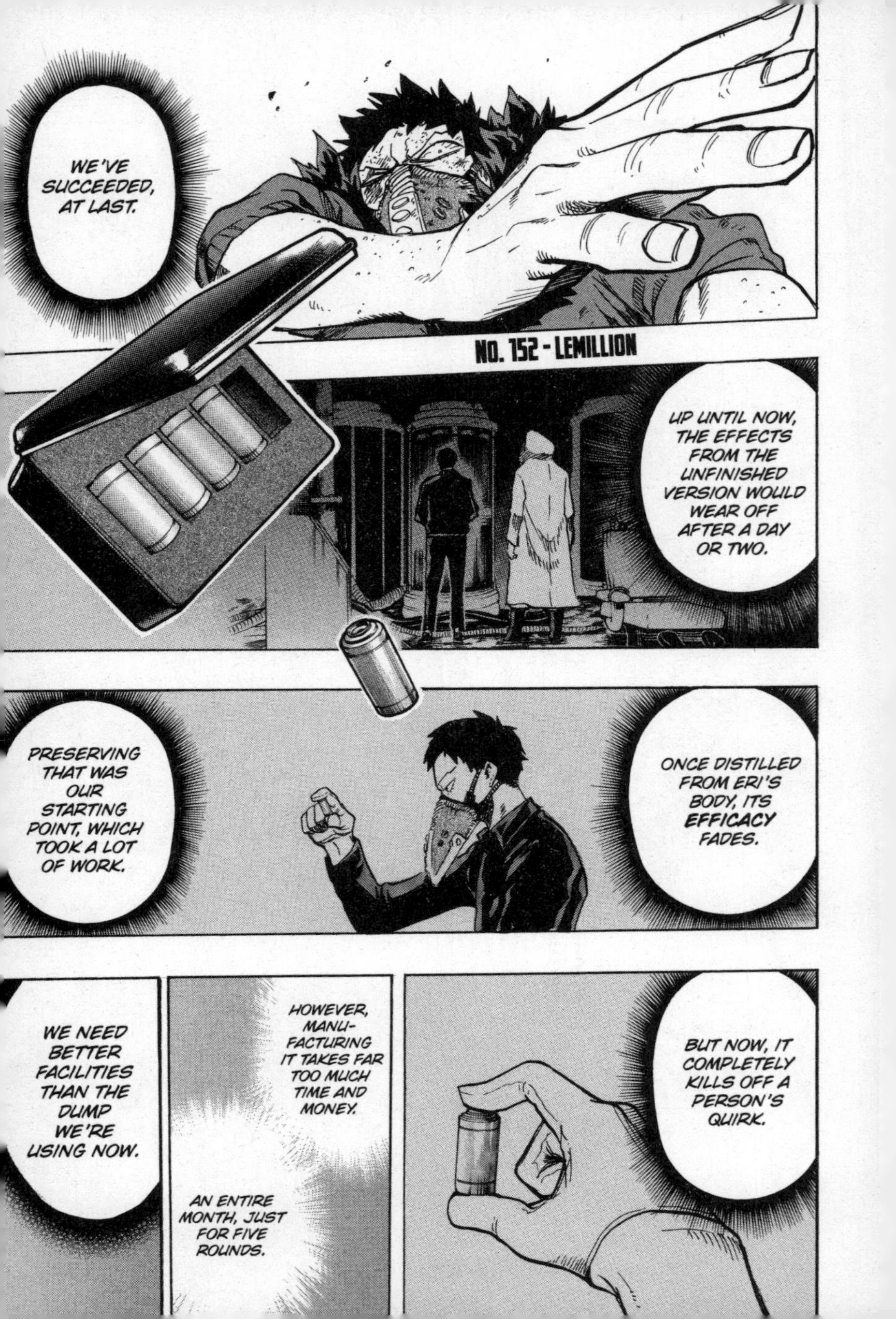
WE'VE SUCCEEDED, AT LAST.
NO. 152 - LEMILLION
UP UNTIL NOW, THE EFFECTS FROM THE UNFINISHED VERSION WOULD WEAR OFF AFTER A DAY OR TWO.
ONCE DISTILLED FROM ERI'S BODY, ITS **EFFICACY** FADES.
PRESERVING THAT WAS OUR STARTING POINT, WHICH TOOK A LOT OF WORK.
BUT NOW, IT COMPLETELY KILLS OFF A PERSON'S QUIRK.
HOWEVER, MANU-FACTURING IT TAKES FAR TOO MUCH TIME AND MONEY.
AN ENTIRE MONTH, JUST FOR FIVE ROUNDS.
WE NEED BETTER FACILITIES THAN THE DUMP WE'RE USING NOW.

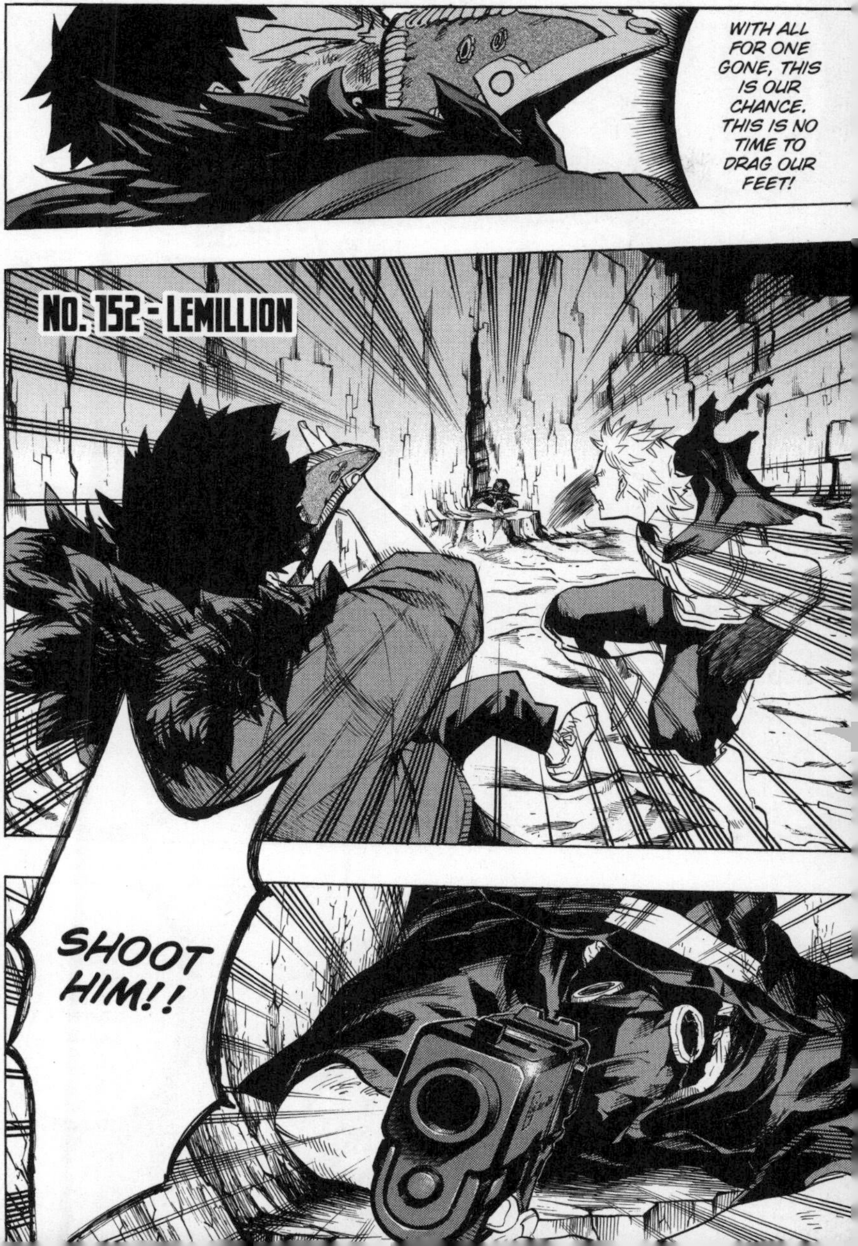
WITH ALL FOR ONE GONE, THIS IS OUR CHANCE. THIS IS NO TIME TO DRAG OUR FEET!
NO. 152 - LEMILLION
SHOOT HIM!!

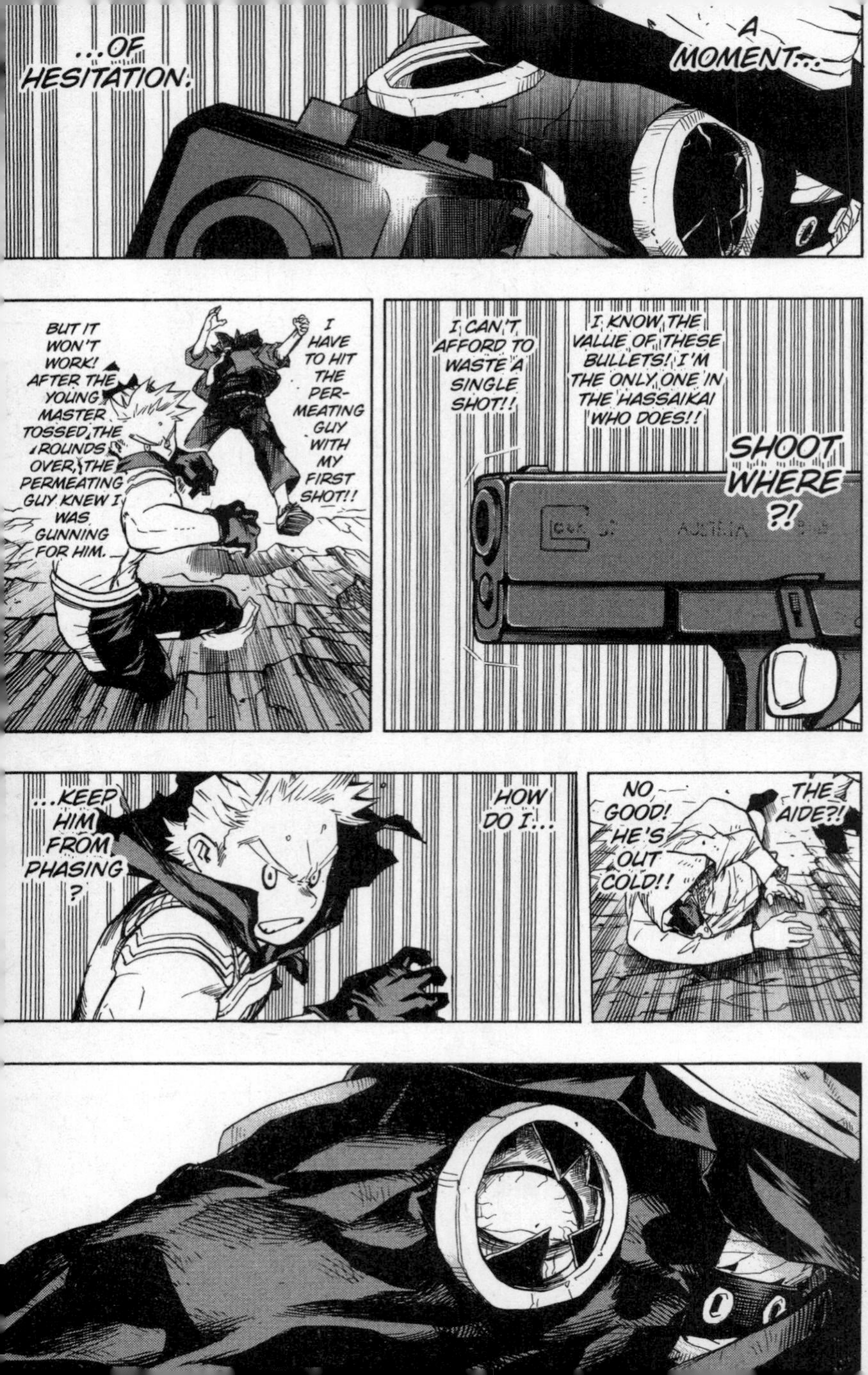
A MOMENT...
...OF HESITATION.
I KNOW THE VALUE OF THESE BULLETS! I'M THE ONLY ONE IN THE HASSAIKAI WHO DOES!!
I CAN'T AFFORD TO WASTE A SINGLE SHOT!!
SHOOT WHERE?!
I HAVE TO HIT THE PER-MEATING GUY WITH MY FIRST SHOT!!
BUT IT WON'T WORK! AFTER THE YOUNG MASTER TOSSED THE ROUNDS OVER, THE PERMEATING GUY KNEW I WAS GUNNING FOR HIM.
THE AIDE?!
NO GOOD! HE'S OUT COLD!!
HOW DO I...
...KEEP HIM FROM PHASING?

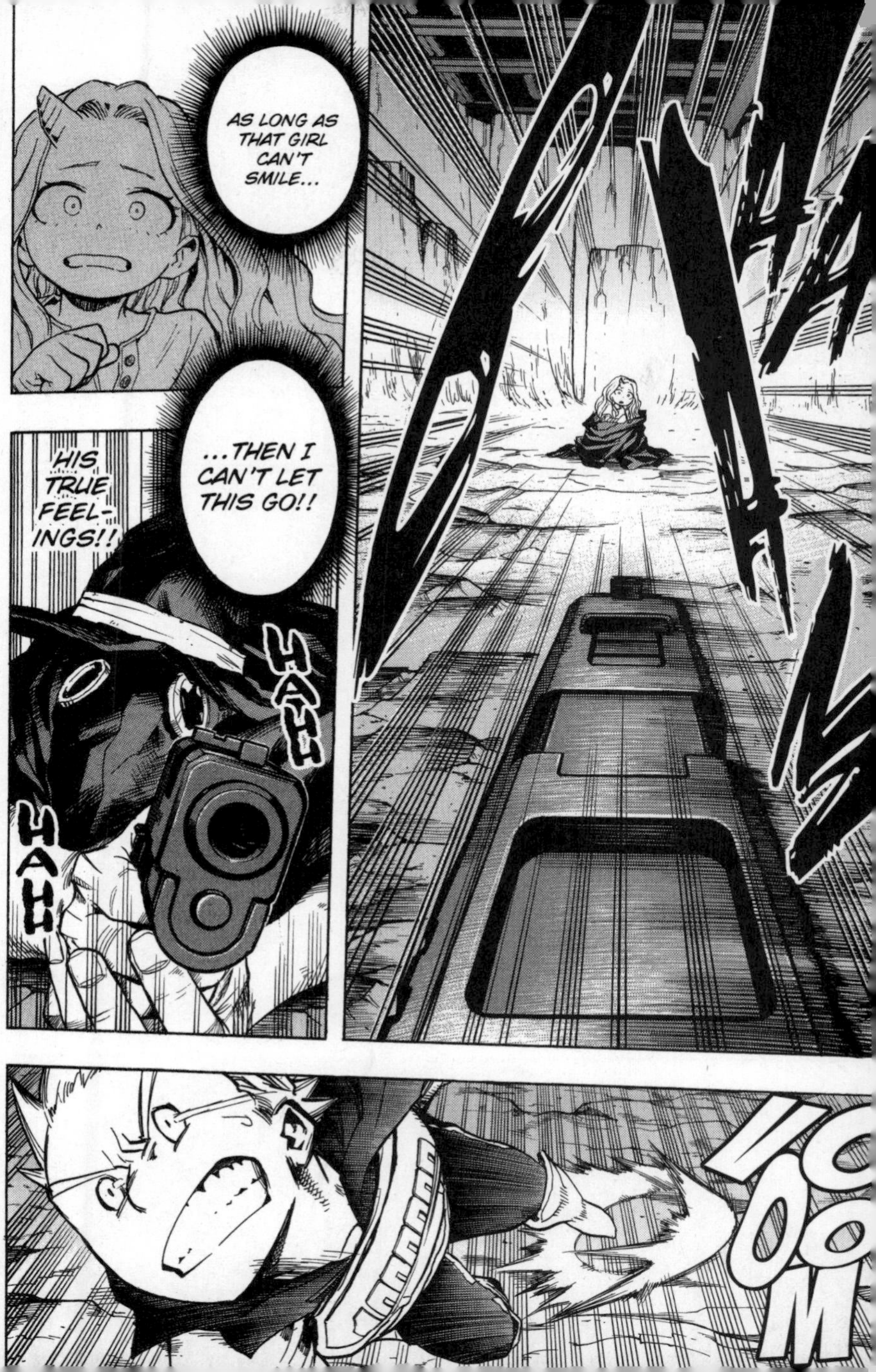
AS LONG AS THAT GIRL CAN'T SMILE...
...THEN I CAN'T LET THIS GO!!
HIS TRUE FEEL-INGS!!
HAHH
HAHH

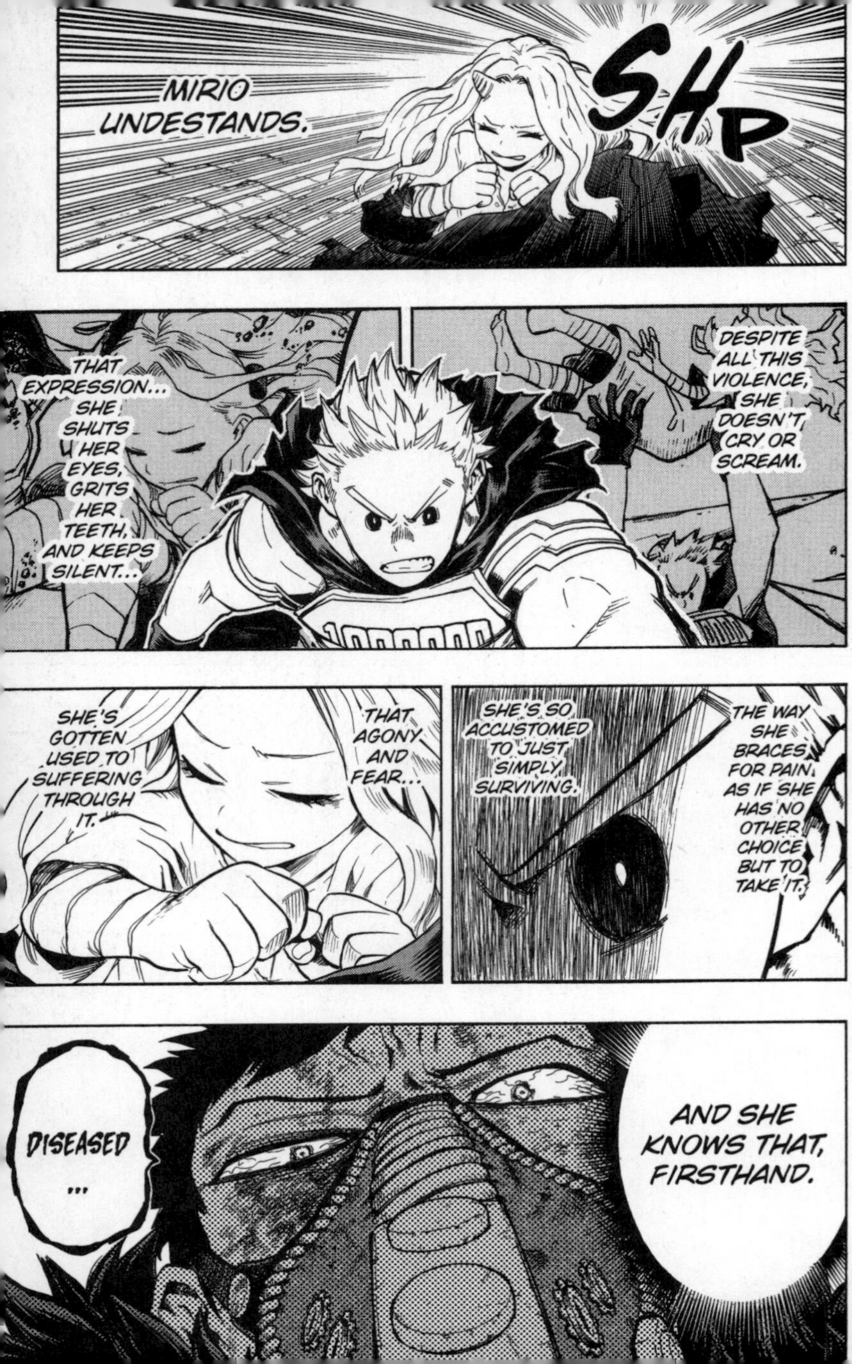
SHP
MIRIO UNDESTANDS.
DESPITE ALL THIS VIOLENCE, SHE DOESN'T CRY OR SCREAM.
THAT EXPRESSION... SHE SHUTS HER EYES, GRITS HER TEETH, AND KEEPS SILENT...
THE WAY SHE BRACES FOR PAIN AS IF SHE HAS NO OTHER CHOICE BUT TO TAKE IT.
SHE'S SO ACCUSTOMED TO JUST SIMPLY SURVIVING.
THAT AGONY AND FEAR...
SHE'S GOTTEN USED TO SUFFERING THROUGH IT.
AND SHE KNOWS THAT, FIRSTHAND.
DISEASED ...

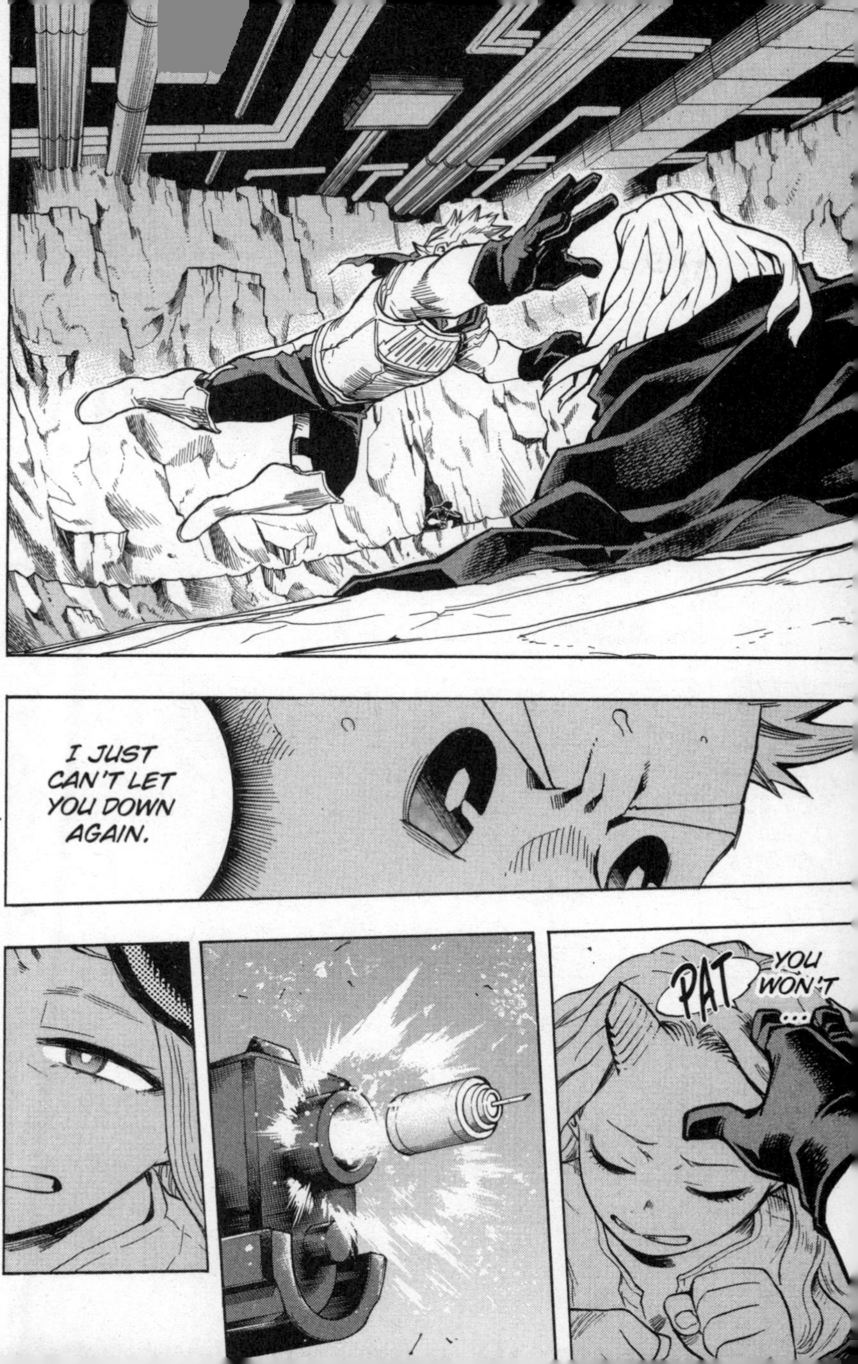
I JUST CAN'T LET YOU DOWN AGAIN.
PAT
YOU WON'T ...

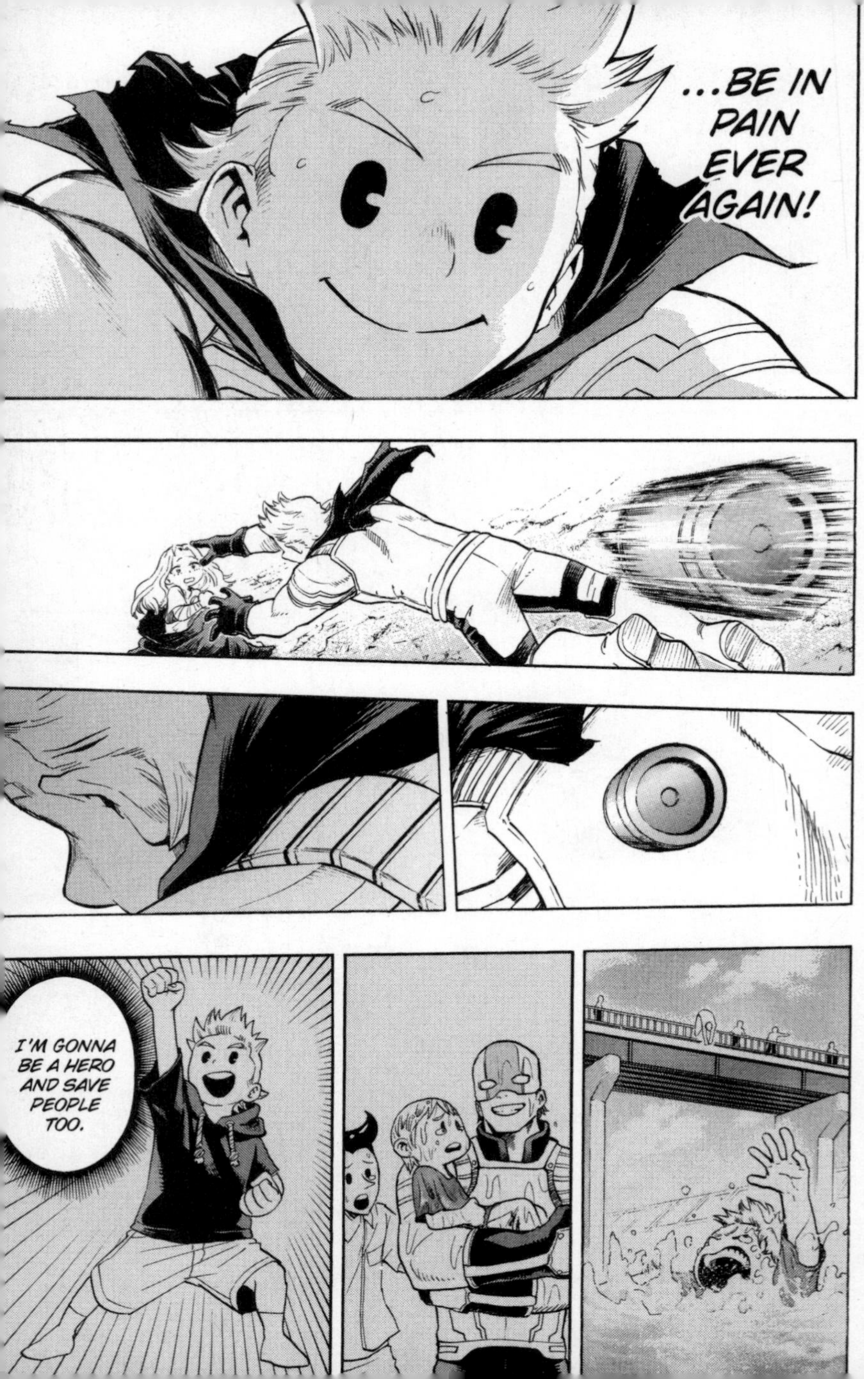
...BE IN PAIN EVER AGAIN!
I'M GONNA BE A HERO AND SAVE PEOPLE TOO.

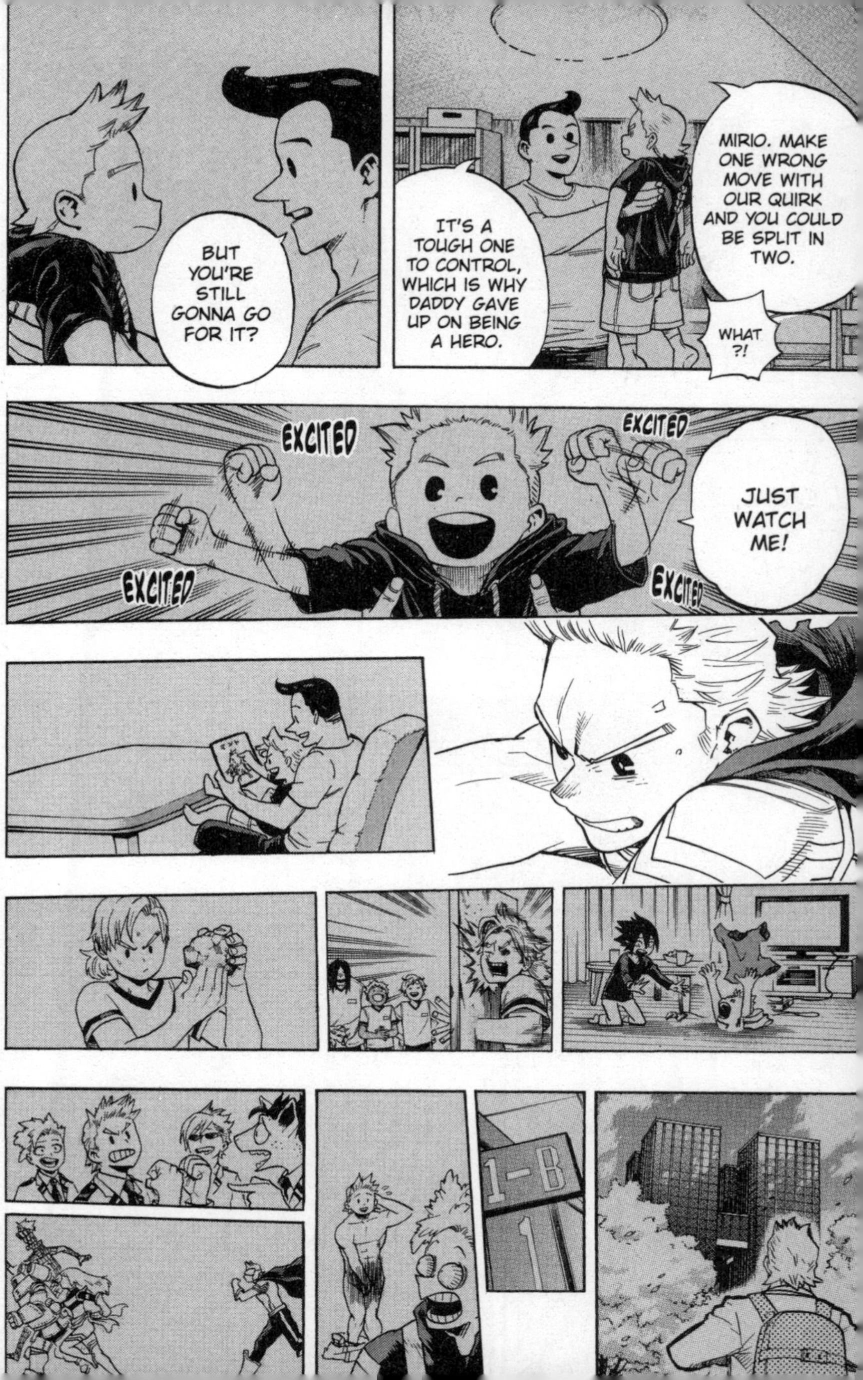
MIRIO. MAKE ONE WRONG MOVE WITH OUR QUIRK AND YOU COULD BE SPLIT IN TWO.
WHAT ?!
IT'S A TOUGH ONE TO CONTROL, WHICH IS WHY DADDY GAVE UP ON BEING A HERO.
BUT YOU'RE STILL GONNA GO FOR IT?
JUST WATCH ME!
EXCITED
EXCITED
EXCITED
EXCITED
1-B

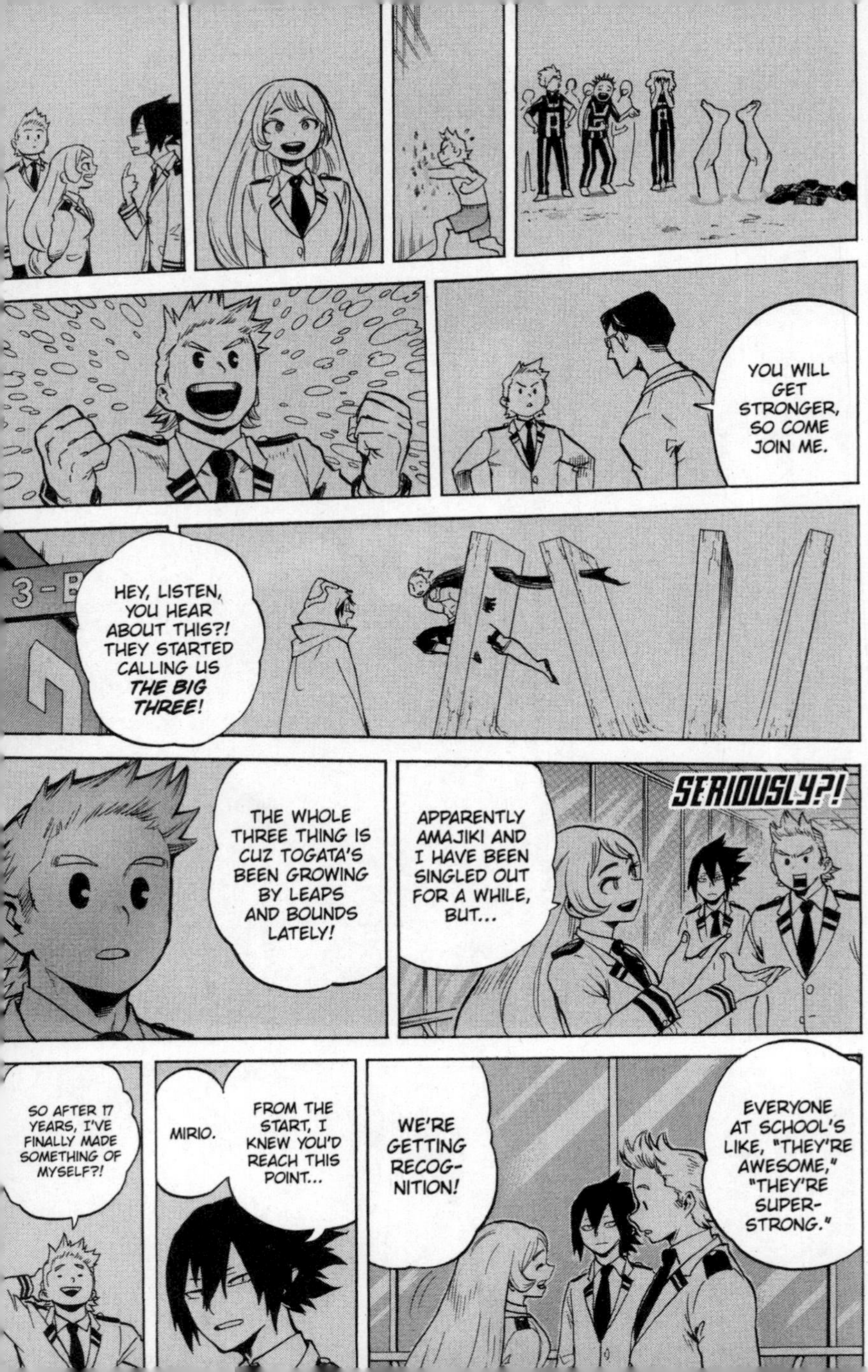
YOU WILL GET STRONGER, SO COME JOIN ME.
HEY, LISTEN, YOU HEAR ABOUT THIS?! THEY STARTED CALLING US *THE BIG THREE!*
SERIOUSLY?!
APPARENTLY AMAJIKI AND I HAVE BEEN SINGLED OUT FOR A WHILE, BUT...
THE WHOLE THREE THING IS CUZ TOGATA'S BEEN GROWING BY LEAPS AND BOUNDS LATELY!
EVERYONE AT SCHOOL'S LIKE, "THEY'RE AWESOME," "THEY'RE SUPER-STRONG."
WE'RE GETTING RECOG-NITION!
FROM THE START, I KNEW YOU'D REACH THIS POINT...
MIRIO.
SO AFTER 17 YEARS, I'VE FINALLY MADE SOMETHING OF MYSELF?!

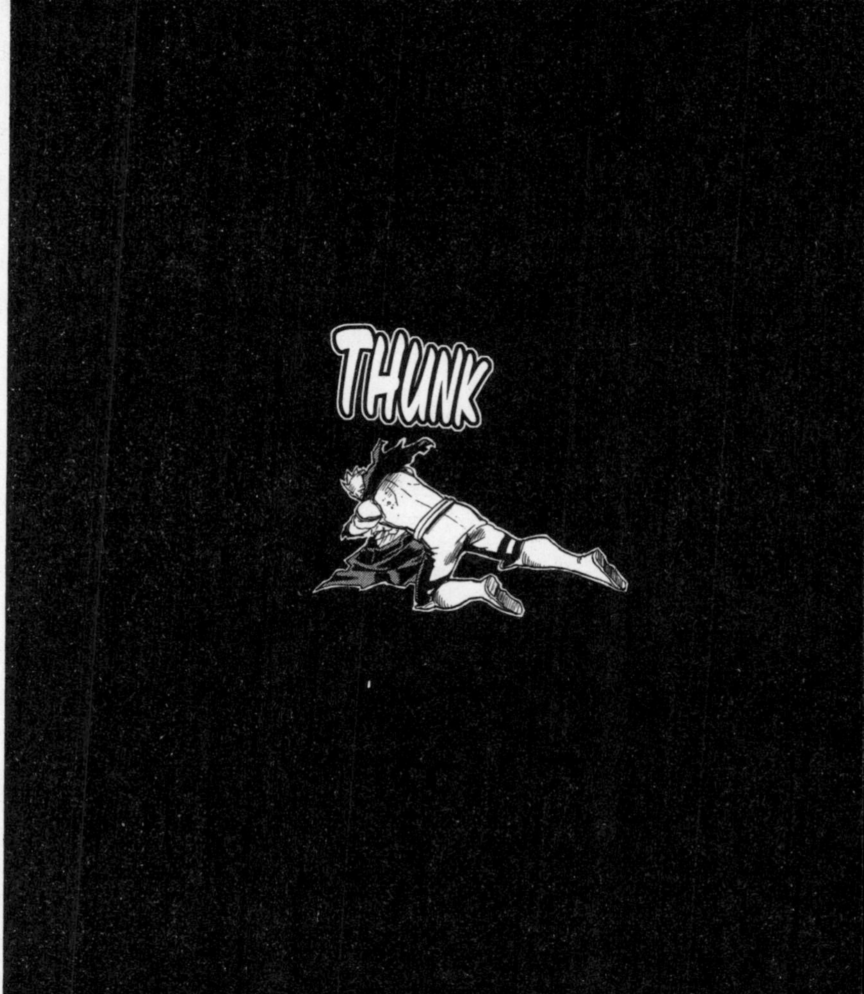
THUNK
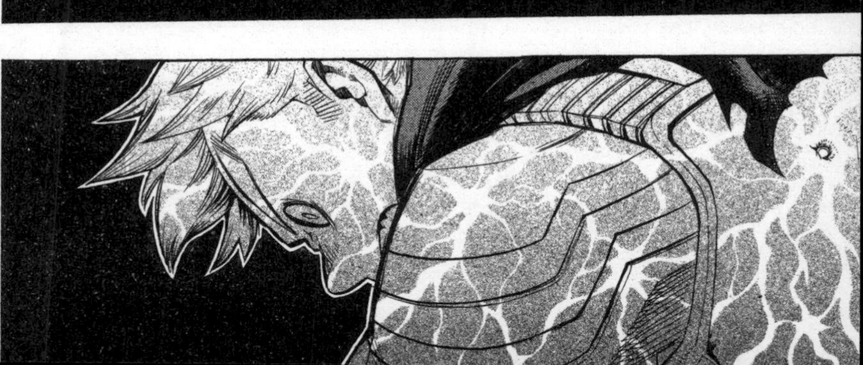

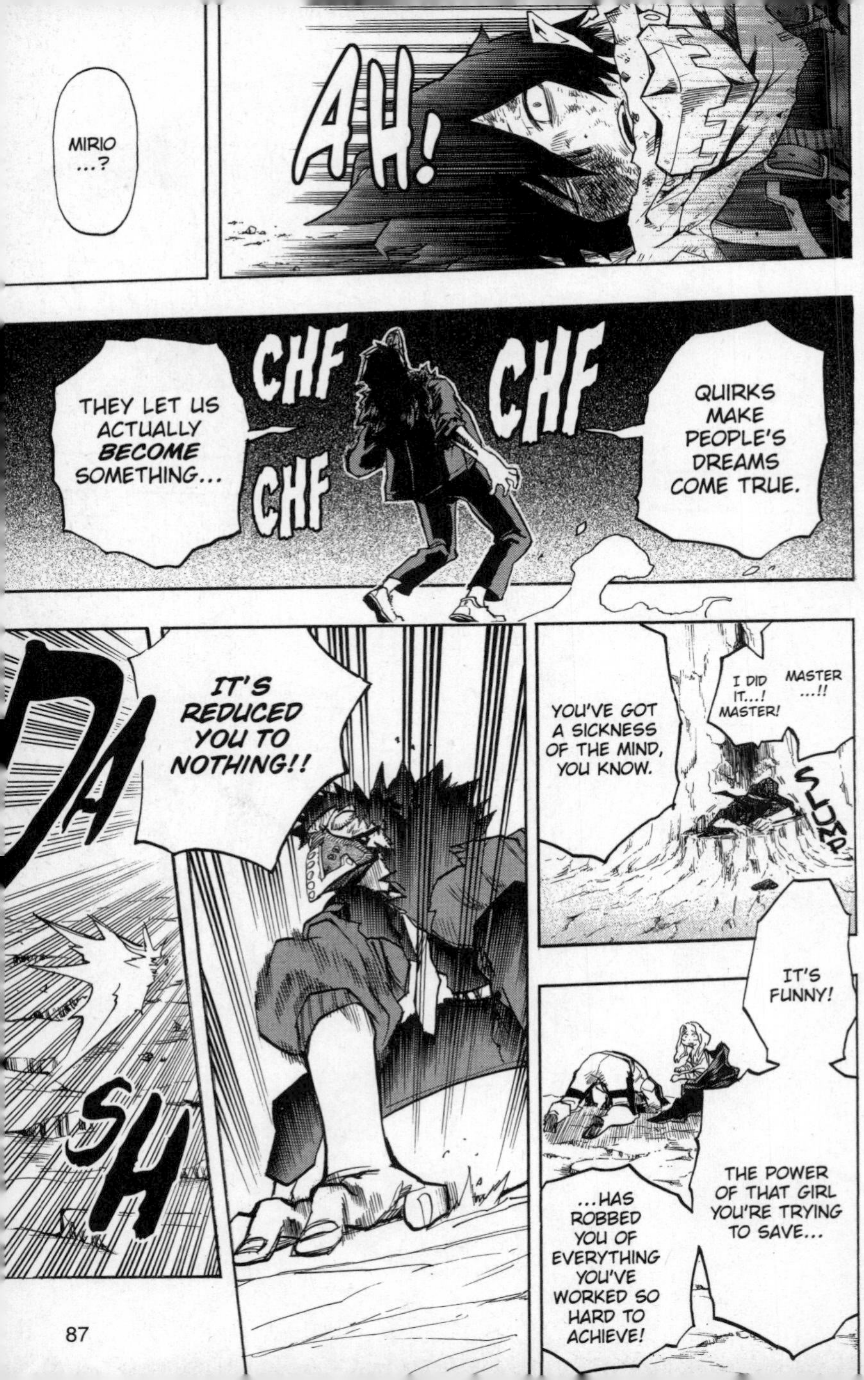
AH!
MIRIO ...?
QUIRKS MAKE PEOPLE'S DREAMS COME TRUE.
CHF CHF CHF
THEY LET US ACTUALLY *BECOME* SOMETHING...
MASTER ...!!
I DID IT...! MASTER!
SLUMP
YOU'VE GOT A SICKNESS OF THE MIND, YOU KNOW.
IT'S FUNNY!
THE POWER OF THAT GIRL YOU'RE TRYING TO SAVE...
...HAS ROBBED YOU OF EVERYTHING YOU'VE WORKED SO HARD TO ACHIEVE!
IT'S REDUCED YOU TO NOTHING!!
DASH

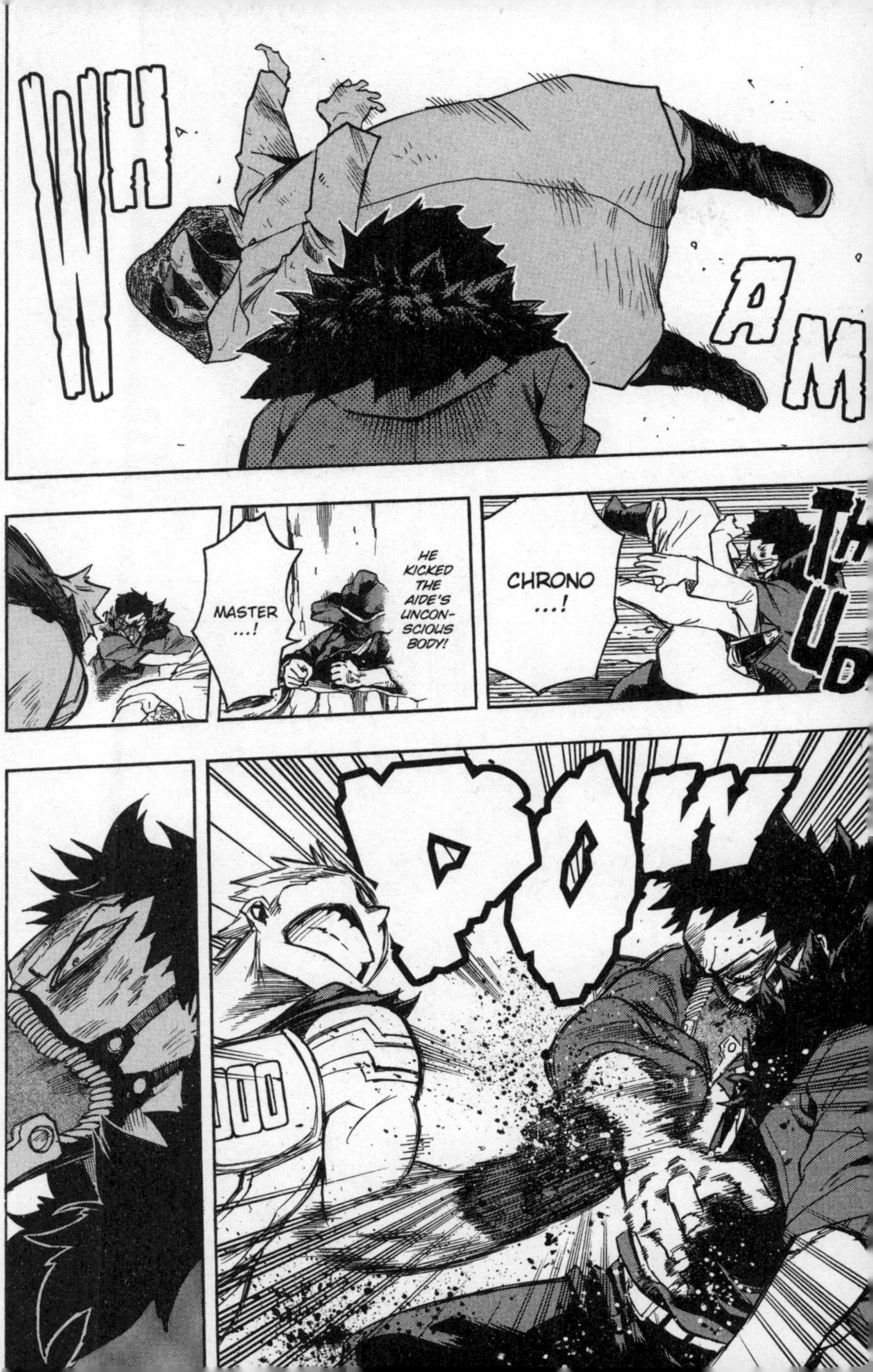
WHAM
THUD
CHRONO ...!
HE KICKED THE AIDE'S UNCONSCIOUS BODY!
MASTER ...!
POW

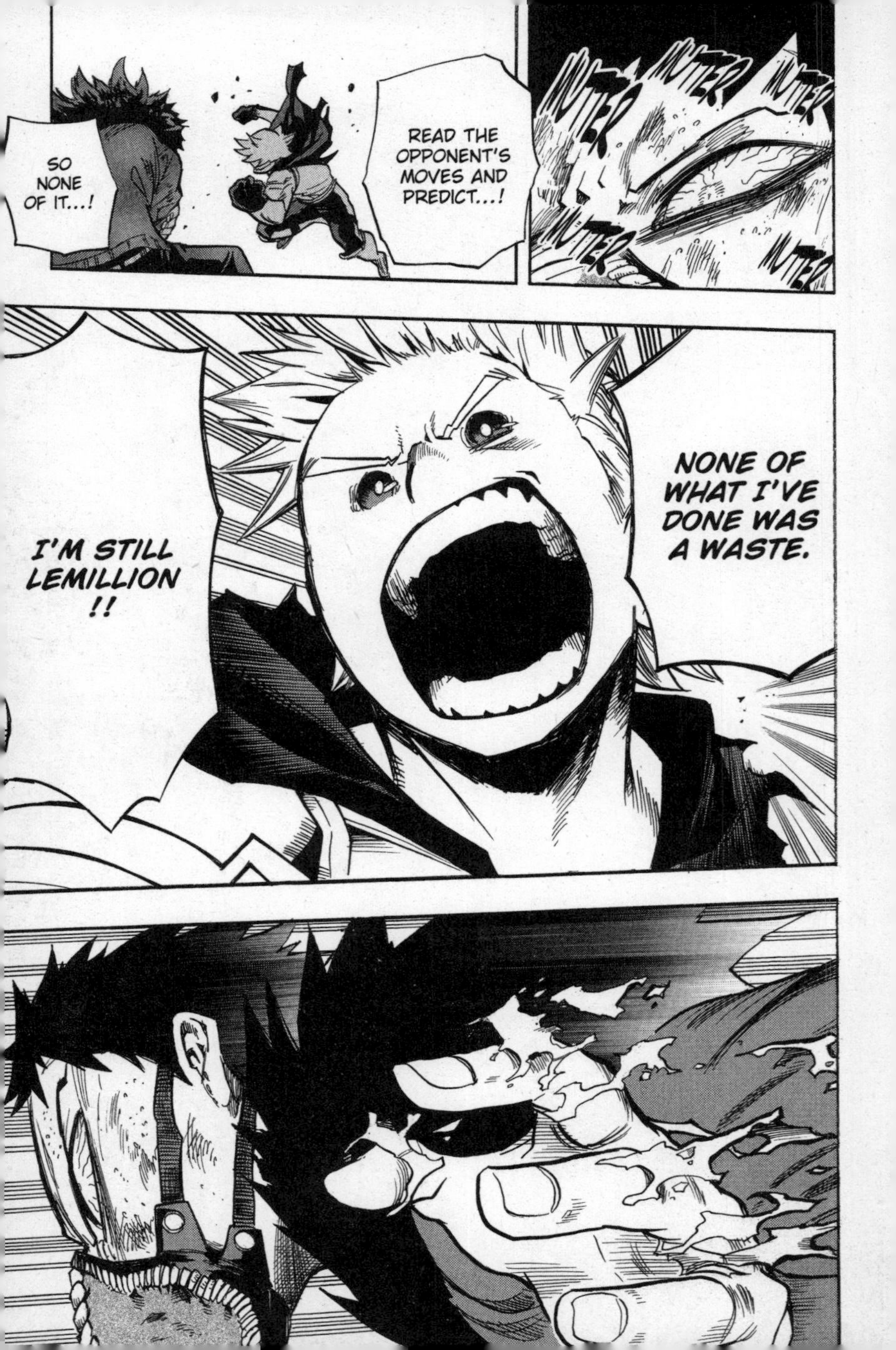
READ THE OPPONENT'S MOVES AND PREDICT...!
SO NONE OF IT...!
NONE OF WHAT I'VE DONE WAS A WASTE.
I'M STILL LEMILLION!!

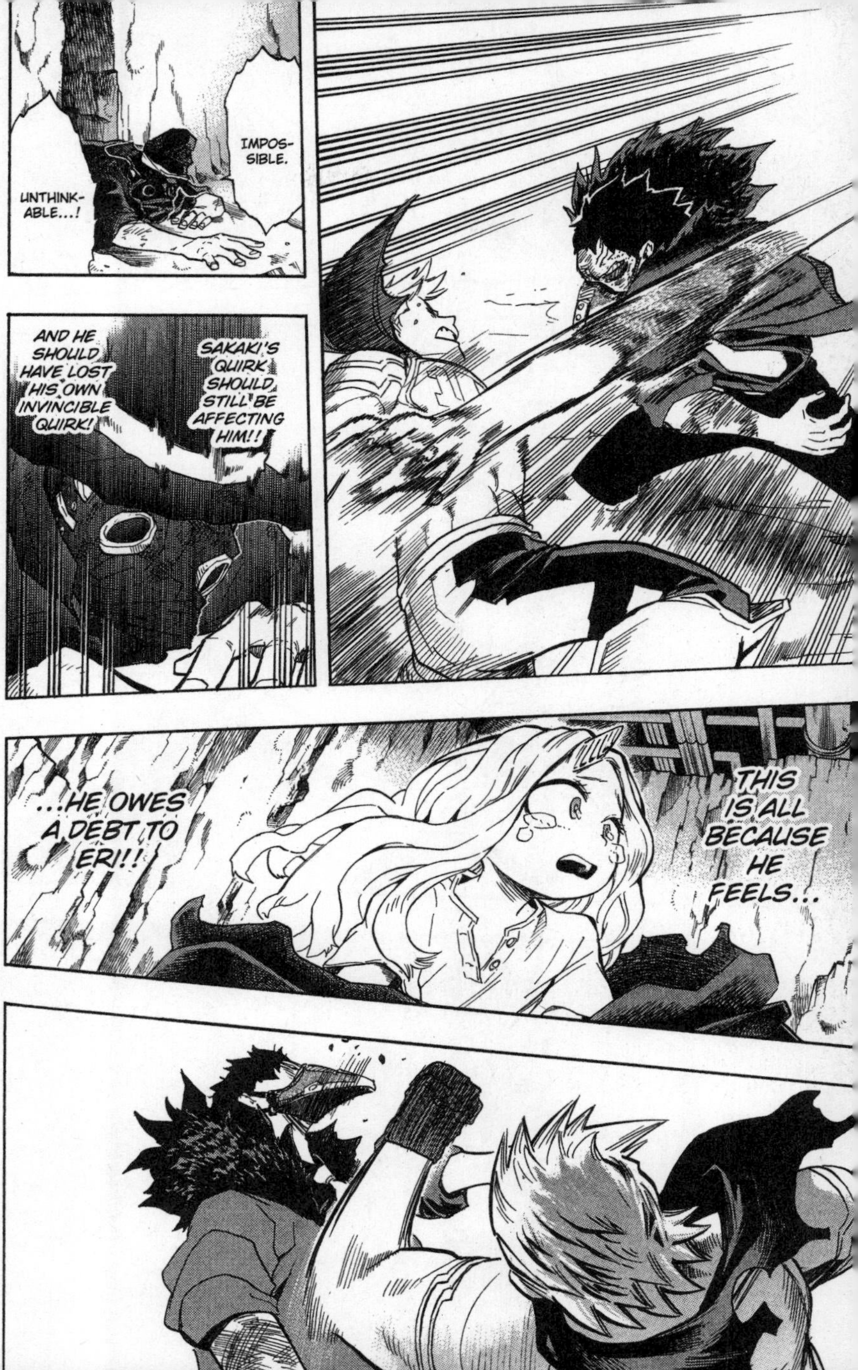
IMPOSSIBLE.
UNTHINKABLE...!
SAKAKI'S QUIRK SHOULD STILL BE AFFECTING HIM!!
AND HE SHOULD HAVE LOST HIS OWN INVINCIBLE QUIRK!
THIS IS ALL BECAUSE HE FEELS...
...HE OWES A DEBT TO ERI!!

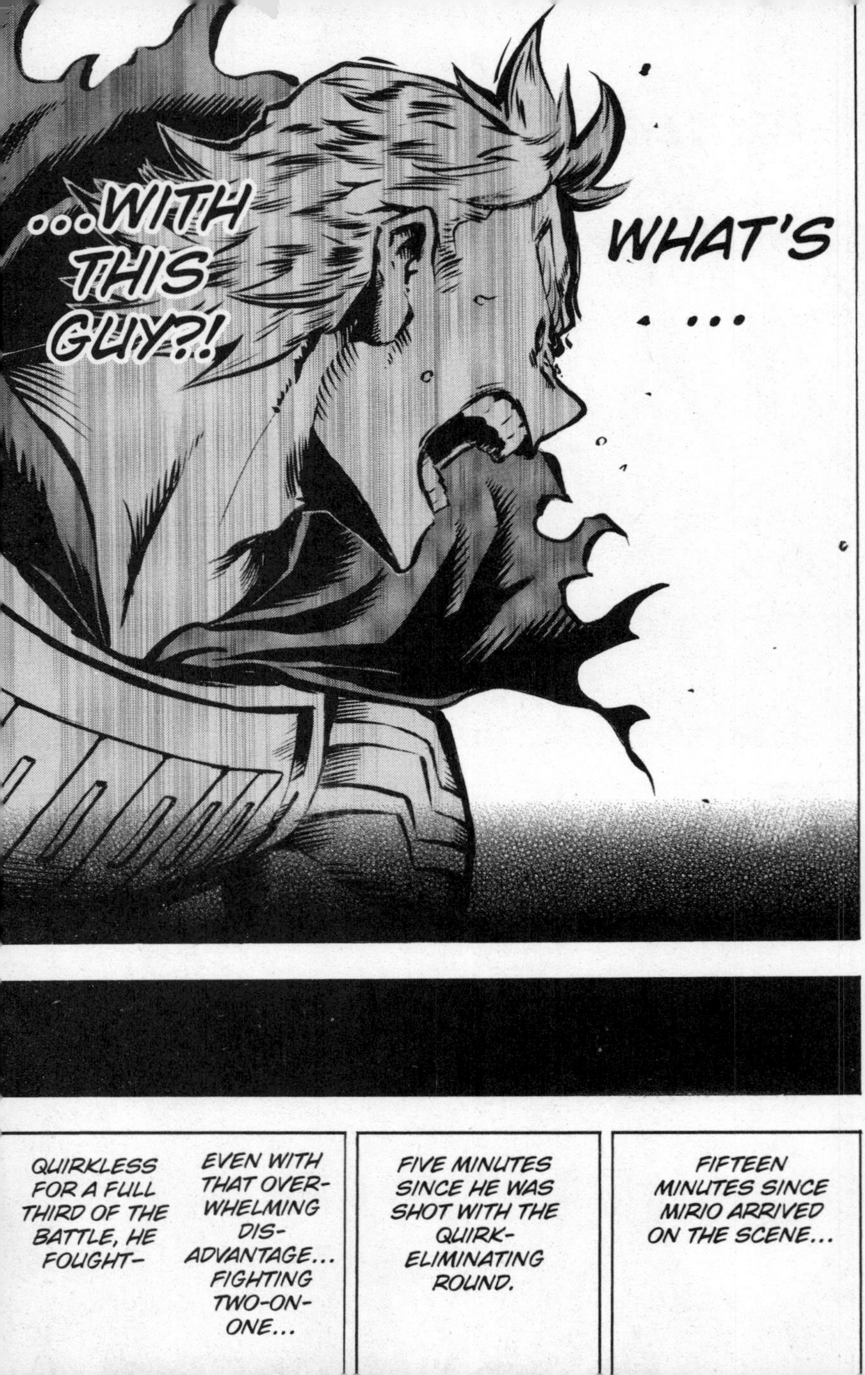
WHAT'S
...WITH THIS GUY?!
FIFTEEN MINUTES SINCE MIRIO ARRIVED ON THE SCENE...
FIVE MINUTES SINCE HE WAS SHOT WITH THE QUIRK-ELIMINATING ROUND.
EVEN WITH THAT OVERWHELMING DISADVANTAGE... FIGHTING TWO-ON-ONE...
QUIRKLESS FOR A FULL THIRD OF THE BATTLE, HE FOUGHT-

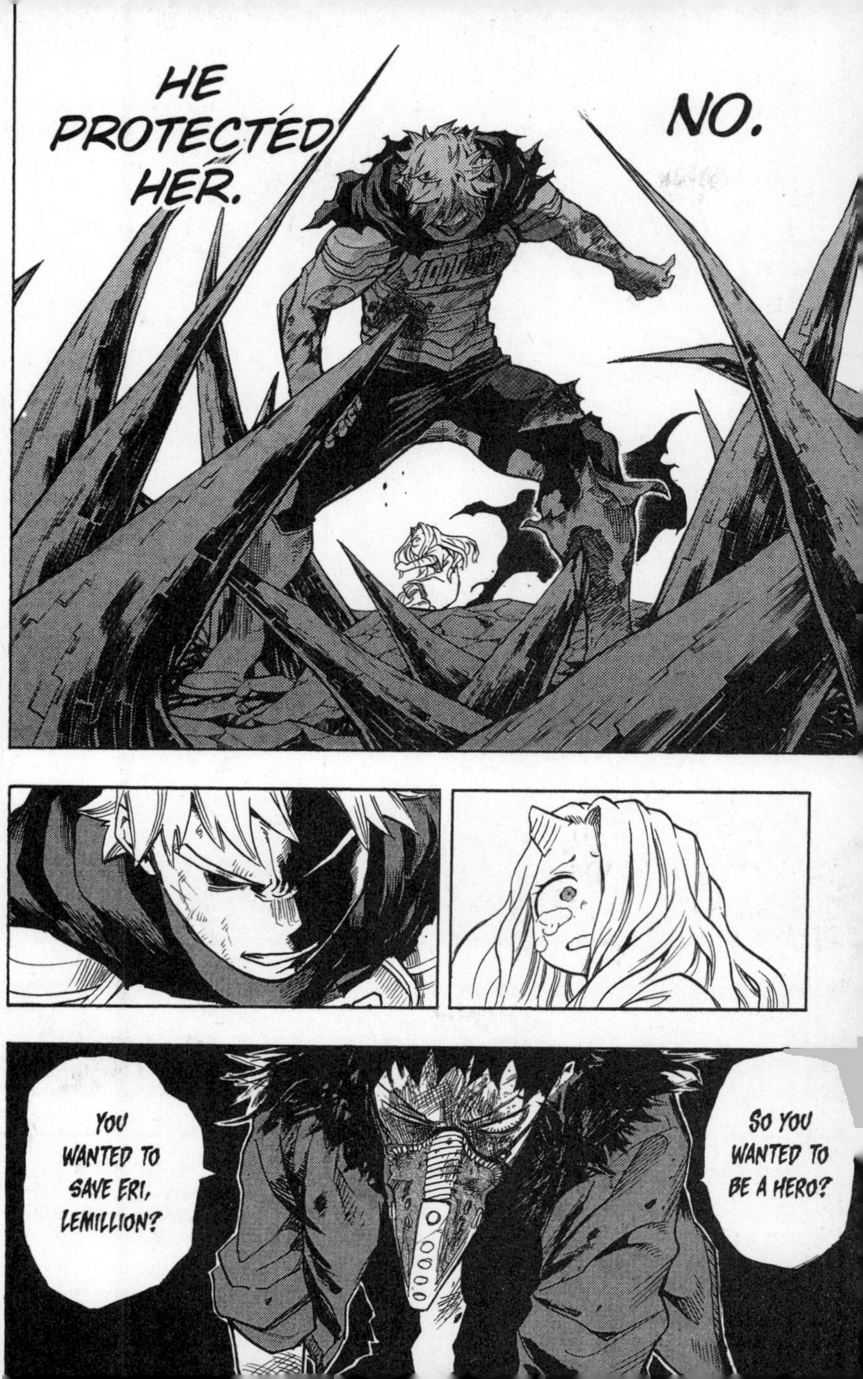
NO.
HE PROTECTED HER.
SO YOU WANTED TO BE A HERO?
YOU WANTED TO SAVE ERI, LEMILLION?

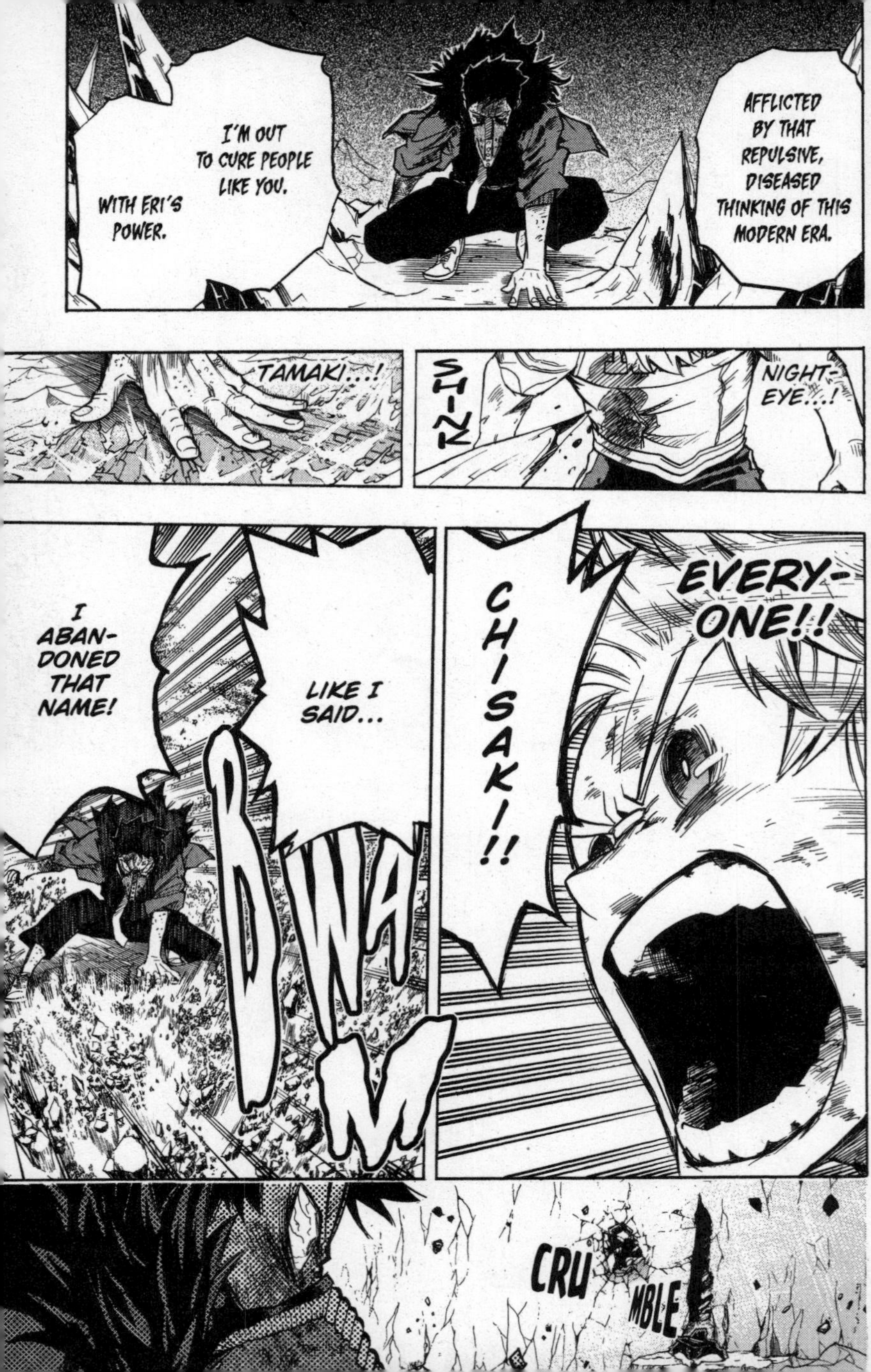
AFFLICTED BY THAT REPULSIVE, DISEASED THINKING OF THIS MODERN ERA.
I'M OUT TO CURE PEOPLE LIKE YOU.
WITH ERI'S POWER.
SHINK
NIGHT-EYE...!
TAMAKI...!
EVERY-ONE!!
CHISAKI!!
LIKE I SAID...
I ABAN-DONED THAT NAME!
BWAM
CRU MBLE

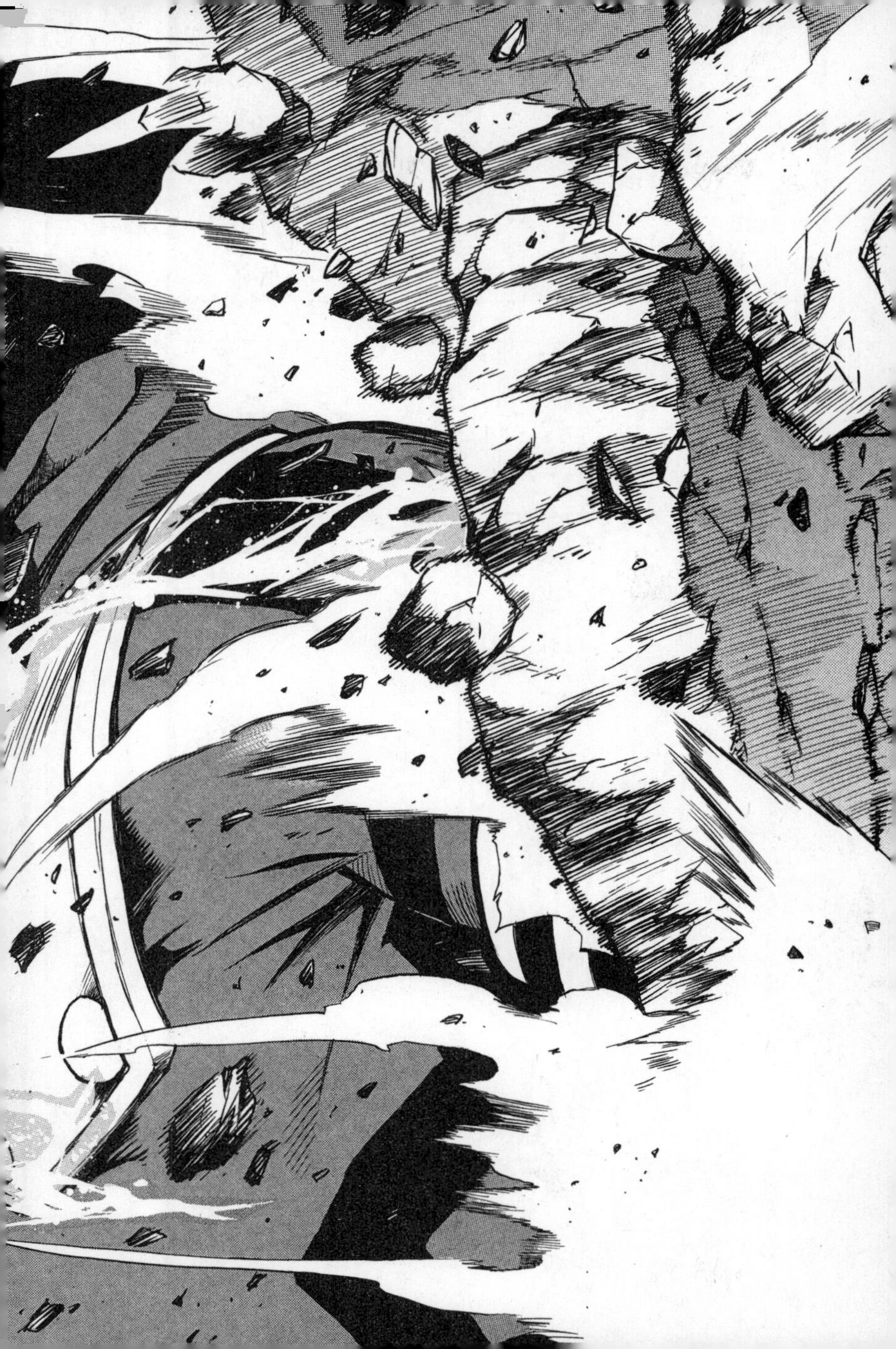

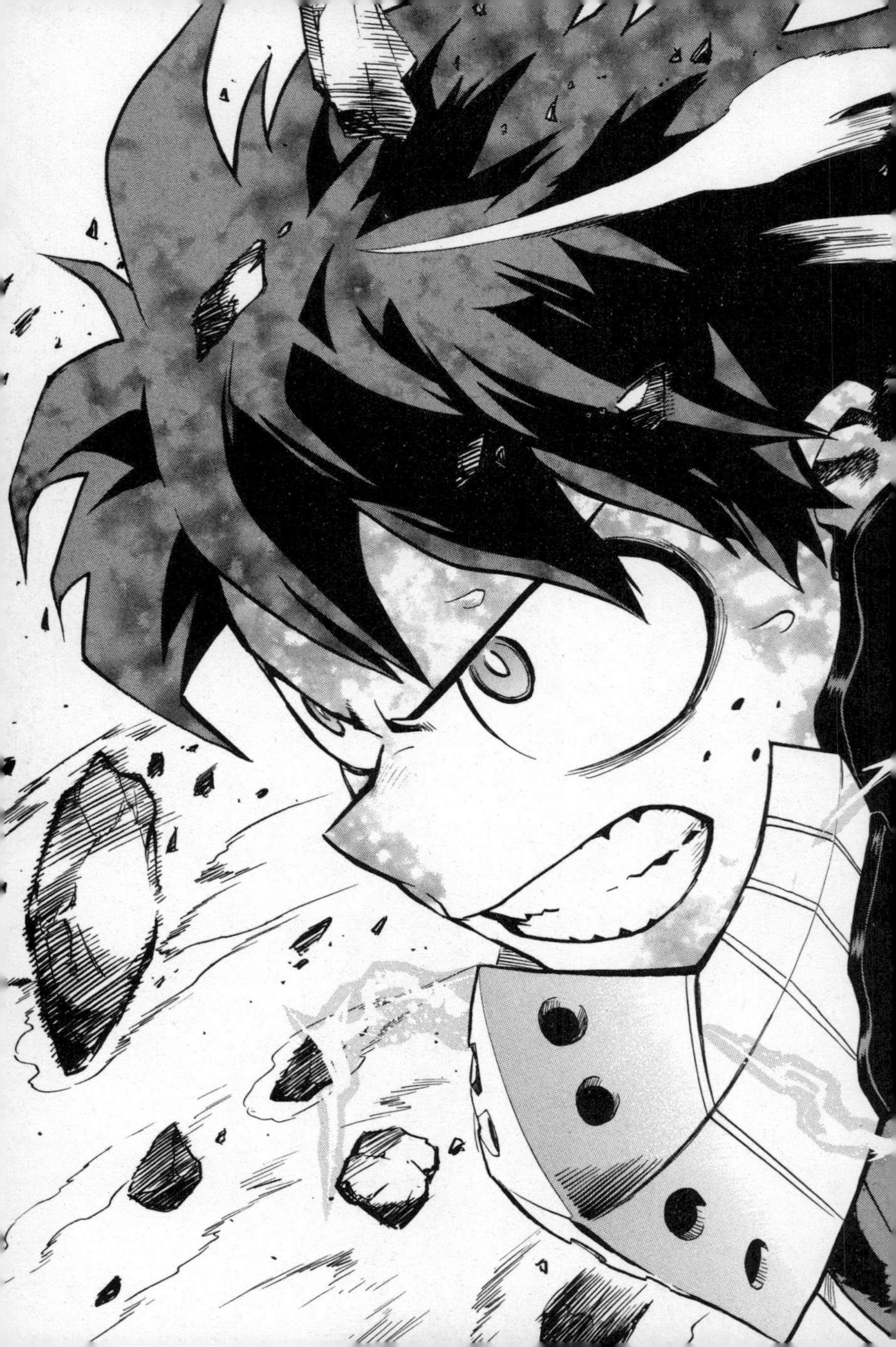

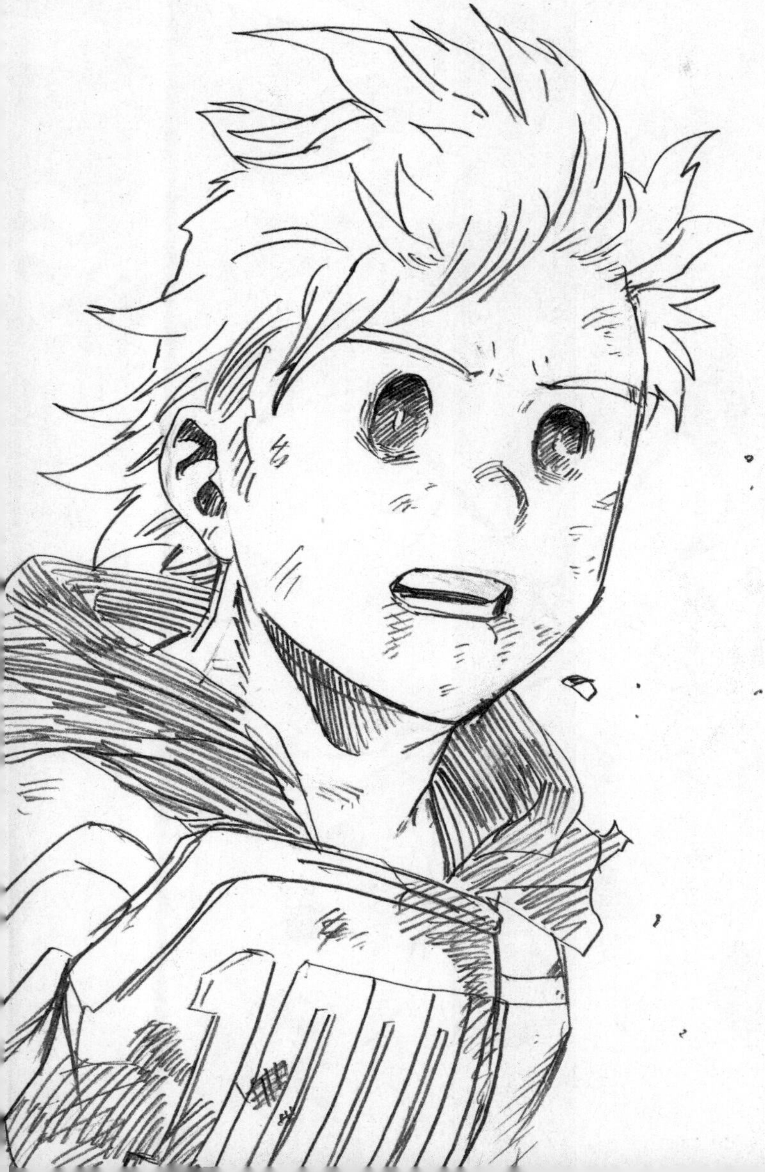

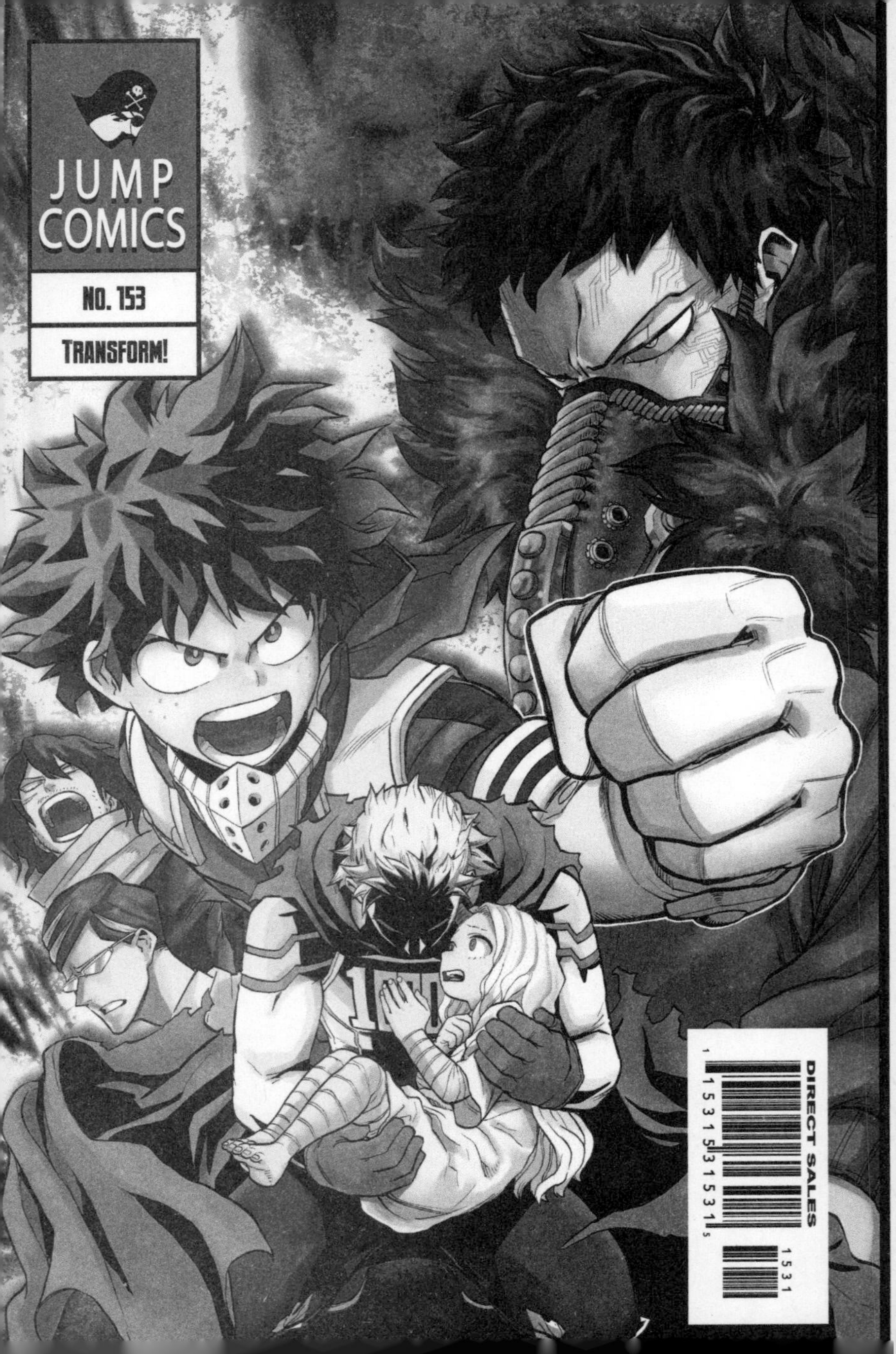
JUMP COMICS
NO. 153
TRANSFORM!
DIRECT SALES

MY HERO
ACADEMIA

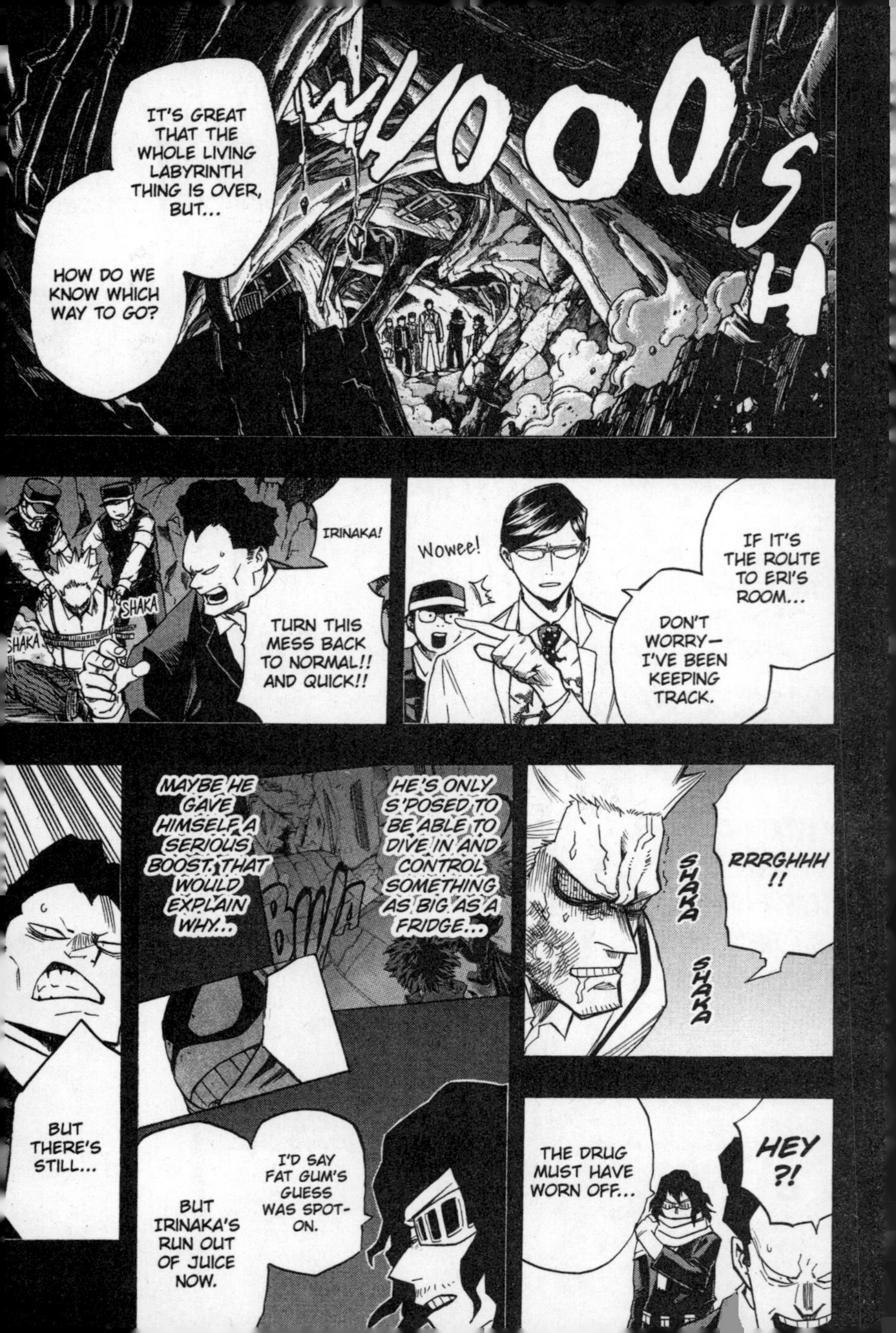
WHOOOSH
IT'S GREAT THAT THE WHOLE LIVING LABYRINTH THING IS OVER, BUT...
HOW DO WE KNOW WHICH WAY TO GO?
IF IT'S THE ROUTE TO ERI'S ROOM...
DON'T WORRY— I'VE BEEN KEEPING TRACK.
Wowee!
IRINAKA!
TURN THIS MESS BACK TO NORMAL!! AND QUICK!!
SHAKA
SHAKA
RRRGHHH!!
SHAKA
SHAKA
HE'S ONLY S'POSED TO BE ABLE TO DIVE IN AND CONTROL SOMETHING AS BIG AS A FRIDGE...
MAYBE HE GAVE HIMSELF A SERIOUS BOOST. THAT WOULD EXPLAIN WHY...
HEY?!
THE DRUG MUST HAVE WORN OFF...
I'D SAY FAT GUM'S GUESS WAS SPOT-ON.
BUT IRINAKA'S RUN OUT OF JUICE NOW.
BUT THERE'S STILL...

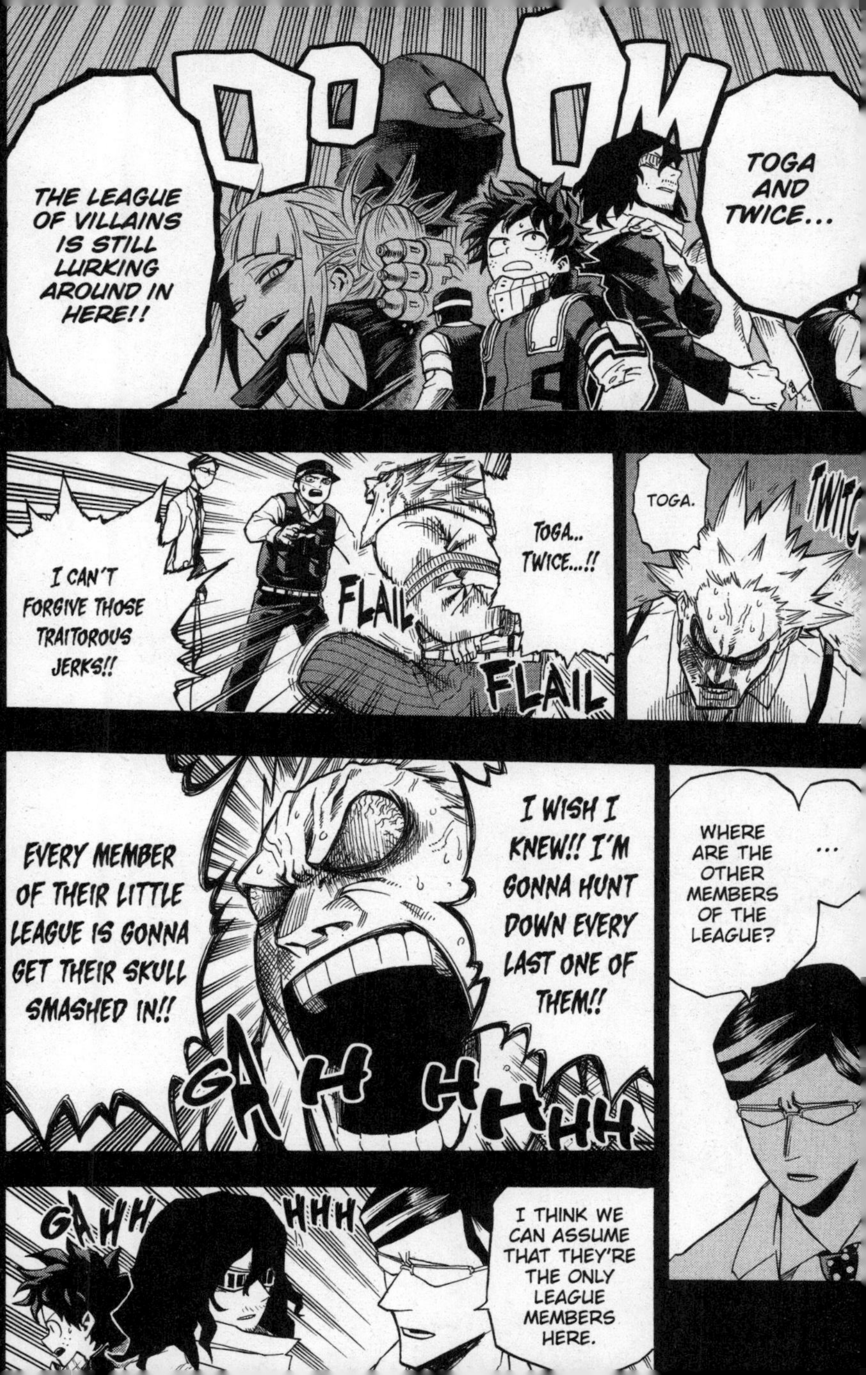
TOGA AND TWICE...
DOOM
THE LEAGUE OF VILLAINS IS STILL LURKING AROUND IN HERE!!
TOGA.
TWITC
TOGA... TWICE...!!
FLAIL
I CAN'T FORGIVE THOSE TRAITOROUS JERKS!!
FLAIL
WHERE ARE THE OTHER MEMBERS OF THE LEAGUE?
...
I WISH I KNEW!! I'M GONNA HUNT DOWN EVERY LAST ONE OF THEM!!
EVERY MEMBER OF THEIR LITTLE LEAGUE IS GONNA GET THEIR SKULL SMASHED IN!!
GAHHHHHH
I THINK WE CAN ASSUME THAT THEY'RE THE ONLY LEAGUE MEMBERS HERE.
GAHHHHH

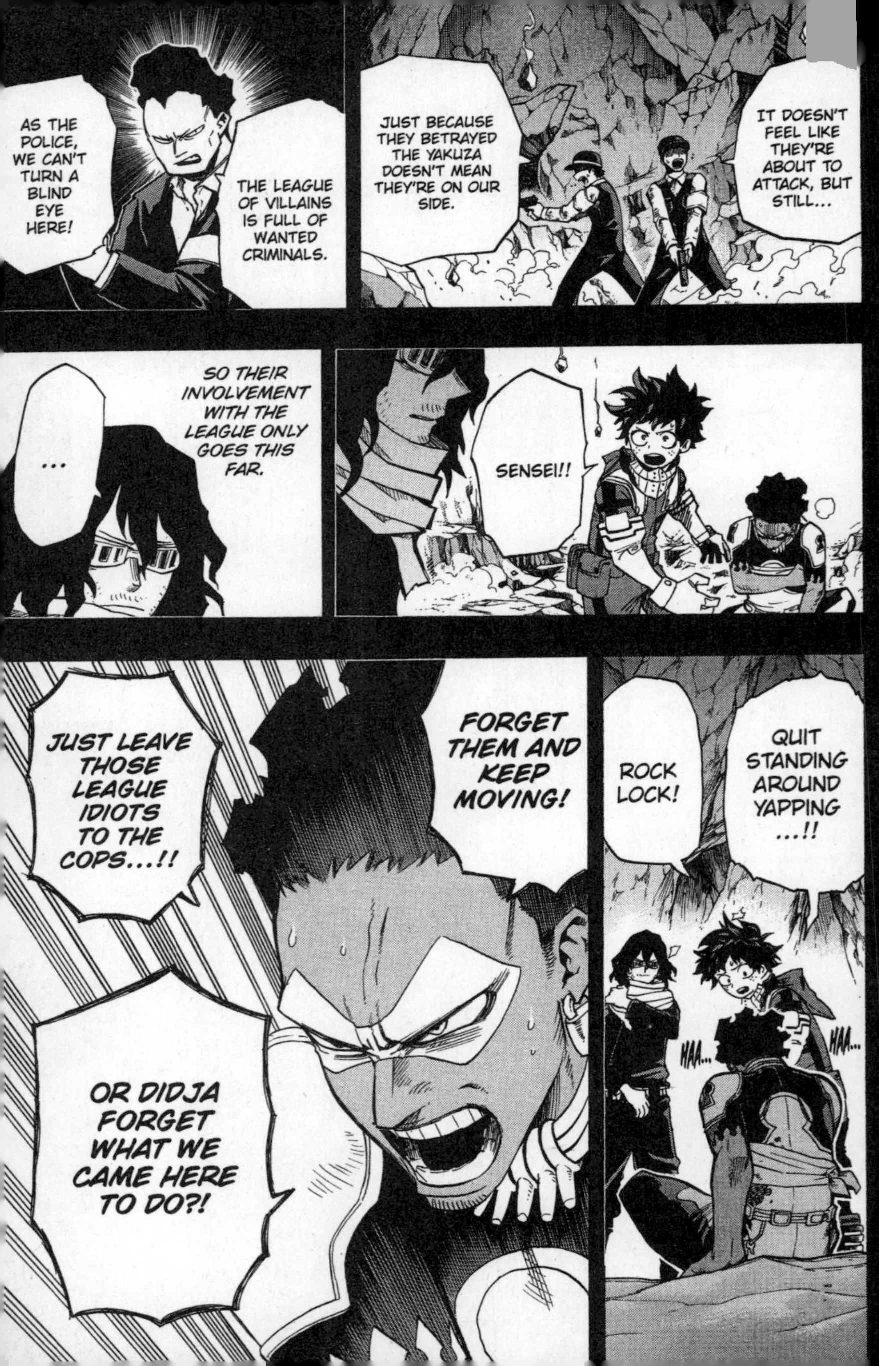
IT DOESN'T FEEL LIKE THEY'RE ABOUT TO ATTACK, BUT STILL...
JUST BECAUSE THEY BETRAYED THE YAKUZA DOESN'T MEAN THEY'RE ON OUR SIDE.
THE LEAGUE OF VILLAINS IS FULL OF WANTED CRIMINALS.
AS THE POLICE, WE CAN'T TURN A BLIND EYE HERE!
SENSEI!!
SO THEIR INVOLVEMENT WITH THE LEAGUE ONLY GOES THIS FAR.
...
QUIT STANDING AROUND YAPPING ...!!
ROCK LOCK!
HAA...
HAA...
FORGET THEM AND KEEP MOVING!
JUST LEAVE THOSE LEAGUE IDIOTS TO THE COPS...!!
OR DIDJA FORGET WHAT WE CAME HERE TO DO?!

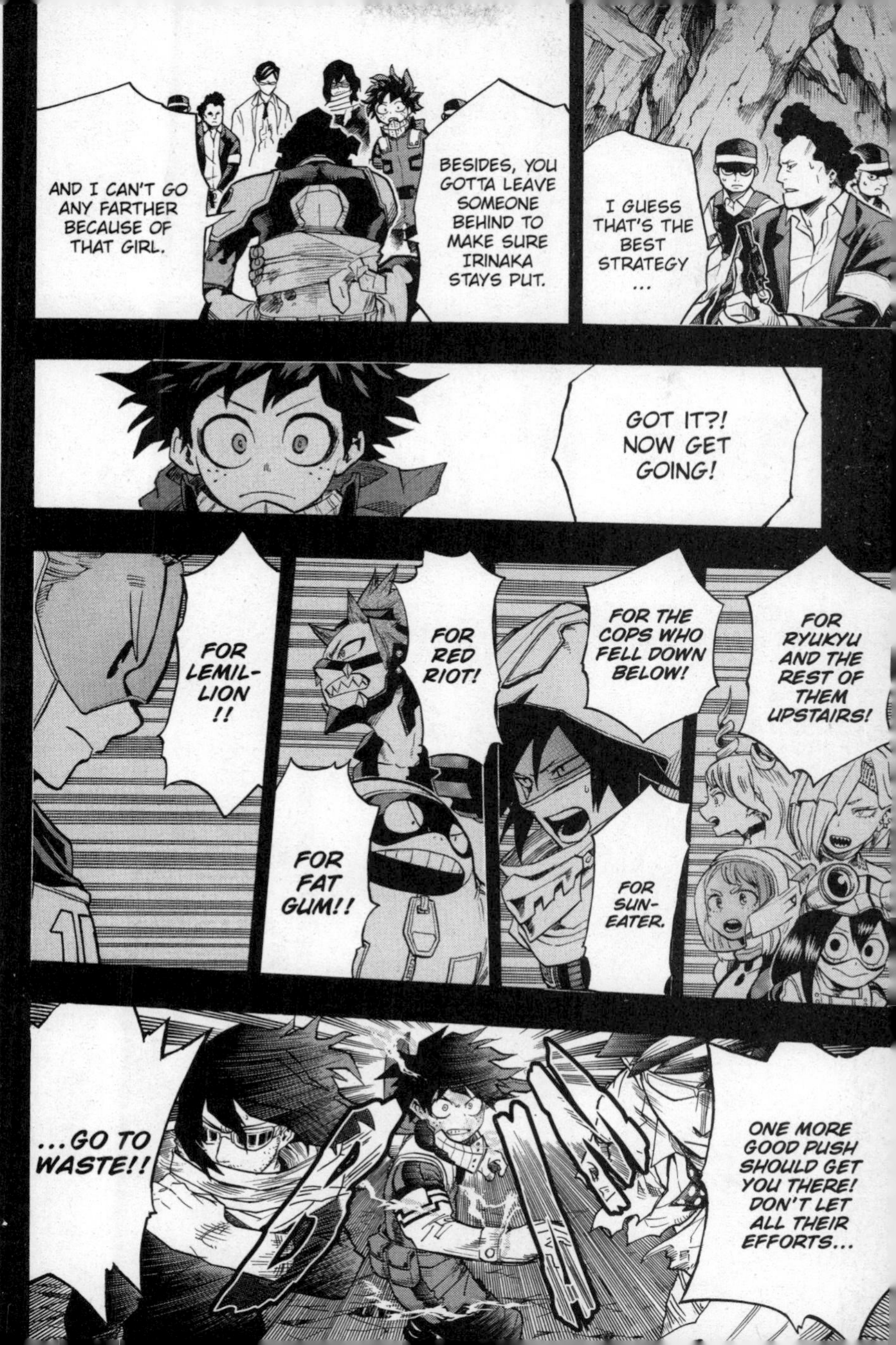
I GUESS THAT'S THE BEST STRATEGY ...
BESIDES, YOU GOTTA LEAVE SOMEONE BEHIND TO MAKE SURE IRINAKA STAYS PUT.
AND I CAN'T GO ANY FARTHER BECAUSE OF THAT GIRL.
GOT IT?! NOW GET GOING!
FOR RYUKYU AND THE REST OF THEM UPSTAIRS!
FOR THE COPS WHO FELL DOWN BELOW!
FOR SUN-EATER.
FOR RED RIOT!
FOR FAT GUM!!
FOR LEMIL-LION !!
ONE MORE GOOD PUSH SHOULD GET YOU THERE! DON'T LET ALL THEIR EFFORTS...
...GO TO WASTE!!

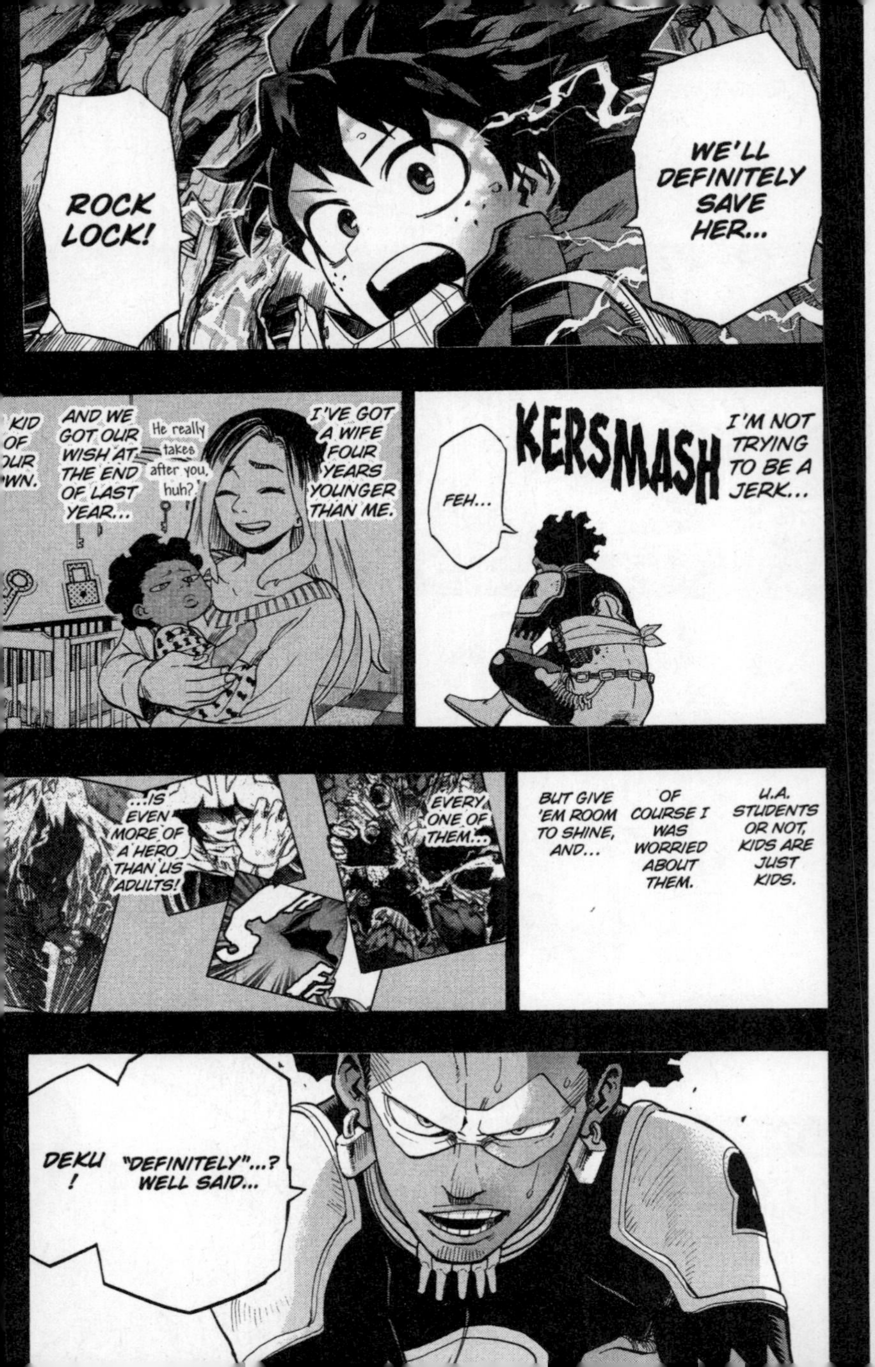
WE'LL DEFINITELY SAVE HER...
ROCK LOCK!
I'M NOT TRYING TO BE A JERK...
KERSMASH
FEH...
I'VE GOT A WIFE FOUR YEARS YOUNGER THAN ME.
He really takes after you, huh?
AND WE GOT OUR WISH AT THE END OF LAST YEAR...
KID OF
U.A. STUDENTS OR NOT, KIDS ARE JUST KIDS.
OF COURSE I WAS WORRIED ABOUT THEM.
BUT GIVE 'EM ROOM TO SHINE, AND...
EVERY ONE OF THEM...
...IS EVEN MORE OF A HERO THAN US ADULTS!
"DEFINITELY"...? WELL SAID...
DEKU!

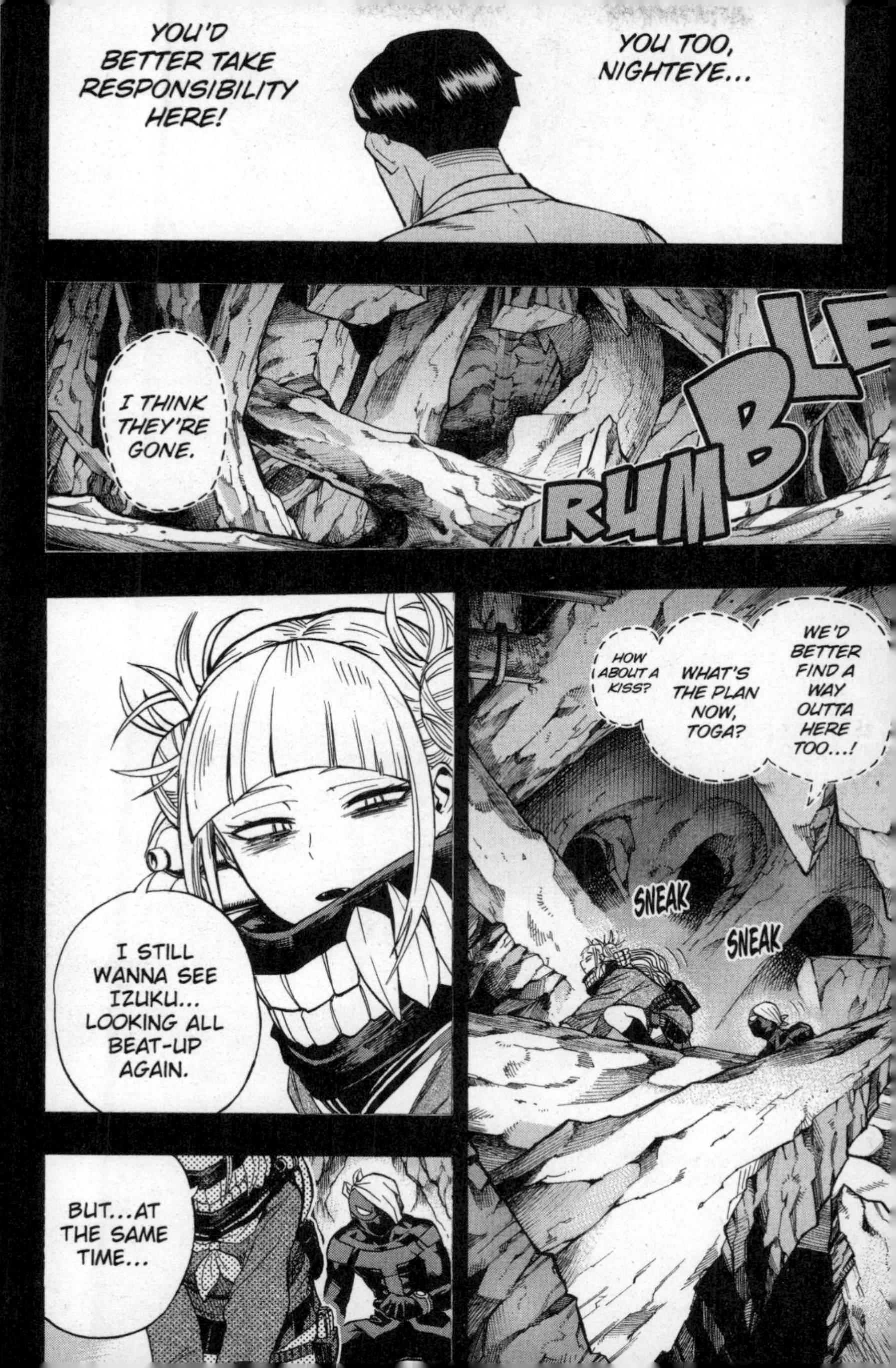
YOU TOO, NIGHTEYE...
YOU'D BETTER TAKE RESPONSIBILITY HERE!
RUMBLE
I THINK THEY'RE GONE.
WE'D BETTER FIND A WAY OUTTA HERE TOO...!
WHAT'S THE PLAN NOW, TOGA?
HOW ABOUT A KISS?
SNEAK
SNEAK
I STILL WANNA SEE IZUKU... LOOKING ALL BEAT-UP AGAIN.
BUT...AT THE SAME TIME...

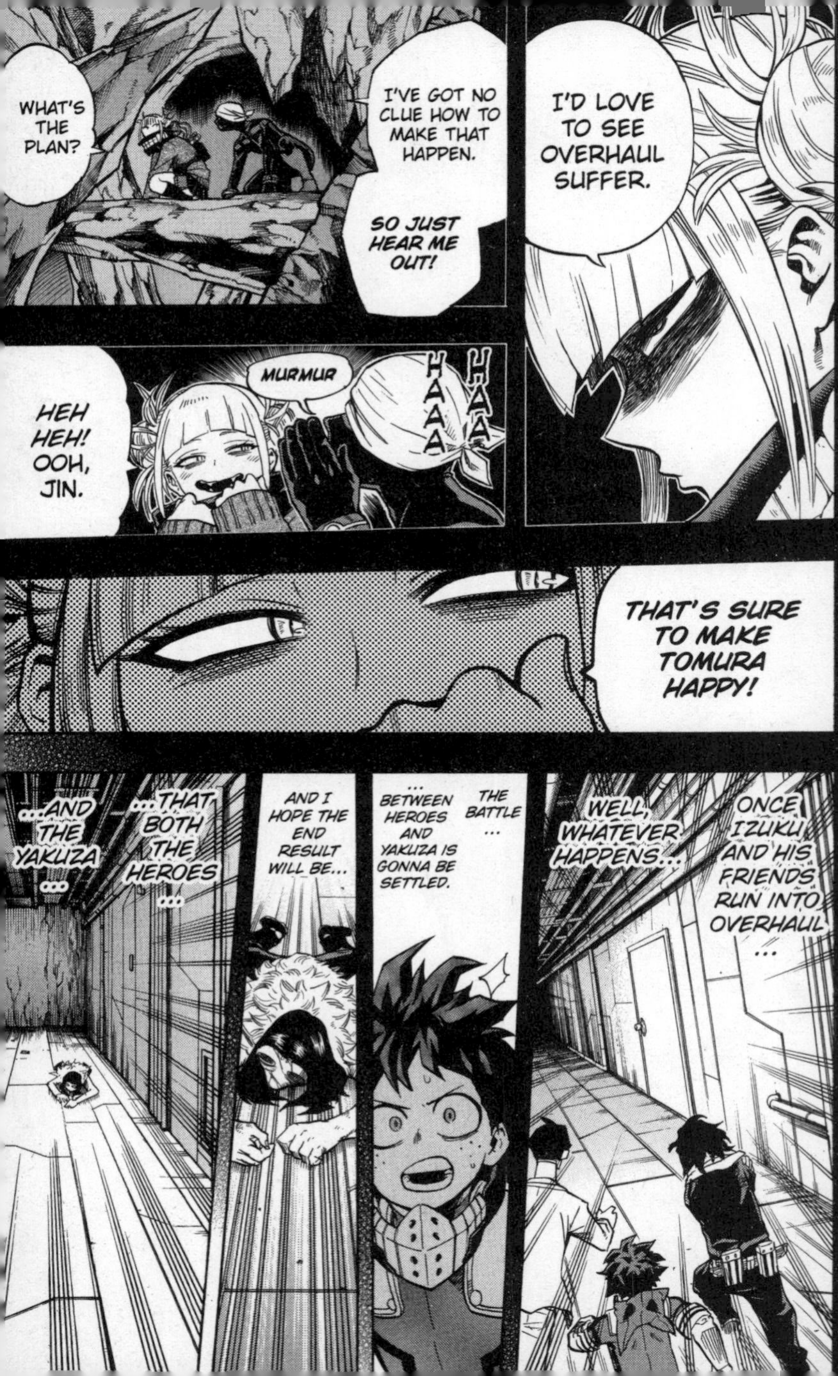
I'D LOVE TO SEE OVERHAUL SUFFER.
I'VE GOT NO CLUE HOW TO MAKE THAT HAPPEN.
SO JUST HEAR ME OUT!
WHAT'S THE PLAN?
HAA HAA
MURMUR
HEH HEH! OOH, JIN.
THAT'S SURE TO MAKE TOMURA HAPPY!
ONCE IZUKU AND HIS FRIENDS RUN INTO OVERHAUL...
WELL, WHATEVER HAPPENS...
THE BATTLE...
...BETWEEN HEROES AND YAKUZA IS GONNA BE SETTLED.
AND I HOPE THE END RESULT WILL BE...
...THAT BOTH THE HEROES...
...AND THE YAKUZA...

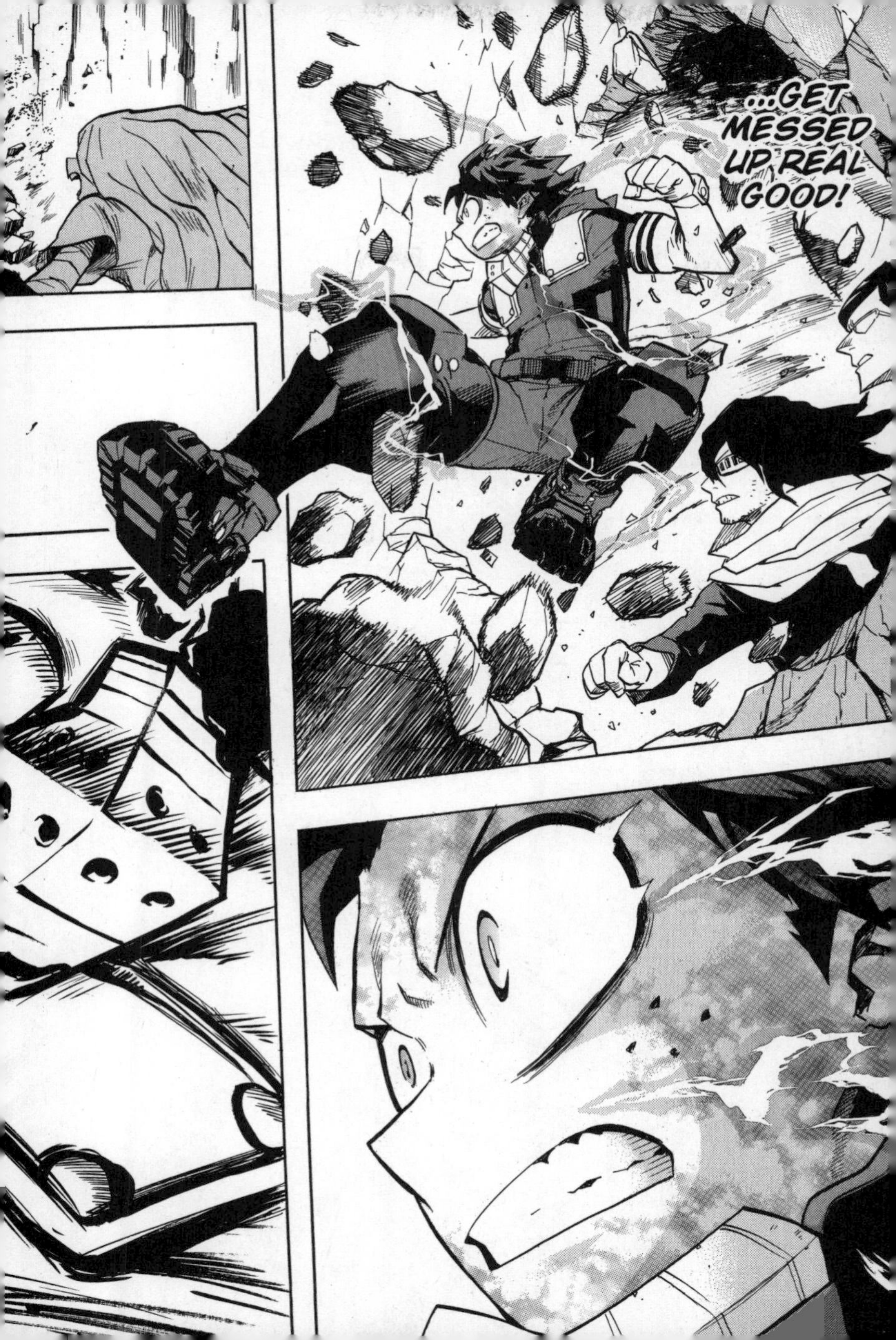
...GET MESSED UP REAL GOOD!

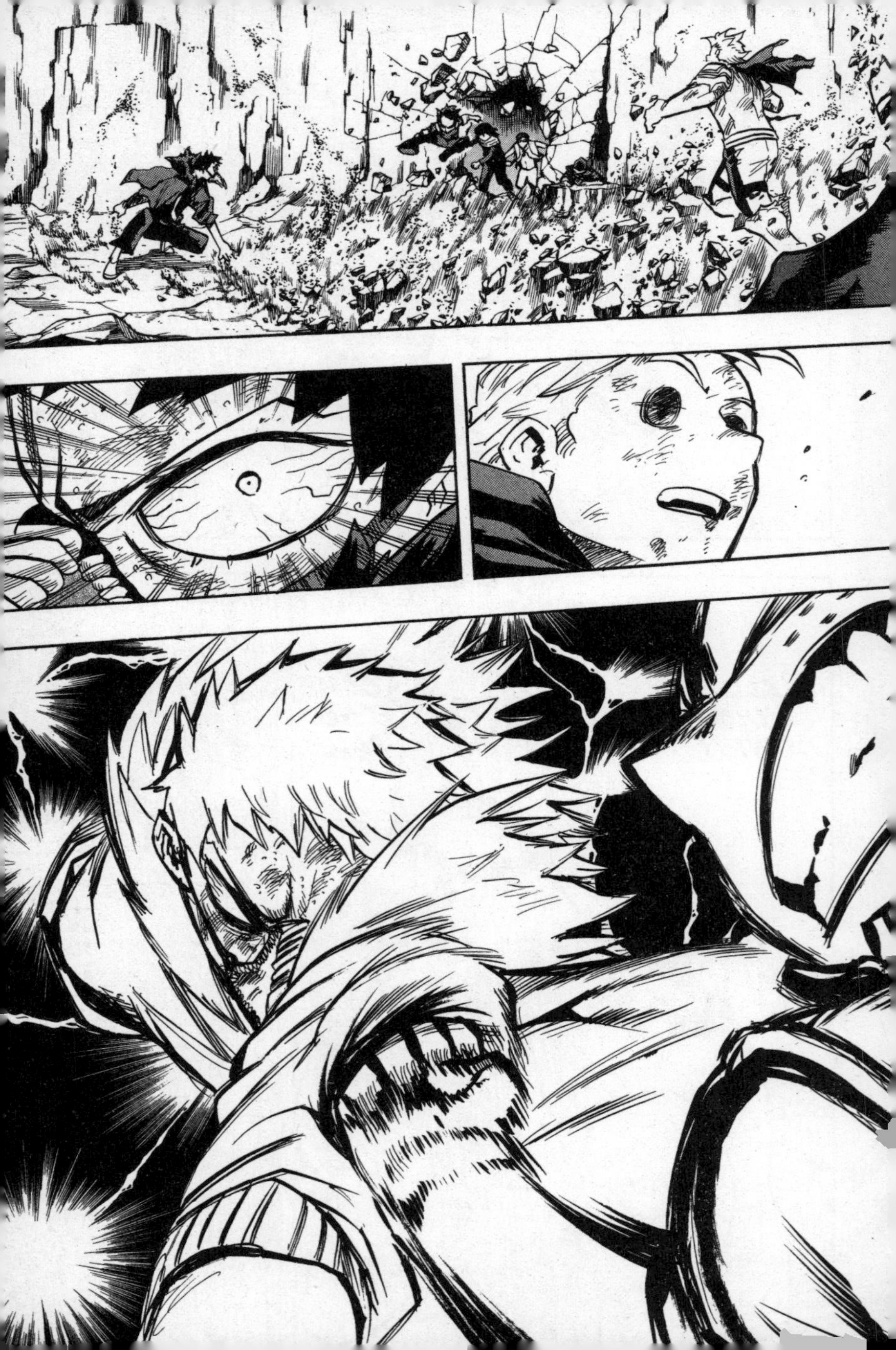

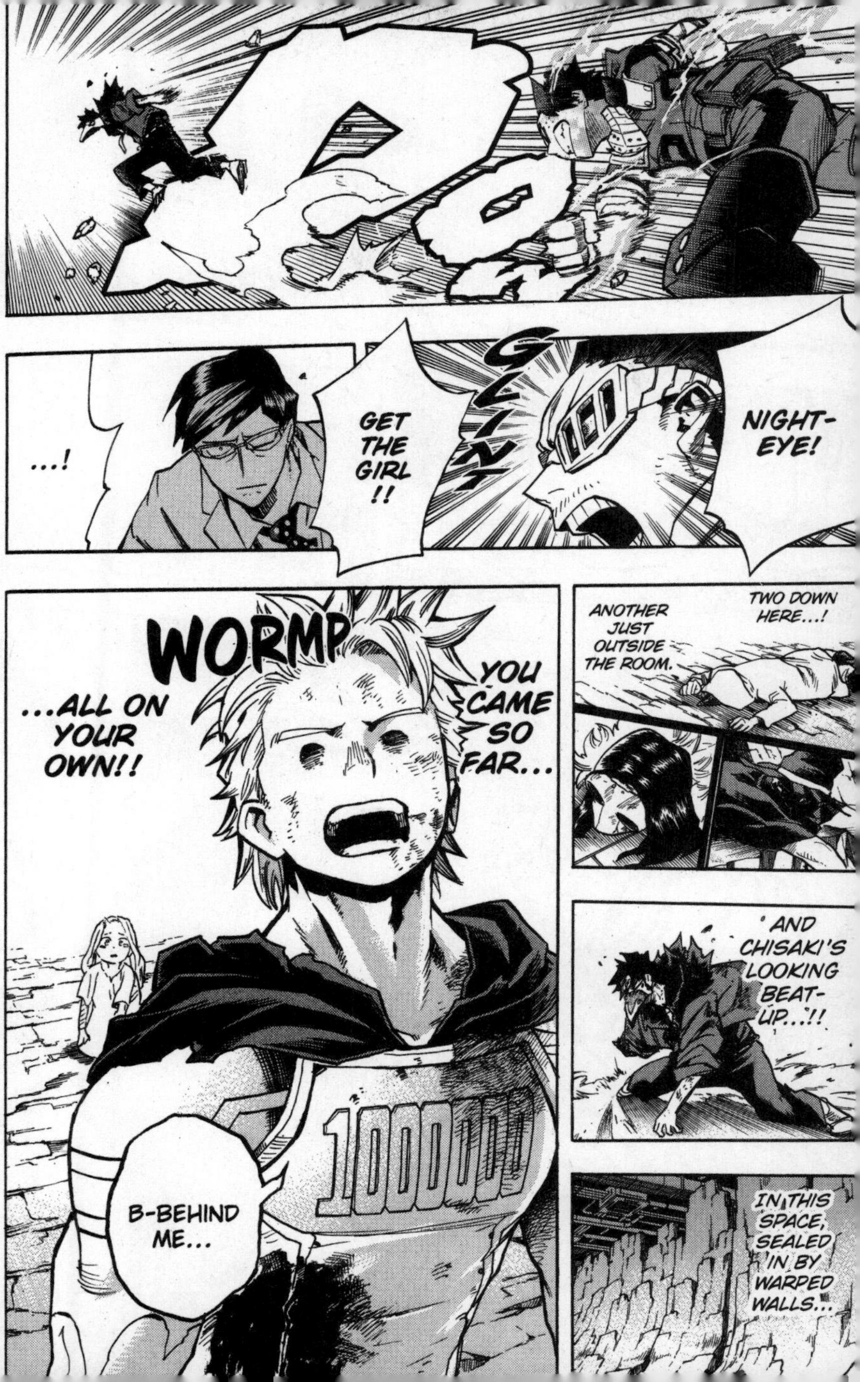
NIGHT-EYE!
GLINT
GET THE GIRL!!
...!
TWO DOWN HERE...!
ANOTHER JUST OUTSIDE THE ROOM.
AND CHISAKI'S LOOKING BEAT-UP...!!
IN THIS SPACE, SEALED IN BY WARPED WALLS...
YOU CAME SO FAR...
WORMP
...ALL ON YOUR OWN!!
1000000
B-BEHIND ME...

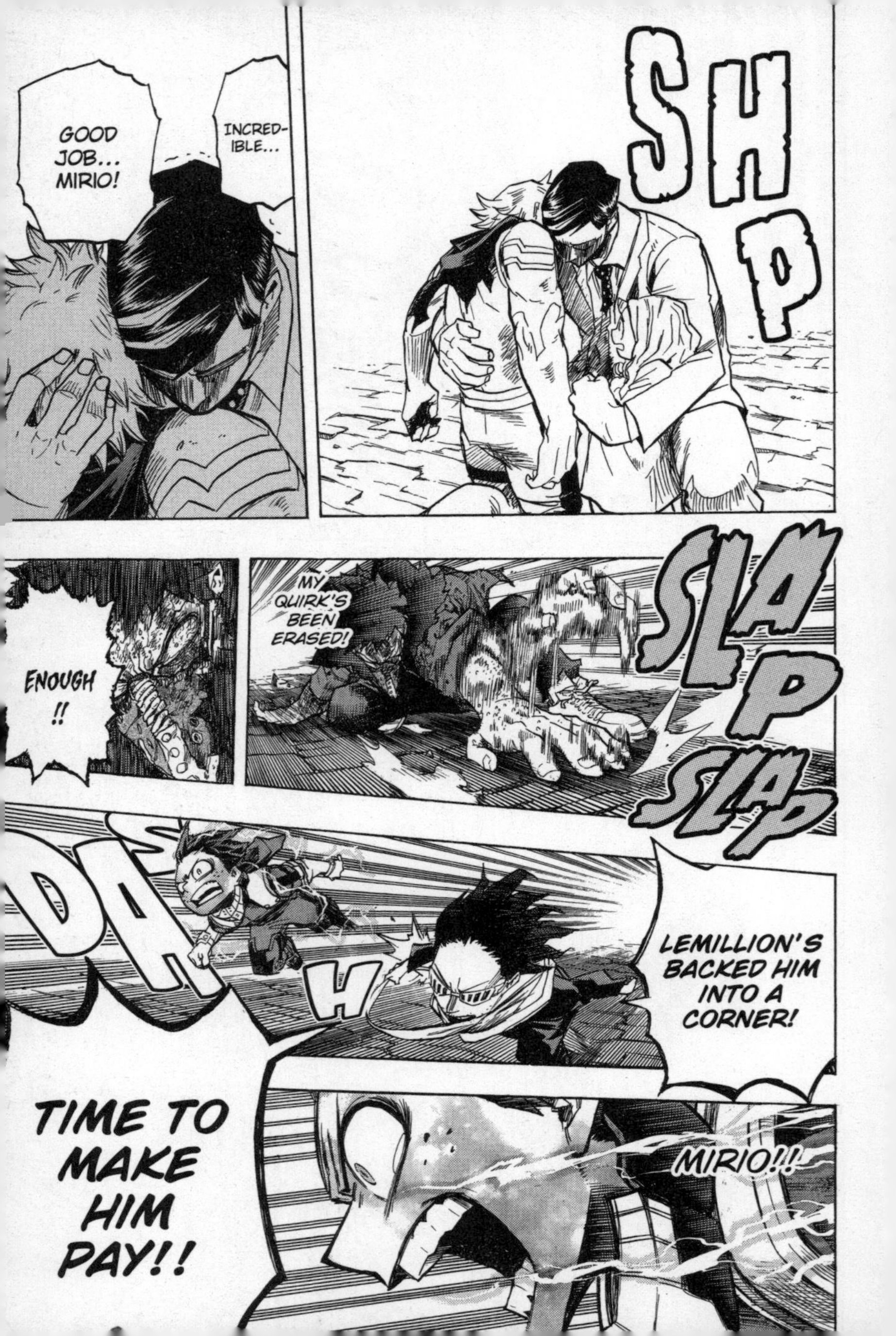
SHP
INCRED-IBLE...
GOOD JOB... MIRIO!
SLAP
SLAP
MY QUIRK'S BEEN ERASED!
ENOUGH!!
LEMILLION'S BACKED HIM INTO A CORNER!
DA
H
MIRIO!!
TIME TO MAKE HIM PAY!!

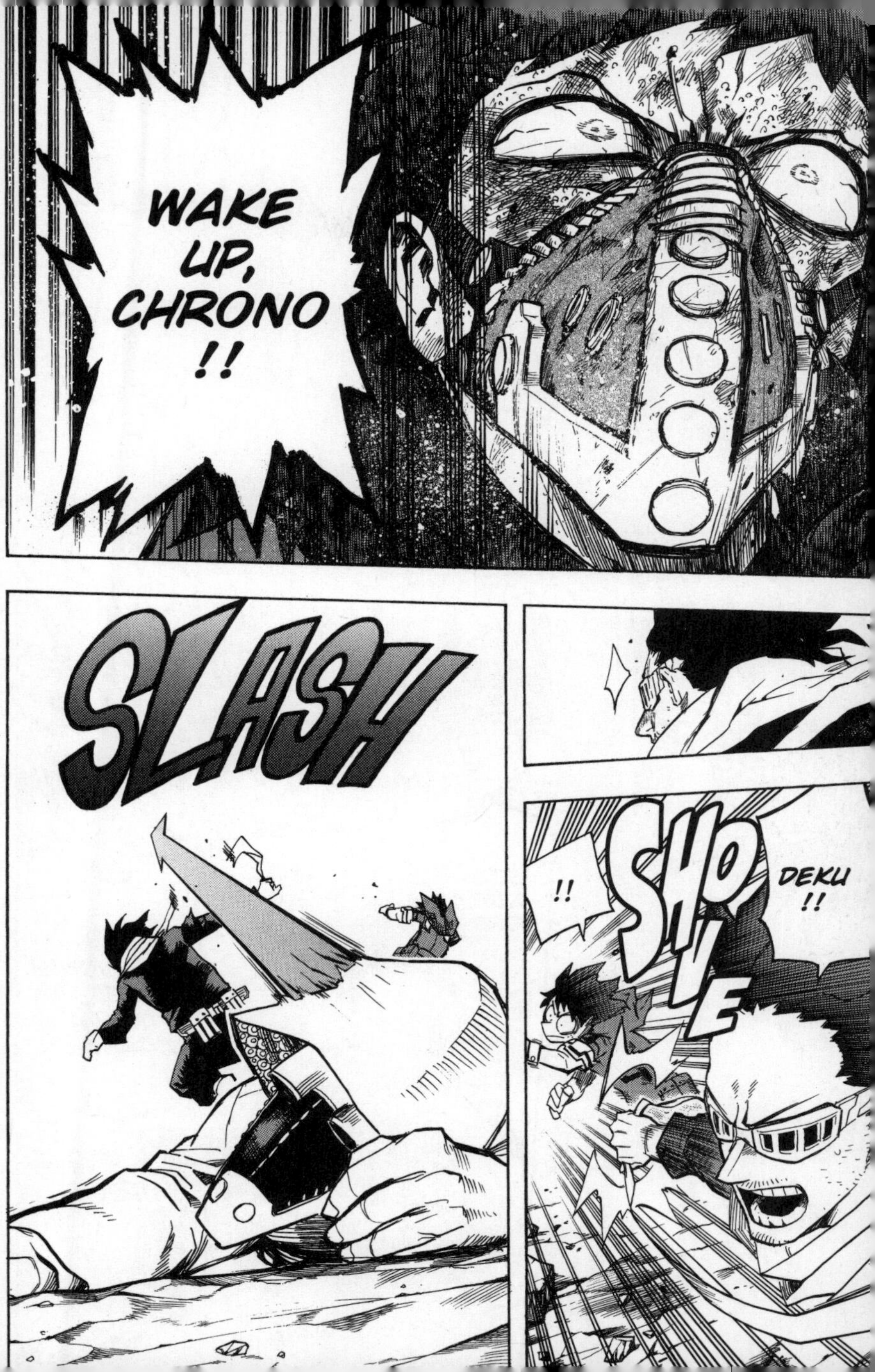
WAKE UP, CHRONO !!
SHOVE
!!
DEKU !!
SLASH

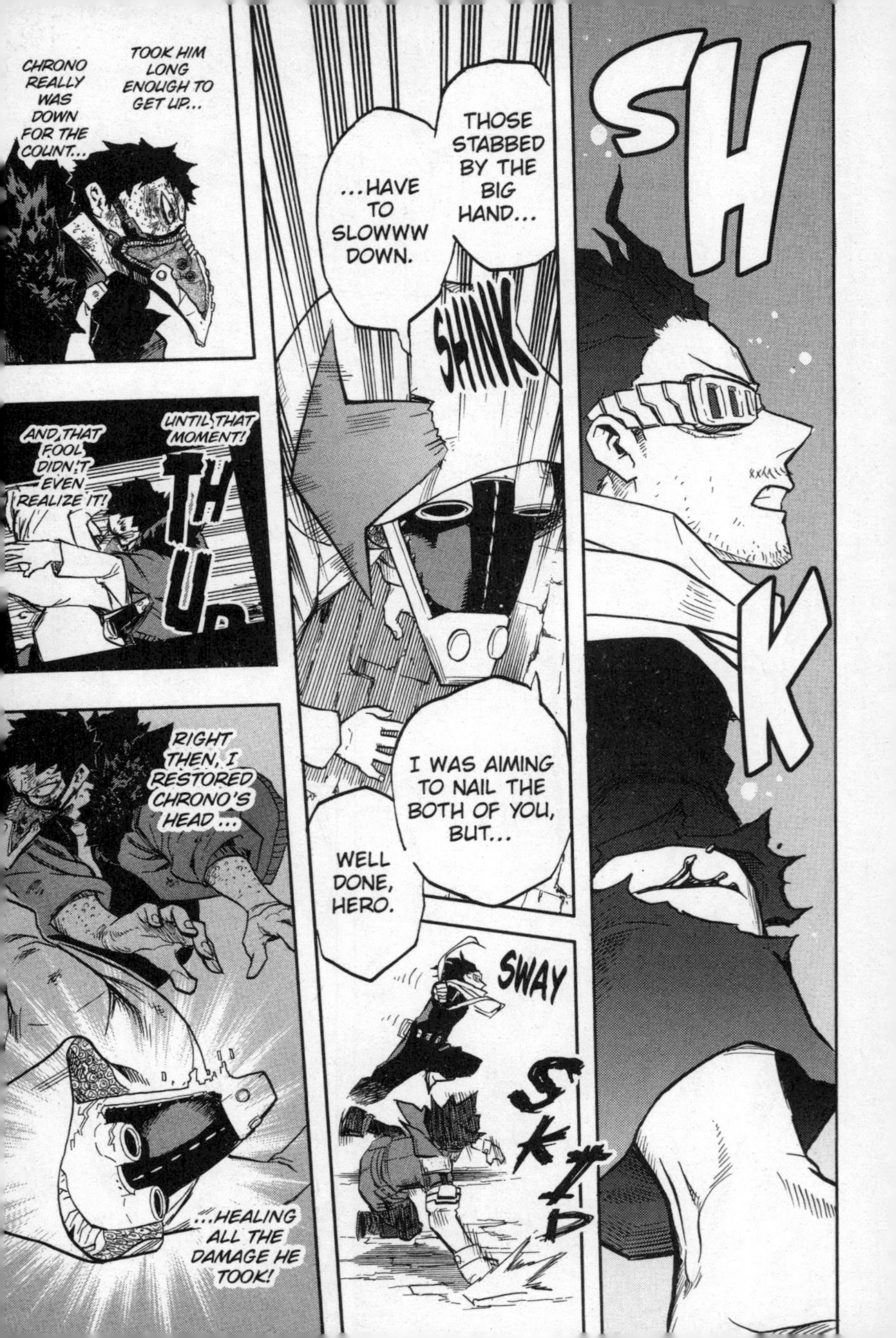
SHK
THOSE STABBED BY THE BIG HAND...
...HAVE TO SLOWWW DOWN.
SHINK
I WAS AIMING TO NAIL THE BOTH OF YOU, BUT...
WELL DONE, HERO.
SWAY
SKID
TOOK HIM LONG ENOUGH TO GET UP...
CHRONO REALLY WAS DOWN FOR THE COUNT...
UNTIL THAT MOMENT!
AND THAT FOOL DIDN'T EVEN REALIZE IT!
THUD
RIGHT THEN, I RESTORED CHRONO'S HEAD...
...HEALING ALL THE DAMAGE HE TOOK!

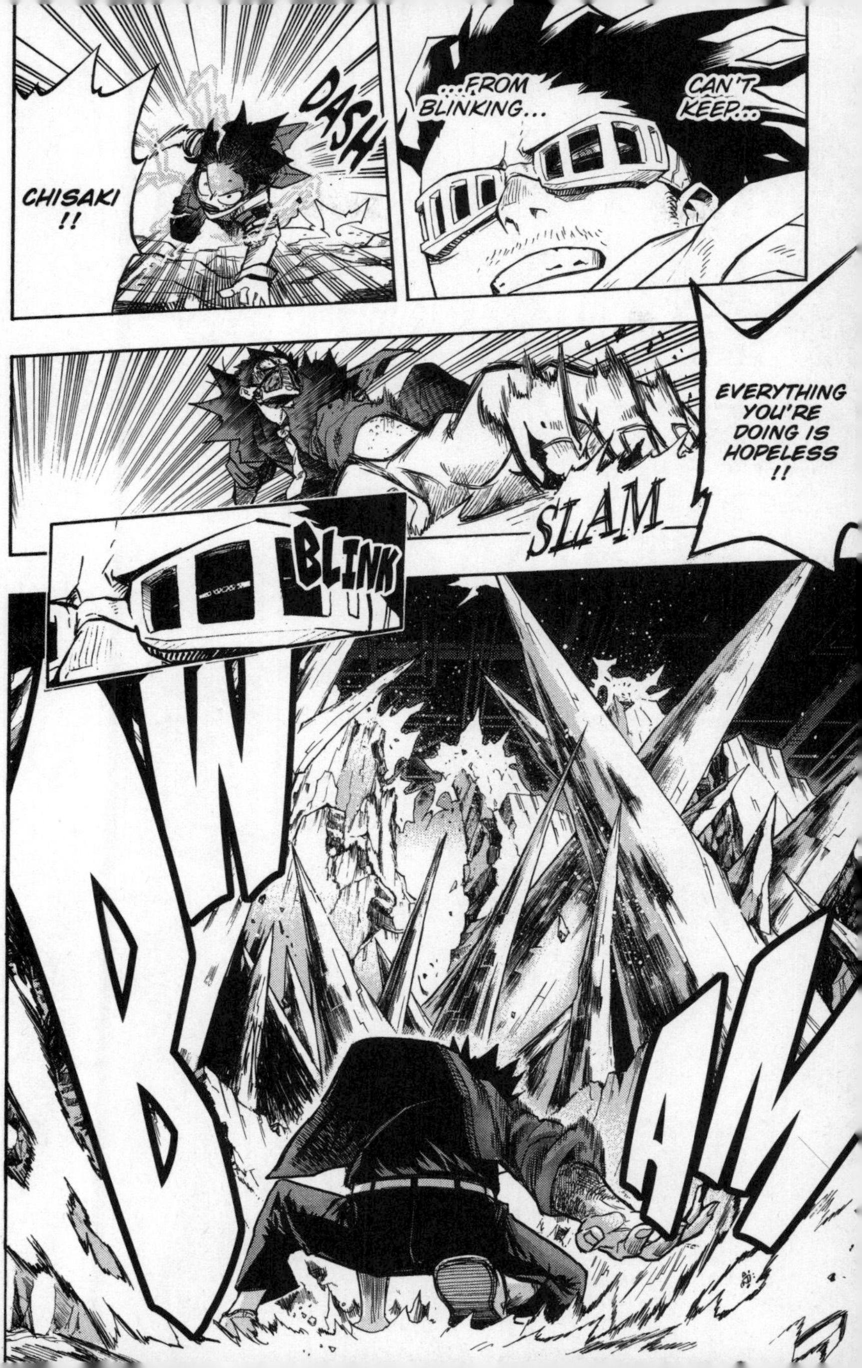
CAN'T KEEP...
...FROM BLINKING...
DASH
CHISAKI !!
EVERYTHING YOU'RE DOING IS HOPELESS !!
SLAM
BLINK

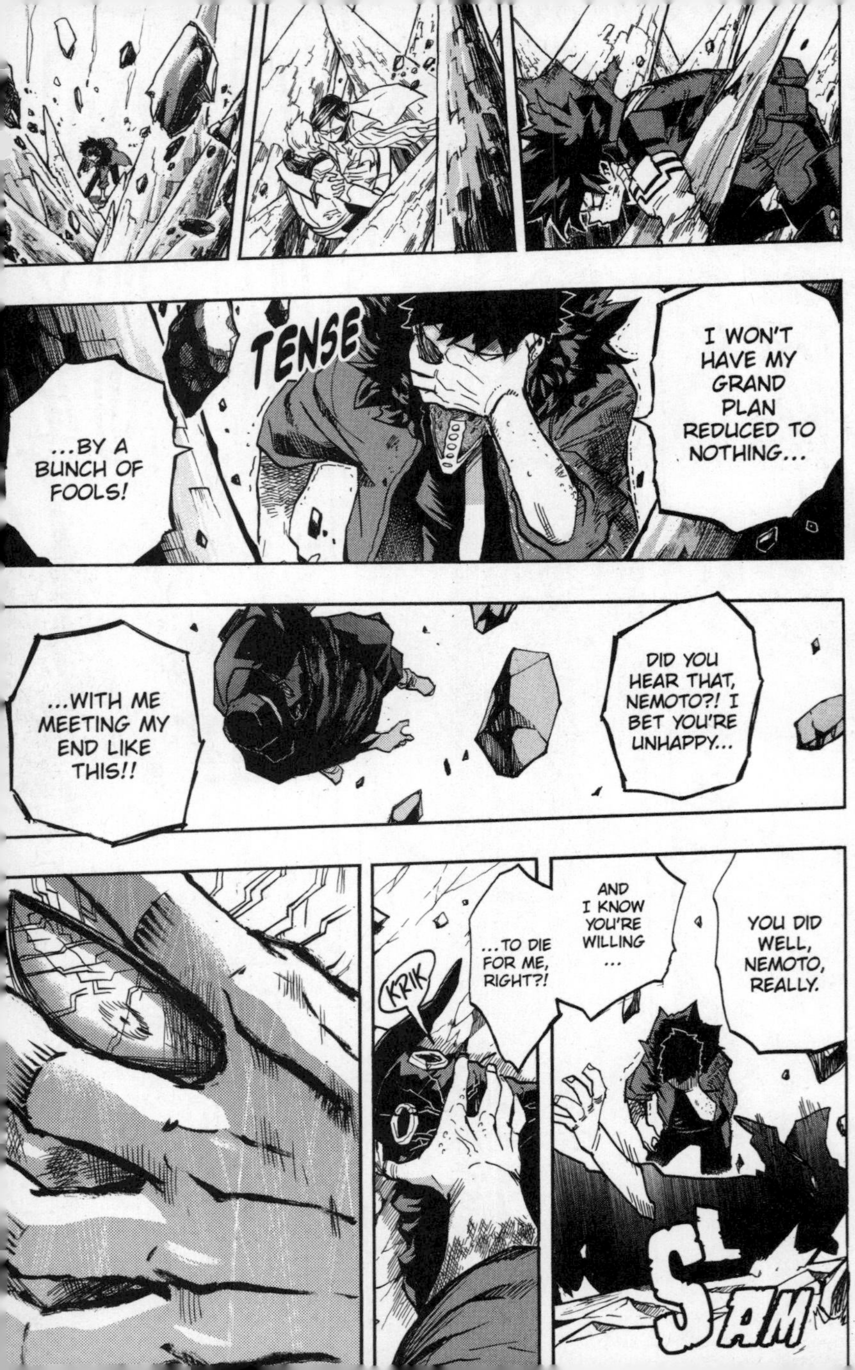
I WON'T HAVE MY GRAND PLAN REDUCED TO NOTHING...
TENSE
...BY A BUNCH OF FOOLS!
DID YOU HEAR THAT, NEMOTO?! I BET YOU'RE UNHAPPY...
...WITH ME MEETING MY END LIKE THIS!!
YOU DID WELL, NEMOTO, REALLY.
AND I KNOW YOU'RE WILLING ...
...TO DIE FOR ME, RIGHT?!
SLAM
KRIK

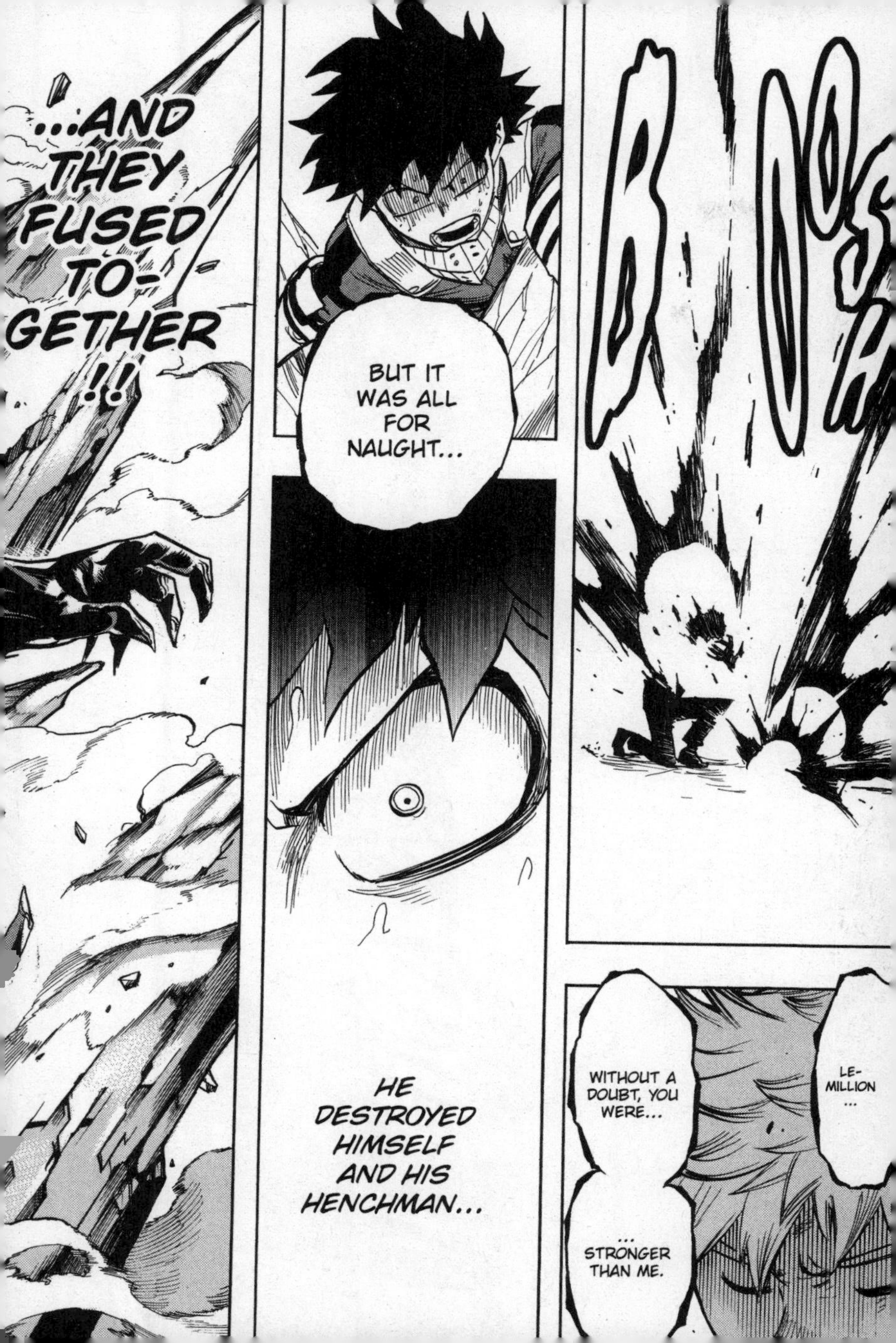
LE-MILLION...
WITHOUT A DOUBT, YOU WERE...
...STRONGER THAN ME.
BUT IT WAS ALL FOR NAUGHT...
HE DESTROYED HIMSELF AND HIS HENCHMAN...
...AND THEY FUSED TO-GETHER!!

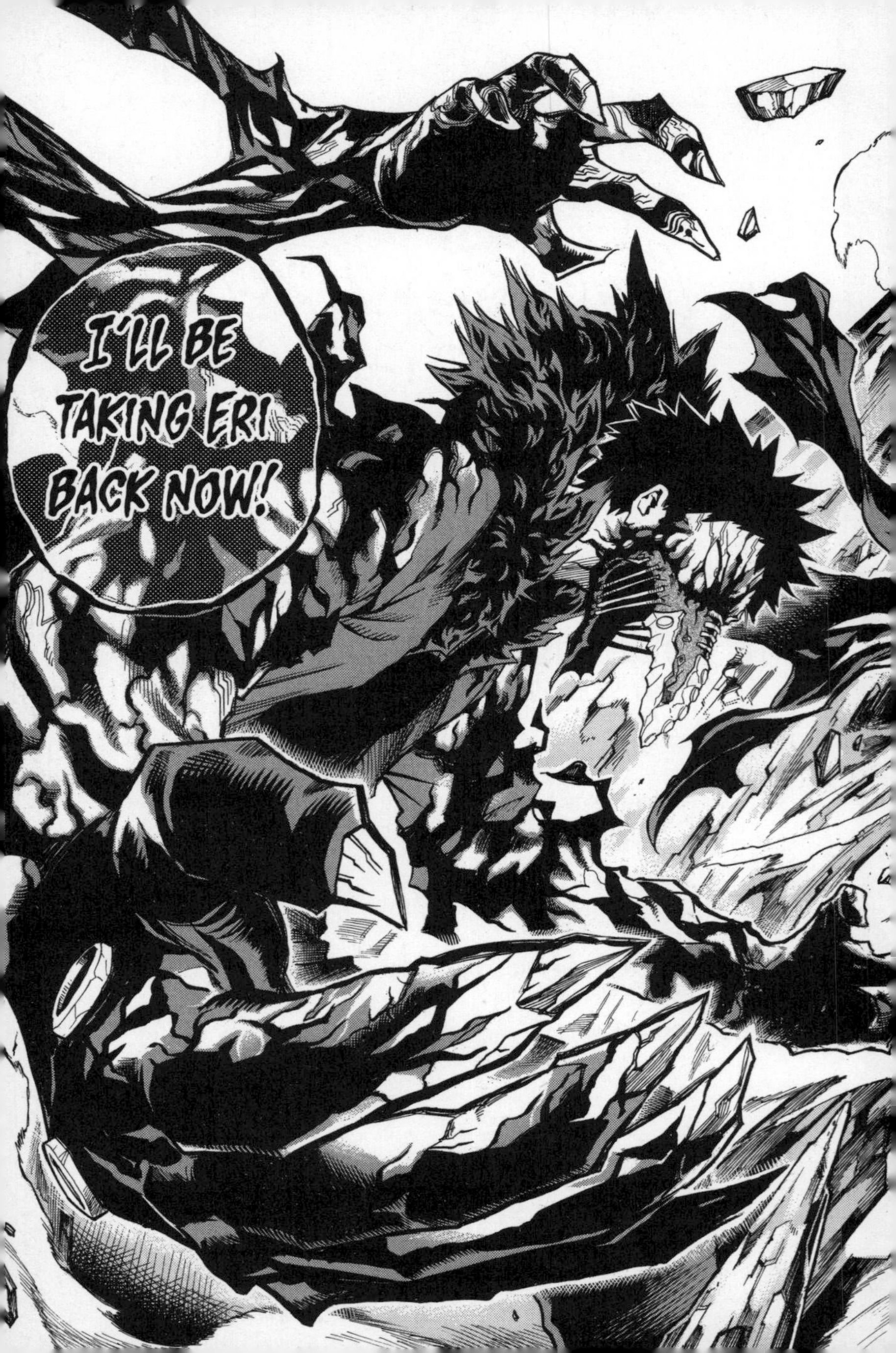
I'LL BE TAKING ERI BACK NOW!

KYOKA JIRO MAKES SOME NOISE!!

(FINAL EDITION)

Q. I WANT TO HIT THOSE HIGH NOTES DURING KARAOKE. ANY QUICK TIPS TO HELP ME OUT?

(FROM E-SAN, AGE 41)

A: BEFORE SINGING, TRY BUZZING YOUR LIPS WHILE GOING FOR THOSE HIGH PITCHES!

IT'S EVEN BETTER IF YOU TUG UP ON THE CORNERS OF YOUR MOUTH AT THE SAME TIME!

I WAS SURPRISED HOW WELL THIS WORKS, SERIOUSLY!

GOOD LUCK!

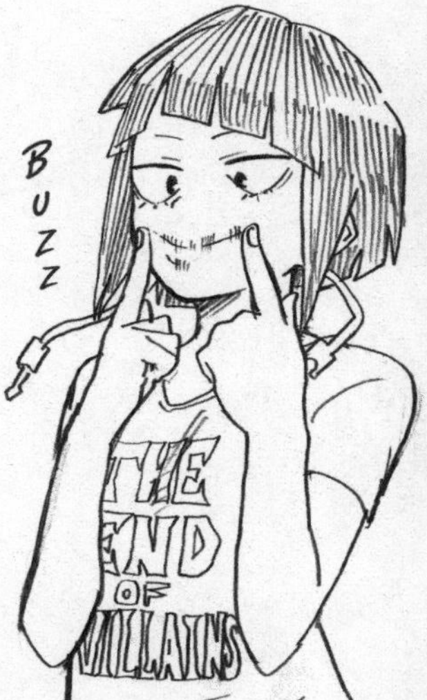
BUZZ
THE END OF VILLAINS

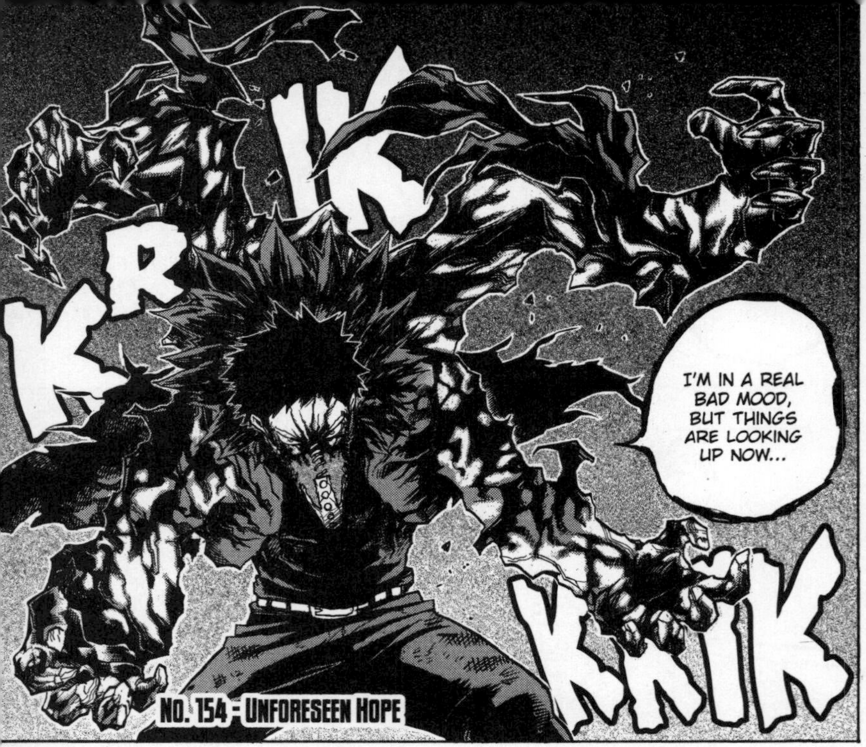
KRIK
KRIK
I'M IN A REAL BAD MOOD, BUT THINGS ARE LOOKING UP NOW...
KRIK
No. 154 - Unforeseen Hope

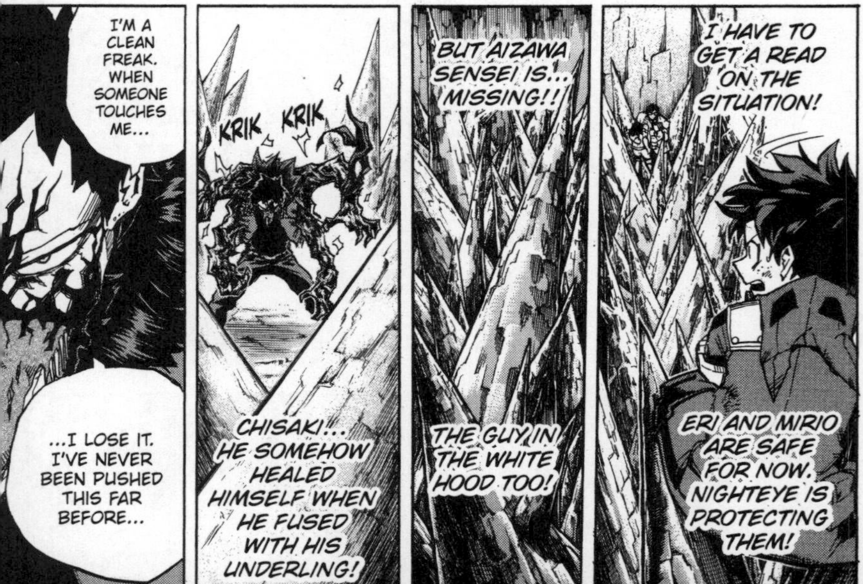
I HAVE TO GET A READ ON THE SITUATION!
ERI AND MIRIO ARE SAFE FOR NOW. NIGHTEYE IS PROTECTING THEM!
BUT AIZAWA SENSEI IS... MISSING!!
THE GUY IN THE WHITE HOOD TOO!
KRIK KRIK
CHISAKI... HE SOMEHOW HEALED HIMSELF WHEN HE FUSED WITH HIS UNDERLING!
I'M A CLEAN FREAK. WHEN SOMEONE TOUCHES ME...
...I LOSE IT. I'VE NEVER BEEN PUSHED THIS FAR BEFORE...

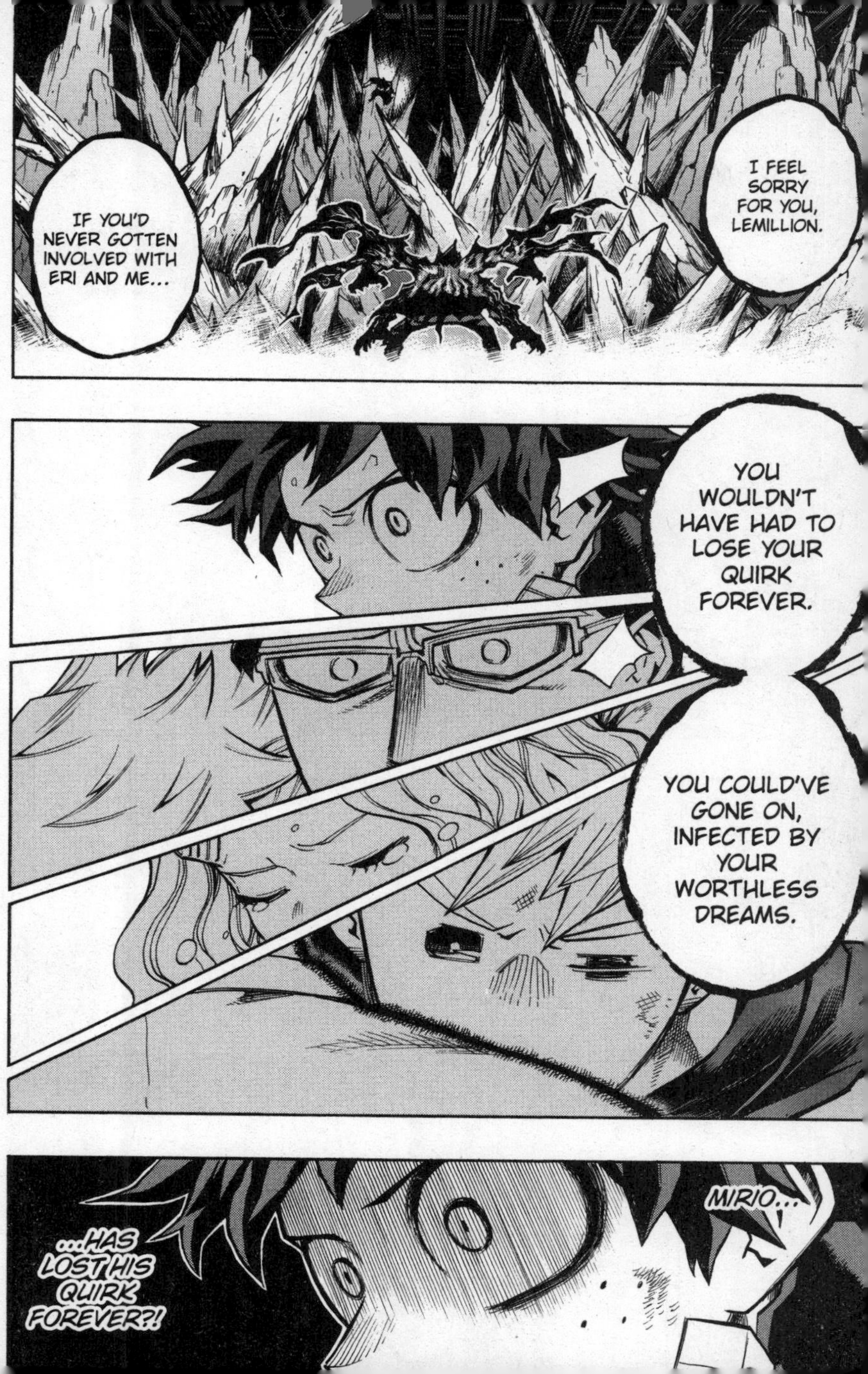
I FEEL SORRY FOR YOU, LEMILLION.
IF YOU'D NEVER GOTTEN INVOLVED WITH ERI AND ME...
YOU WOULDN'T HAVE HAD TO LOSE YOUR QUIRK FOREVER.
YOU COULD'VE GONE ON, INFECTED BY YOUR WORTHLESS DREAMS.
MIRIO...
...HAS LOST HIS QUIRK FOREVER?!

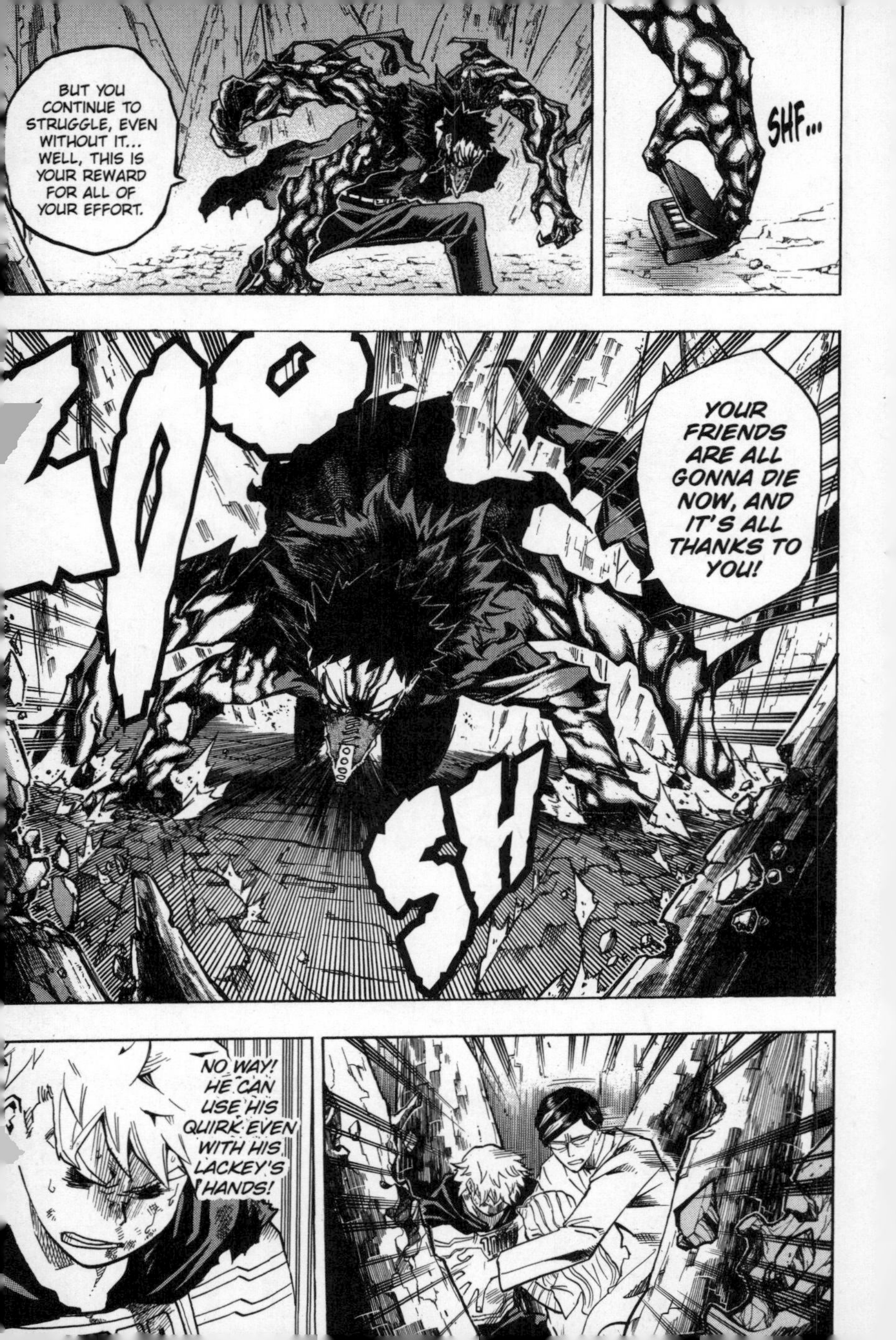
SHF...
BUT YOU CONTINUE TO STRUGGLE, EVEN WITHOUT IT... WELL, THIS IS YOUR REWARD FOR ALL OF YOUR EFFORT.
YOUR FRIENDS ARE ALL GONNA DIE NOW, AND IT'S ALL THANKS TO YOU!
SH
NO WAY! HE CAN USE HIS QUIRK EVEN WITH HIS LACKEY'S HANDS!

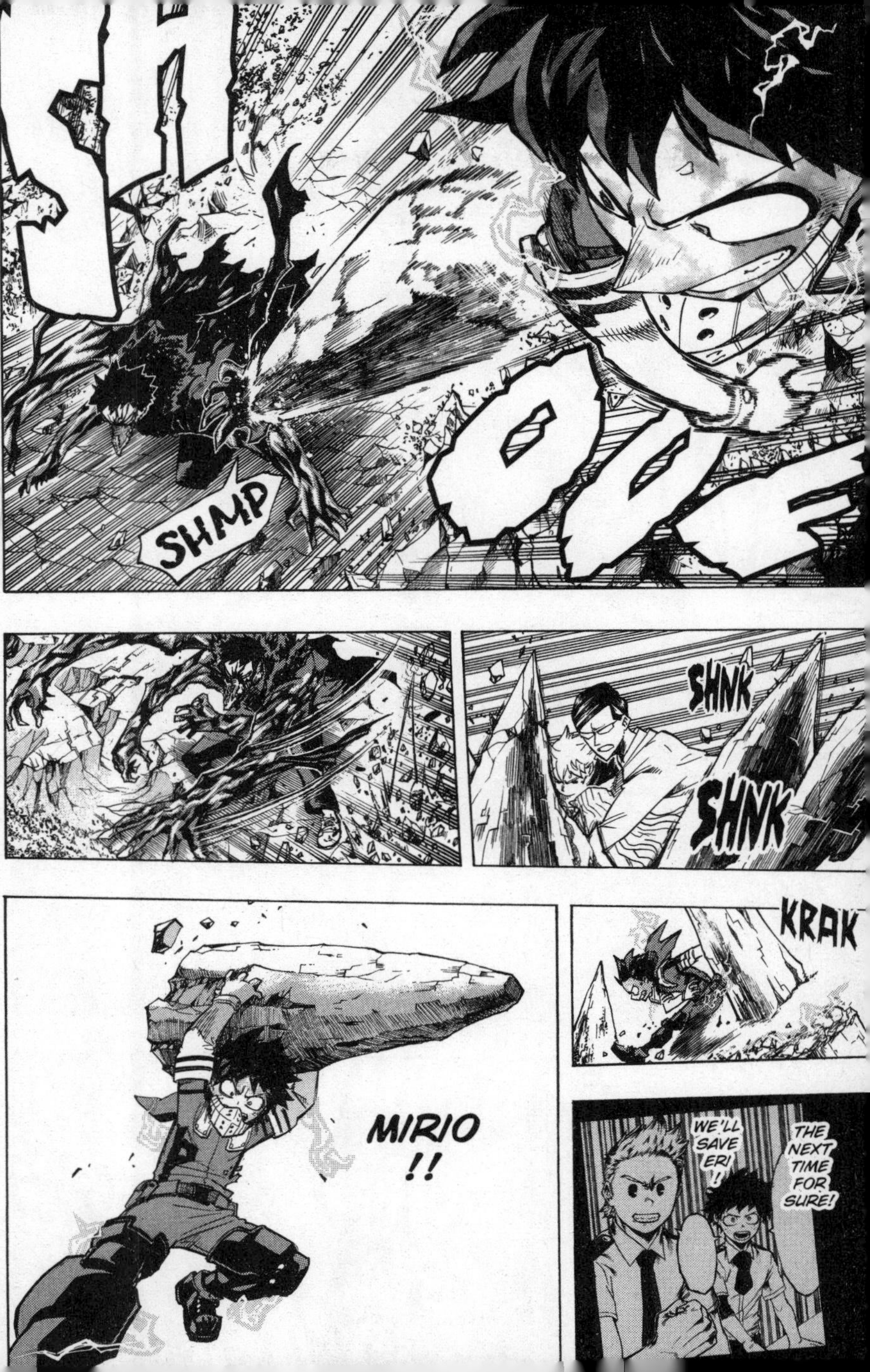
SHMP
SHNK
SHNK
KRAK
THE NEXT TIME FOR SURE!
WE'LL SAVE ERI!
MIRIO!!

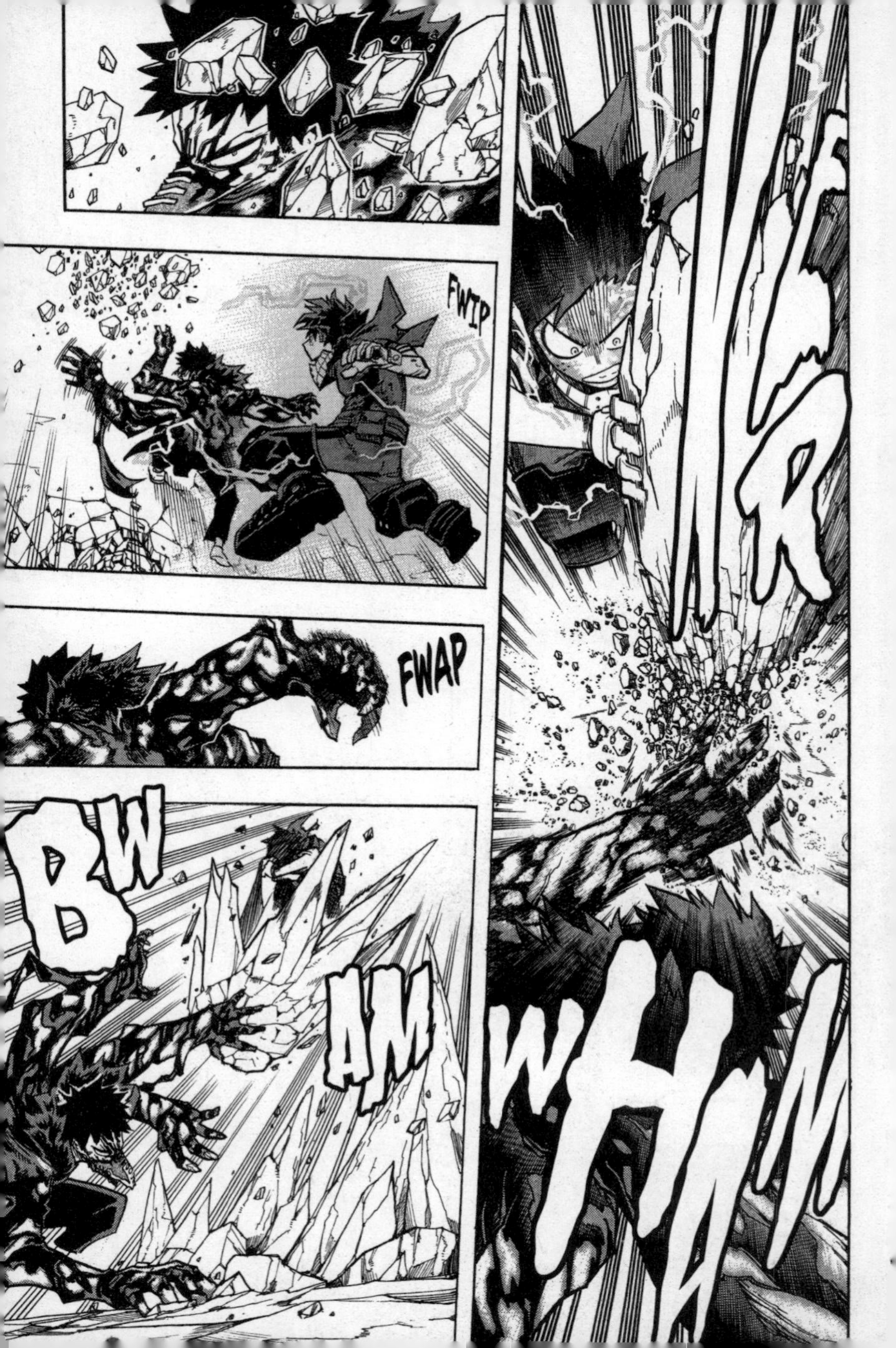
FWIP
FWAP
BWAM

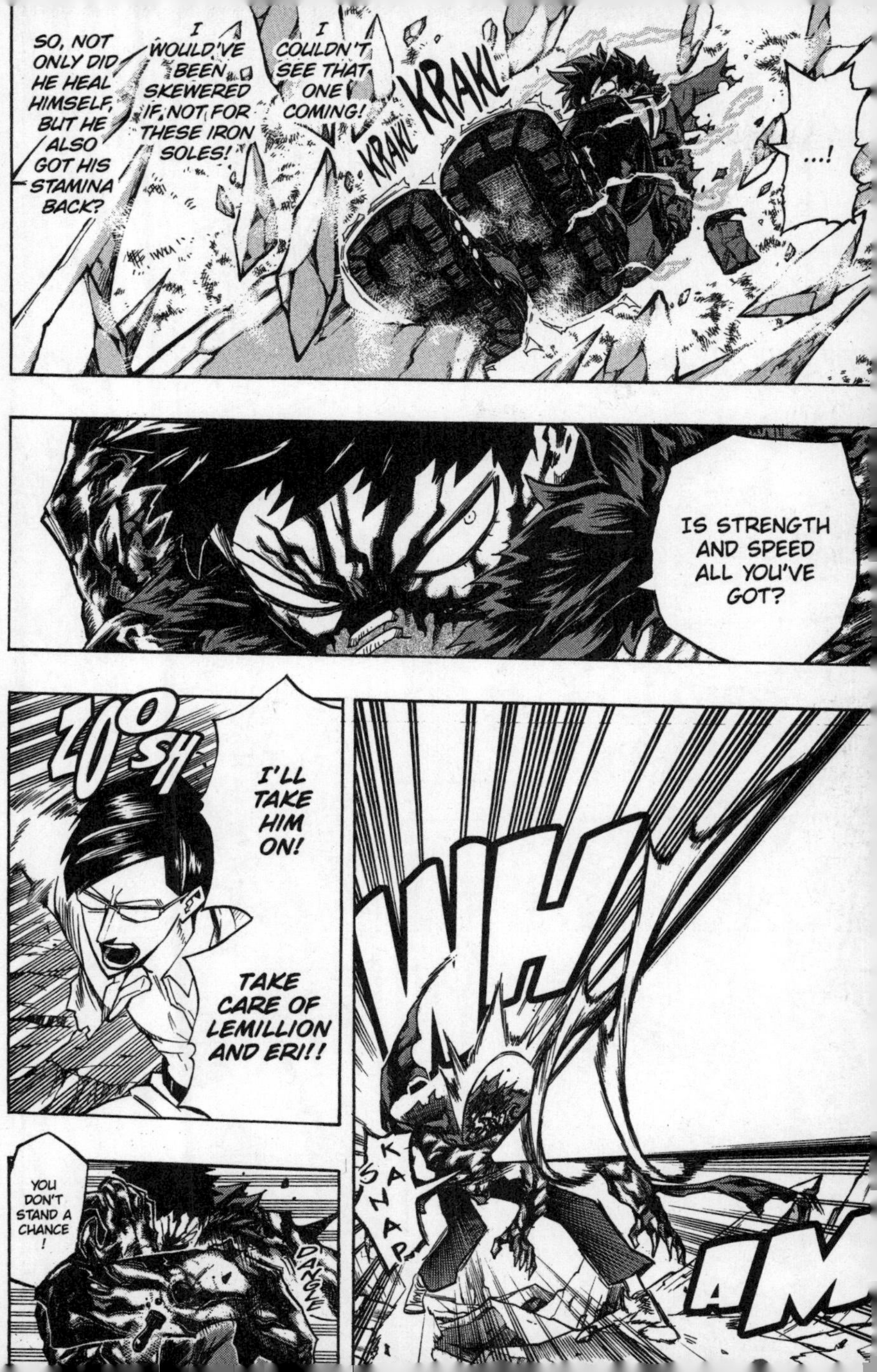
...!
KRAKL KRAKL KRAKL
I COULDN'T SEE THAT ONE COMING!
I WOULD'VE BEEN SKEWERED IF NOT FOR THESE IRON SOLES!
SO, NOT ONLY DID HE HEAL HIMSELF, BUT HE ALSO GOT HIS STAMINA BACK?
IS STRENGTH AND SPEED ALL YOU'VE GOT?
WHAM
SNAP
ZOOSH
I'LL TAKE HIM ON!
TAKE CARE OF LEMILLION AND ERI!!
YOU DON'T STAND A CHANCE!
DANGLE

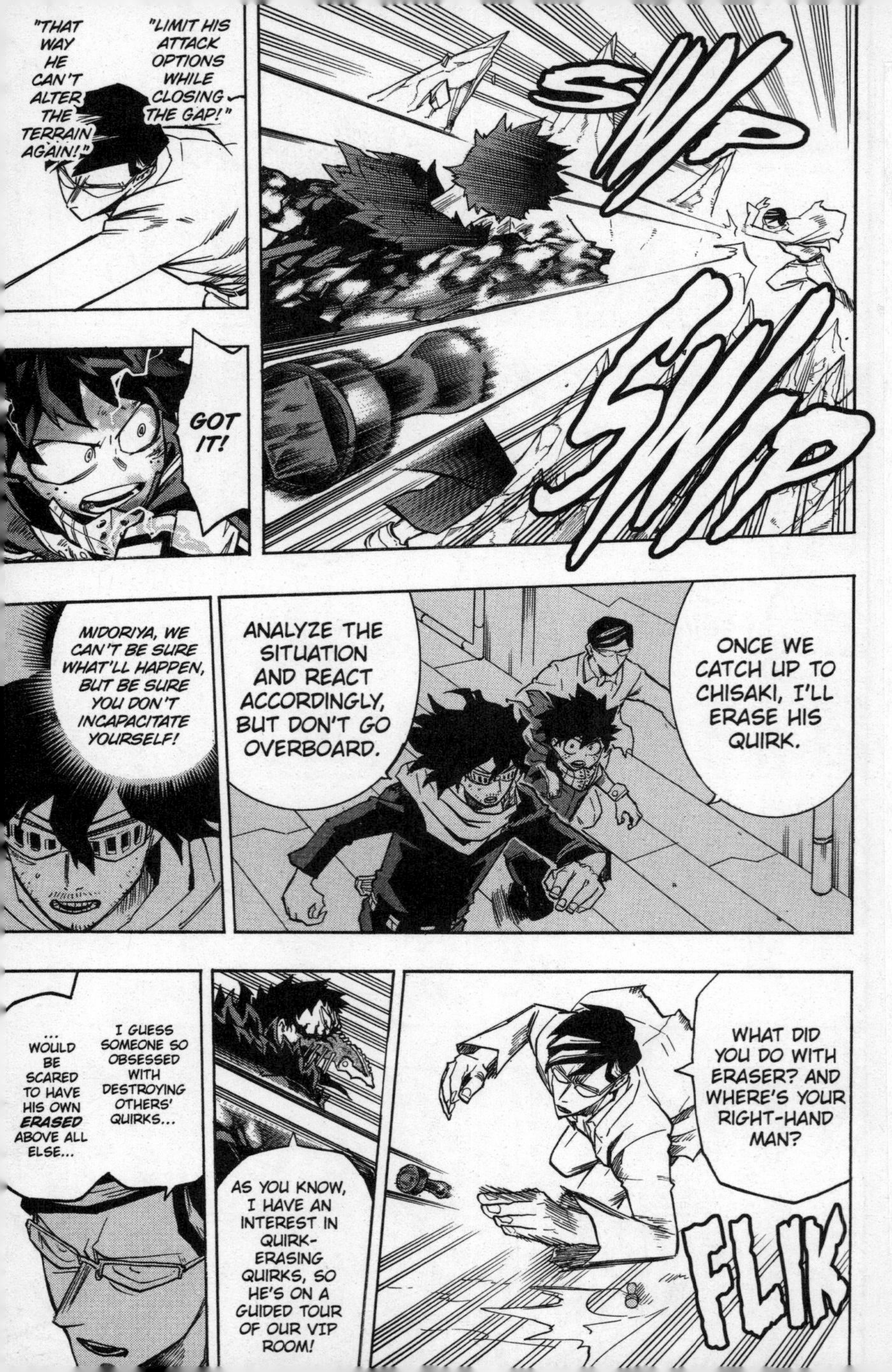
SWIP
SWIP
"LIMIT HIS ATTACK OPTIONS WHILE CLOSING THE GAP!"
"THAT WAY HE CAN'T ALTER THE TERRAIN AGAIN!"
GOT IT!
ONCE WE CATCH UP TO CHISAKI, I'LL ERASE HIS QUIRK.
ANALYZE THE SITUATION AND REACT ACCORDINGLY, BUT DON'T GO OVERBOARD.
MIDORIYA, WE CAN'T BE SURE WHAT'LL HAPPEN, BUT BE SURE YOU DON'T INCAPACITATE YOURSELF!
WHAT DID YOU DO WITH ERASER? AND WHERE'S YOUR RIGHT-HAND MAN?
FLIK
AS YOU KNOW, I HAVE AN INTEREST IN QUIRK-ERASING QUIRKS, SO HE'S ON A GUIDED TOUR OF OUR VIP ROOM!
I GUESS SOMEONE SO OBSESSED WITH DESTROYING OTHERS' QUIRKS...
...WOULD BE SCARED TO HAVE HIS OWN ERASED ABOVE ALL ELSE...

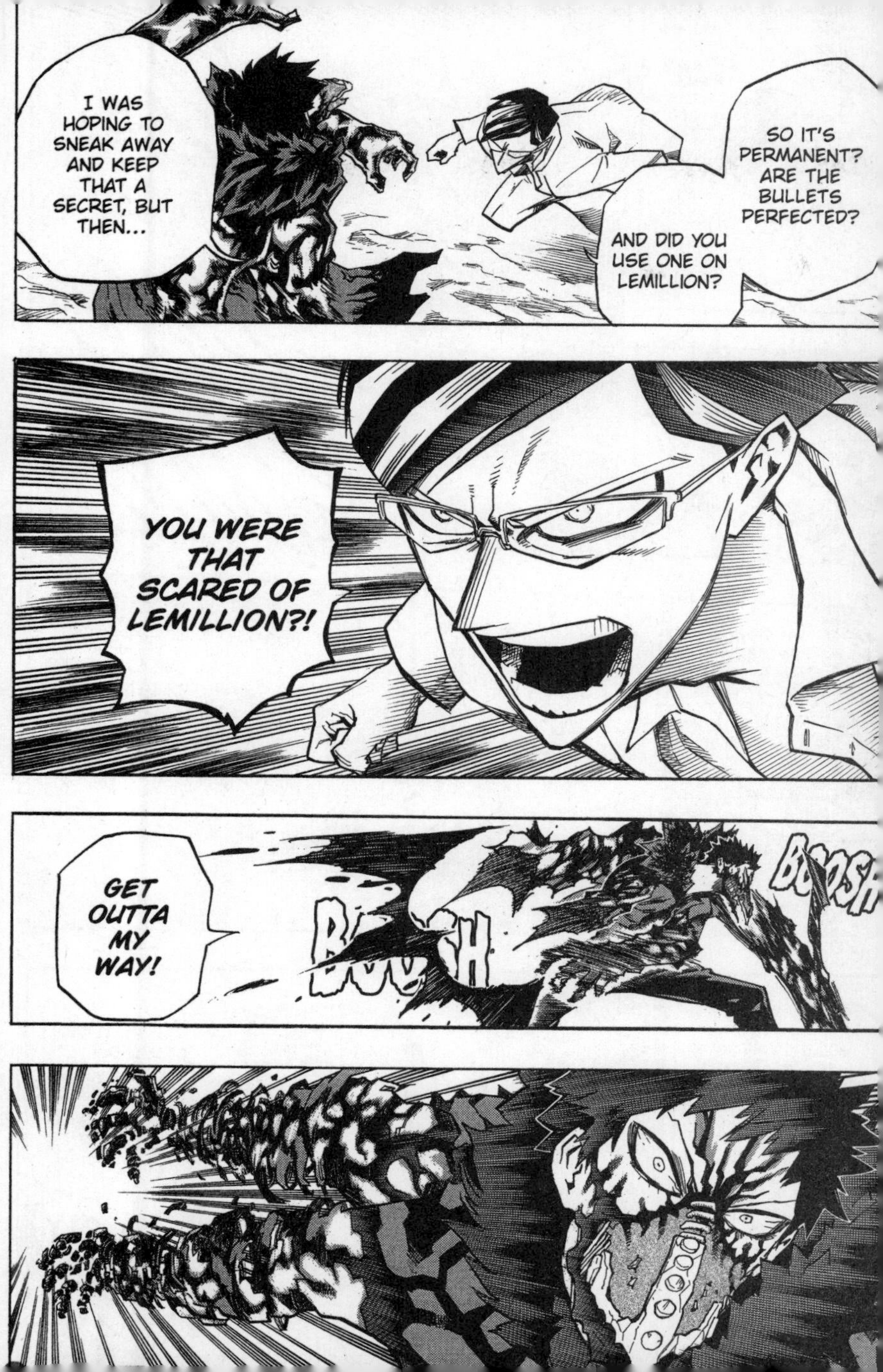
SO IT'S PERMANENT? ARE THE BULLETS PERFECTED?
AND DID YOU USE ONE ON LEMILLION?
I WAS HOPING TO SNEAK AWAY AND KEEP THAT A SECRET, BUT THEN...
YOU WERE THAT SCARED OF LEMILLION?!
BOOSH
GET OUTTA MY WAY!

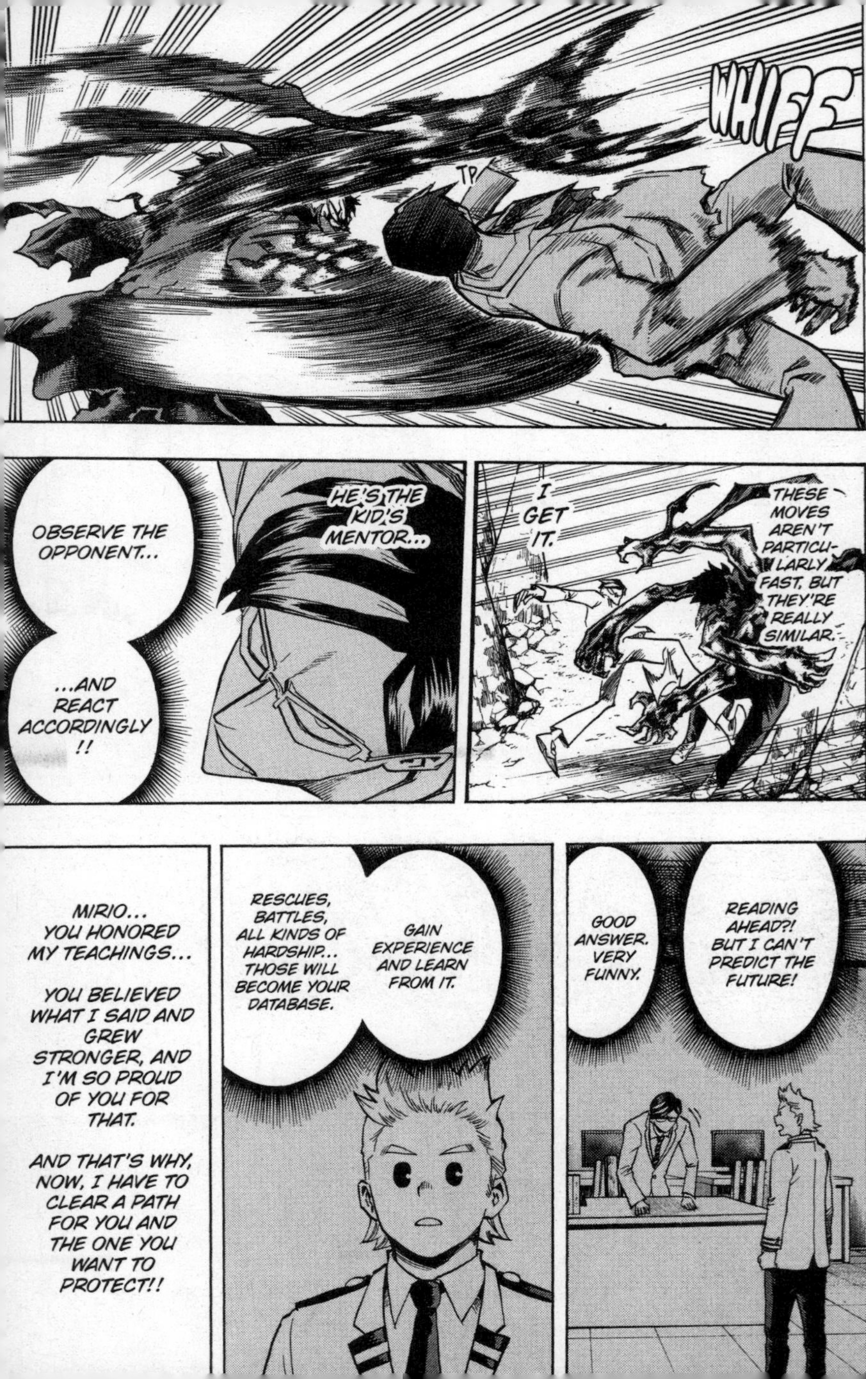

WHIFF
TP
THESE MOVES AREN'T PARTICULARLY FAST, BUT THEY'RE REALLY SIMILAR.
I GET IT.
HE'S THE KID'S MENTOR...
OBSERVE THE OPPONENT...
...AND REACT ACCORDINGLY!!
READING AHEAD?! BUT I CAN'T PREDICT THE FUTURE!
GOOD ANSWER. VERY FUNNY.
GAIN EXPERIENCE AND LEARN FROM IT.
RESCUES, BATTLES, ALL KINDS OF HARDSHIP... THOSE WILL BECOME YOUR DATABASE.
MIRIO... YOU HONORED MY TEACHINGS...
YOU BELIEVED WHAT I SAID AND GREW STRONGER, AND I'M SO PROUD OF YOU FOR THAT.
AND THAT'S WHY, NOW, I HAVE TO CLEAR A PATH FOR YOU AND THE ONE YOU WANT TO PROTECT!!

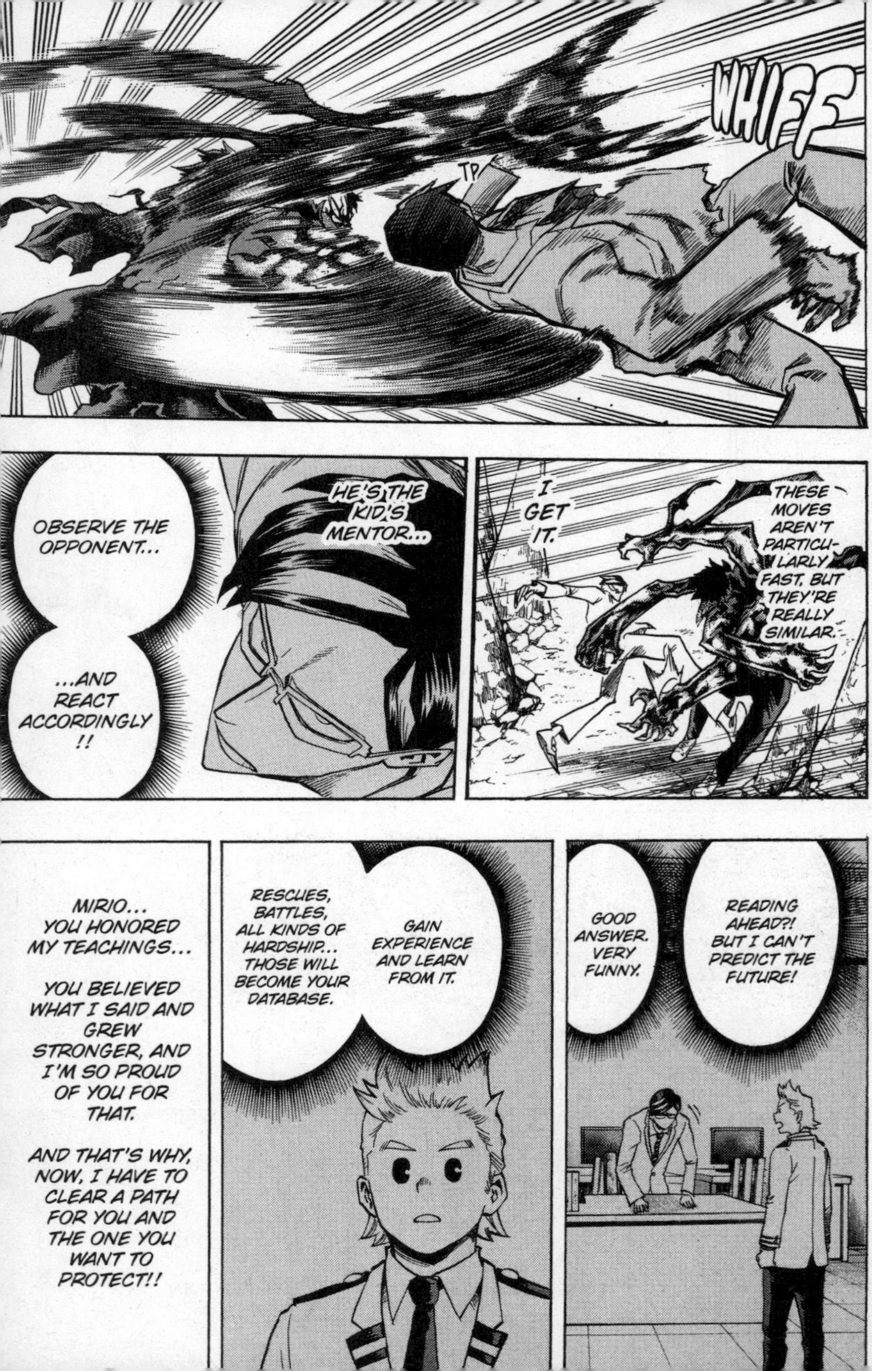
WHIFF
TP
THESE MOVES AREN'T PARTICU-LARLY FAST, BUT THEY'RE REALLY SIMILAR.
I GET IT.
HE'S THE KID'S MENTOR...
OBSERVE THE OPPONENT...
...AND REACT ACCORDINGLY!!
READING AHEAD?! BUT I CAN'T PREDICT THE FUTURE!
GOOD ANSWER. VERY FUNNY.
GAIN EXPERIENCE AND LEARN FROM IT.
RESCUES, BATTLES, ALL KINDS OF HARDSHIP... THOSE WILL BECOME YOUR DATABASE.
MIRIO... YOU HONORED MY TEACHINGS...
YOU BELIEVED WHAT I SAID AND GREW STRONGER, AND I'M SO PROUD OF YOU FOR THAT.
AND THAT'S WHY, NOW, I HAVE TO CLEAR A PATH FOR YOU AND THE ONE YOU WANT TO PROTECT!!

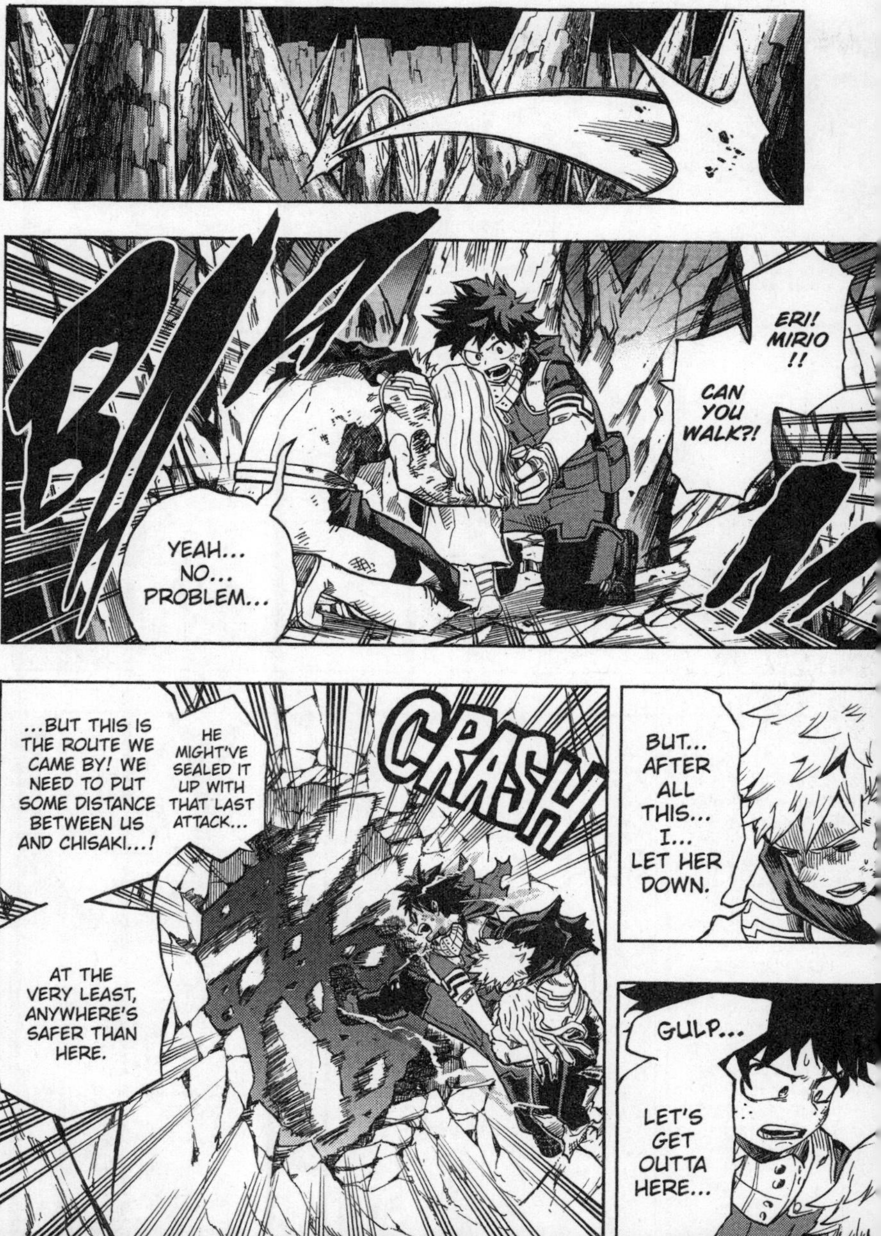
ERI! MIRIO!!
CAN YOU WALK?!
YEAH... NO... PROBLEM...
BUT... AFTER ALL THIS... I... LET HER DOWN.
GULP...
LET'S GET OUTTA HERE...
CRASH
HE MIGHT'VE SEALED IT UP WITH THAT LAST ATTACK...
...BUT THIS IS THE ROUTE WE CAME BY! WE NEED TO PUT SOME DISTANCE BETWEEN US AND CHISAKI...!
AT THE VERY LEAST, ANYWHERE'S SAFER THAN HERE.

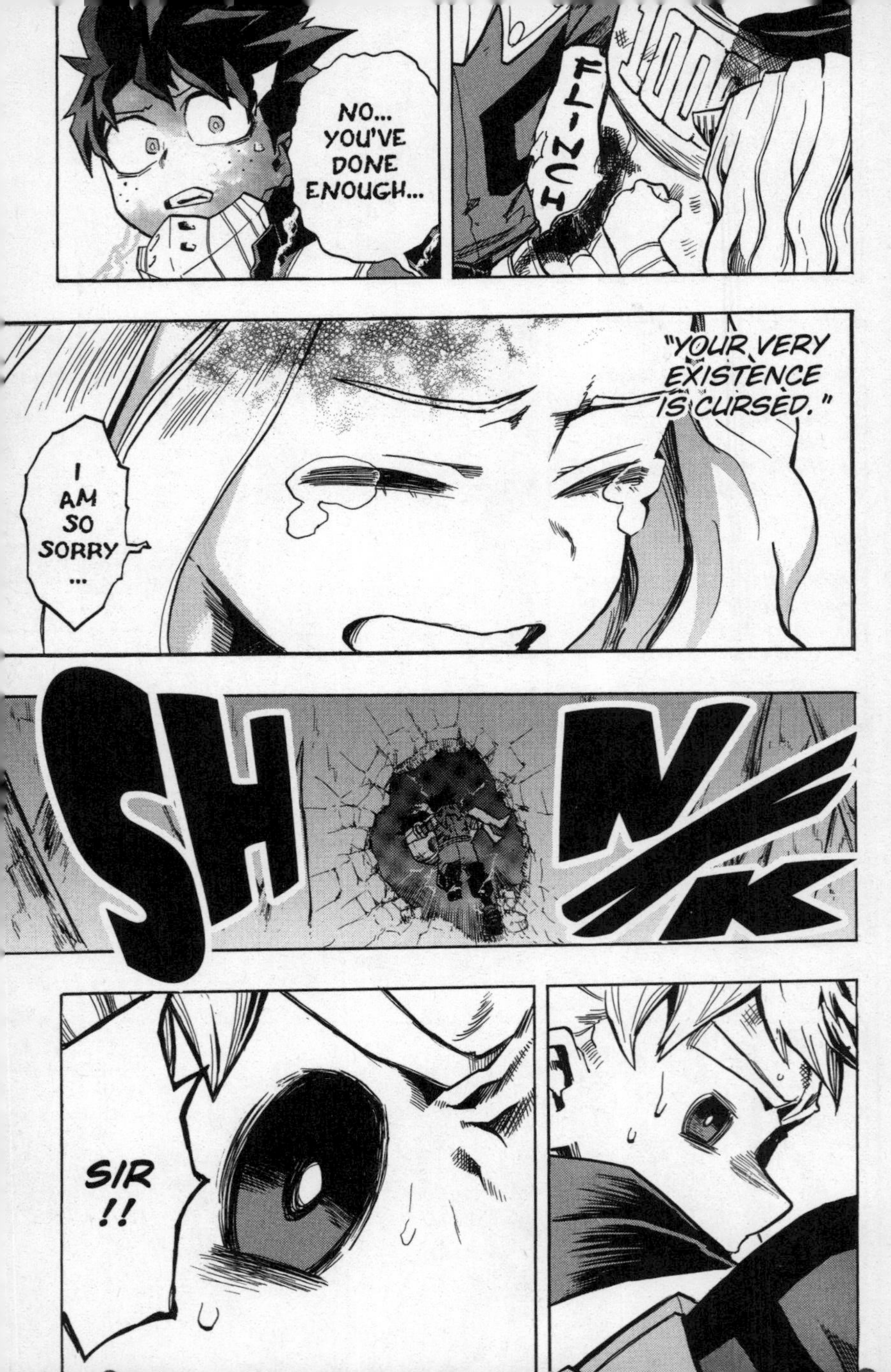
FLINCH
NO... YOU'VE DONE ENOUGH...
"YOUR VERY EXISTENCE IS CURSED."
I AM SO SORRY ...
SHNK
SIR !!

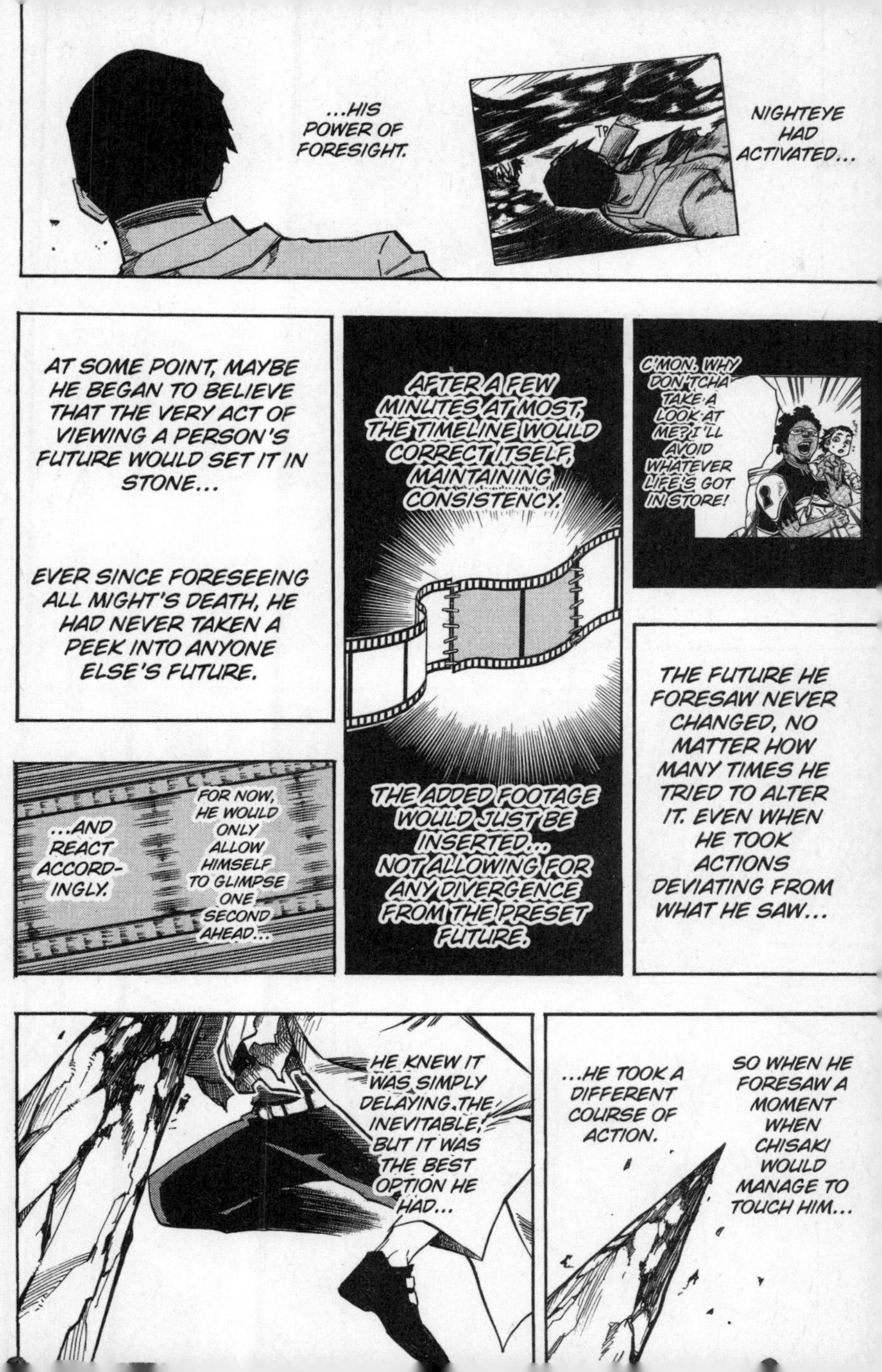
NIGHTEYE HAD ACTIVATED...
...HIS POWER OF FORESIGHT.
C'MON. WHY DON'TCHA TAKE A LOOK AT ME? I'LL AVOID WHATEVER LIFE'S GOT IN STORE!
THE FUTURE HE FORESAW NEVER CHANGED, NO MATTER HOW MANY TIMES HE TRIED TO ALTER IT. EVEN WHEN HE TOOK ACTIONS DEVIATING FROM WHAT HE SAW...
AFTER A FEW MINUTES AT MOST, THE TIMELINE WOULD CORRECT ITSELF, MAINTAINING CONSISTENCY.
THE ADDED FOOTAGE WOULD JUST BE INSERTED... NOT ALLOWING FOR ANY DIVERGENCE FROM THE PRESET FUTURE.
AT SOME POINT, MAYBE HE BEGAN TO BELIEVE THAT THE VERY ACT OF VIEWING A PERSON'S FUTURE WOULD SET IT IN STONE...
EVER SINCE FORESEEING ALL MIGHT'S DEATH, HE HAD NEVER TAKEN A PEEK INTO ANYONE ELSE'S FUTURE.
FOR NOW, HE WOULD ONLY ALLOW HIMSELF TO GLIMPSE ONE SECOND AHEAD...
...AND REACT ACCORDINGLY.
SO WHEN HE FORESAW A MOMENT WHEN CHISAKI WOULD MANAGE TO TOUCH HIM...
...HE TOOK A DIFFERENT COURSE OF ACTION.
HE KNEW IT WAS SIMPLY DELAYING THE INEVITABLE, BUT IT WAS THE BEST OPTION HE HAD...

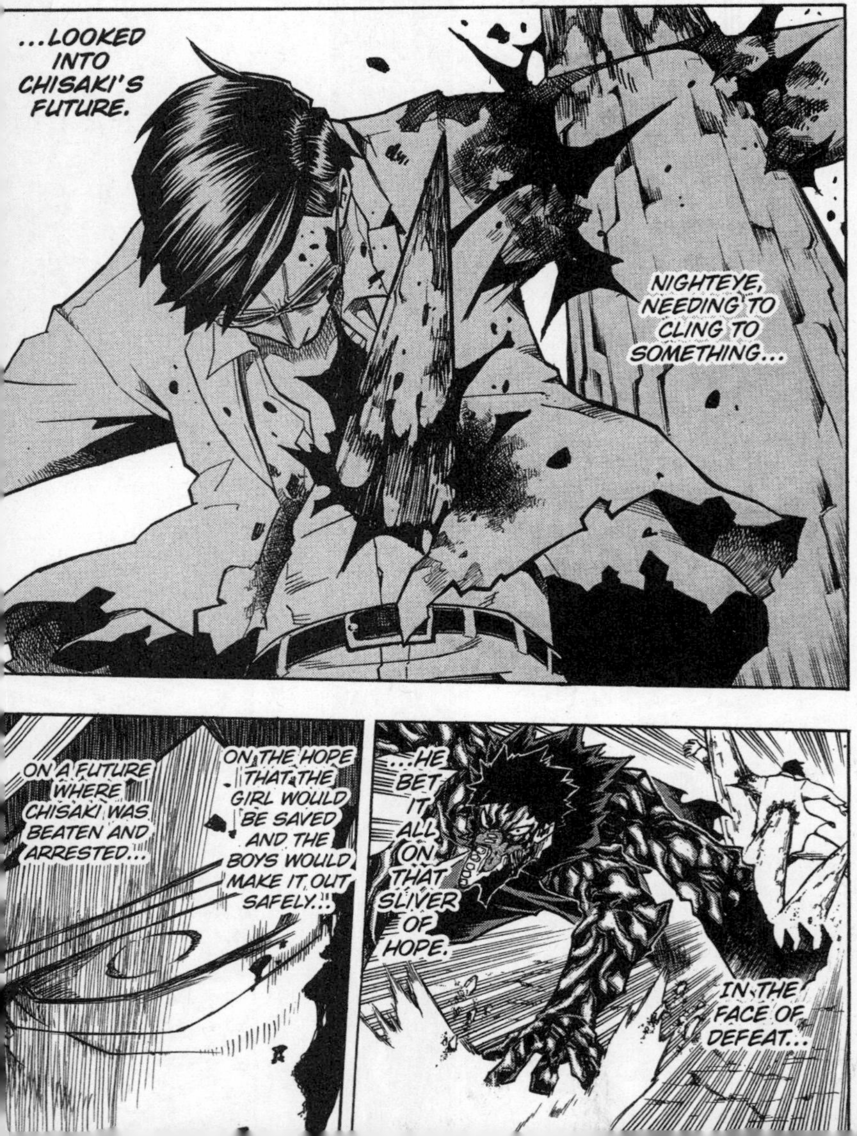

NIGHTEYE, NEEDING TO CLING TO SOMETHING...
...LOOKED INTO CHISAKI'S FUTURE.
IN THE FACE OF DEFEAT...
...HE BET IT ALL ON THAT SLIVER OF HOPE.
ON THE HOPE THAT THE GIRL WOULD BE SAVED AND THE BOYS WOULD MAKE IT OUT SAFELY...
ON A FUTURE WHERE CHISAKI WAS BEATEN AND ARRESTED...

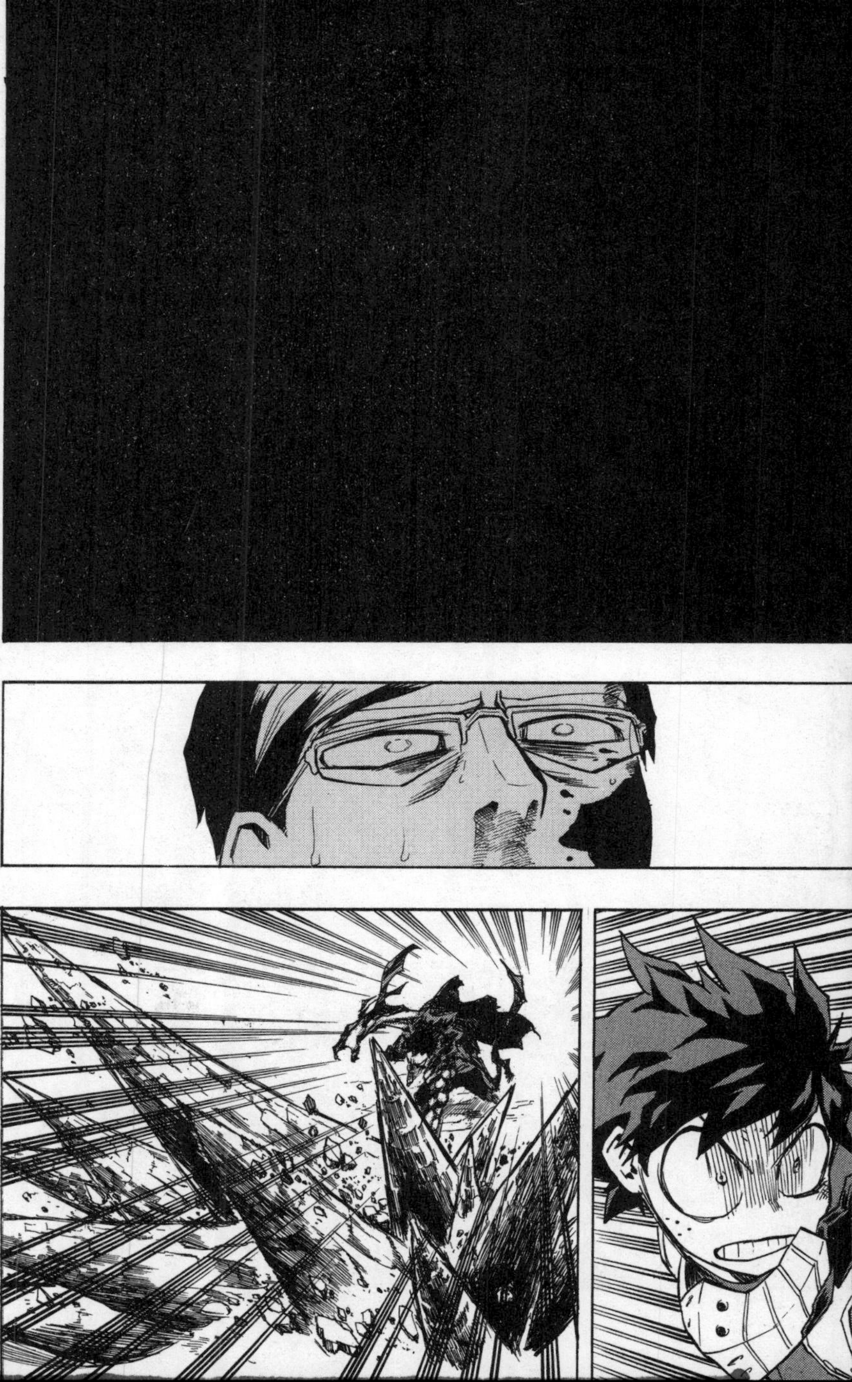

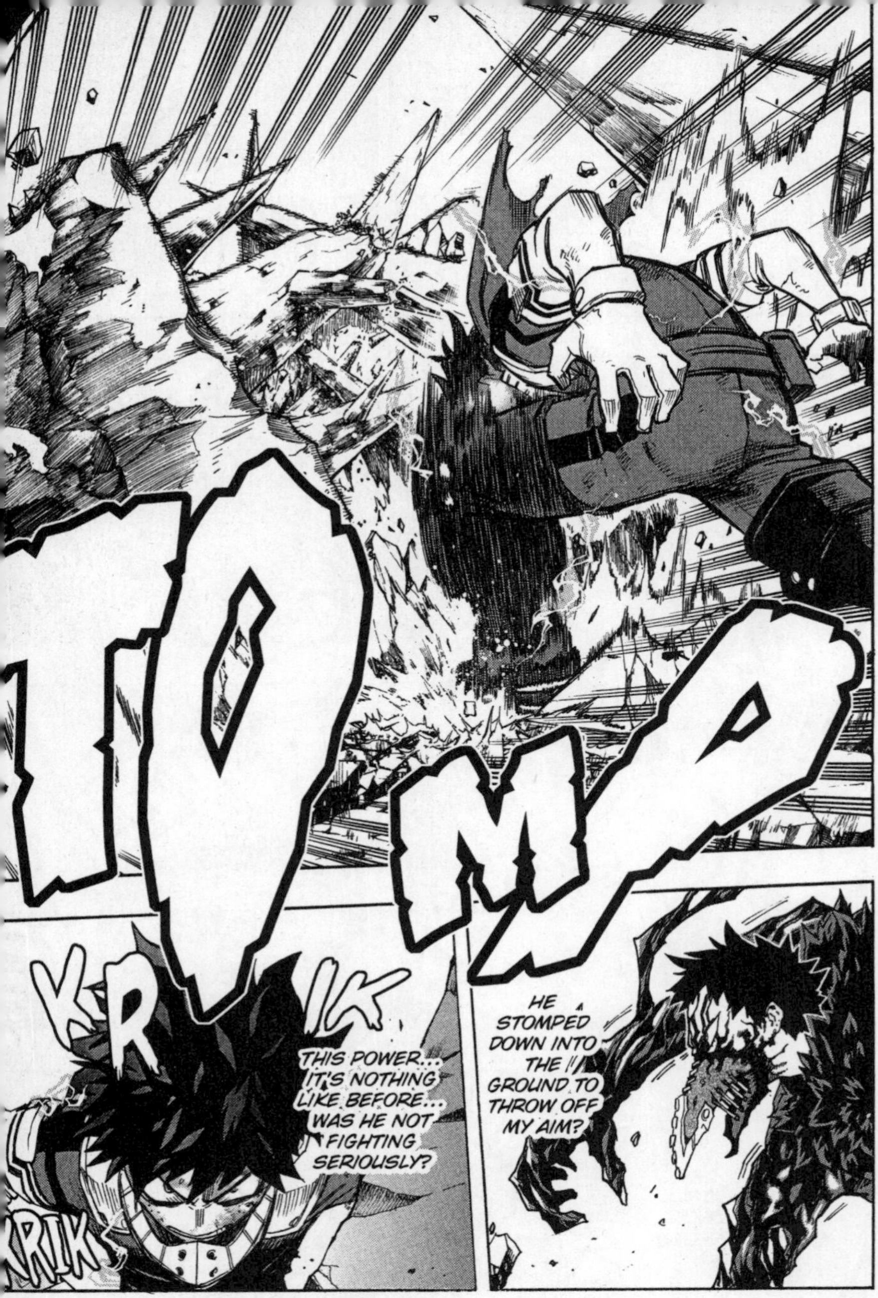
TOMP
HE STOMPED DOWN INTO THE GROUND TO THROW OFF MY AIM?
KRIK
THIS POWER... IT'S NOTHING LIKE BEFORE... WAS HE NOT FIGHTING SERIOUSLY?
RIK

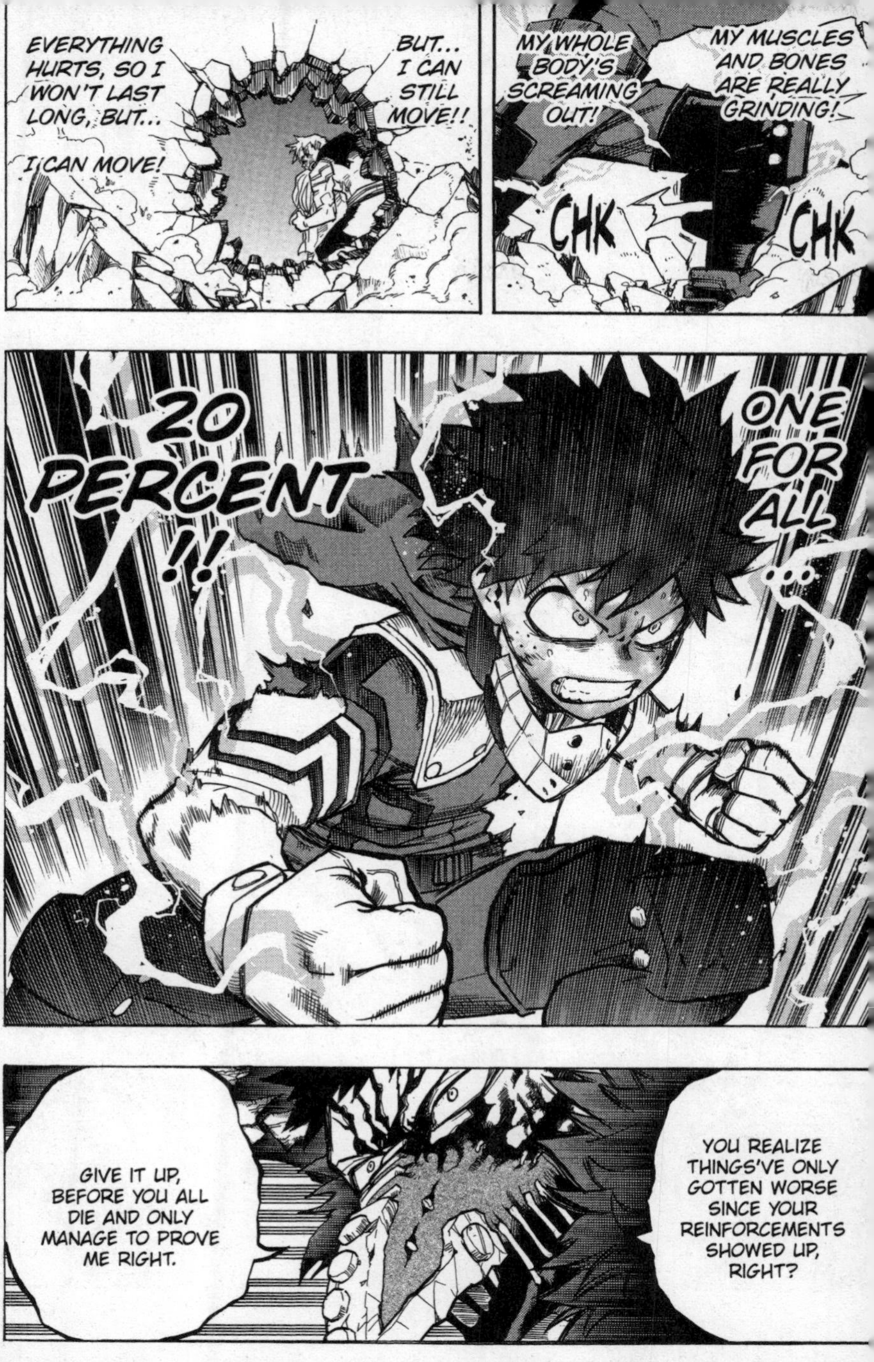
MY MUSCLES AND BONES ARE REALLY GRINDING!
MY WHOLE BODY'S SCREAMING OUT!
CHK
CHK
BUT... I CAN STILL MOVE!!
EVERYTHING HURTS, SO I WON'T LAST LONG, BUT...
I CAN MOVE!
ONE FOR ALL...
20 PERCENT!!
YOU REALIZE THINGS'VE ONLY GOTTEN WORSE SINCE YOUR REINFORCEMENTS SHOWED UP, RIGHT?
GIVE IT UP, BEFORE YOU ALL DIE AND ONLY MANAGE TO PROVE ME RIGHT.

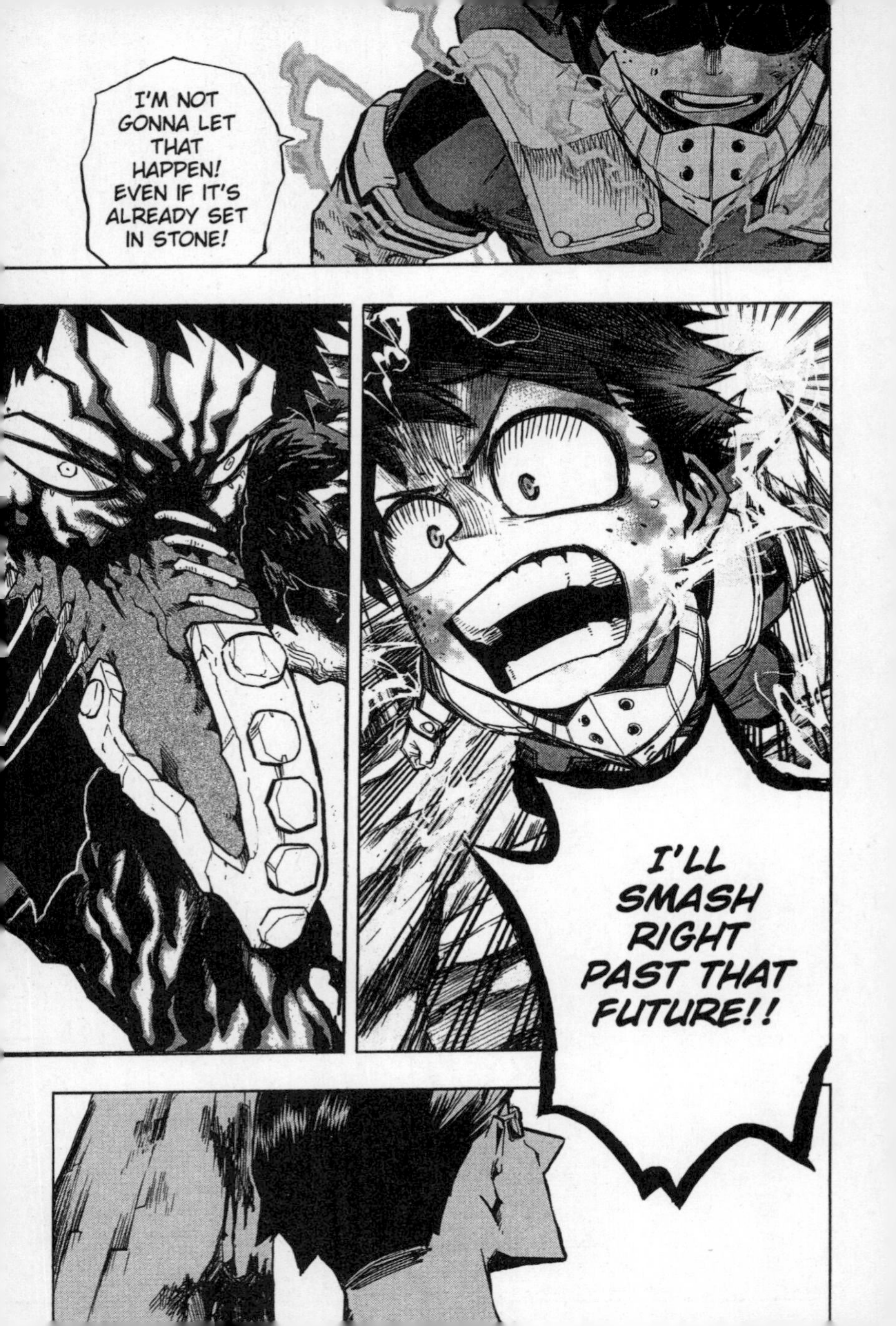
I'M NOT GONNA LET THAT HAPPEN! EVEN IF IT'S ALREADY SET IN STONE!
I'LL SMASH RIGHT PAST THAT FUTURE!!

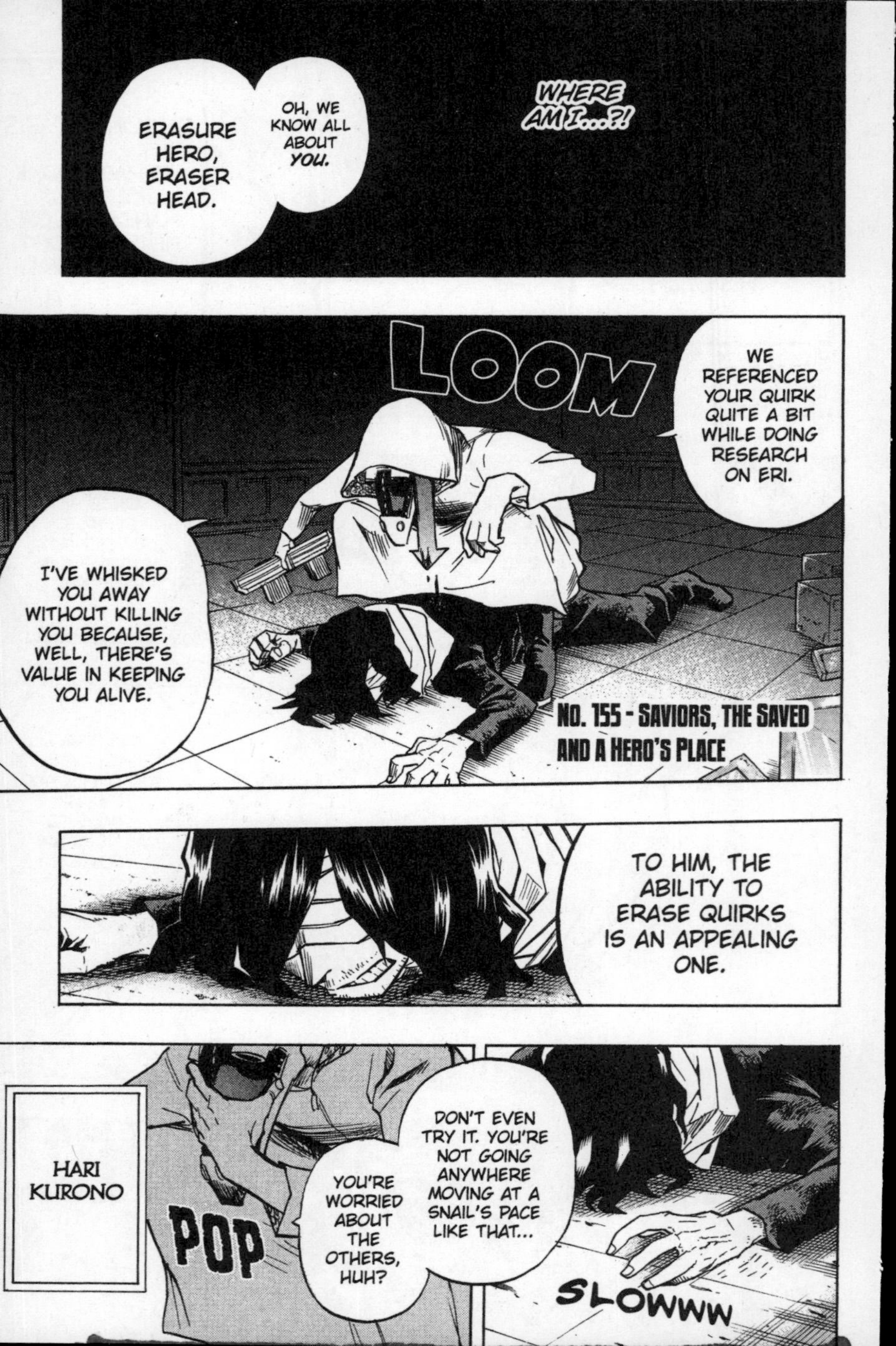
WHERE AM I...?!
OH, WE KNOW ALL ABOUT YOU.
ERASURE HERO, ERASER HEAD.
LOOM
WE REFERENCED YOUR QUIRK QUITE A BIT WHILE DOING RESEARCH ON ERI.
I'VE WHISKED YOU AWAY WITHOUT KILLING YOU BECAUSE, WELL, THERE'S VALUE IN KEEPING YOU ALIVE.
No. 155 - SAVIORS, THE SAVED AND A HERO'S PLACE
TO HIM, THE ABILITY TO ERASE QUIRKS IS AN APPEALING ONE.
SLOWWW
DON'T EVEN TRY IT. YOU'RE NOT GOING ANYWHERE MOVING AT A SNAIL'S PACE LIKE THAT...
YOU'RE WORRIED ABOUT THE OTHERS, HUH?
POP
HARI KURONO

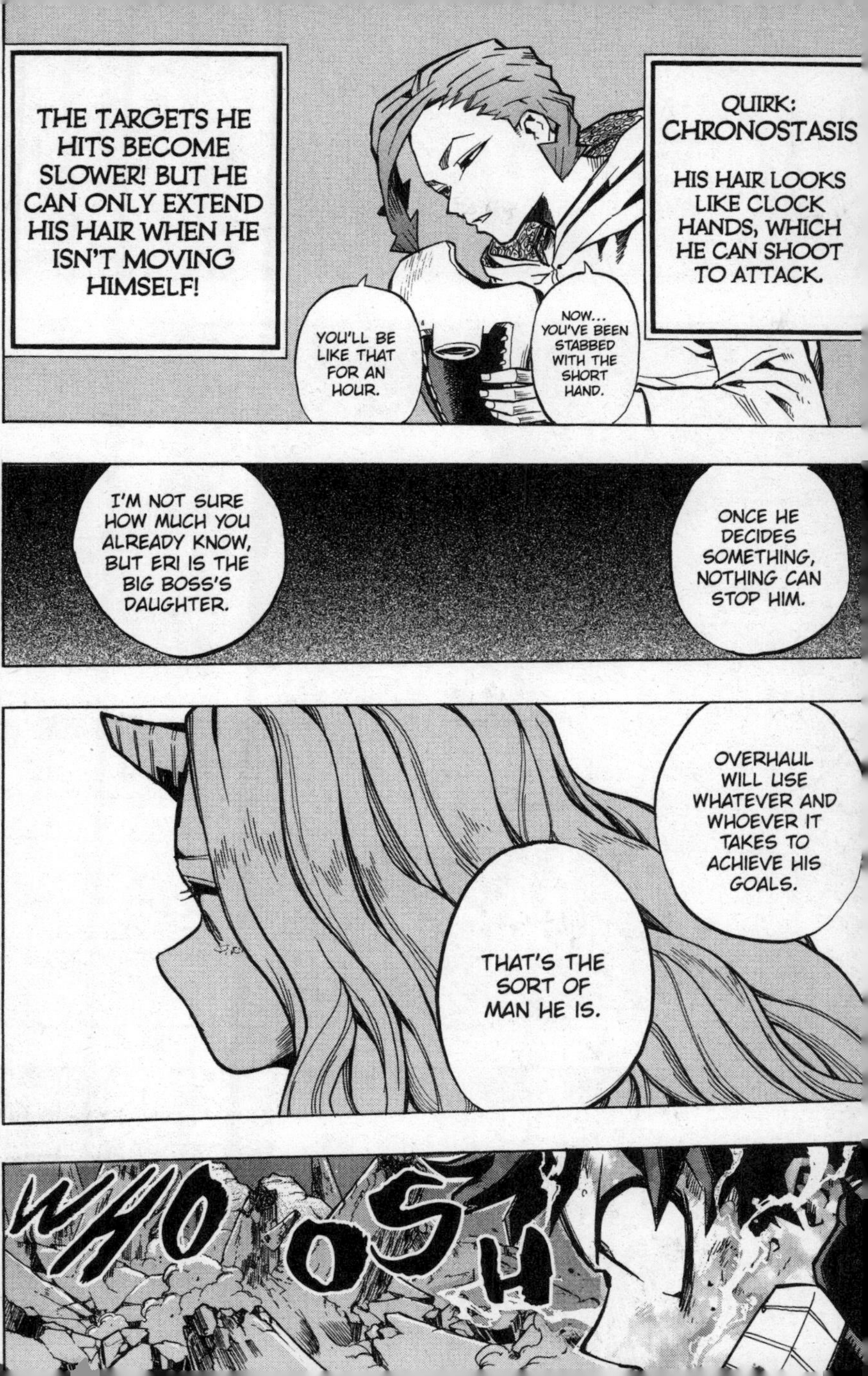
QUIRK: CHRONOSTASIS
HIS HAIR LOOKS LIKE CLOCK HANDS, WHICH HE CAN SHOOT TO ATTACK.
NOW... YOU'VE BEEN STABBED WITH THE SHORT HAND.
YOU'LL BE LIKE THAT FOR AN HOUR.
THE TARGETS HE HITS BECOME SLOWER! BUT HE CAN ONLY EXTEND HIS HAIR WHEN HE ISN'T MOVING HIMSELF!
I'M NOT SURE HOW MUCH YOU ALREADY KNOW, BUT ERI IS THE BIG BOSS'S DAUGHTER.
ONCE HE DECIDES SOMETHING, NOTHING CAN STOP HIM.
OVERHAUL WILL USE WHATEVER AND WHOEVER IT TAKES TO ACHIEVE HIS GOALS.
THAT'S THE SORT OF MAN HE IS.
WHOOSH

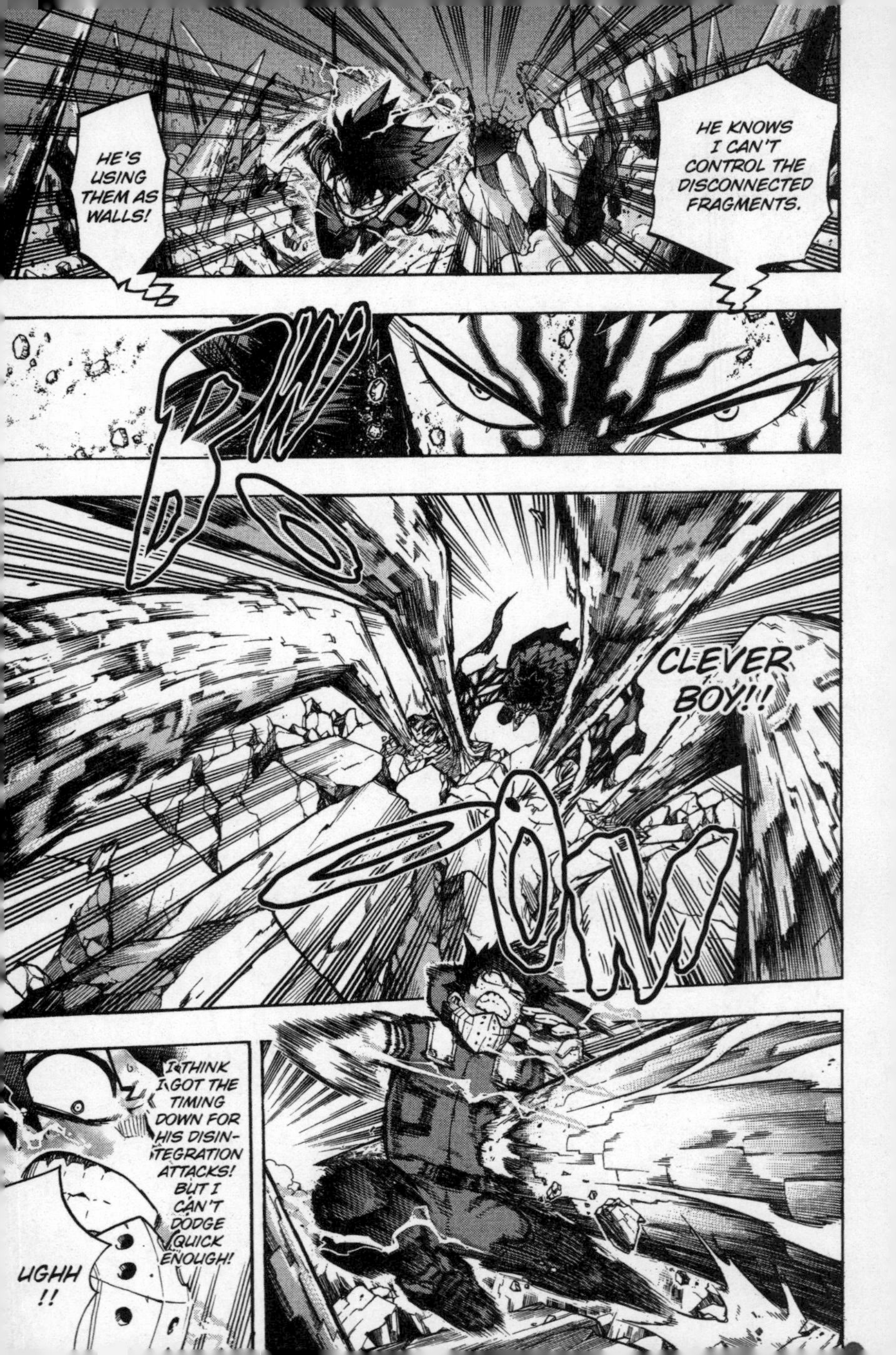
HE KNOWS I CAN'T CONTROL THE DISCONNECTED FRAGMENTS.
HE'S USING THEM AS WALLS!
CLEVER BOY!!
I THINK I GOT THE TIMING DOWN FOR HIS DISIN-TEGRATION ATTACKS! BUT I CAN'T DODGE QUICK ENOUGH!
UGHH!!

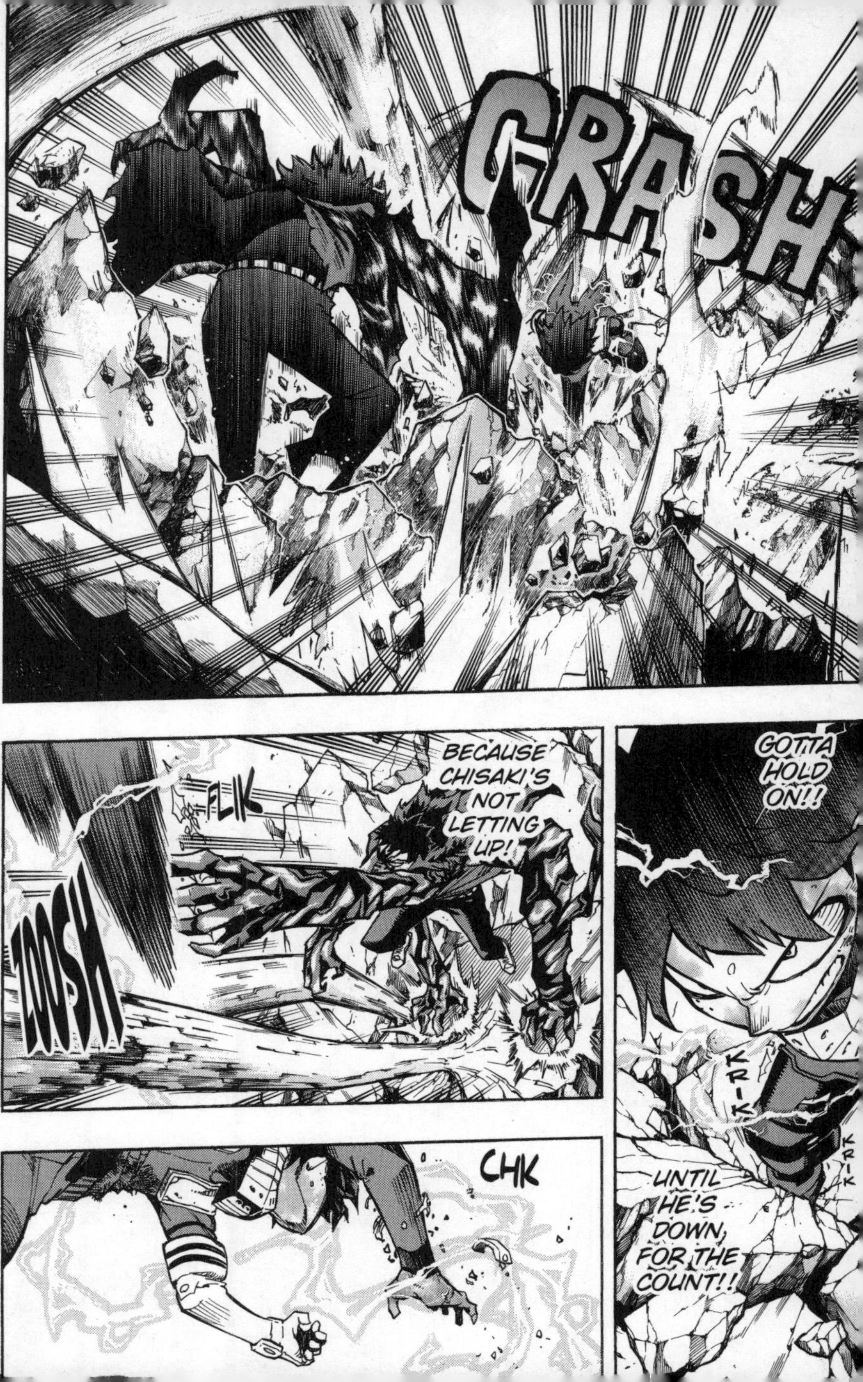

CRASH
GOTTA HOLD ON!!
KRIK
KRIK
UNTIL HE'S DOWN, FOR THE COUNT!!
BECAUSE CHISAKI'S NOT LETTING UP!
FLIK
ZOOSH
CHK

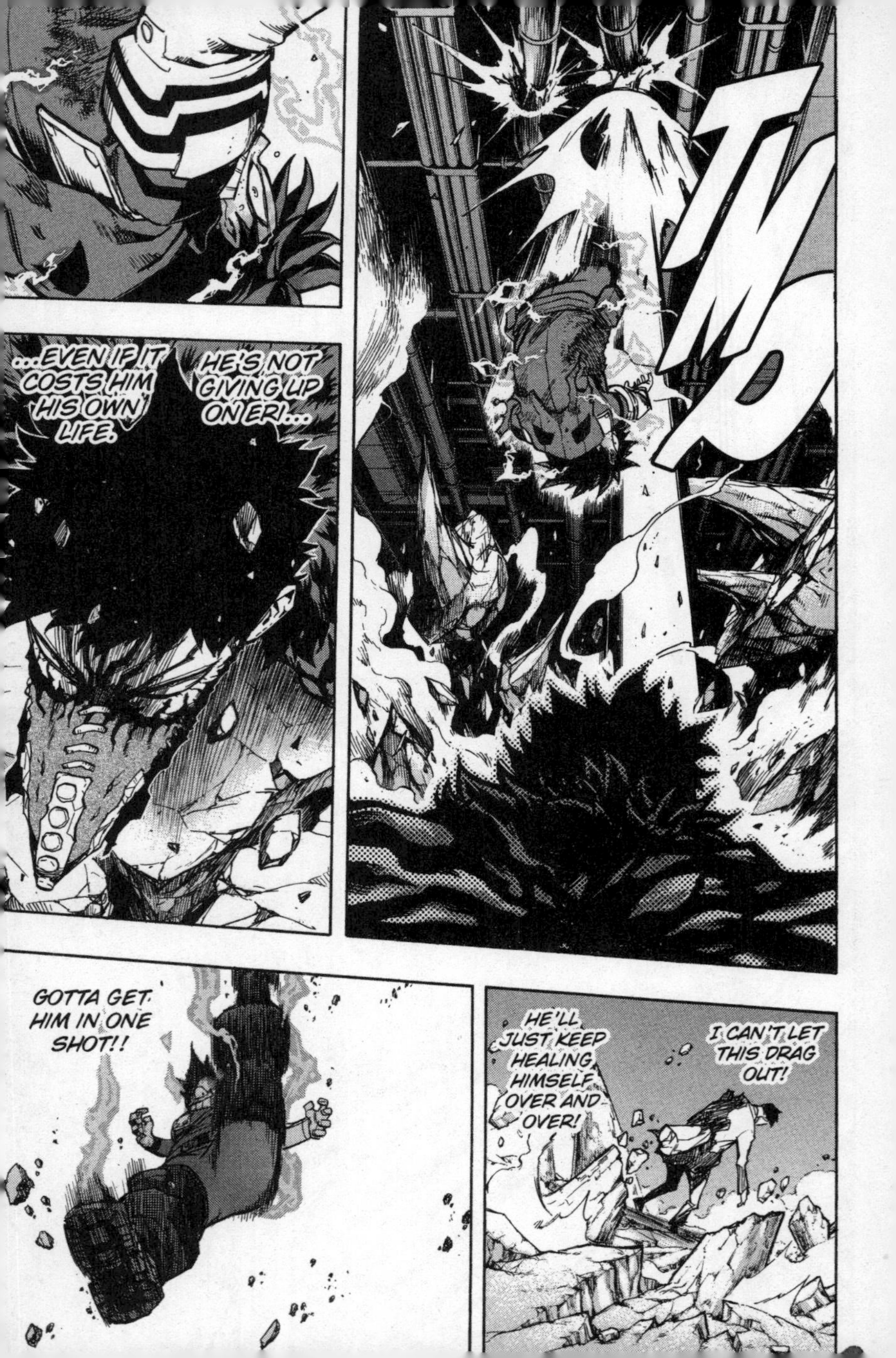
HE'S NOT GIVING UP ON ERI...
...EVEN IF IT COSTS HIM HIS OWN LIFE.
I CAN'T LET THIS DRAG OUT!
HE'LL JUST KEEP HEALING HIMSELF OVER AND OVER!
GOTTA GET HIM IN ONE SHOT!!

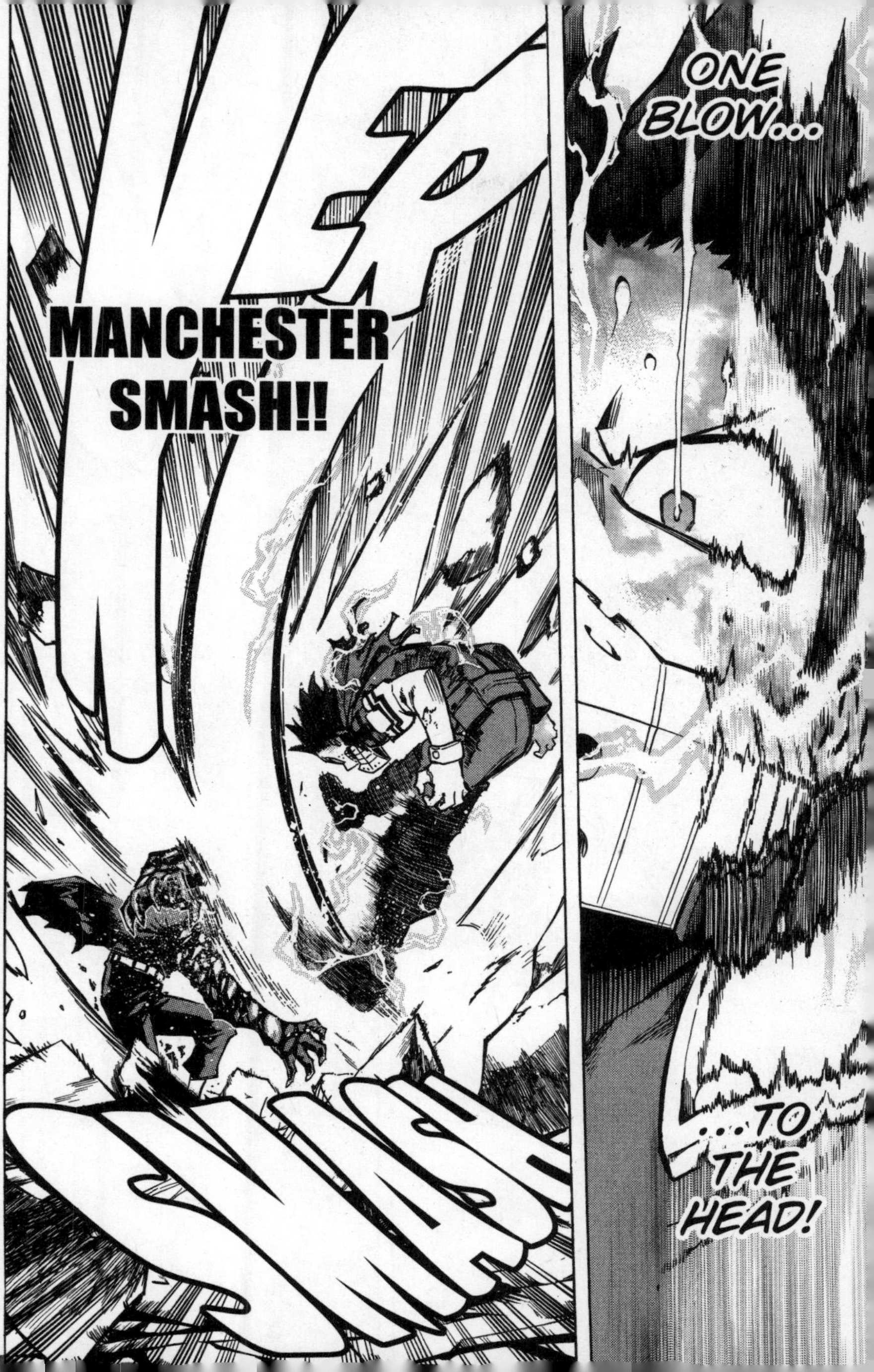
ONE BLOW...
...TO THE HEAD!
MANCHESTER SMASH!!

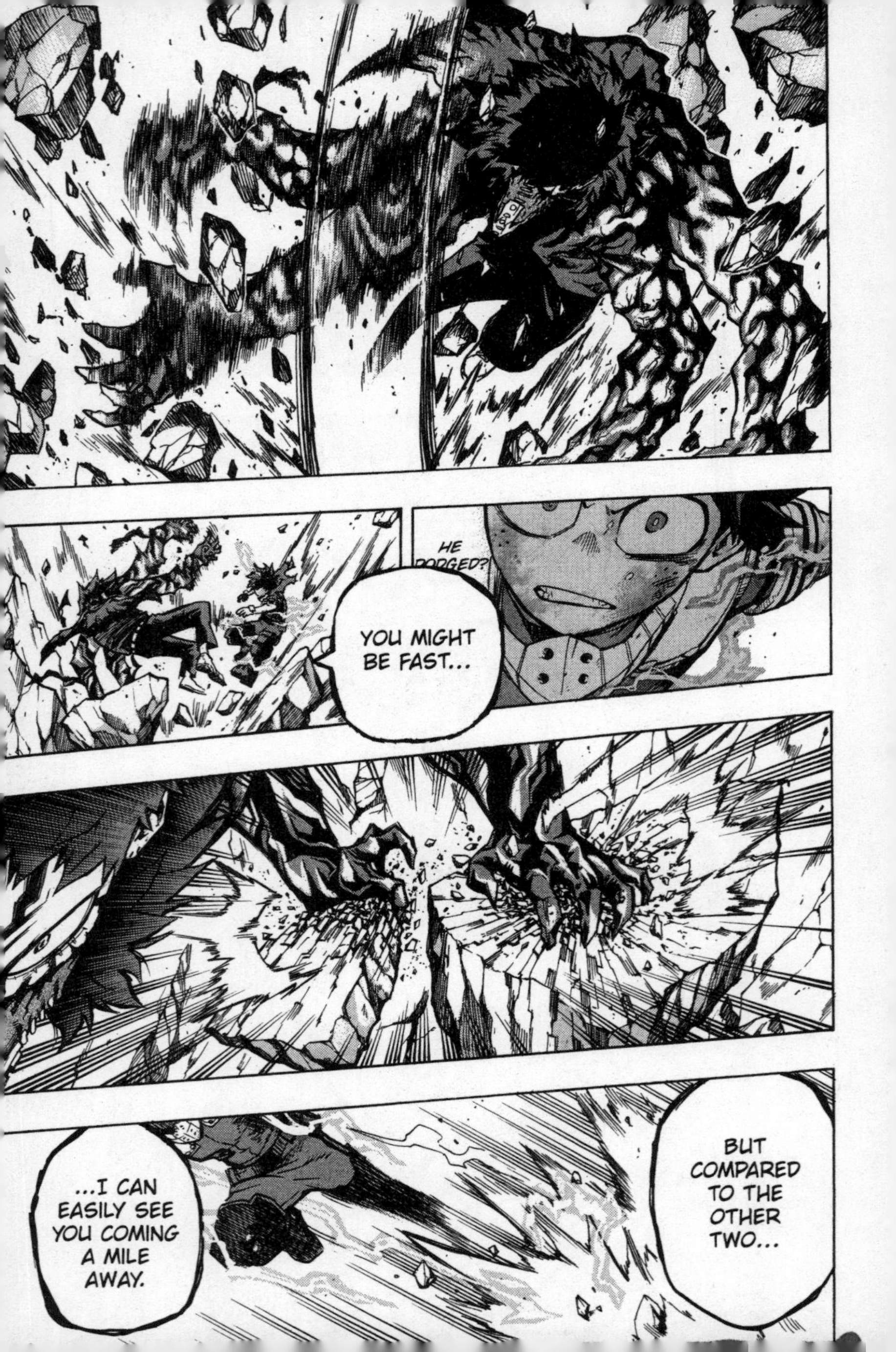
HE DODGED?
YOU MIGHT BE FAST...
BUT COMPARED TO THE OTHER TWO...
...I CAN EASILY SEE YOU COMING A MILE AWAY.

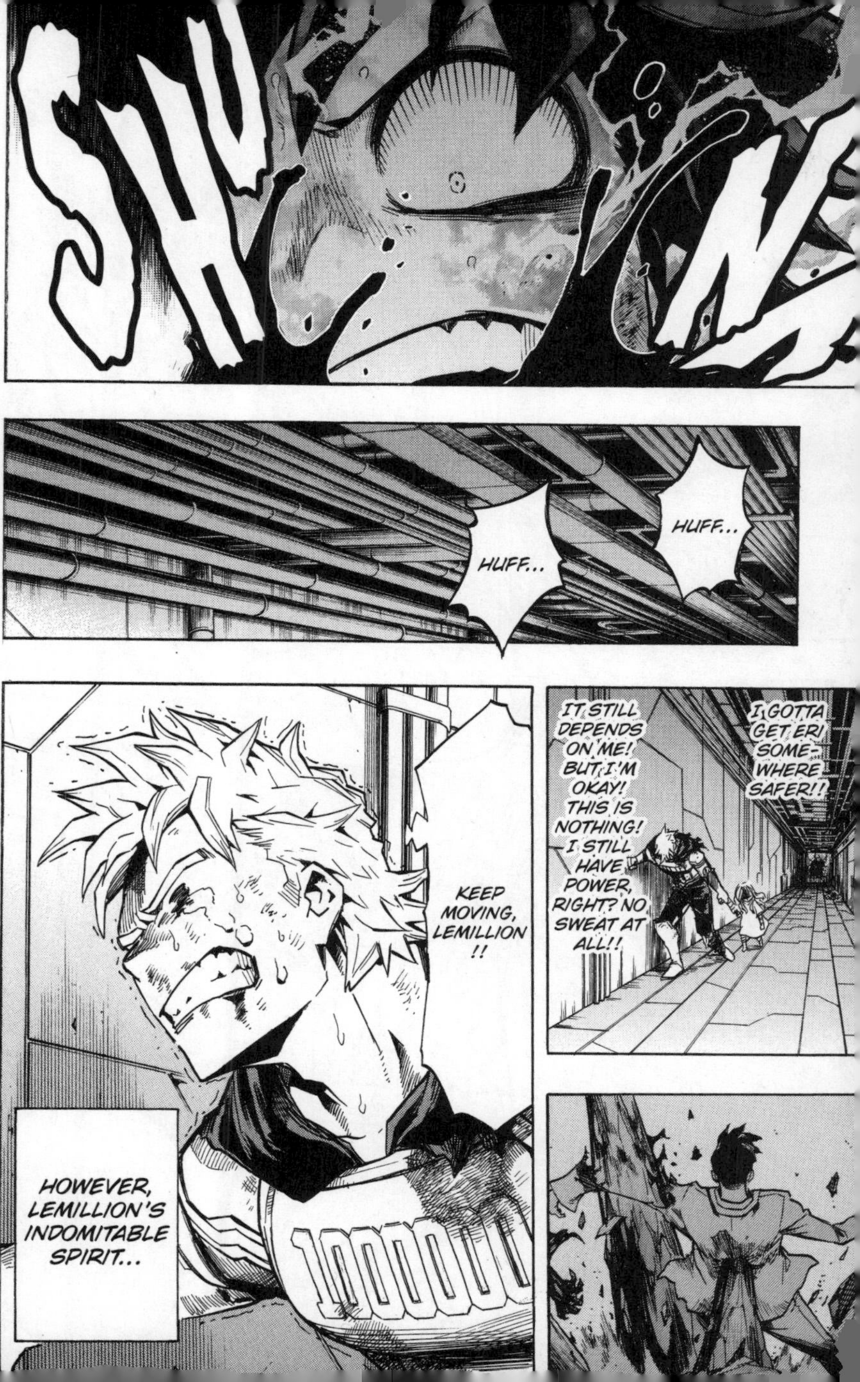

SHU
HUFF...
HUFF...
I GOTTA GET ERI SOME-WHERE SAFER!!
IT STILL DEPENDS ON ME! BUT I'M OKAY! THIS IS NOTHING! I STILL HAVE POWER, RIGHT? NO SWEAT AT ALL!!
KEEP MOVING, LEMILLION!!
HOWEVER, LEMILLION'S INDOMITABLE SPIRIT...

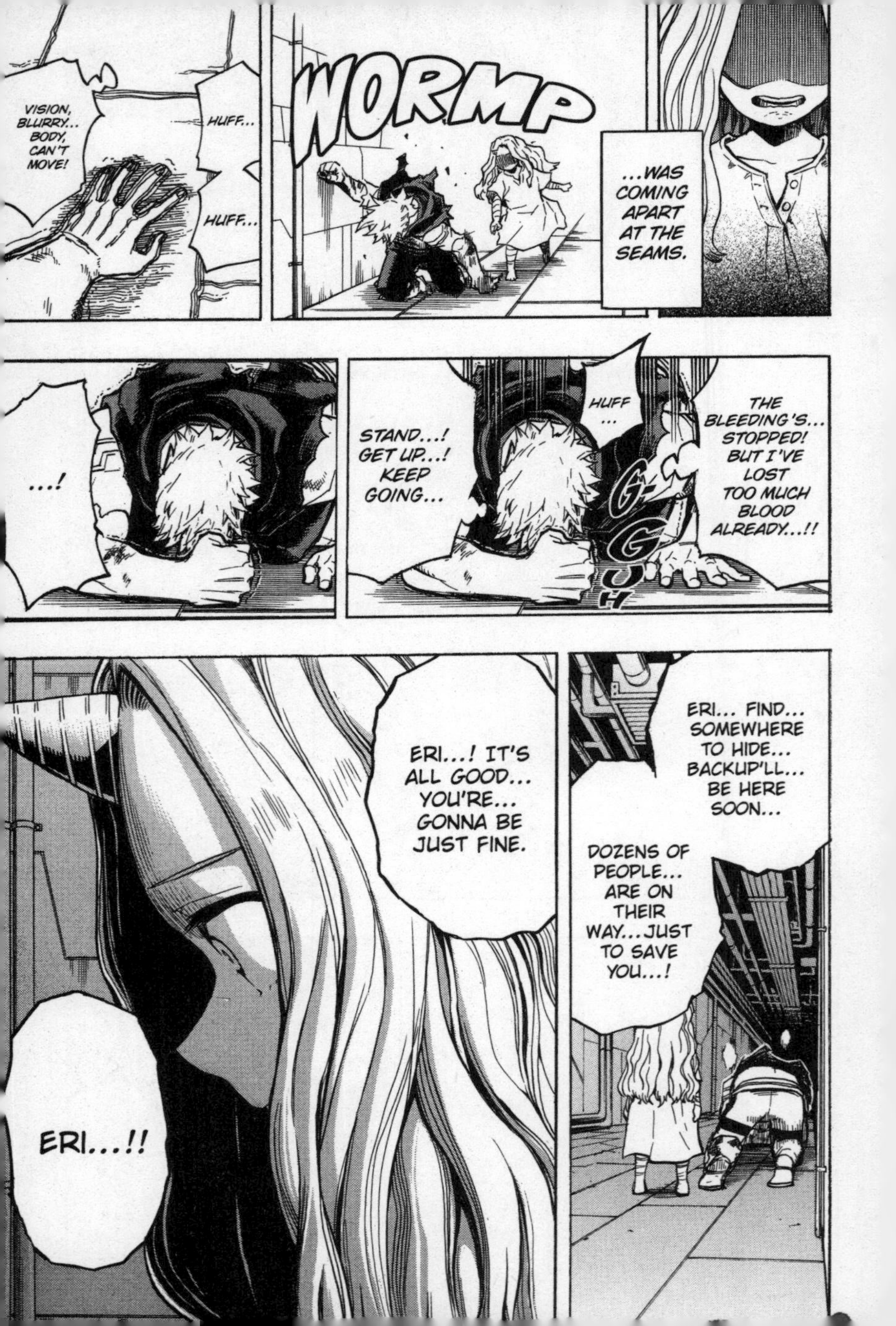

...WAS COMING APART AT THE SEAMS.
WORMP
HUFF...
VISION, BLURRY... BODY, CAN'T MOVE!
HUFF...
THE BLEEDING'S... STOPPED! BUT I'VE LOST TOO MUCH BLOOD ALREADY...!!
HUFF...
G-G-UGH
STAND...! GET UP...! KEEP GOING...
...!
ERI... FIND... SOMEWHERE TO HIDE... BACKUP'LL... BE HERE SOON...
DOZENS OF PEOPLE... ARE ON THEIR WAY... JUST TO SAVE YOU...!
ERI...! IT'S ALL GOOD... YOU'RE... GONNA BE JUST FINE.
ERI...!!

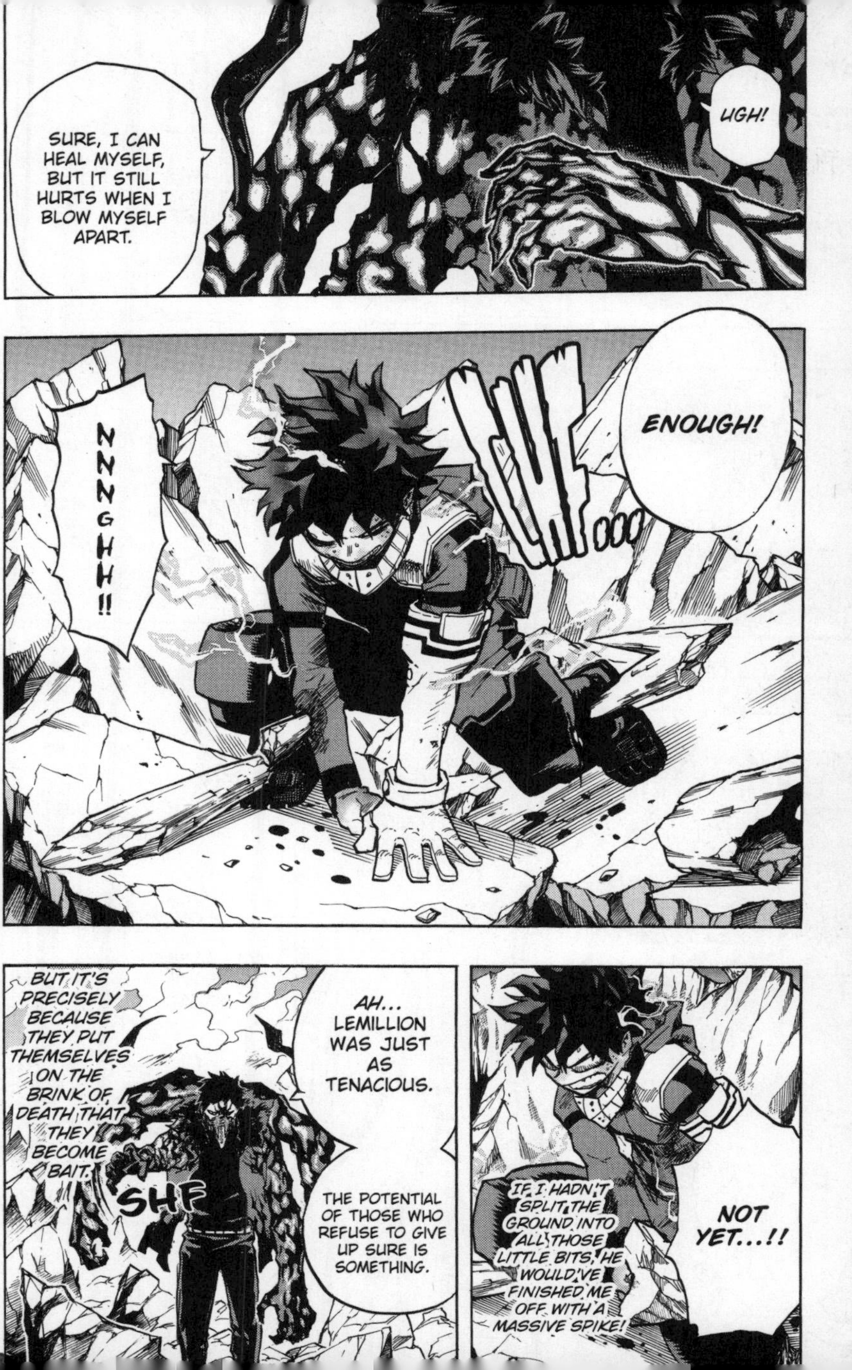
UGH!
SURE, I CAN HEAL MYSELF, BUT IT STILL HURTS WHEN I BLOW MYSELF APART.
ENOUGH!
NNNGHHH!!
IF I HADN'T SPLIT THE GROUND INTO ALL THOSE LITTLE BITS, HE WOULD'VE FINISHED ME OFF WITH A MASSIVE SPIKE!
NOT YET...!!
AH... LEMILLION WAS JUST AS TENACIOUS.
THE POTENTIAL OF THOSE WHO REFUSE TO GIVE UP SURE IS SOMETHING.
BUT IT'S PRECISELY BECAUSE THEY PUT THEMSELVES ON THE BRINK OF DEATH THAT THEY BECOME BAIT.
SHF

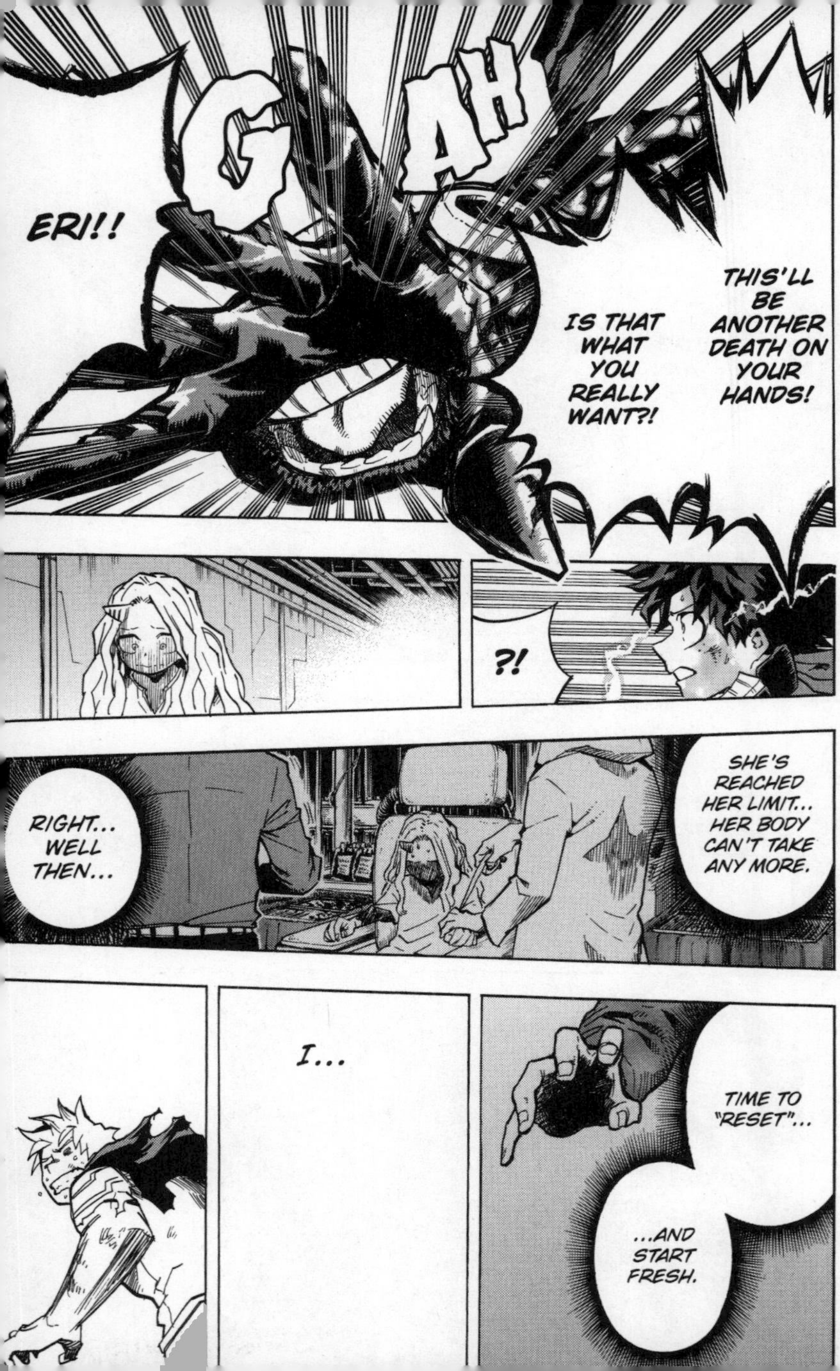
GAH
THIS'LL BE ANOTHER DEATH ON YOUR HANDS!
IS THAT WHAT YOU REALLY WANT?!
ERI!!
?!
SHE'S REACHED HER LIMIT... HER BODY CAN'T TAKE ANY MORE.
RIGHT... WELL THEN...
TIME TO "RESET"...
...AND START FRESH.
I...

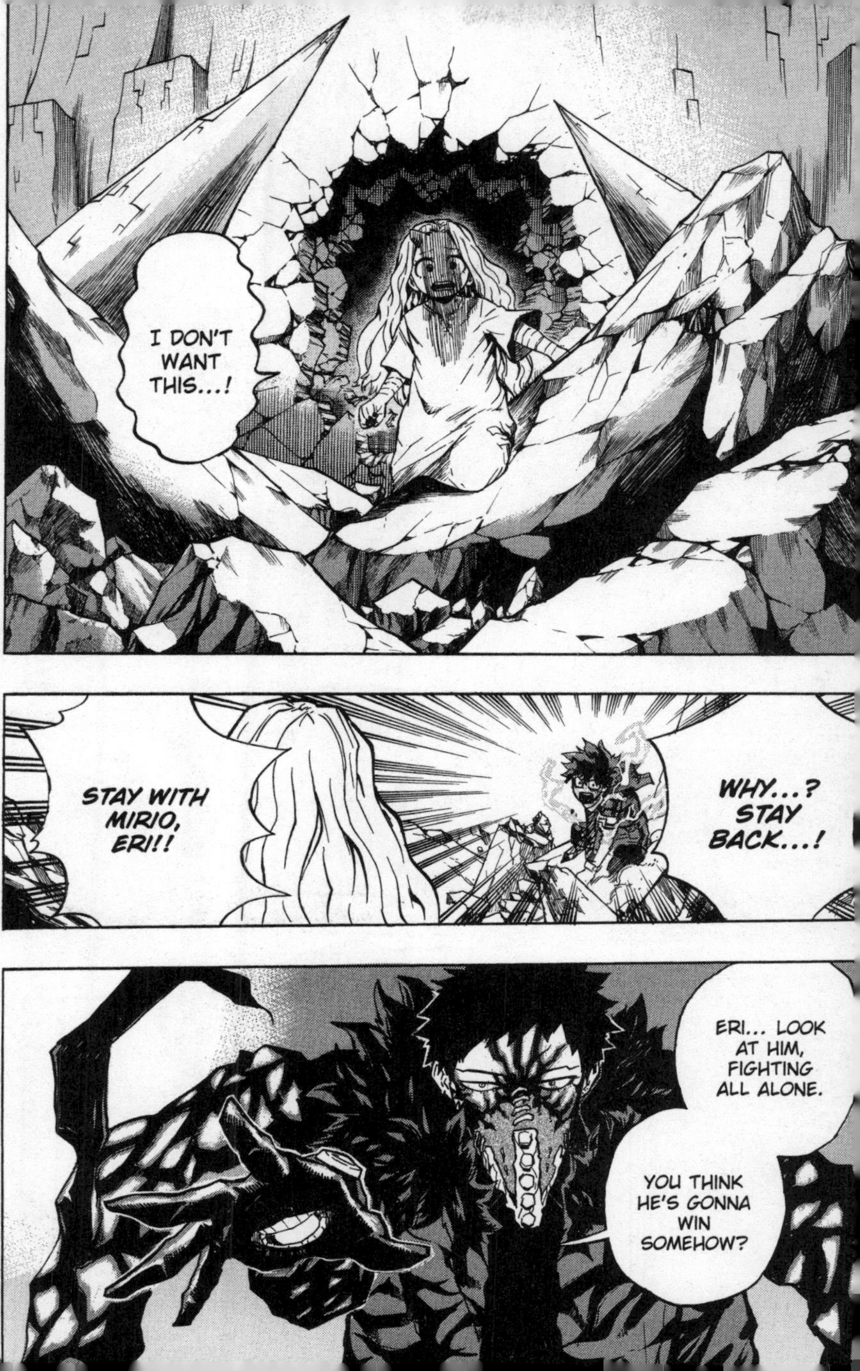
I DON'T WANT THIS...!
WHY...? STAY BACK...!
STAY WITH MIRIO, ERI!!
ERI... LOOK AT HIM, FIGHTING ALL ALONE.
YOU THINK HE'S GONNA WIN SOMEHOW?

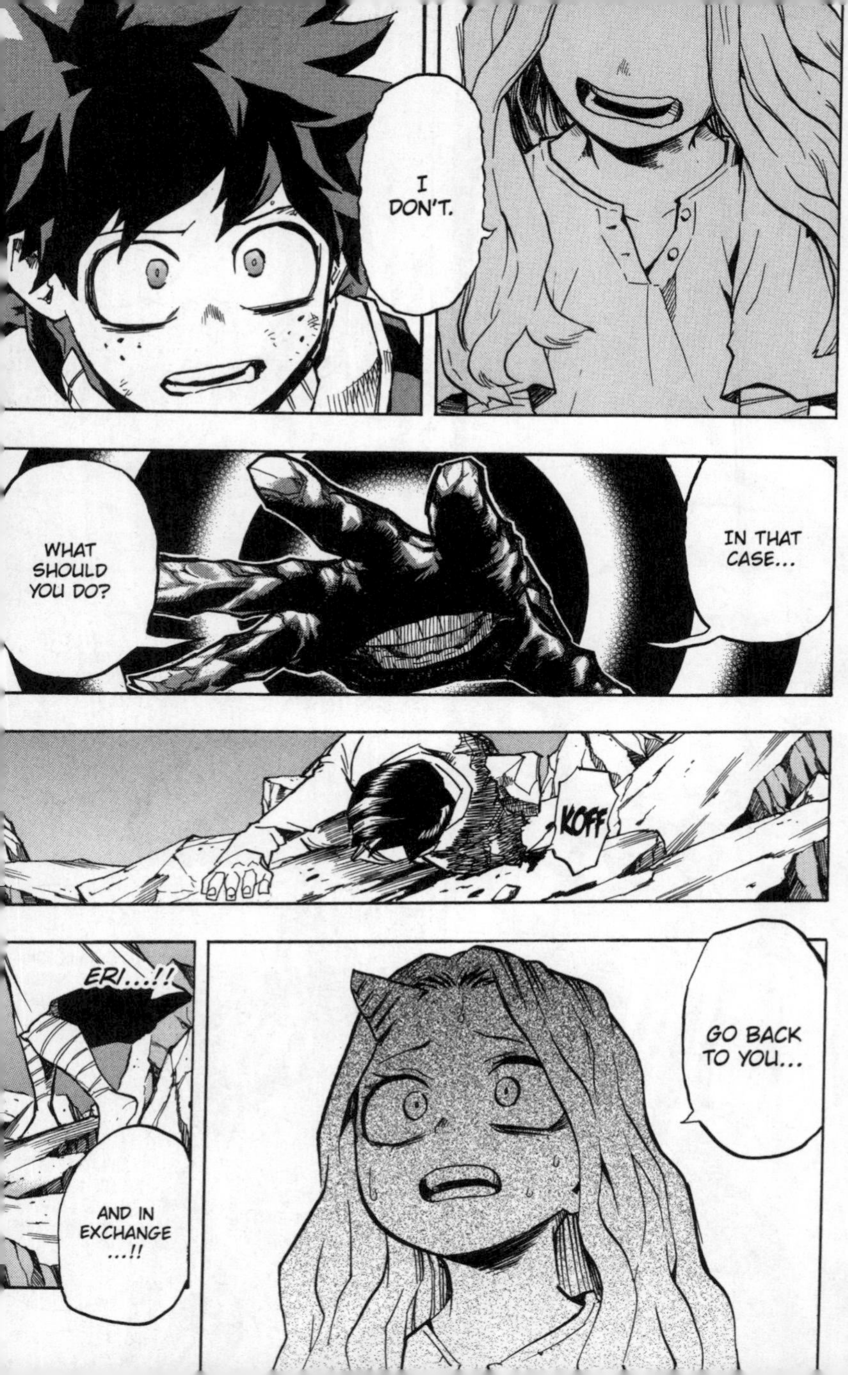
I DON'T.
IN THAT CASE...
WHAT SHOULD YOU DO?
KOFF
GO BACK TO YOU...
ERI...!!
AND IN EXCHANGE ...!!

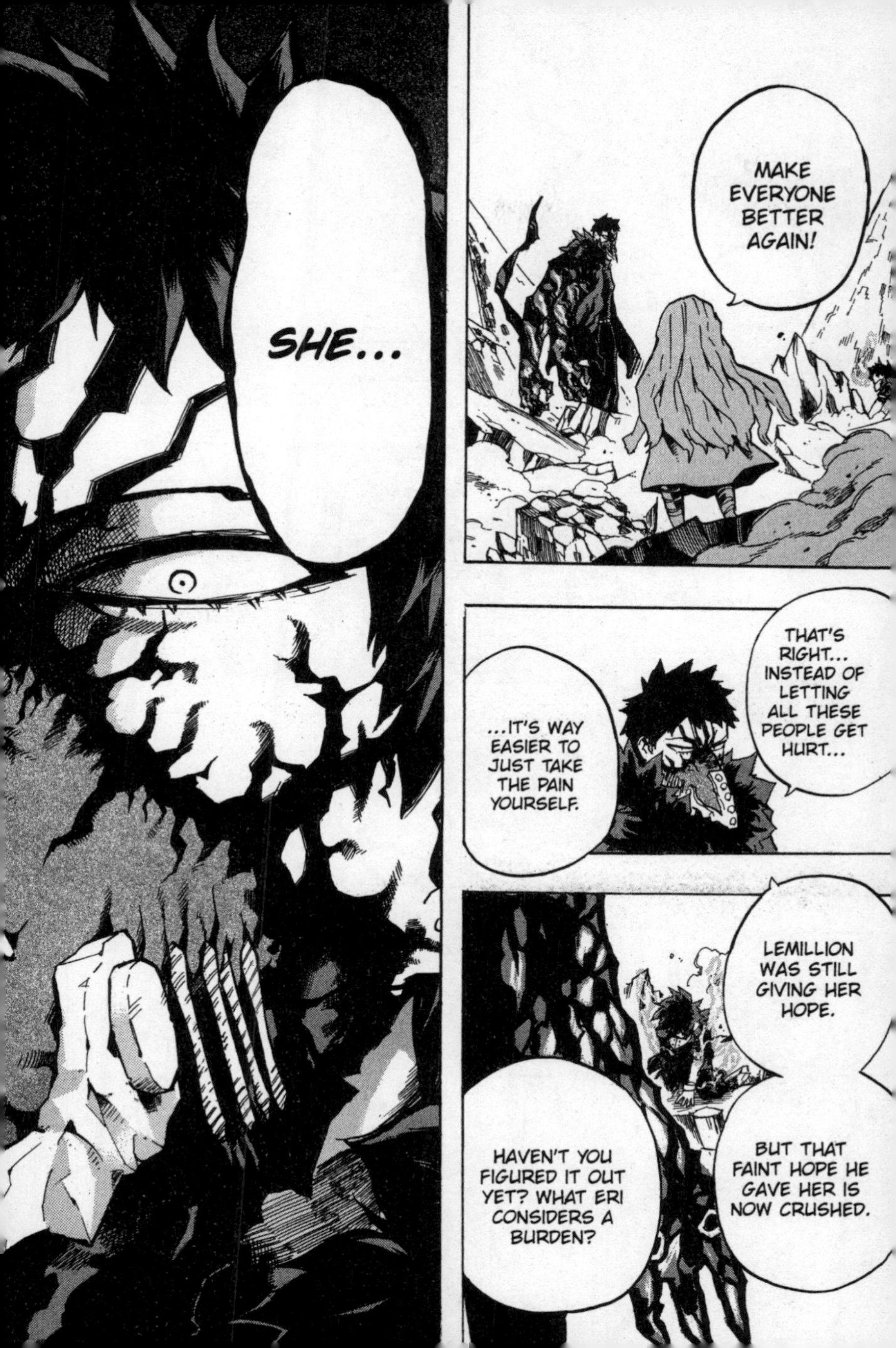
MAKE EVERYONE BETTER AGAIN!
THAT'S RIGHT... INSTEAD OF LETTING ALL THESE PEOPLE GET HURT...
...IT'S WAY EASIER TO JUST TAKE THE PAIN YOURSELF.
LEMILLION WAS STILL GIVING HER HOPE.
BUT THAT FAINT HOPE HE GAVE HER IS NOW CRUSHED.
HAVEN'T YOU FIGURED IT OUT YET? WHAT ERI CONSIDERS A BURDEN?
SHE...

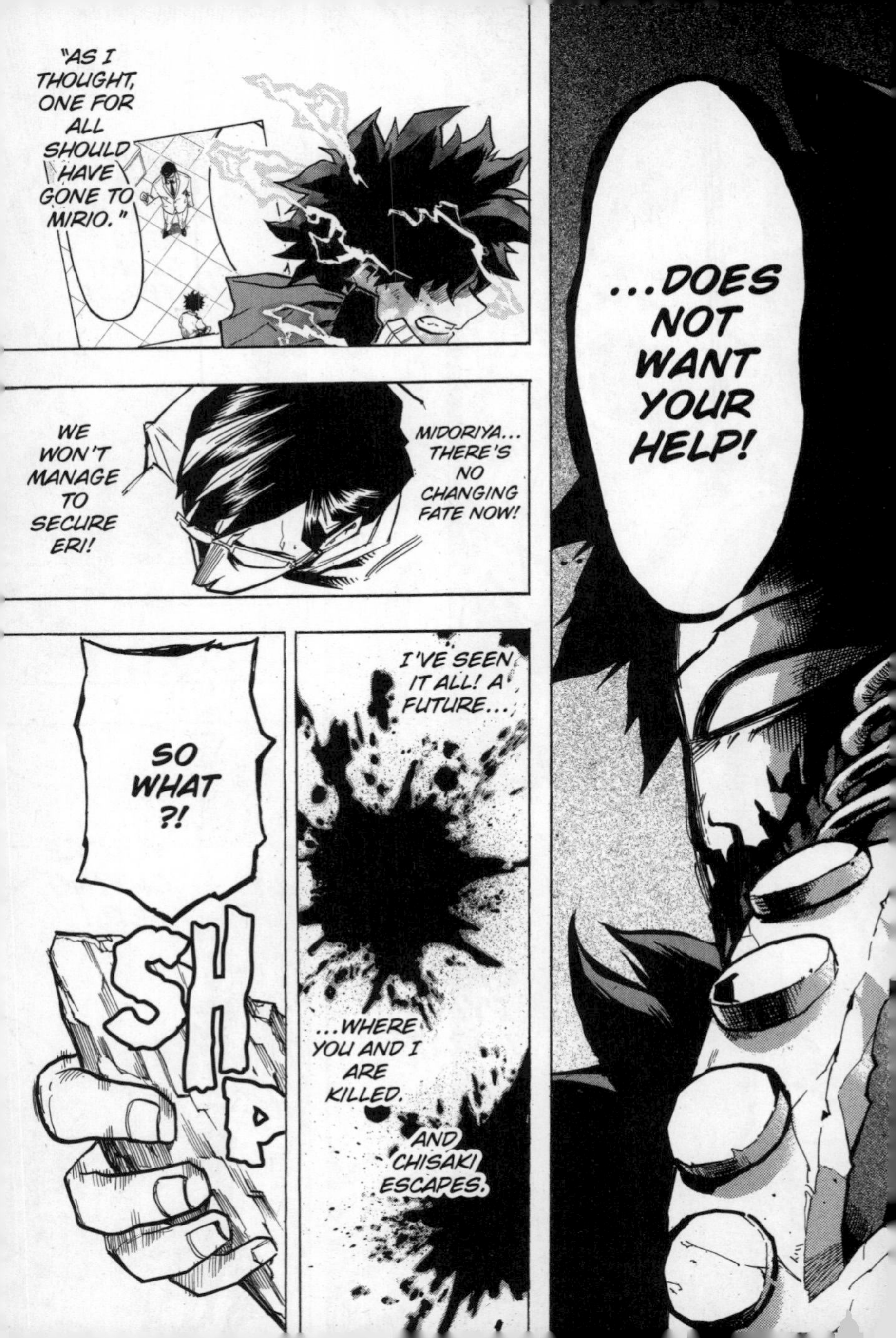
...DOES NOT WANT YOUR HELP!
"AS I THOUGHT, ONE FOR ALL SHOULD HAVE GONE TO MIRIO."
MIDORIYA... THERE'S NO CHANGING FATE NOW!
WE WON'T MANAGE TO SECURE ERI!
I'VE SEEN IT ALL! A FUTURE...
...WHERE YOU AND I ARE KILLED.
AND CHISAKI ESCAPES.
SO WHAT?!
SHP

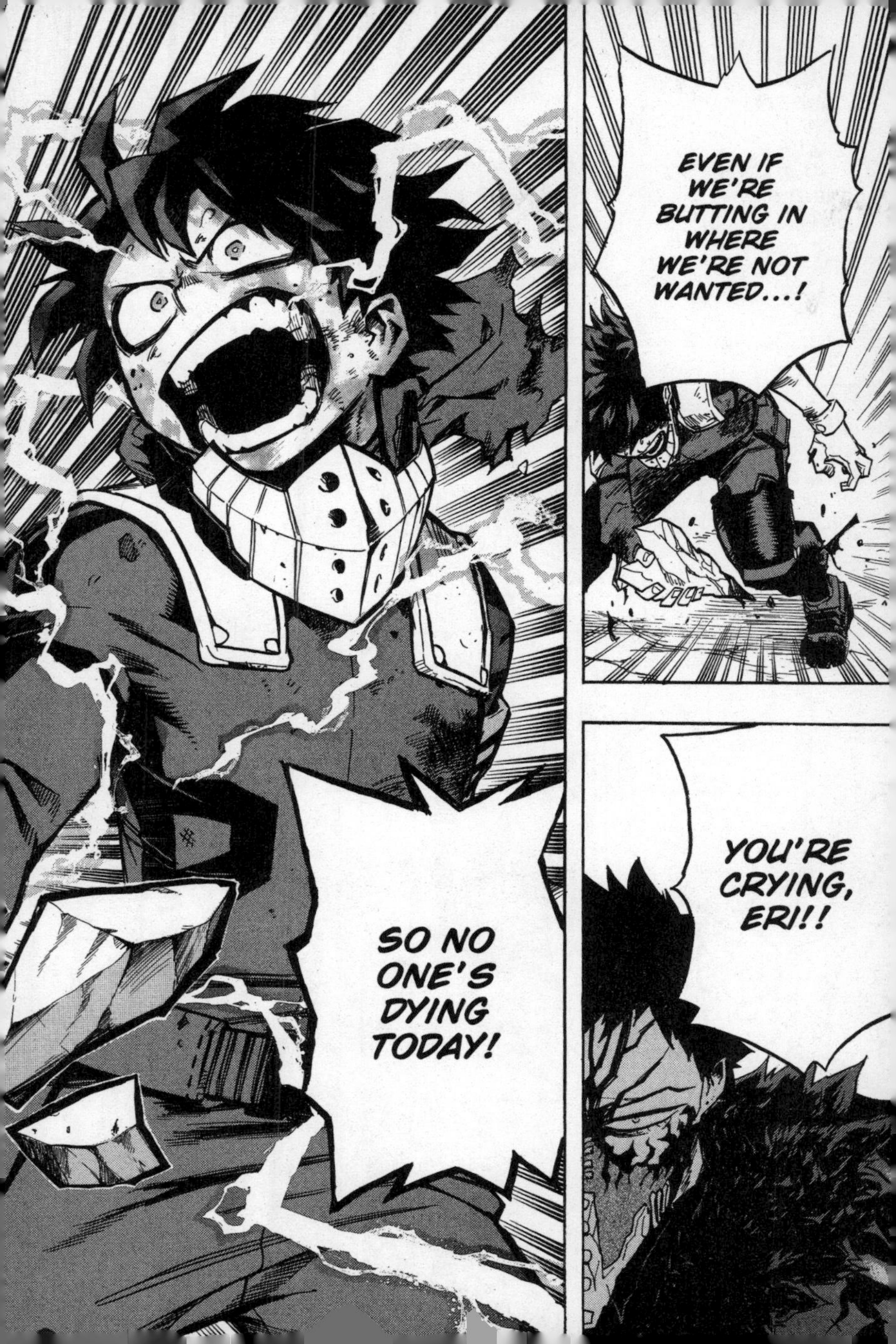
EVEN IF WE'RE BUTTING IN WHERE WE'RE NOT WANTED...!
YOU'RE CRYING, ERI!!
SO NO ONE'S DYING TODAY!

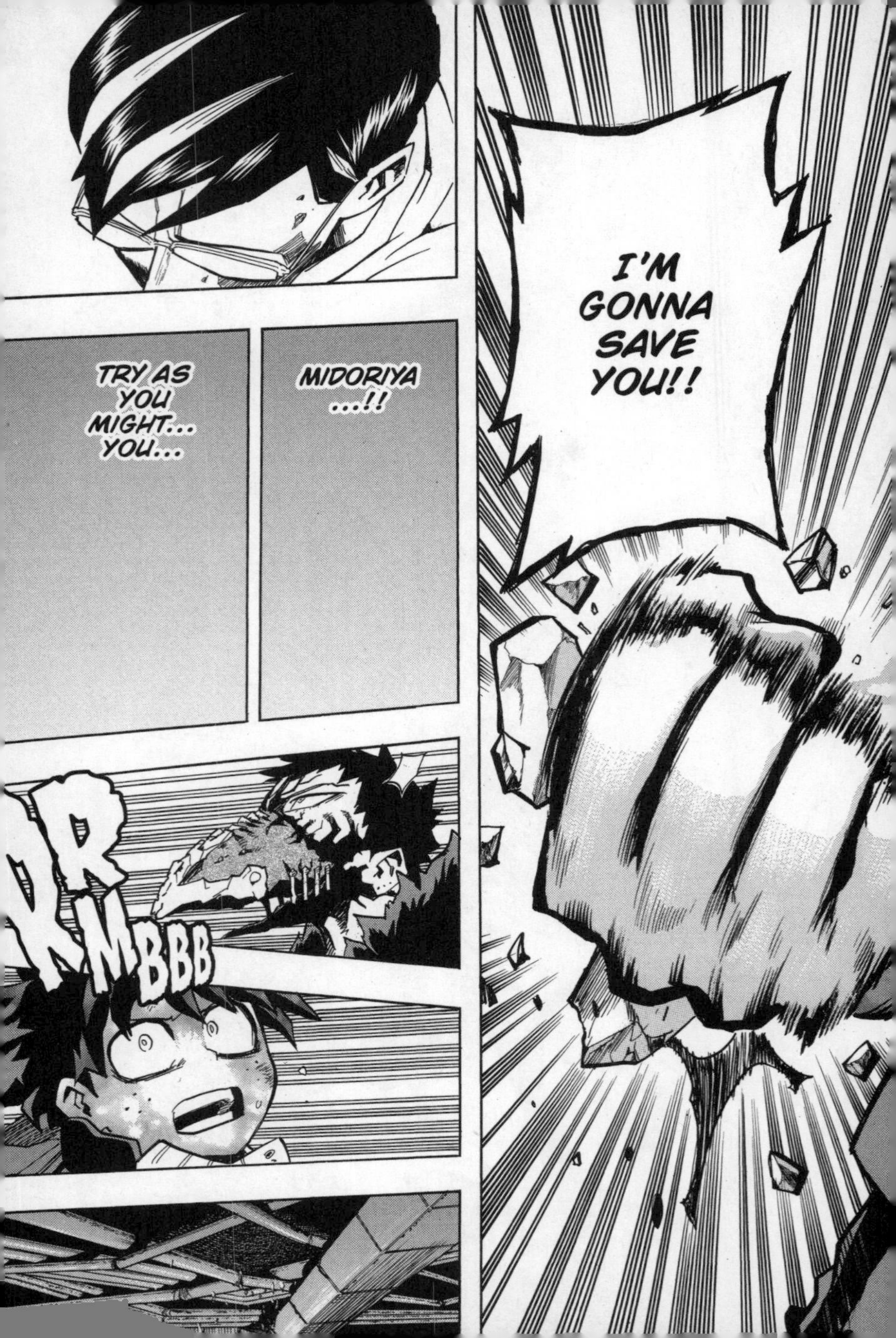
I'M GONNA SAVE YOU!!
MIDORIYA ...!!
TRY AS YOU MIGHT... YOU...
RMBBB

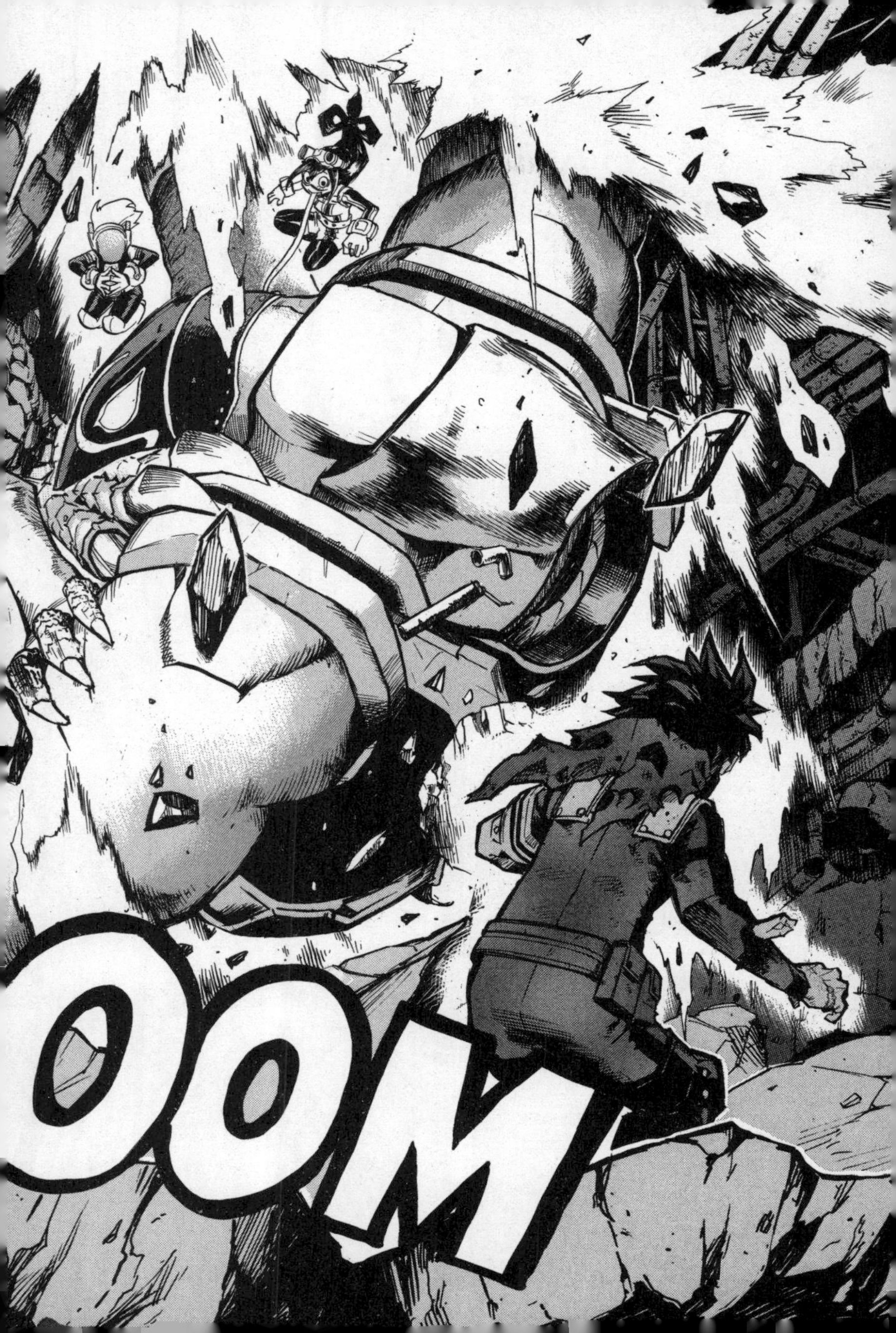
OOM

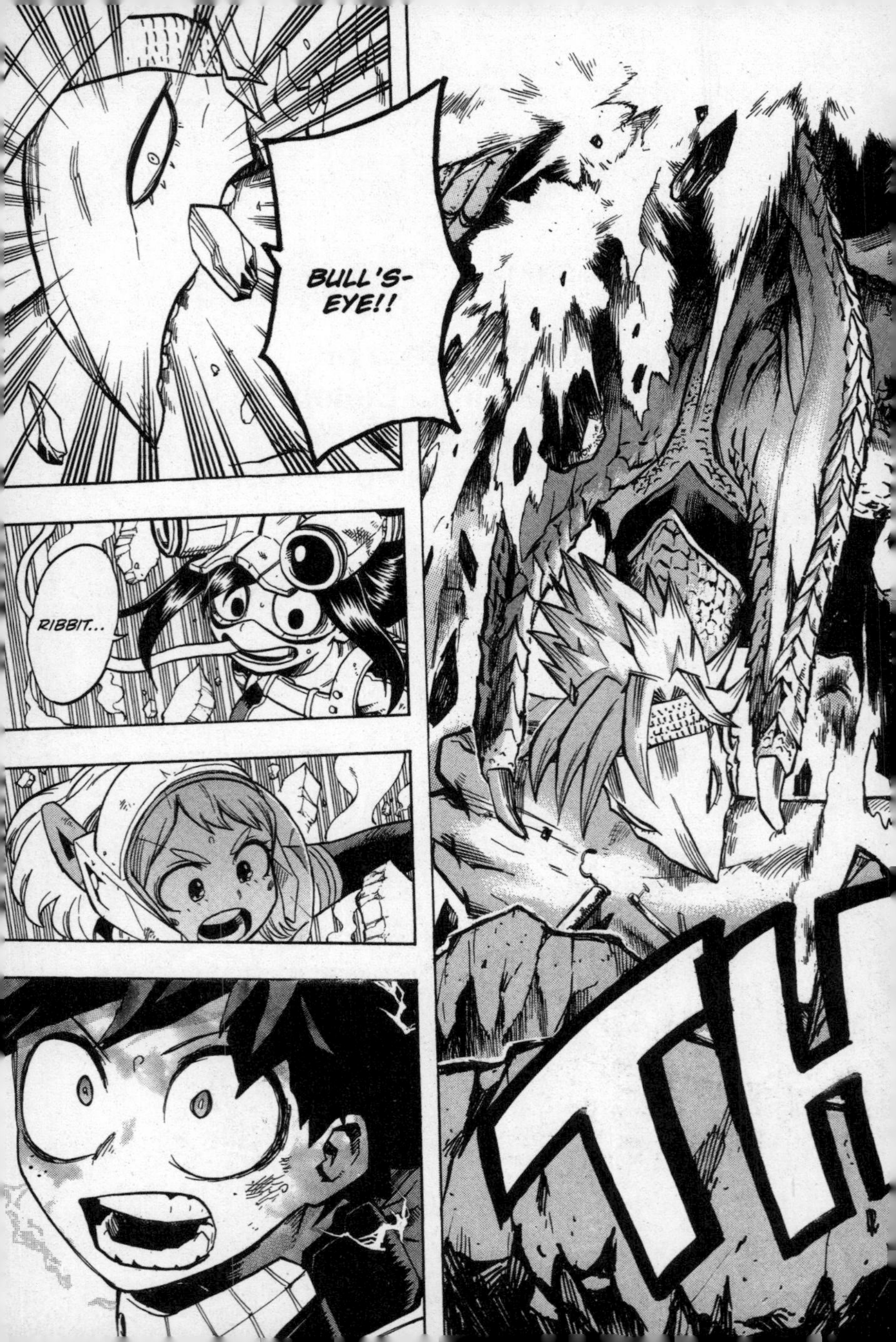
BULL'S-EYE!!
RIBBIT...

Here we are again!!

I've received another piece of commemorative art from Betten Sensei, the artist for the *My Hero Academia: Vigilantes* spin-off series in *JUMP+*.

I'm sure his schedule's packed, so I really appreciate it!!

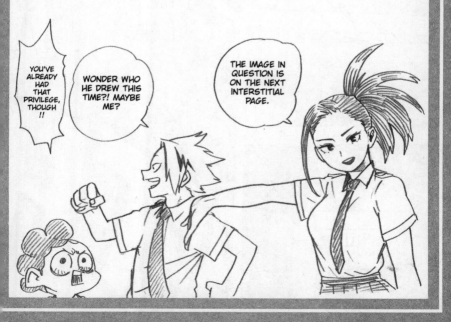

THE IMAGE IN QUESTION IS ON THE NEXT INTERSTITIAL PAGE.
WONDER WHO HE DREW THIS TIME?! MAYBE ME?
YOU'VE ALREADY HAD THAT PRIVILEGE, THOUGH!!

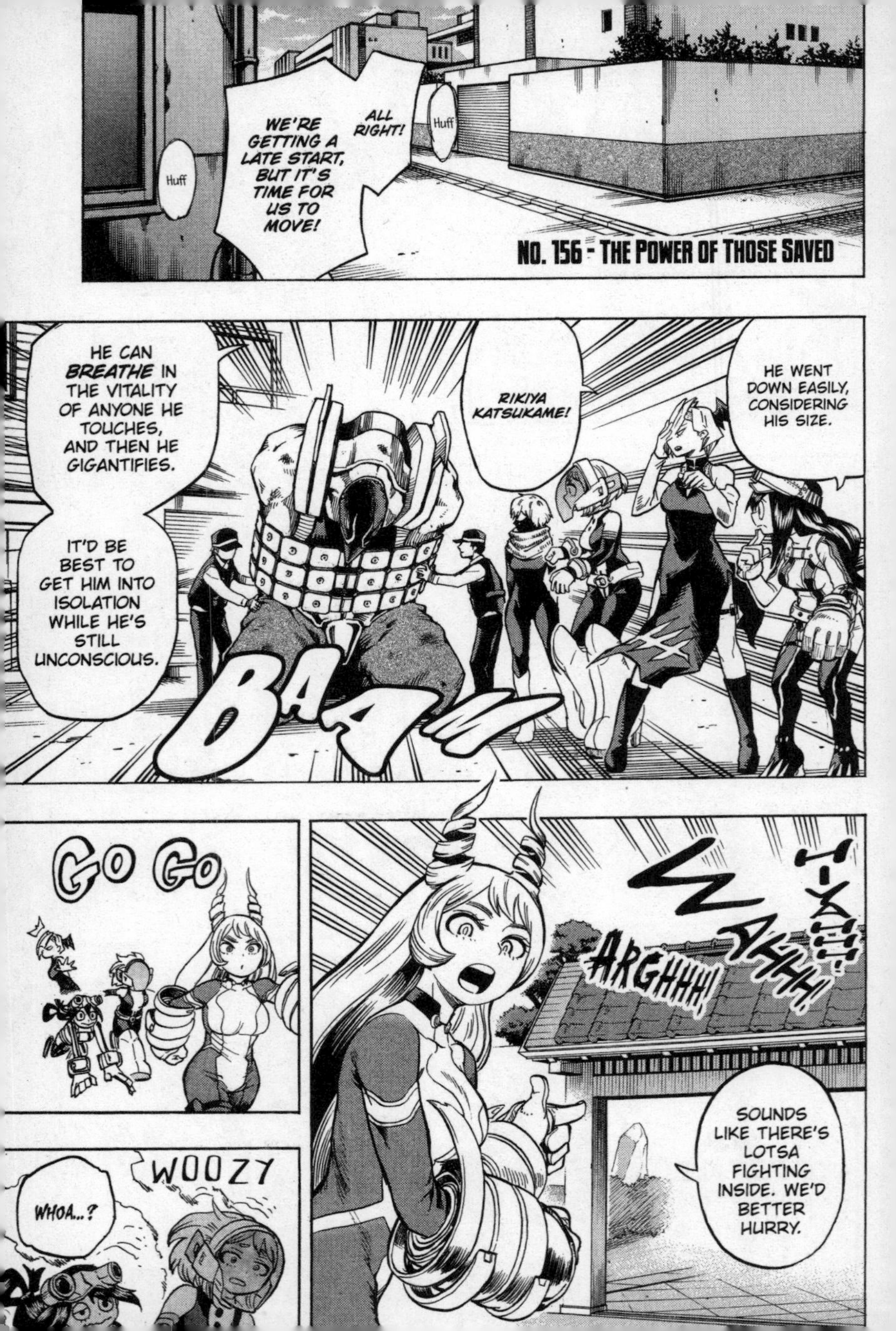
Huff
ALL RIGHT!
WE'RE GETTING A LATE START, BUT IT'S TIME FOR US TO MOVE!
Huff
No. 156 - The Power of Those Saved
HE WENT DOWN EASILY, CONSIDERING HIS SIZE.
RIKIYA KATSUKAME!
HE CAN BREATHE IN THE VITALITY OF ANYONE HE TOUCHES, AND THEN HE GIGANTIFIES.
IT'D BE BEST TO GET HIM INTO ISOLATION WHILE HE'S STILL UNCONSCIOUS.
ARGHHH!
SOUNDS LIKE THERE'S LOTSA FIGHTING INSIDE. WE'D BETTER HURRY.
GO GO
WOOZY
WHOA...?

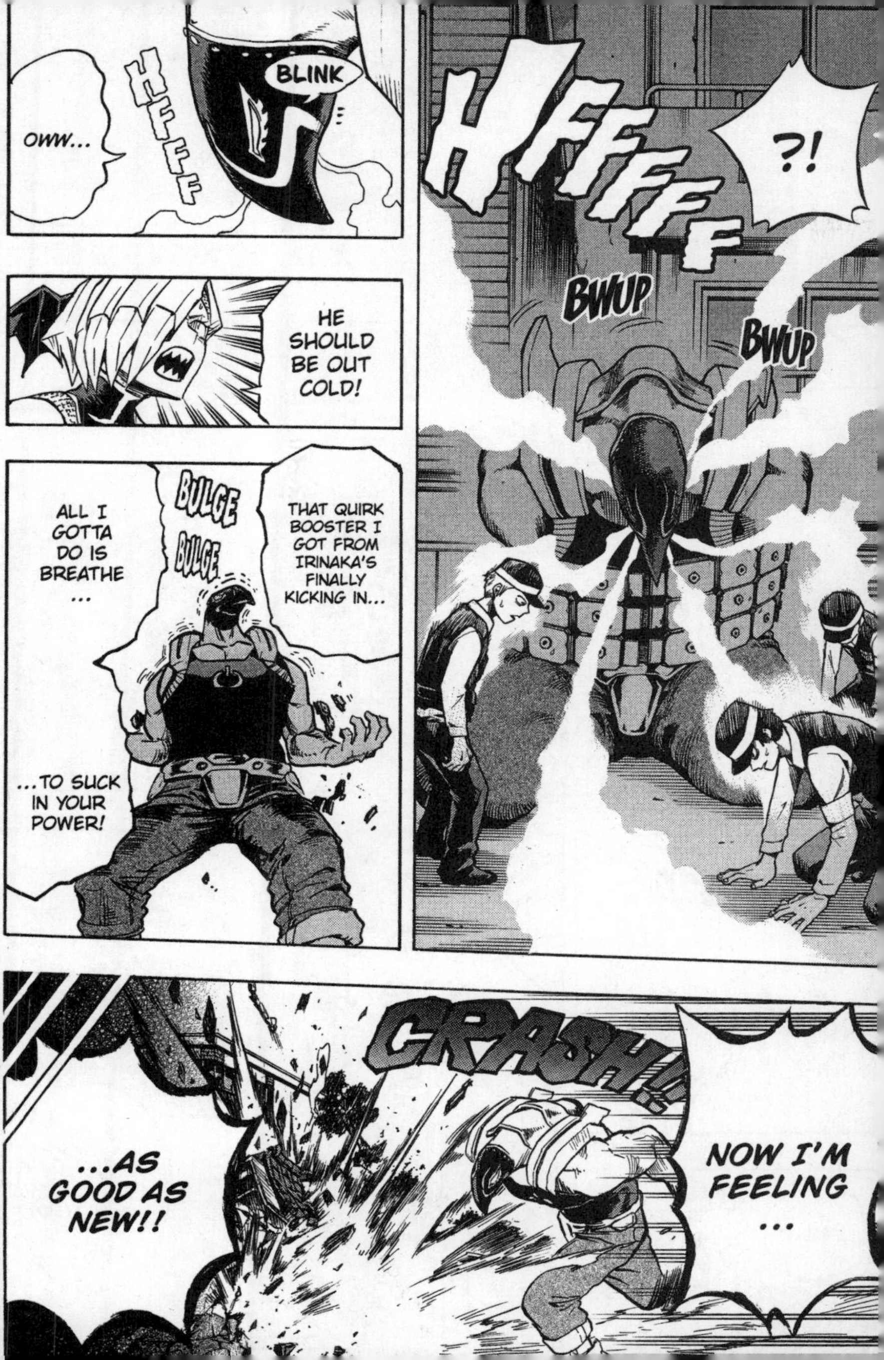
HFFFFF
?!
BWUP
BWUP
BLINK
HFFF
OWW...
HE SHOULD BE OUT COLD!
THAT QUIRK BOOSTER I GOT FROM IRINAKA'S FINALLY KICKING IN...
BULGE
BULGE
ALL I GOTTA DO IS BREATHE...
...TO SUCK IN YOUR POWER!
CRASH!!
NOW I'M FEELING...
...AS GOOD AS NEW!!

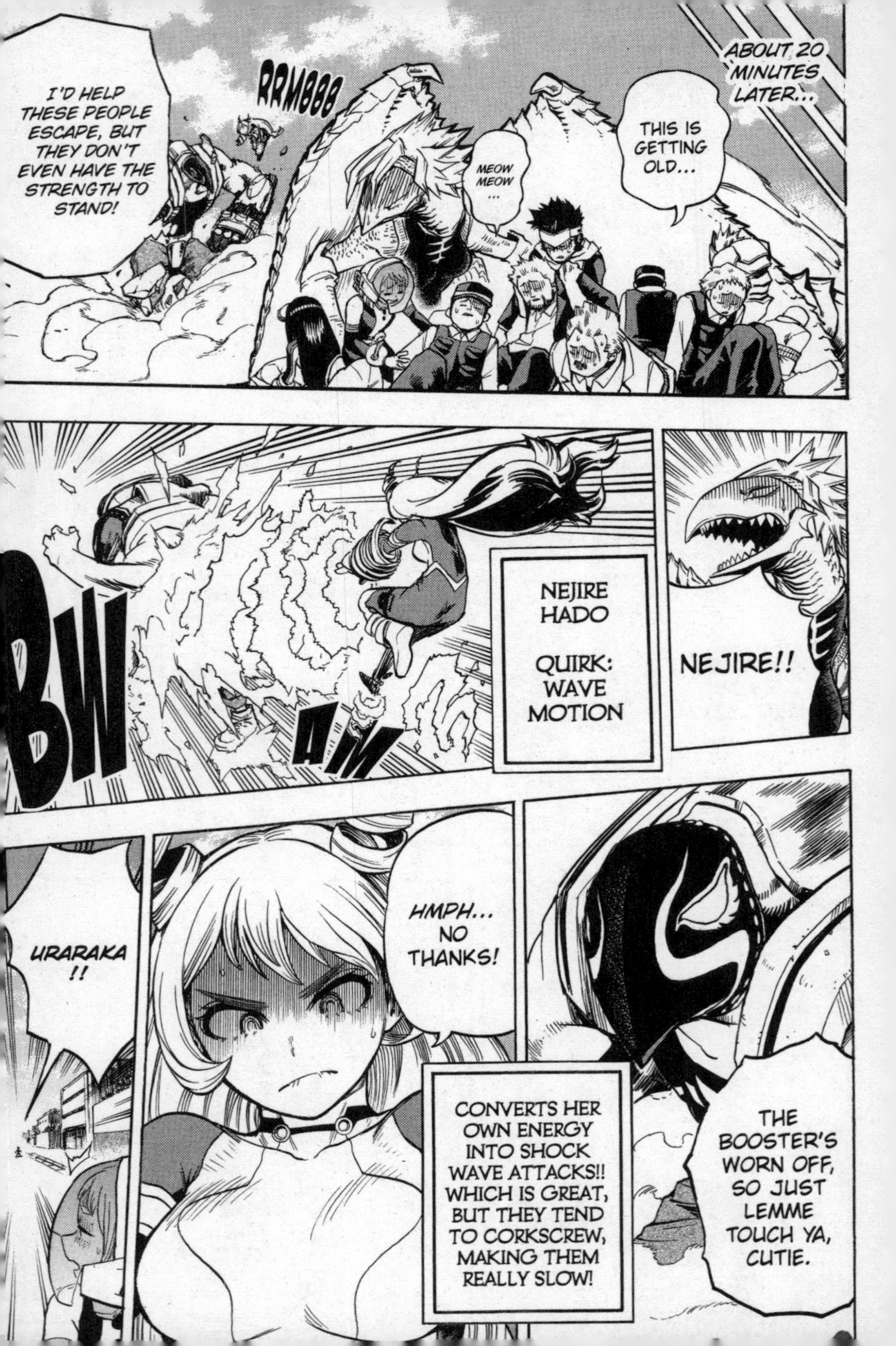
ABOUT 20 MINUTES LATER...
THIS IS GETTING OLD...
MEOW MEOW ...
RRMBBB
I'D HELP THESE PEOPLE ESCAPE, BUT THEY DON'T EVEN HAVE THE STRENGTH TO STAND!
NEJIRE!!
NEJIRE HADO
QUIRK: WAVE MOTION
BWAM
THE BOOSTER'S WORN OFF, SO JUST LEMME TOUCH YA, CUTIE.
HMPH... NO THANKS!
CONVERTS HER OWN ENERGY INTO SHOCK WAVE ATTACKS!! WHICH IS GREAT, BUT THEY TEND TO CORKSCREW, MAKING THEM REALLY SLOW!
URARAKA!!

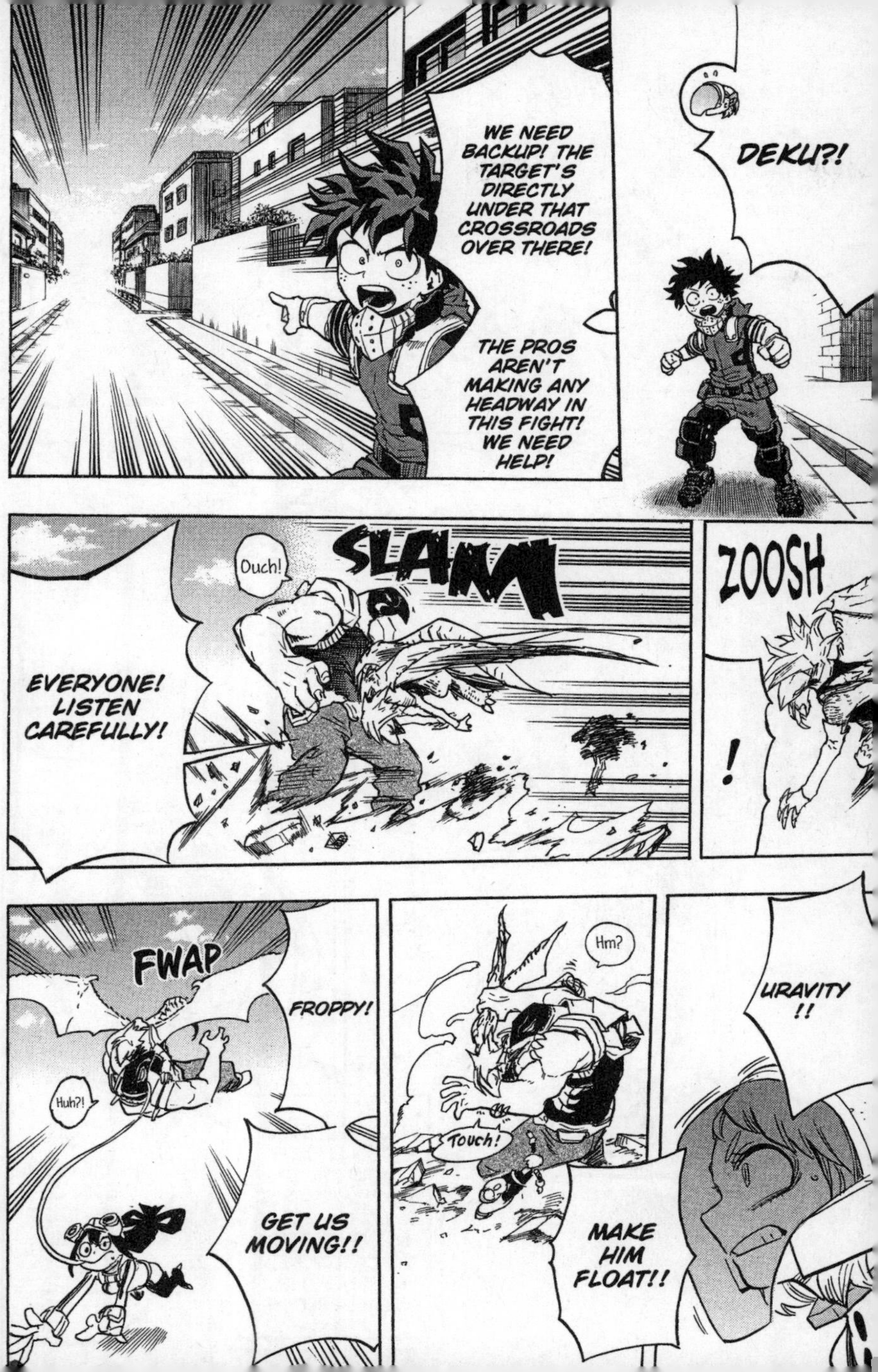
DEKU?!
WE NEED BACKUP! THE TARGET'S DIRECTLY UNDER THAT CROSSROADS OVER THERE!
THE PROS AREN'T MAKING ANY HEADWAY IN THIS FIGHT! WE NEED HELP!
ZOOSH
!
SLAM
Ouch!
EVERYONE! LISTEN CAREFULLY!
URAVITY!!
MAKE HIM FLOAT!!
Hm?
Touch!
FWAP
FROPPY!
Huh?!
GET US MOVING!!

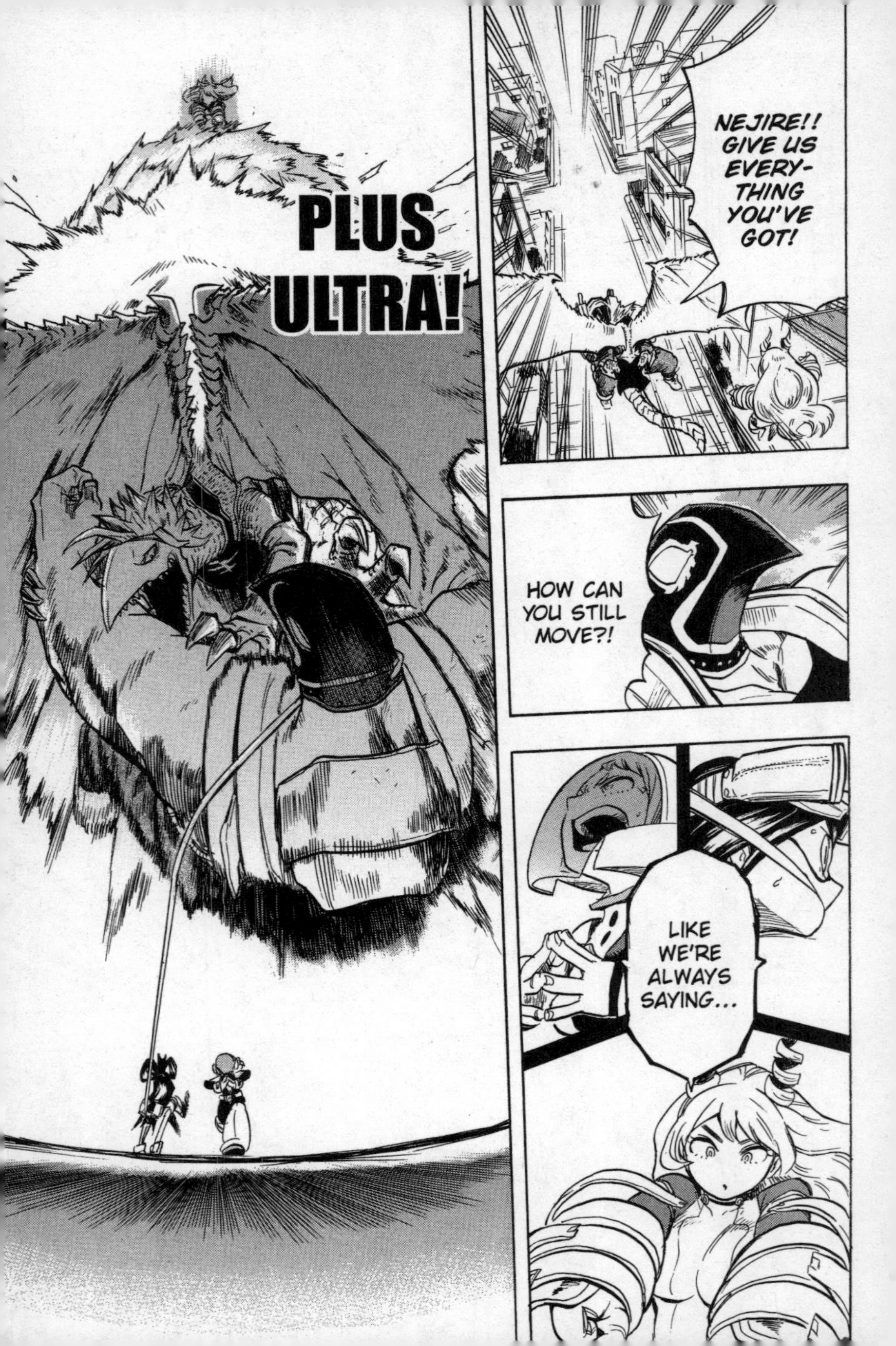
NEJIRE!! GIVE US EVERY-THING YOU'VE GOT!
HOW CAN YOU STILL MOVE?!
LIKE WE'RE ALWAYS SAYING...
PLUS ULTRA!

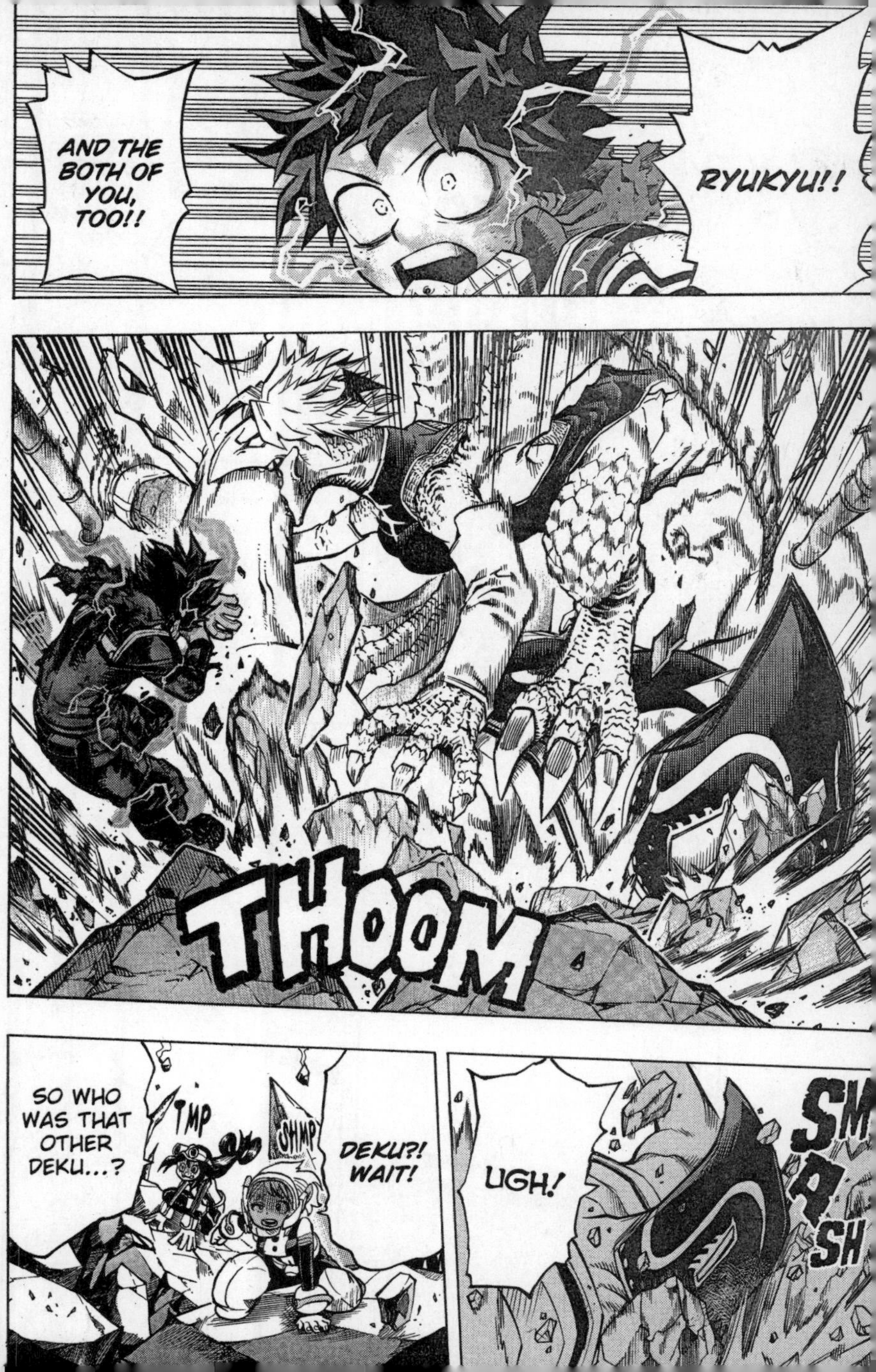
RYUKYU!!
AND THE BOTH OF YOU, TOO!!
THOOM
SMASH
UGH!
SHMP
DEKU?! WAIT!
TMP
SO WHO WAS THAT OTHER DEKU...?

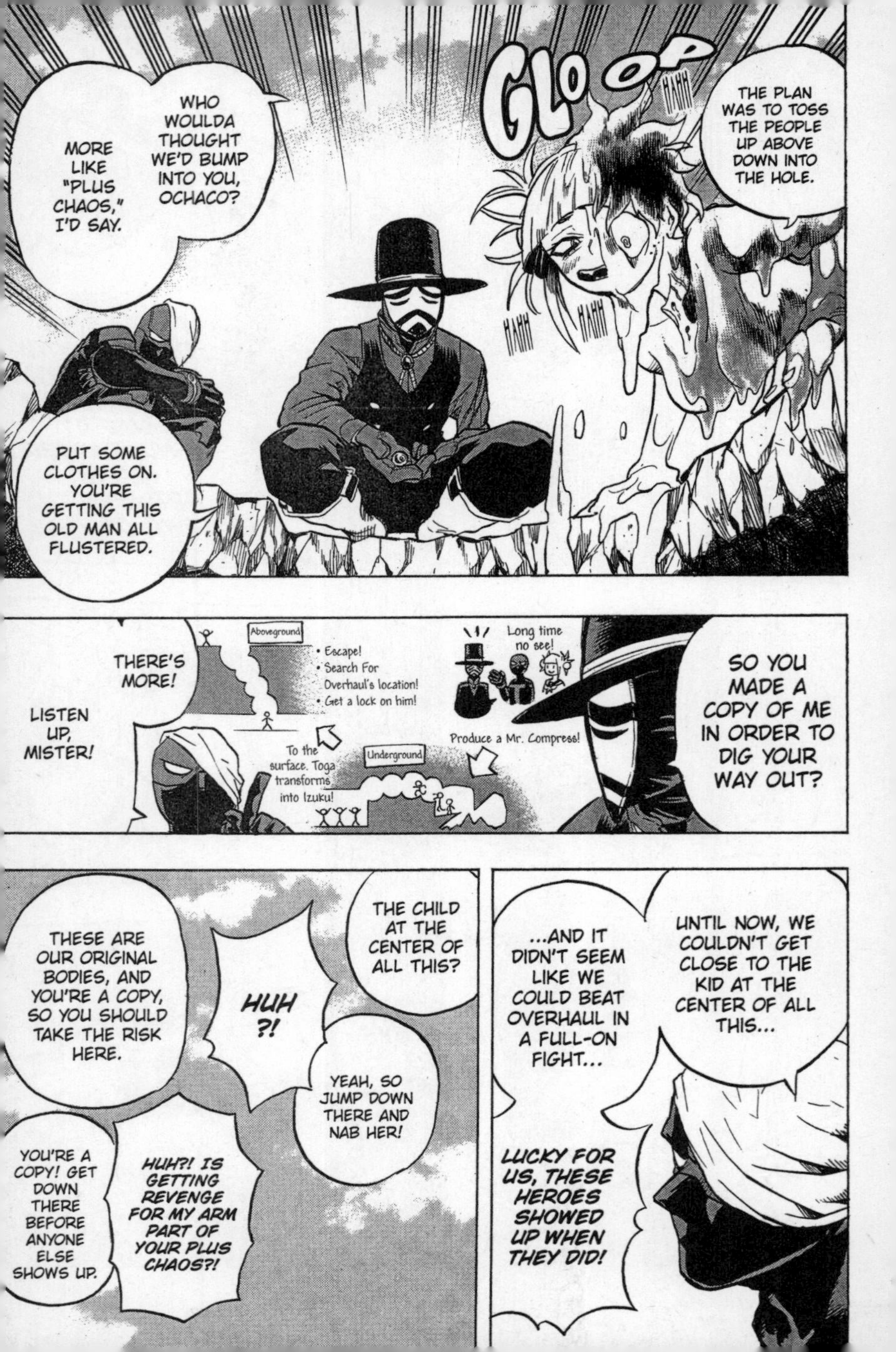
GLOOP
HAHH
THE PLAN WAS TO TOSS THE PEOPLE UP ABOVE DOWN INTO THE HOLE.
HAHH
HAHH
WHO WOULDA THOUGHT WE'D BUMP INTO YOU, OCHACO?
MORE LIKE "PLUS CHAOS," I'D SAY.
PUT SOME CLOTHES ON. YOU'RE GETTING THIS OLD MAN ALL FLUSTERED.
SO YOU MADE A COPY OF ME IN ORDER TO DIG YOUR WAY OUT?
Long time no see!
Aboveground
• Escape!
• Search For Overhaul's location!
• Get a lock on him!
Produce a Mr. Compress!
Underground
To the surface. Toga transforms into Izuku!
THERE'S MORE!
LISTEN UP, MISTER!
UNTIL NOW, WE COULDN'T GET CLOSE TO THE KID AT THE CENTER OF ALL THIS...
...AND IT DIDN'T SEEM LIKE WE COULD BEAT OVERHAUL IN A FULL-ON FIGHT...
LUCKY FOR US, THESE HEROES SHOWED UP WHEN THEY DID!
THE CHILD AT THE CENTER OF ALL THIS?
HUH ?!
THESE ARE OUR ORIGINAL BODIES, AND YOU'RE A COPY, SO YOU SHOULD TAKE THE RISK HERE.
YEAH, SO JUMP DOWN THERE AND NAB HER!
HUH?! IS GETTING REVENGE FOR MY ARM PART OF YOUR PLUS CHAOS?!
YOU'RE A COPY! GET DOWN THERE BEFORE ANYONE ELSE SHOWS UP.

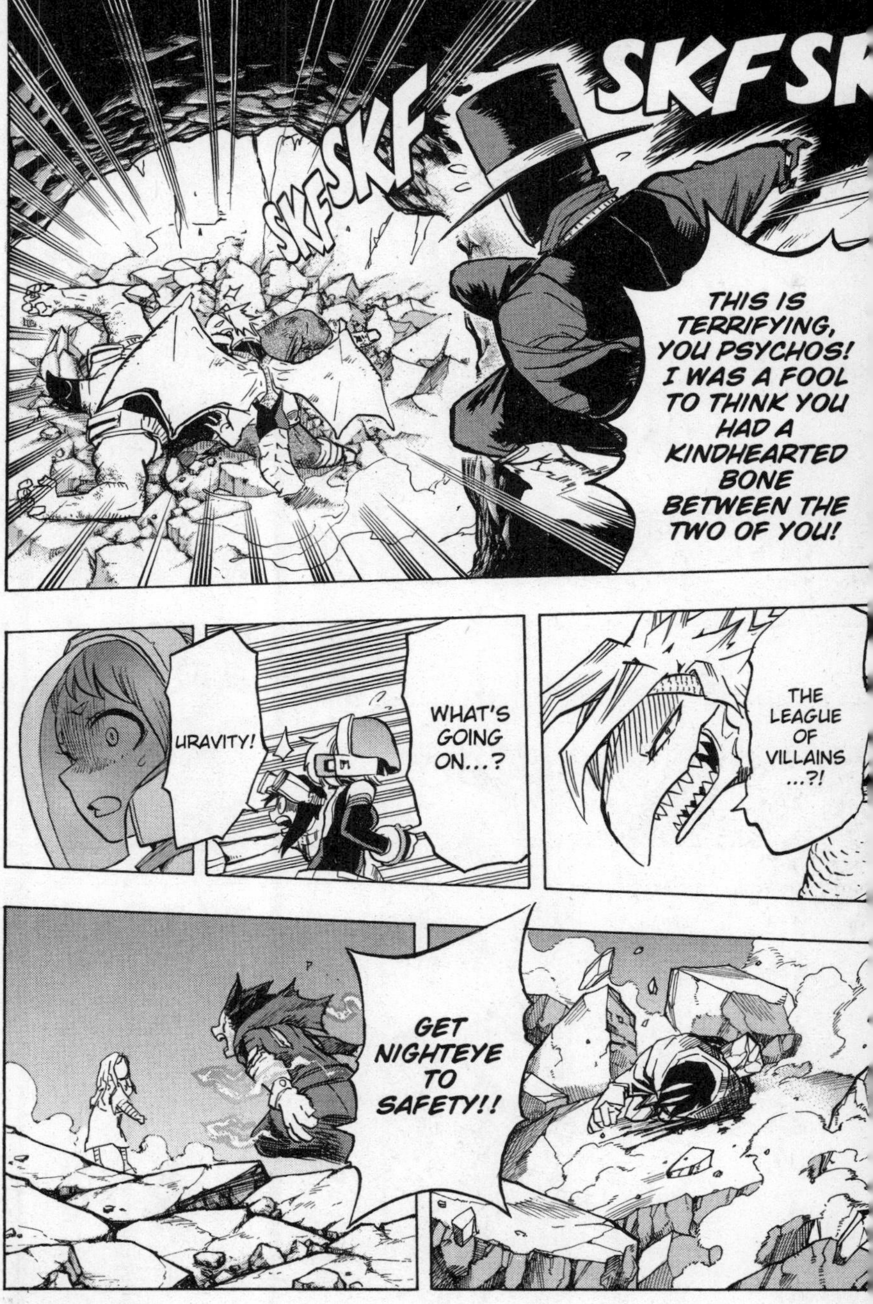
SKF SK
SKF SKF
THIS IS TERRIFYING, YOU PSYCHOS! I WAS A FOOL TO THINK YOU HAD A KINDHEARTED BONE BETWEEN THE TWO OF YOU!
THE LEAGUE OF VILLAINS ...?!
WHAT'S GOING ON...?
URAVITY!
GET NIGHTEYE TO SAFETY!!

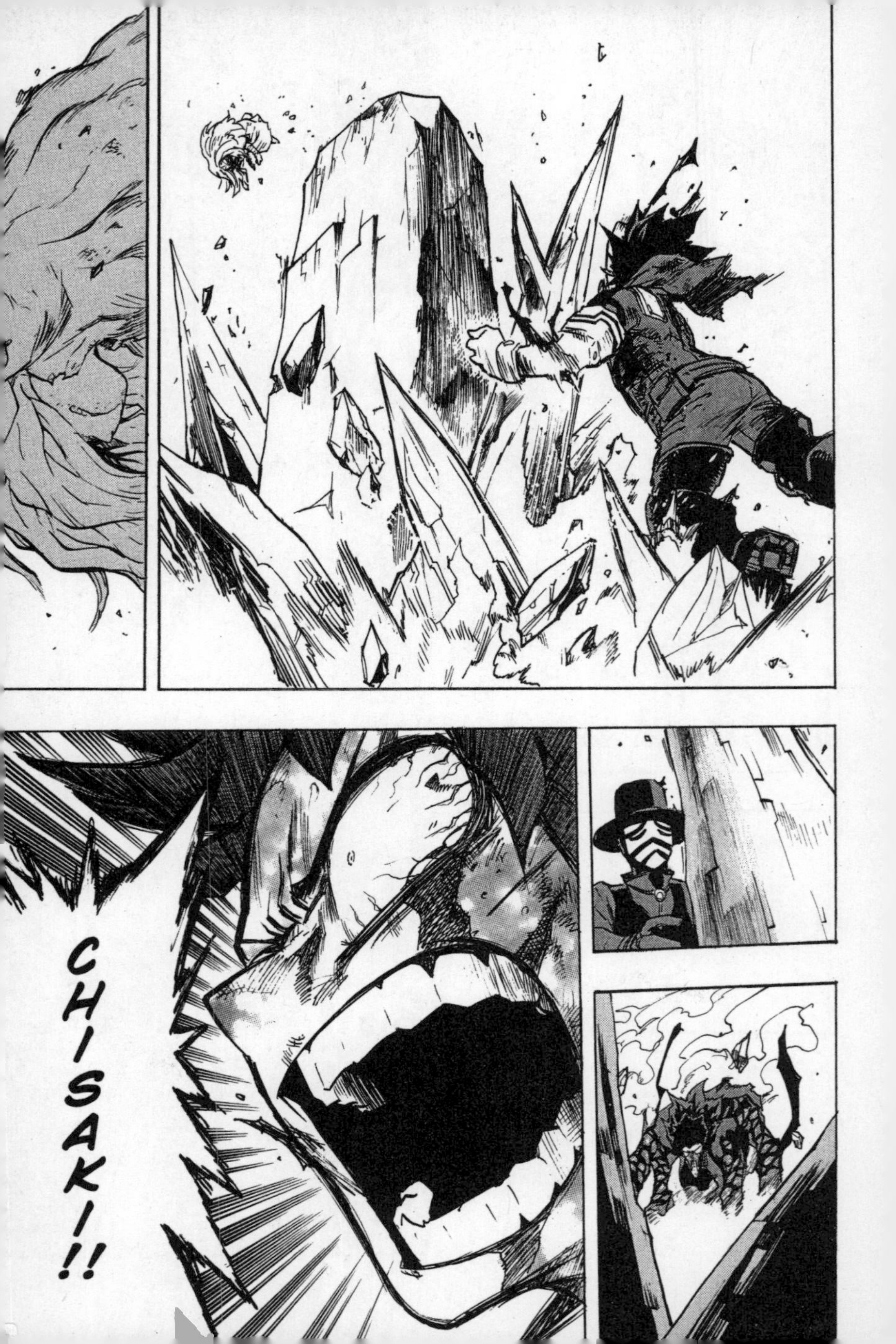
CHISAKI!!

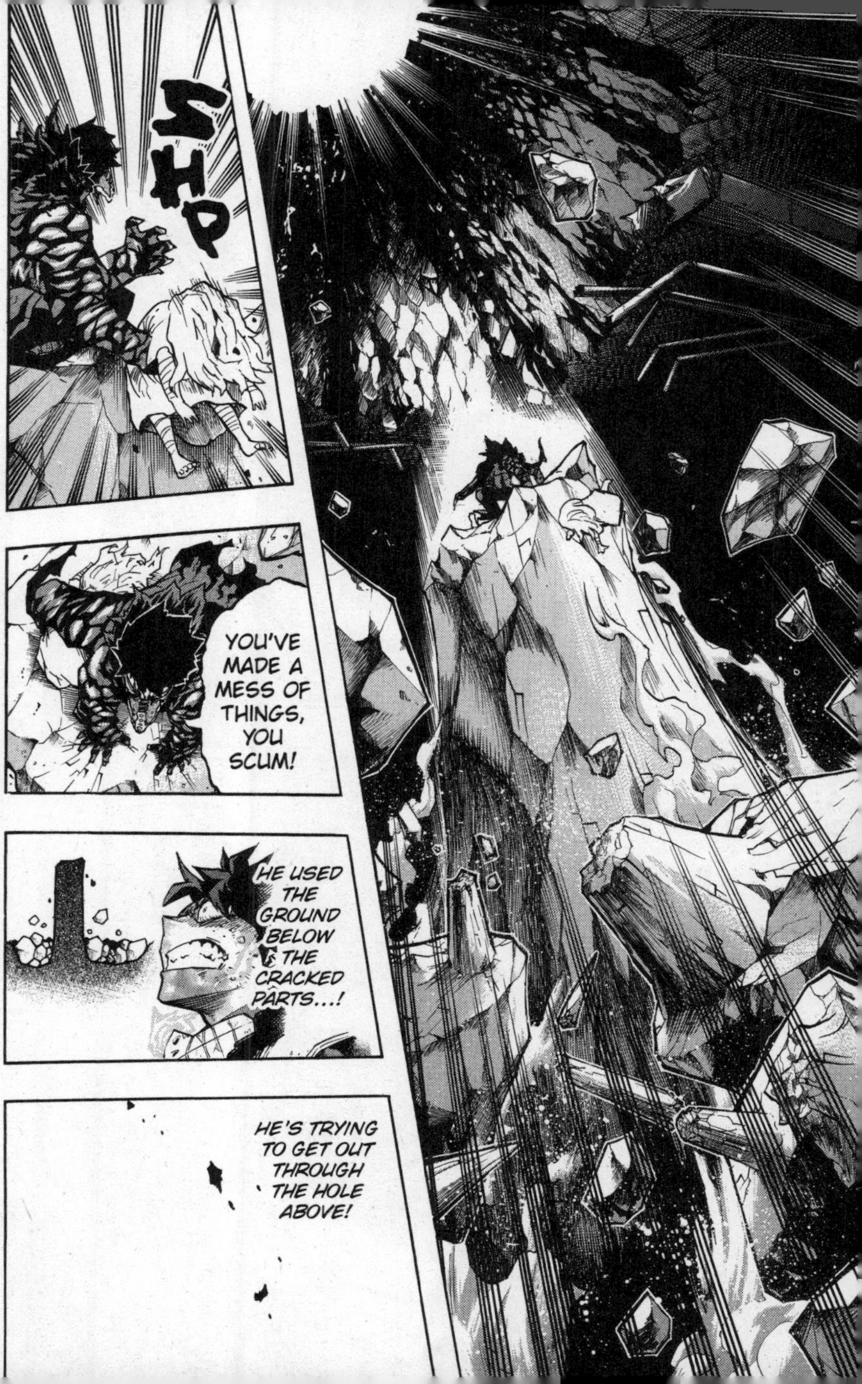
SHP
YOU'VE MADE A MESS OF THINGS, YOU SCUM!
HE USED THE GROUND BELOW THE CRACKED PARTS...!
HE'S TRYING TO GET OUT THROUGH THE HOLE ABOVE!

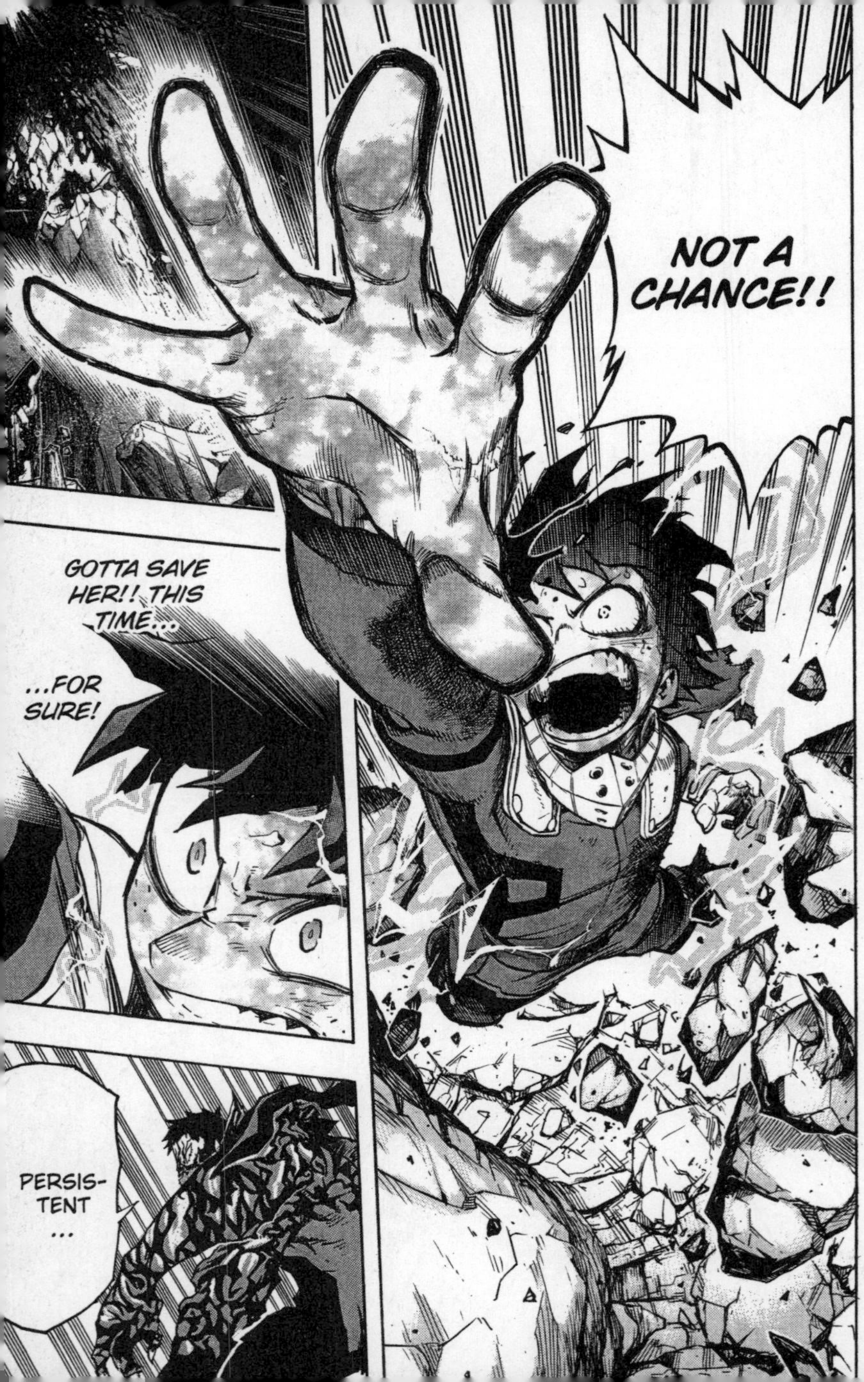
NOT A CHANCE!!
GOTTA SAVE HER!! THIS TIME...
...FOR SURE!
PERSIS-TENT ...

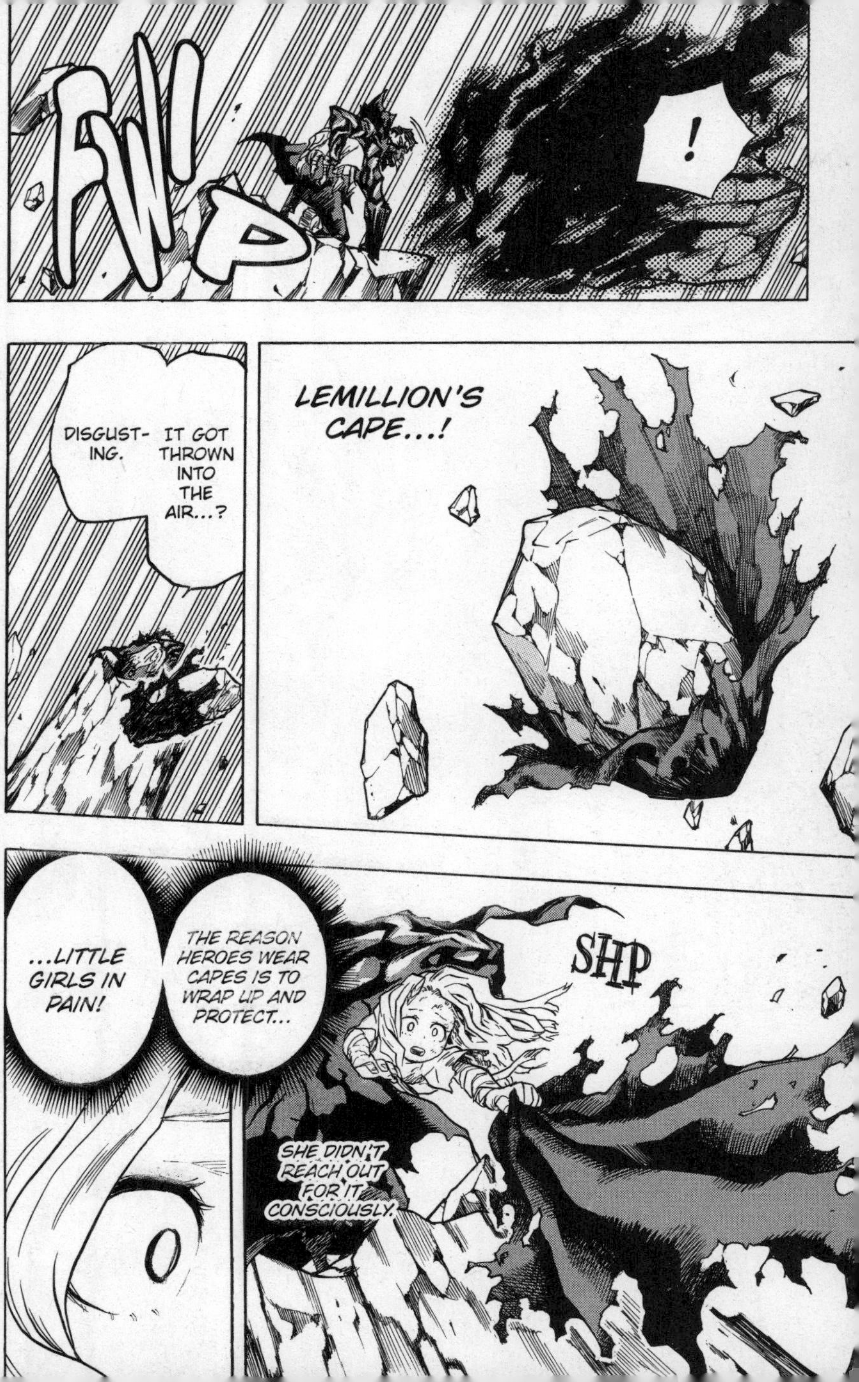
FWIP
!
LEMILLION'S CAPE...!
DISGUST-ING. IT GOT THROWN INTO THE AIR...?
SHP
THE REASON HEROES WEAR CAPES IS TO WRAP UP AND PROTECT...
...LITTLE GIRLS IN PAIN!
SHE DIDN'T REACH OUT FOR IT CONSCIOUSLY.

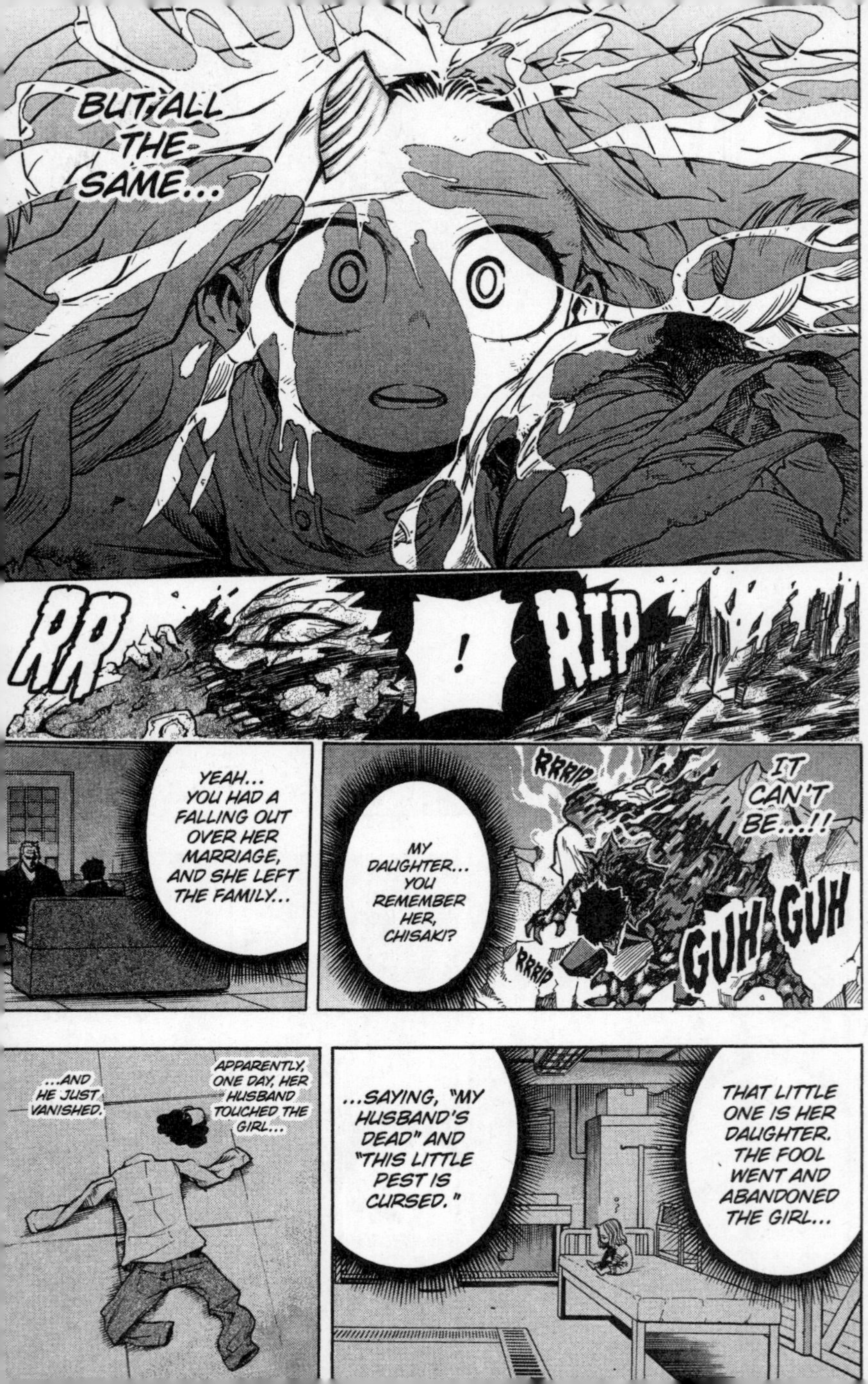
BUT ALL THE SAME...
RR
!
RIP
RRRIP
IT CAN'T BE...!!
MY DAUGHTER... YOU REMEMBER HER, CHISAKI?
GUH GUH
RRRIP
YEAH... YOU HAD A FALLING OUT OVER HER MARRIAGE, AND SHE LEFT THE FAMILY...
THAT LITTLE ONE IS HER DAUGHTER. THE FOOL WENT AND ABANDONED THE GIRL...
...SAYING, "MY HUSBAND'S DEAD" AND "THIS LITTLE PEST IS CURSED."
APPARENTLY, ONE DAY, HER HUSBAND TOUCHED THE GIRL...
...AND HE JUST VANISHED.

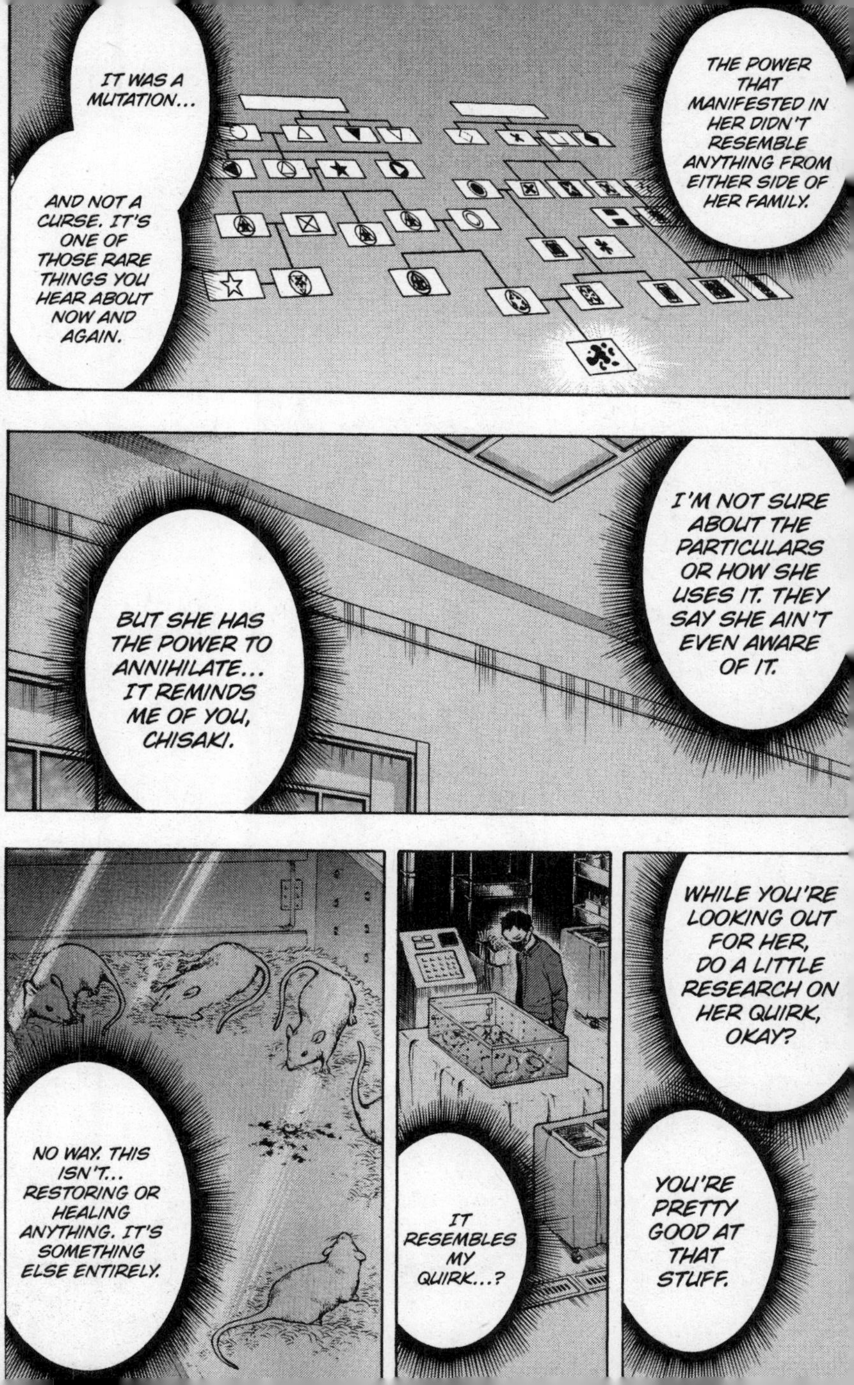
THE POWER THAT MANIFESTED IN HER DIDN'T RESEMBLE ANYTHING FROM EITHER SIDE OF HER FAMILY.
IT WAS A MUTATION...
AND NOT A CURSE. IT'S ONE OF THOSE RARE THINGS YOU HEAR ABOUT NOW AND AGAIN.
I'M NOT SURE ABOUT THE PARTICULARS OR HOW SHE USES IT. THEY SAY SHE AIN'T EVEN AWARE OF IT.
BUT SHE HAS THE POWER TO ANNIHILATE... IT REMINDS ME OF YOU, CHISAKI.
WHILE YOU'RE LOOKING OUT FOR HER, DO A LITTLE RESEARCH ON HER QUIRK, OKAY?
YOU'RE PRETTY GOOD AT THAT STUFF.
IT RESEMBLES MY QUIRK...?
NO WAY. THIS ISN'T... RESTORING OR HEALING ANYTHING. IT'S SOMETHING ELSE ENTIRELY.

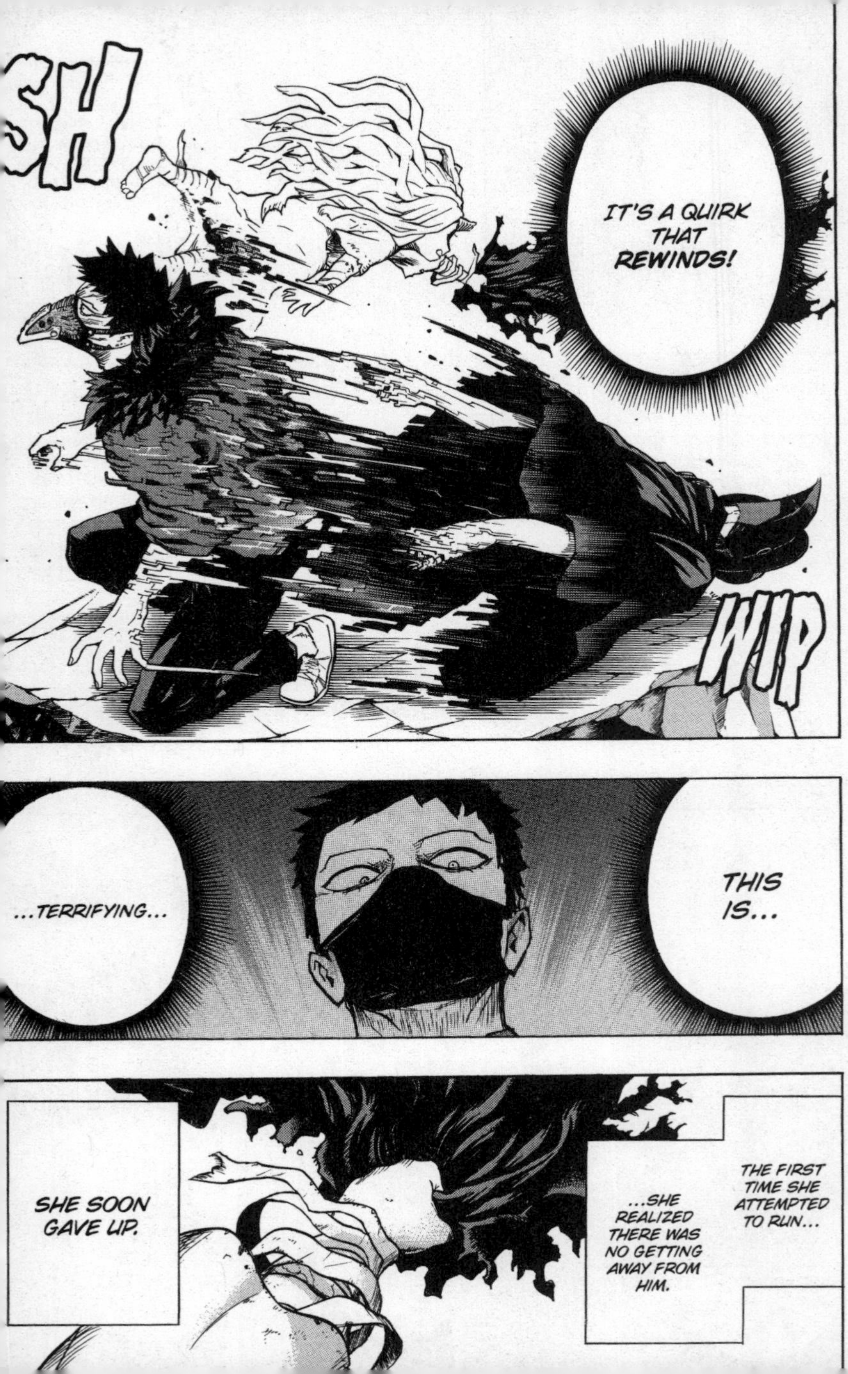
IT'S A QUIRK THAT REWINDS!
SH
WIP
THIS IS...
...TERRIFYING...
THE FIRST TIME SHE ATTEMPTED TO RUN...
...SHE REALIZED THERE WAS NO GETTING AWAY FROM HIM.
SHE SOON GAVE UP.

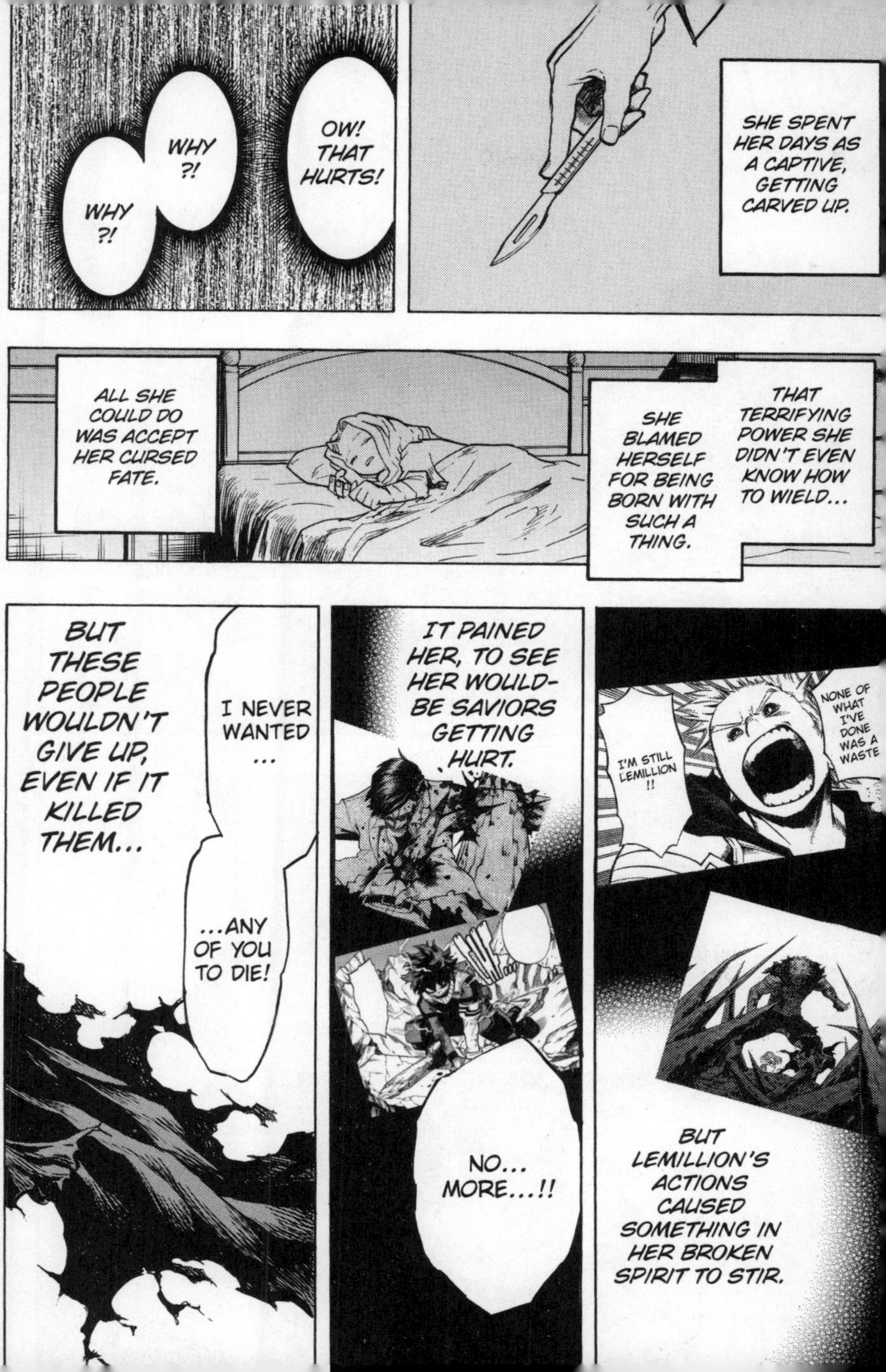
SHE SPENT HER DAYS AS A CAPTIVE, GETTING CARVED UP.
OW! THAT HURTS!
WHY ?!
WHY ?!
THAT TERRIFYING POWER SHE DIDN'T EVEN KNOW HOW TO WIELD...
SHE BLAMED HERSELF FOR BEING BORN WITH SUCH A THING.
ALL SHE COULD DO WAS ACCEPT HER CURSED FATE.
NONE OF WHAT I'VE DONE WAS A WASTE
I'M STILL LEMILLION !!
BUT LEMILLION'S ACTIONS CAUSED SOMETHING IN HER BROKEN SPIRIT TO STIR.
IT PAINED HER, TO SEE HER WOULD-BE SAVIORS GETTING HURT.
NO... MORE...!!
BUT THESE PEOPLE WOULDN'T GIVE UP, EVEN IF IT KILLED THEM...
I NEVER WANTED ...
...ANY OF YOU TO DIE!

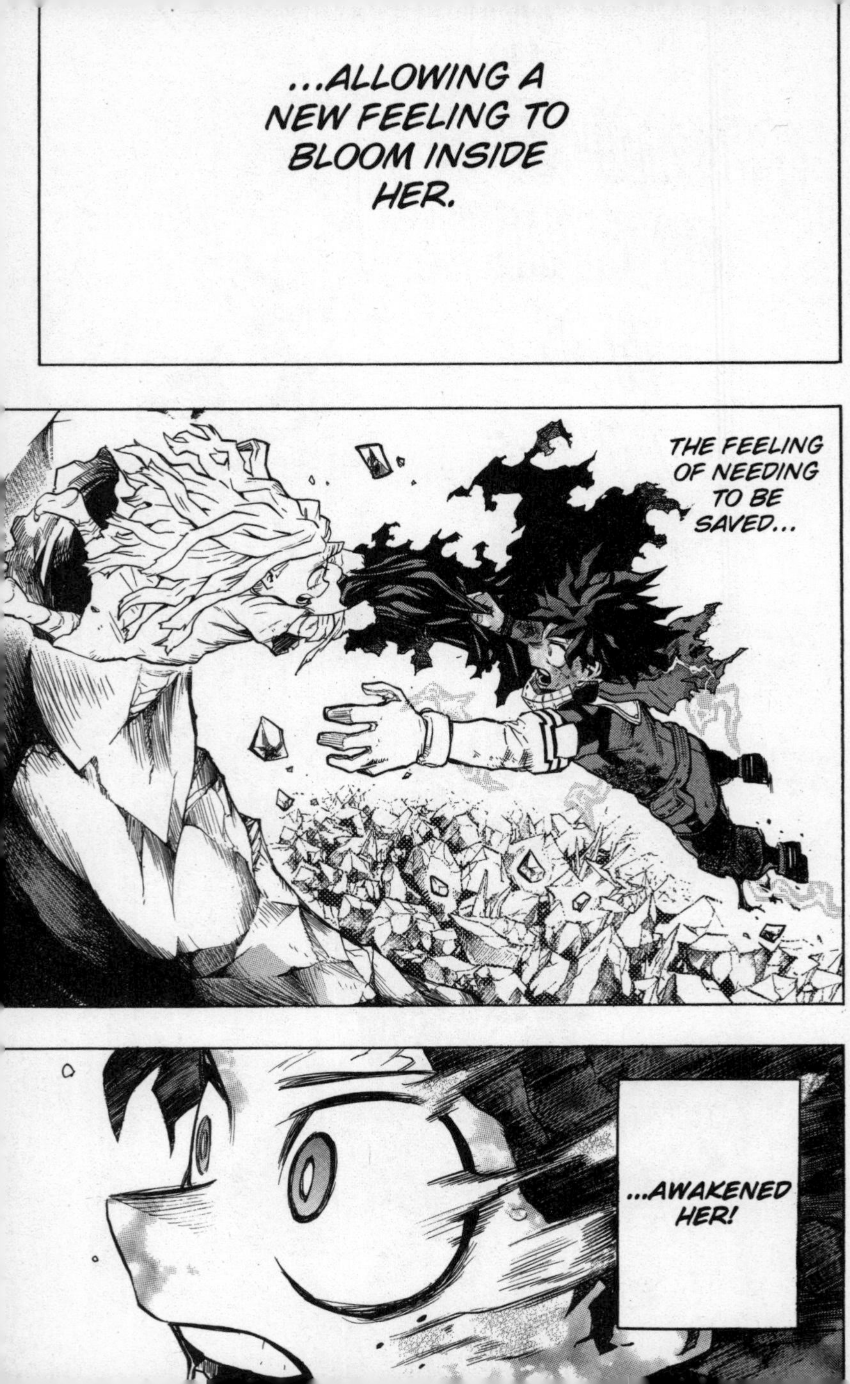
...ALLOWING A NEW FEELING TO BLOOM INSIDE HER.
THE FEELING OF NEEDING TO BE SAVED...
...AWAKENED HER!

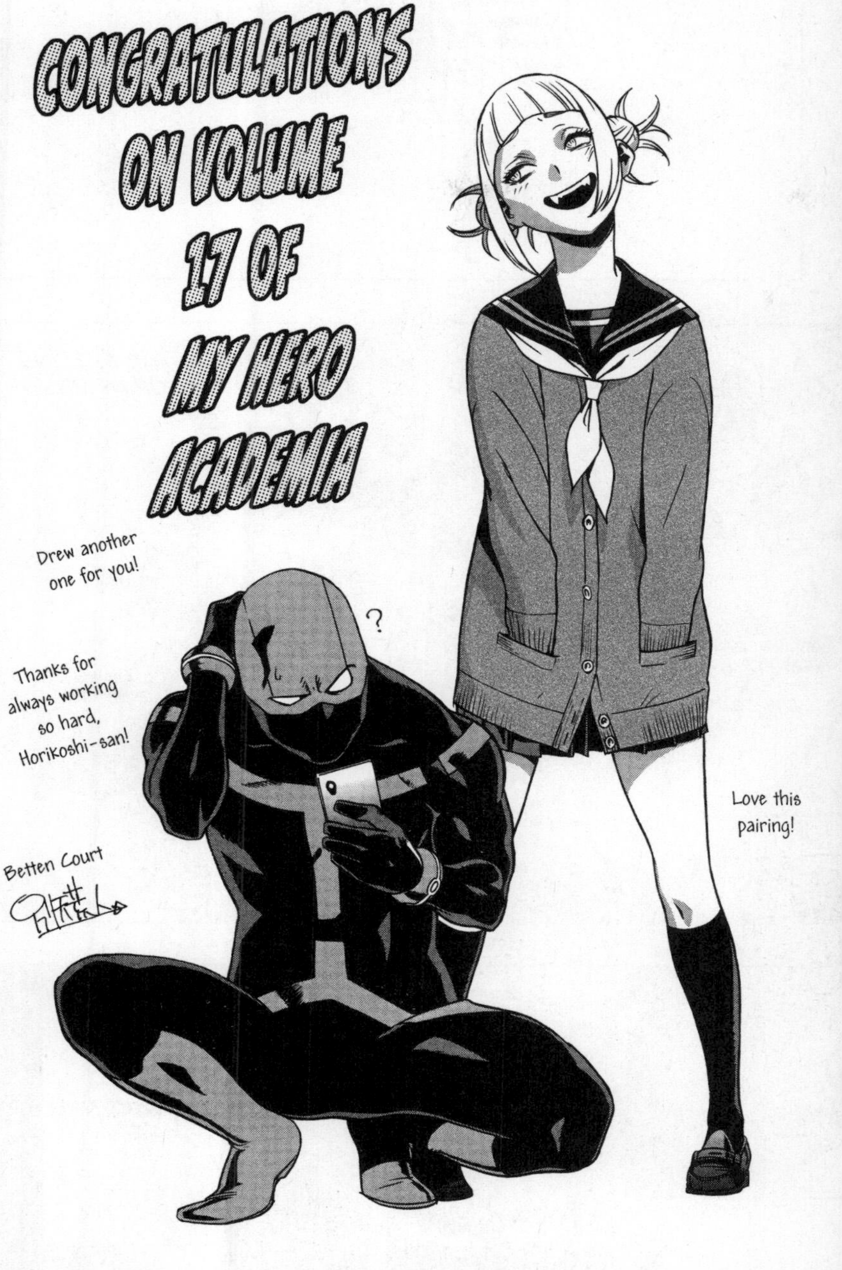
CONGRATULATIONS ON VOLUME 17 OF MY HERO ACADEMIA
Drew another one for you!
?
Thanks for always working so hard, Horikoshi-san!
Love this pairing!
Betten Court

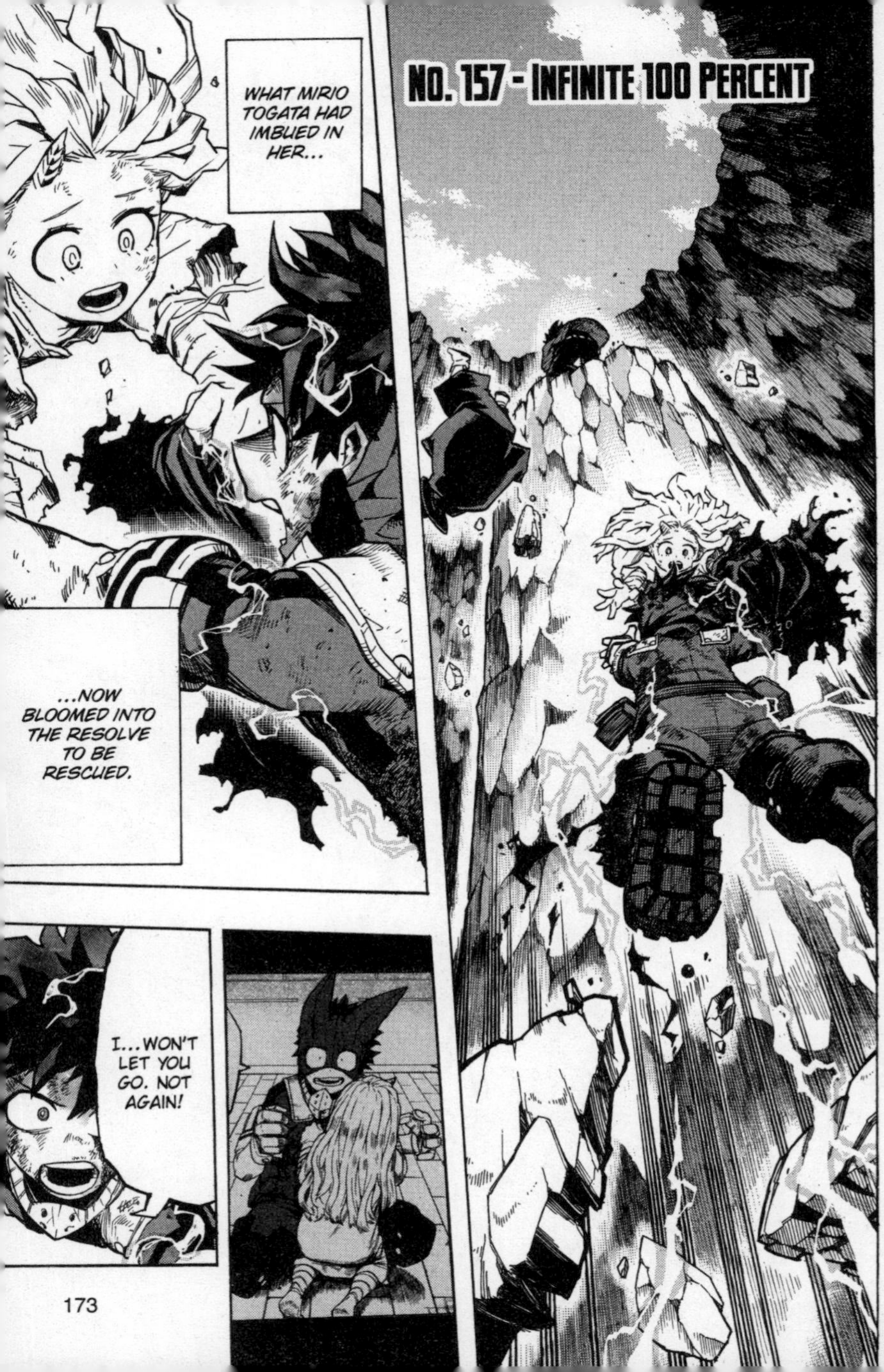
No. 157 - Infinite 100 Percent
WHAT MIRIO TOGATA HAD IMBUED IN HER...
...NOW BLOOMED INTO THE RESOLVE TO BE RESCUED.
I...WON'T LET YOU GO. NOT AGAIN!

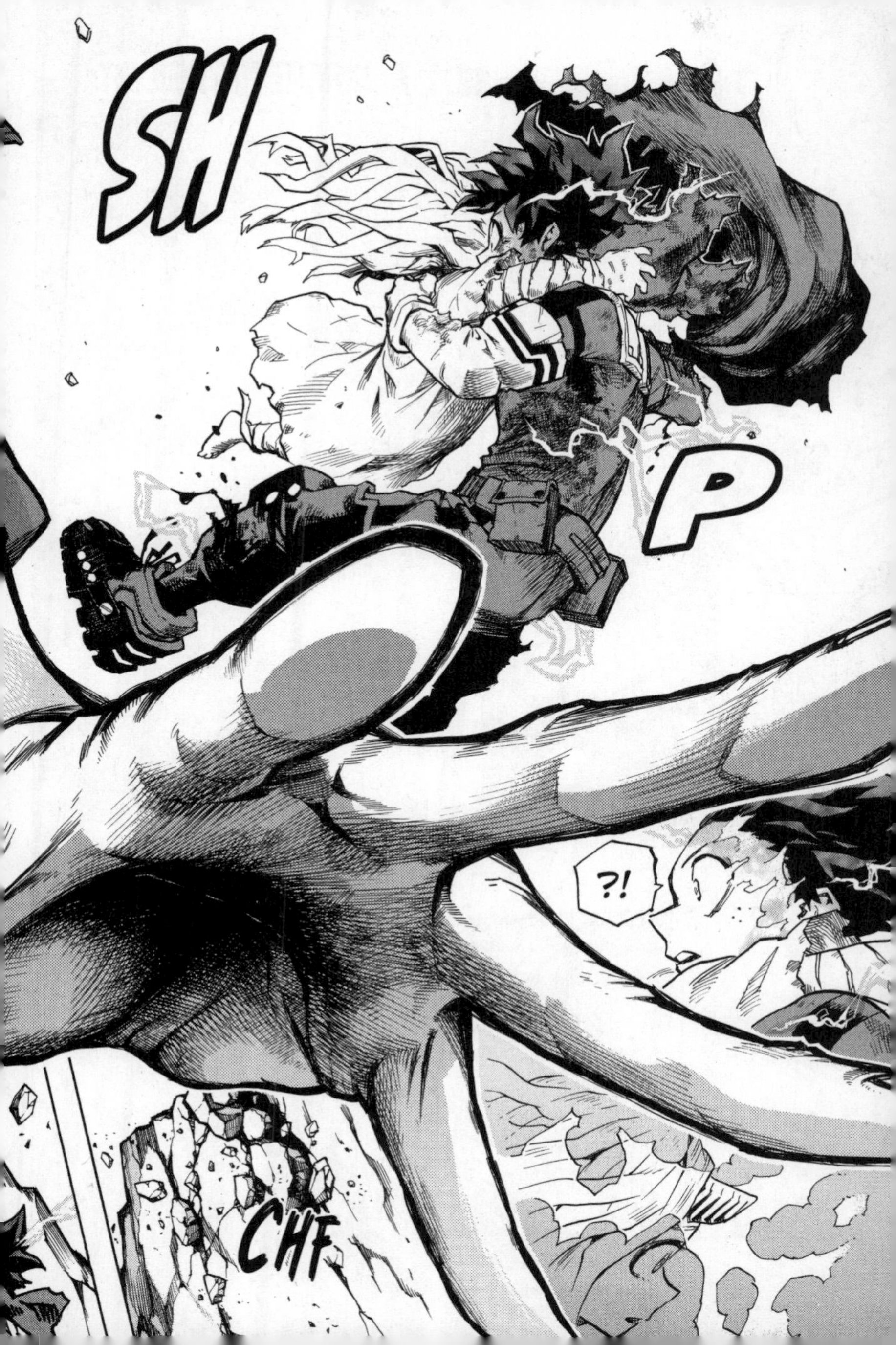
SH
P
?!
CHF

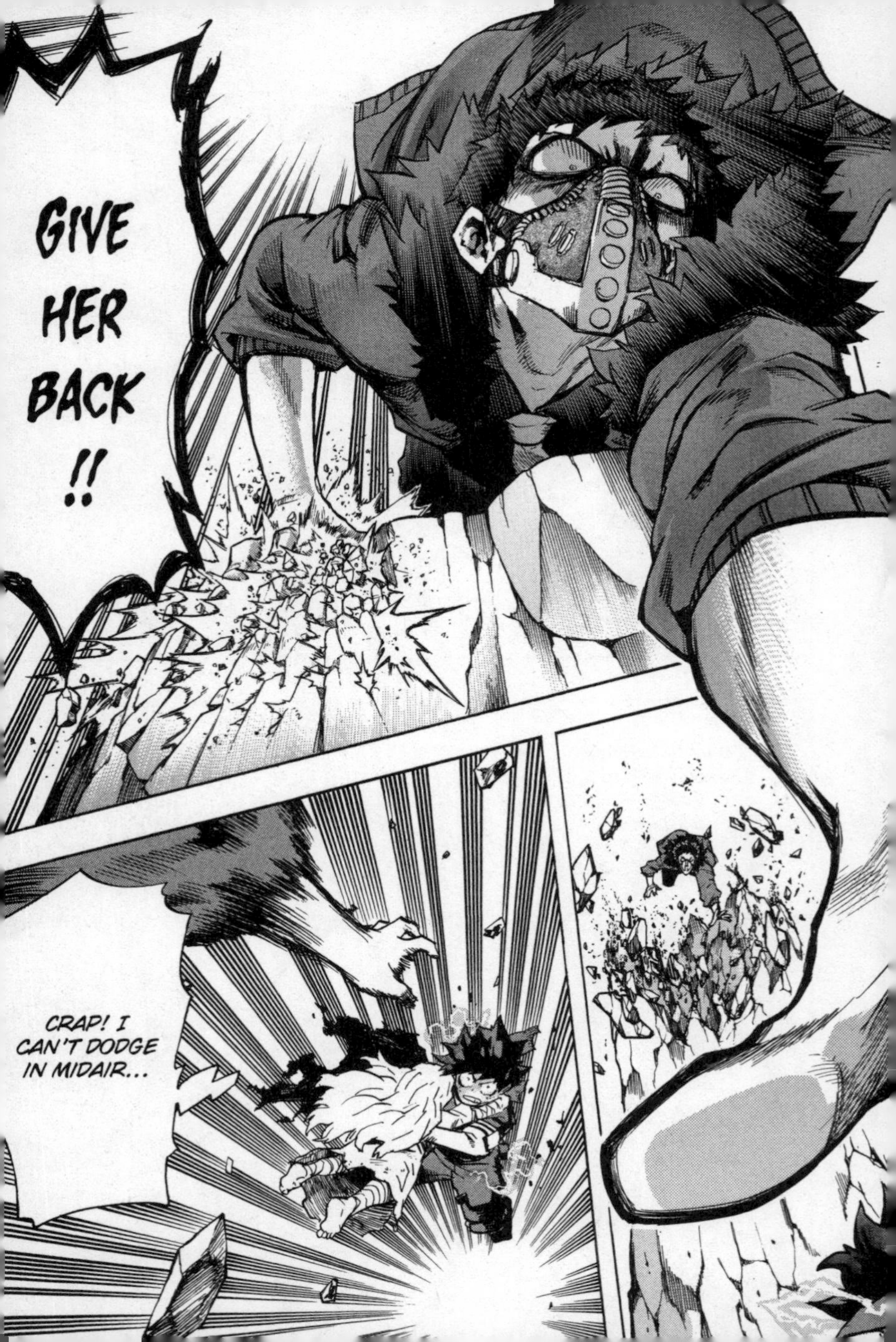
GIVE HER BACK !!
CRAP! I CAN'T DODGE IN MIDAIR...

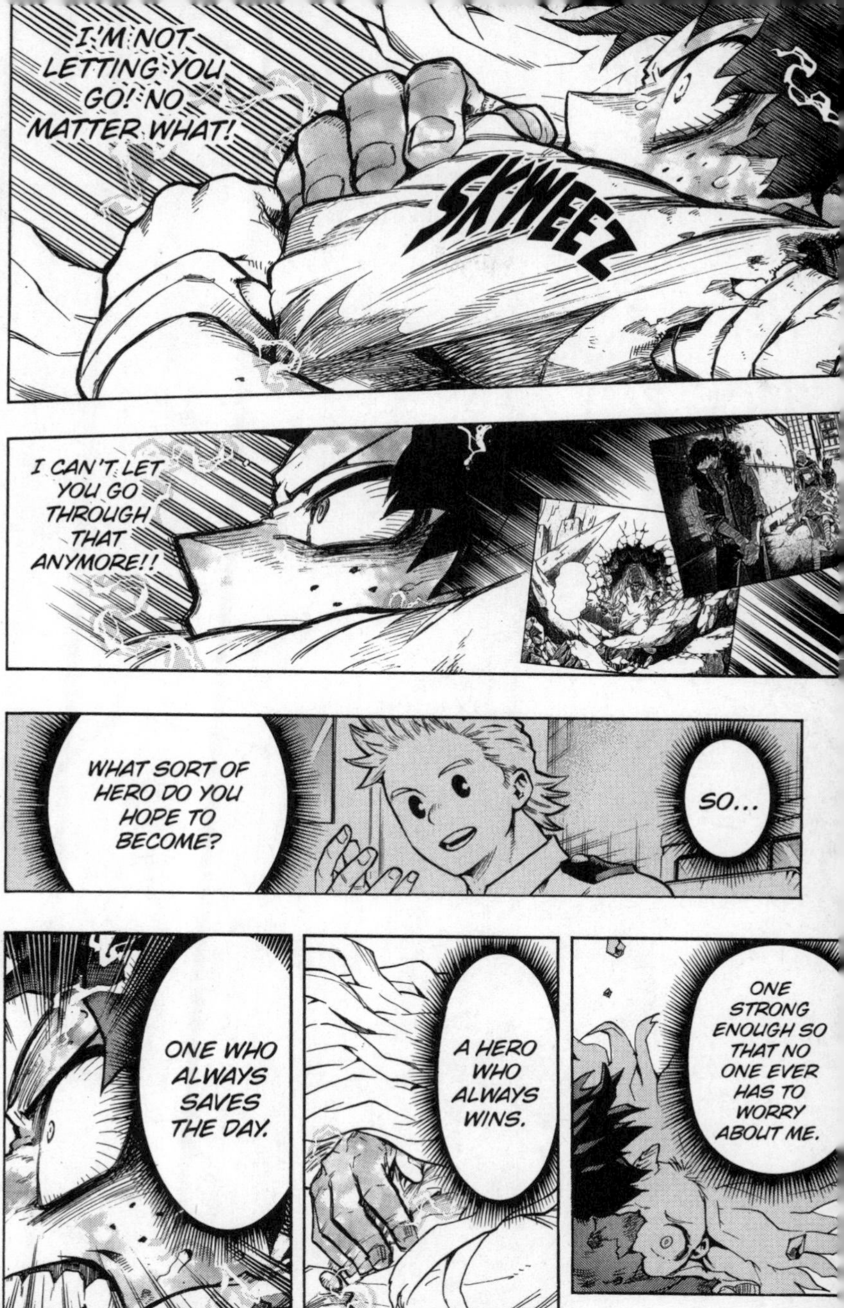
I'M NOT LETTING YOU GO! NO MATTER WHAT!
SKWEEZ
I CAN'T LET YOU GO THROUGH THAT ANYMORE!!
SO...
WHAT SORT OF HERO DO YOU HOPE TO BECOME?
ONE STRONG ENOUGH SO THAT NO ONE EVER HAS TO WORRY ABOUT ME.
A HERO WHO ALWAYS WINS.
ONE WHO ALWAYS SAVES THE DAY.

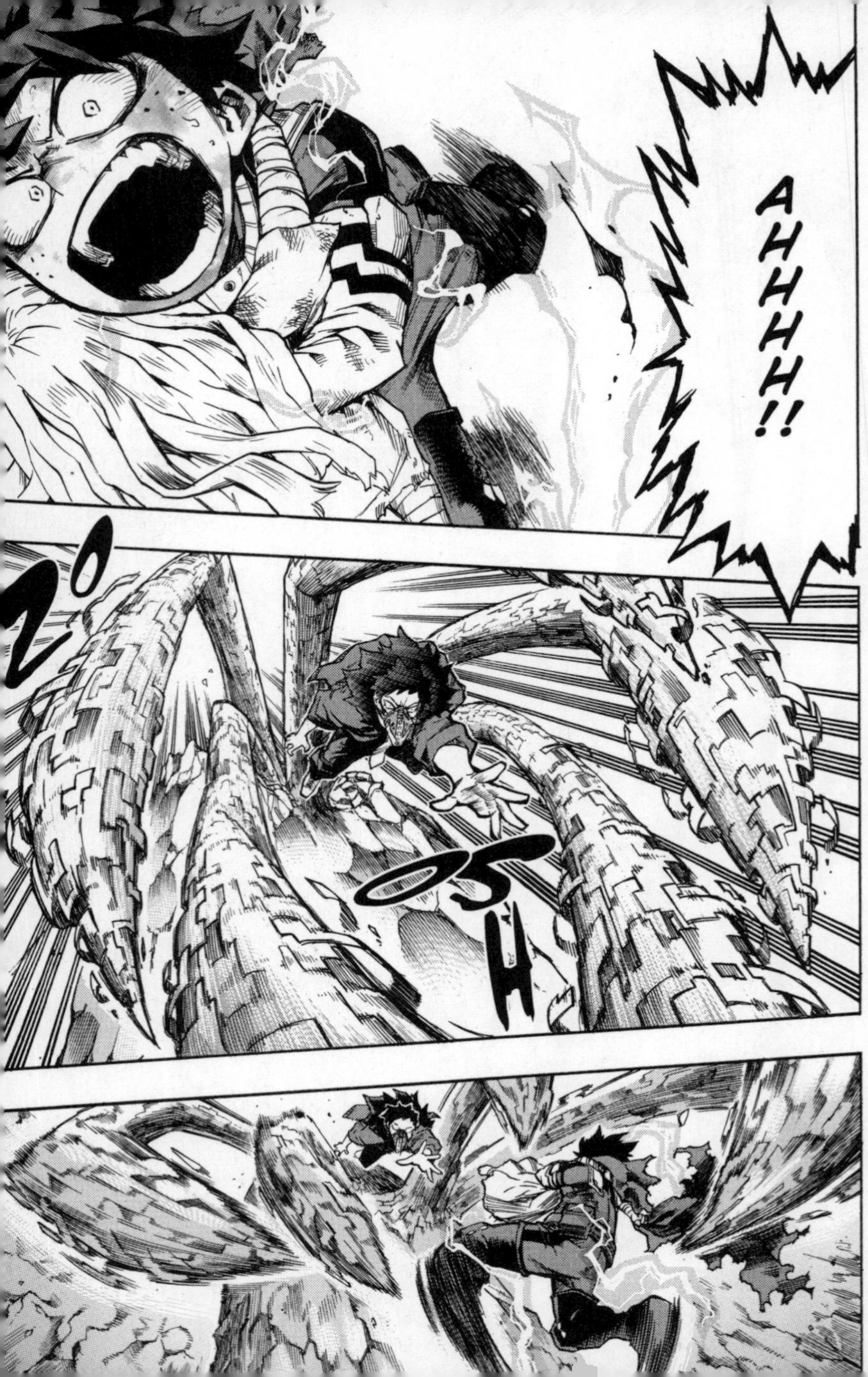
AHHHH!!
ZO

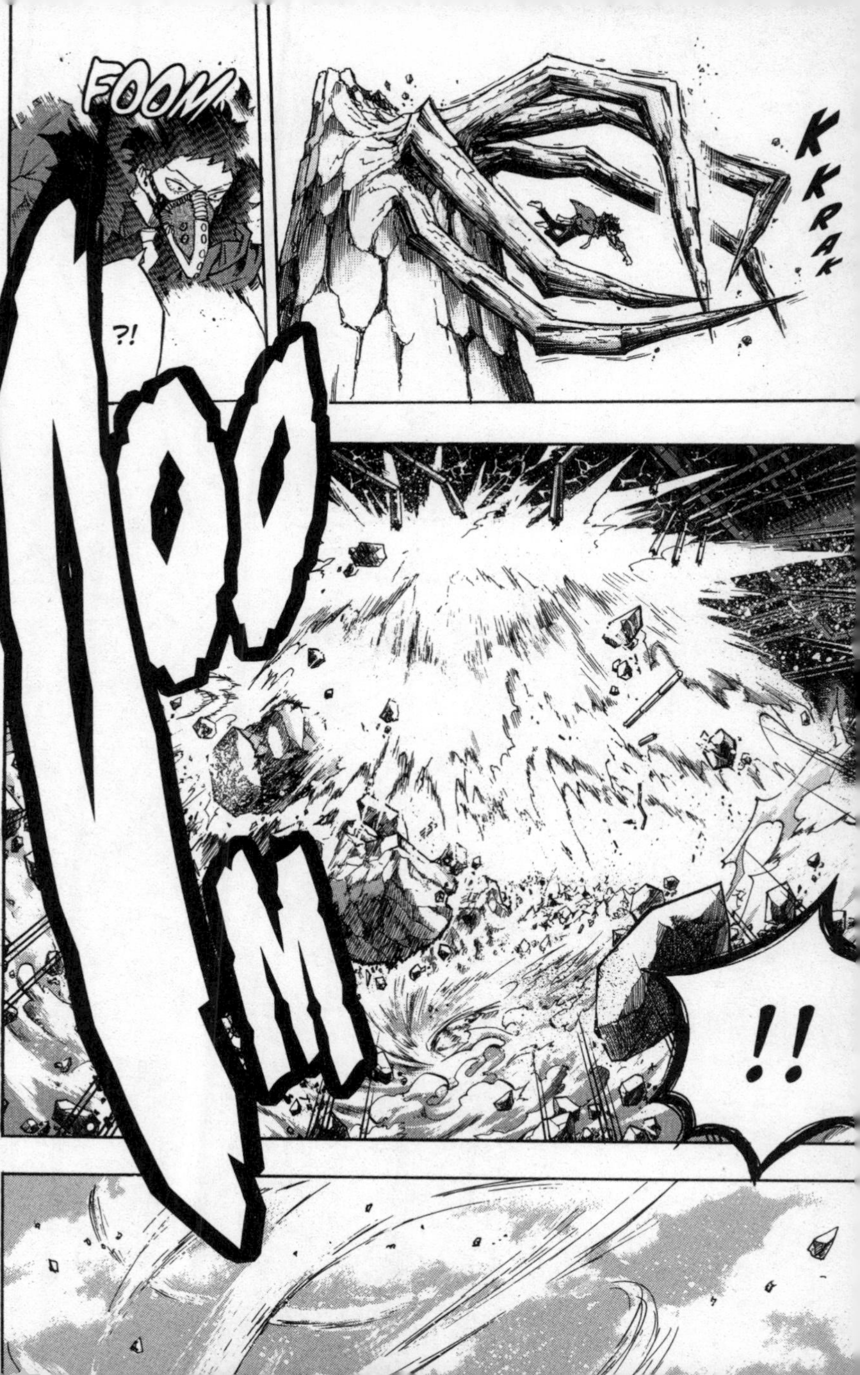
KKRAK
FOOM
?!
!!

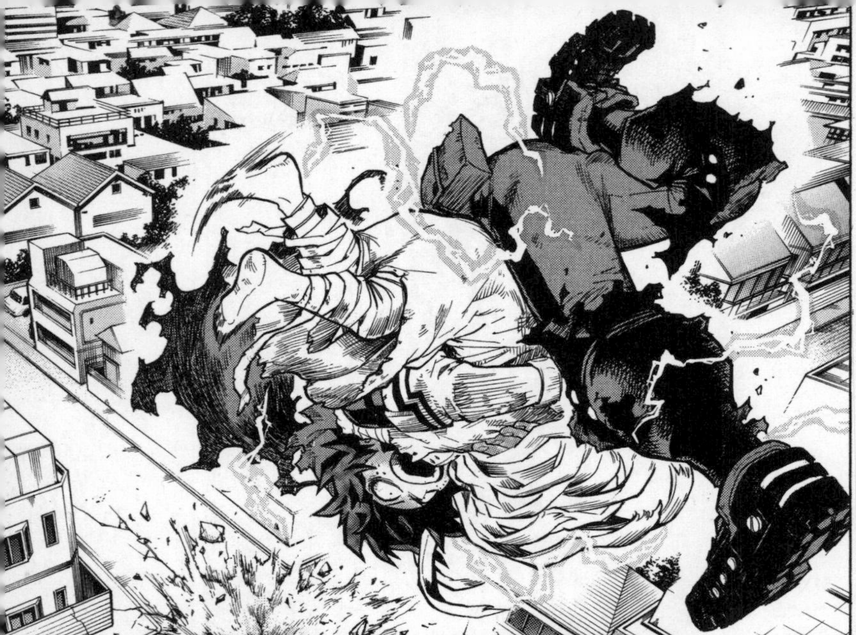

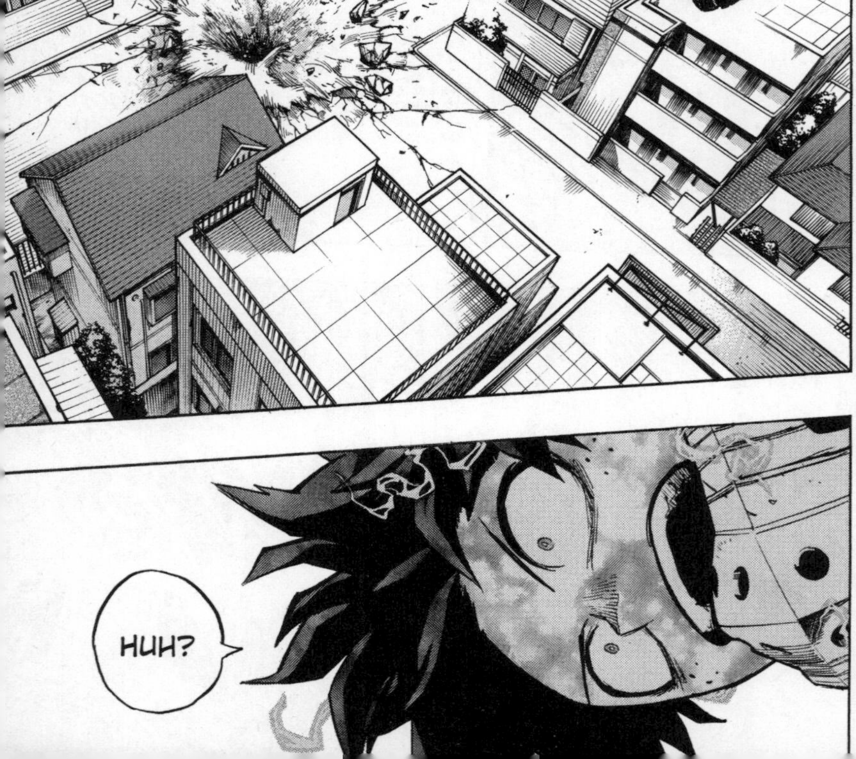
HUH?

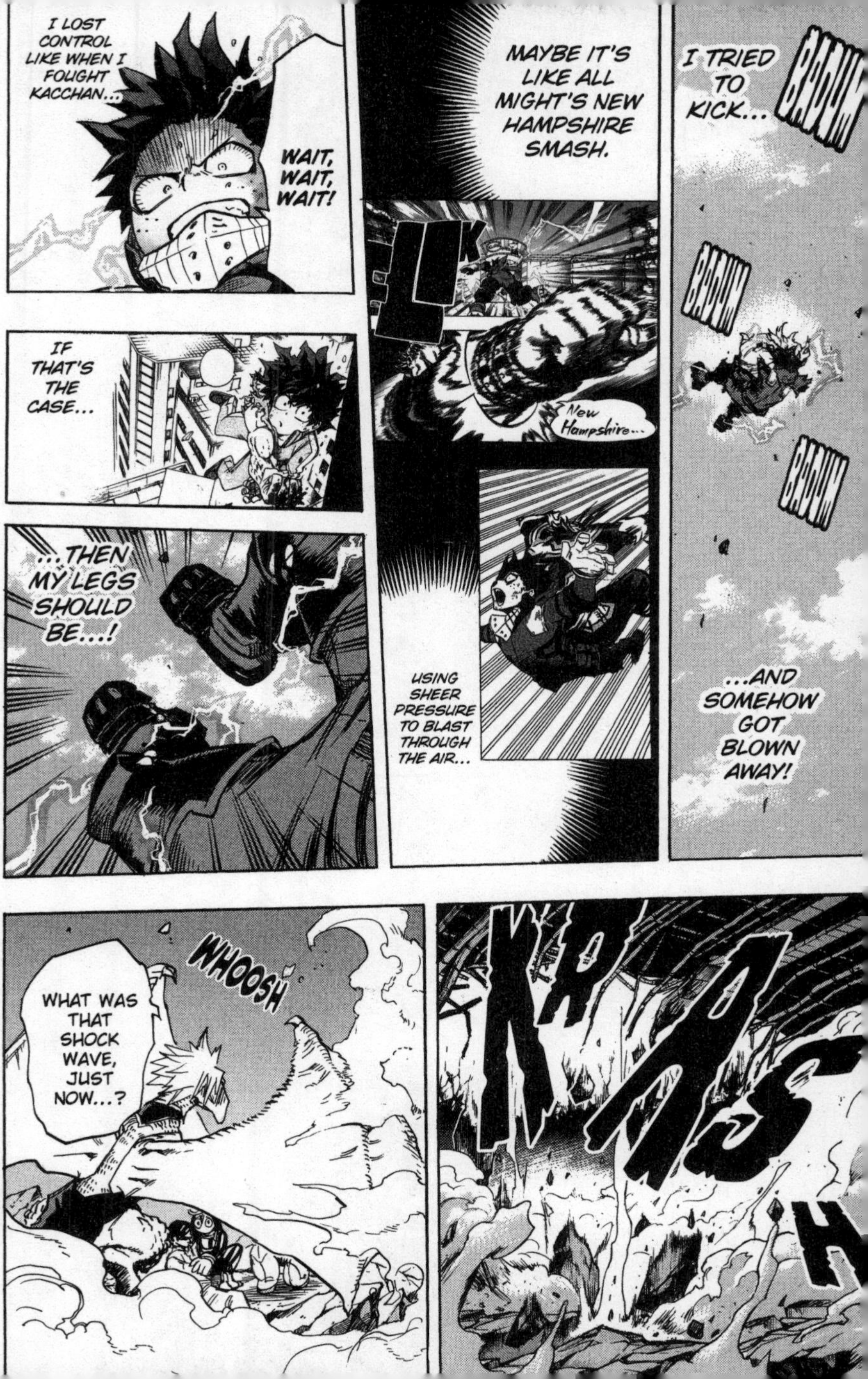
I TRIED TO KICK...
BADUM
BADUM
BADUM
...AND SOMEHOW GOT BLOWN AWAY!
MAYBE IT'S LIKE ALL MIGHT'S NEW HAMPSHIRE SMASH.
New Hampshire...
USING SHEER PRESSURE TO BLAST THROUGH THE AIR...
I LOST CONTROL LIKE WHEN I FOUGHT KACCHAN...
WAIT, WAIT, WAIT!
IF THAT'S THE CASE...
...THEN MY LEGS SHOULD BE...!
KRASH
WHOOSH
WHAT WAS THAT SHOCK WAVE, JUST NOW...?

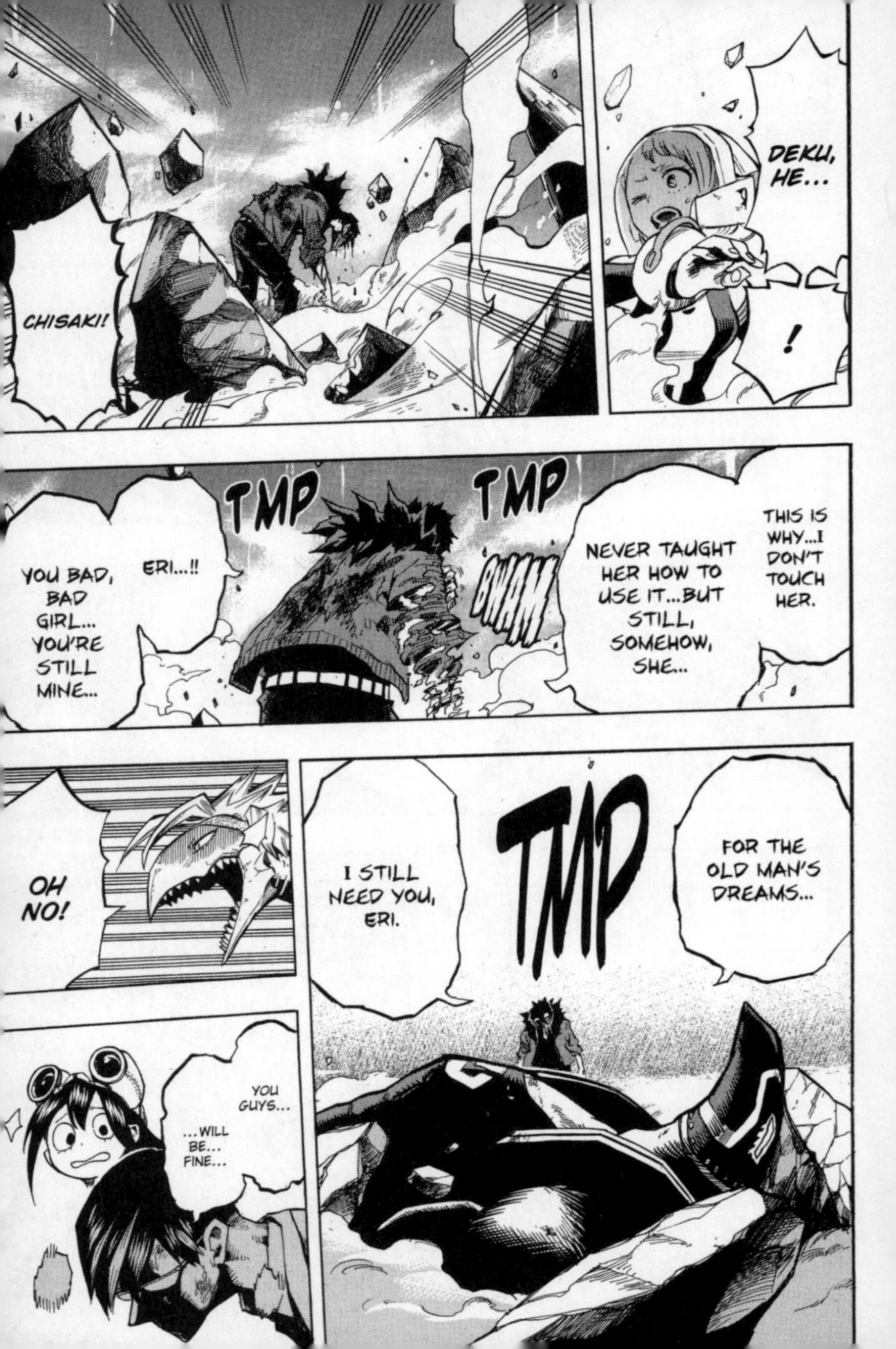
DEKU, HE...
!
CHISAKI!
THIS IS WHY...I DON'T TOUCH HER.
NEVER TAUGHT HER HOW TO USE IT...BUT STILL, SOMEHOW, SHE...
BWAM
TMP
TMP
ERI...!!
YOU BAD, BAD GIRL... YOU'RE STILL MINE...
FOR THE OLD MAN'S DREAMS...
TMP
I STILL NEED YOU, ERI.
OH NO!
YOU GUYS...
...WILL BE... FINE...

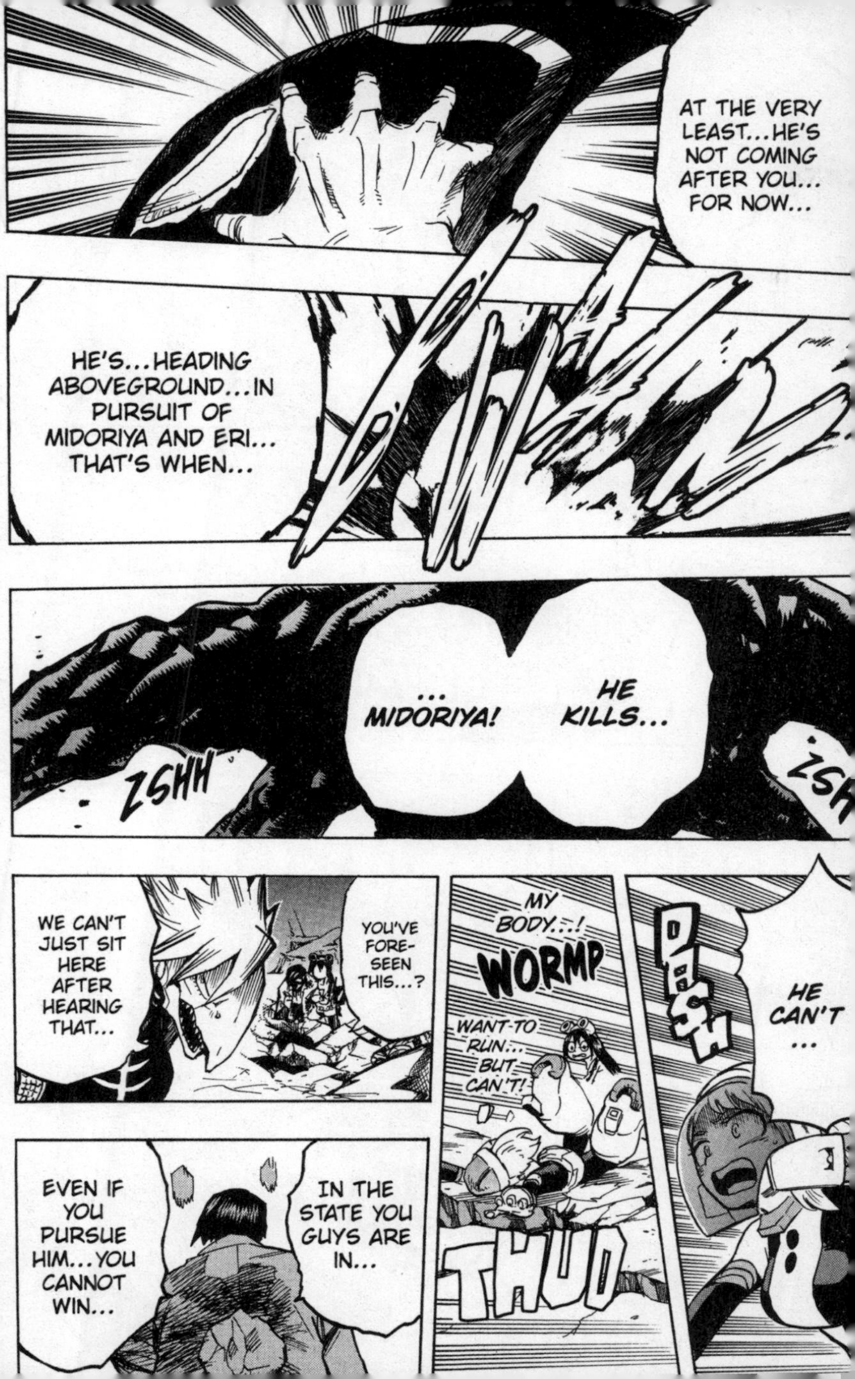
AT THE VERY LEAST...HE'S NOT COMING AFTER YOU... FOR NOW...
HE'S...HEADING ABOVEGROUND...IN PURSUIT OF MIDORIYA AND ERI... THAT'S WHEN...
ZSH
HE KILLS...
...MIDORIYA!
ZSHH
HE CAN'T ...
DASH
MY BODY...!
WORMP
WANT TO RUN... BUT CAN'T!
THUD
YOU'VE FORESEEN THIS...?
WE CAN'T JUST SIT HERE AFTER HEARING THAT...
IN THE STATE YOU GUYS ARE IN...
EVEN IF YOU PURSUE HIM...YOU CANNOT WIN...

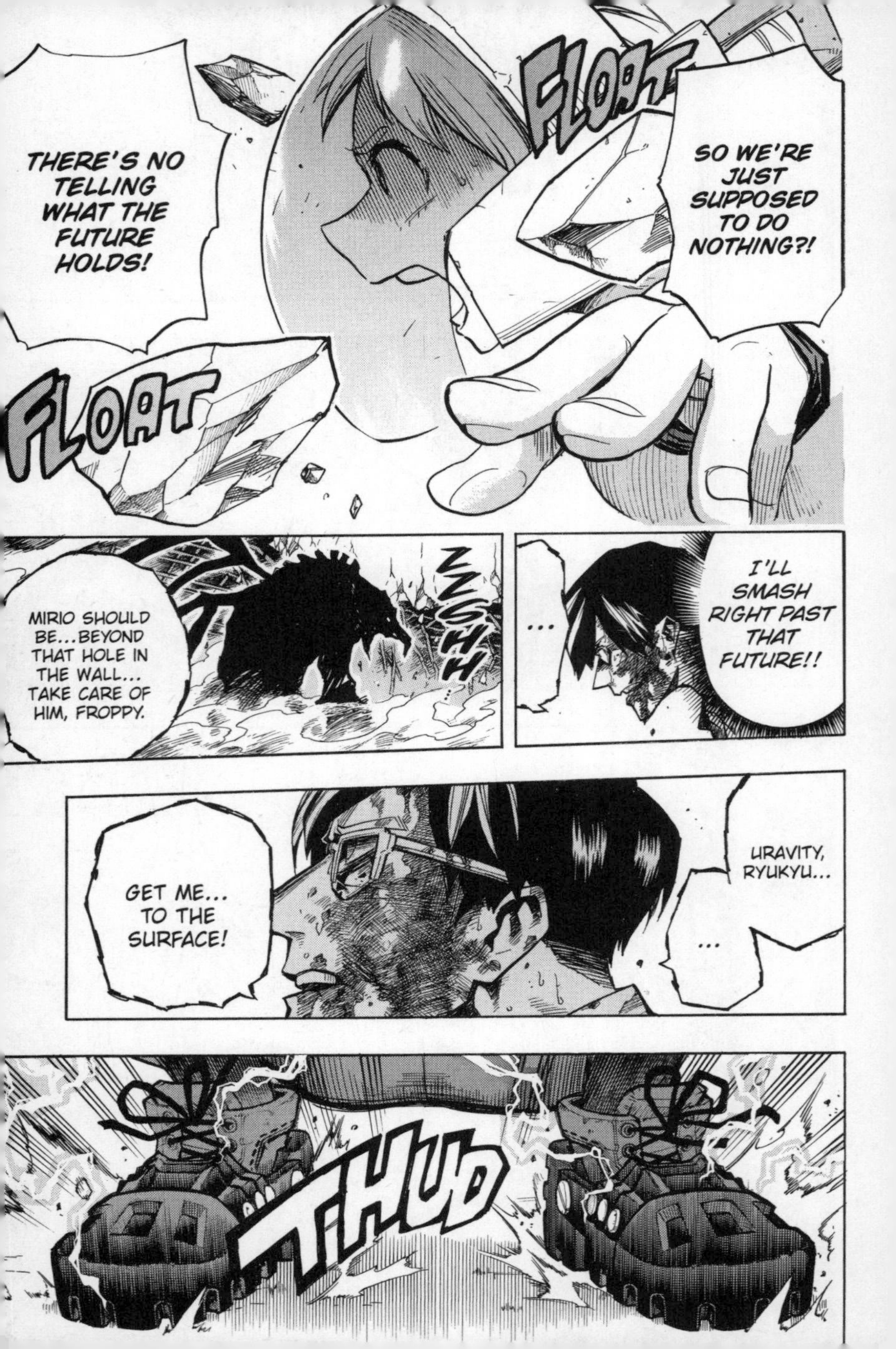
FLOAT
SO WE'RE JUST SUPPOSED TO DO NOTHING?!
THERE'S NO TELLING WHAT THE FUTURE HOLDS!
FLOAT
I'LL SMASH RIGHT PAST THAT FUTURE!!
...
ZWSHH...
MIRIO SHOULD BE...BEYOND THAT HOLE IN THE WALL... TAKE CARE OF HIM, FROPPY.
URAVITY, RYUKYU...
...
GET ME... TO THE SURFACE!
THUD

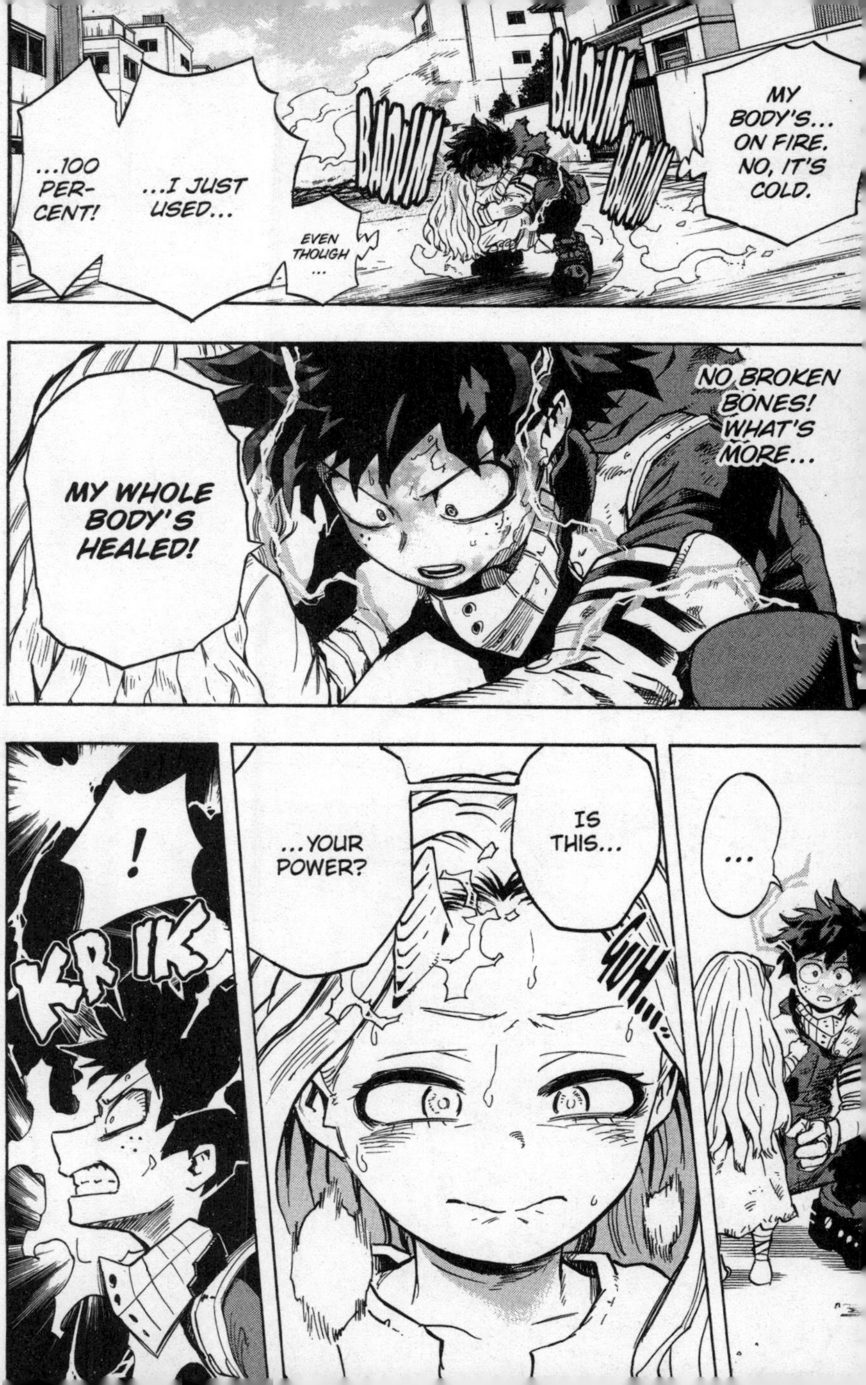
MY BODY'S... ON FIRE. NO, IT'S COLD.
EVEN THOUGH...
...I JUST USED...
...100 PERCENT!
NO BROKEN BONES! WHAT'S MORE...
MY WHOLE BODY'S HEALED!
...
IS THIS...
...YOUR POWER?
!
KRIK

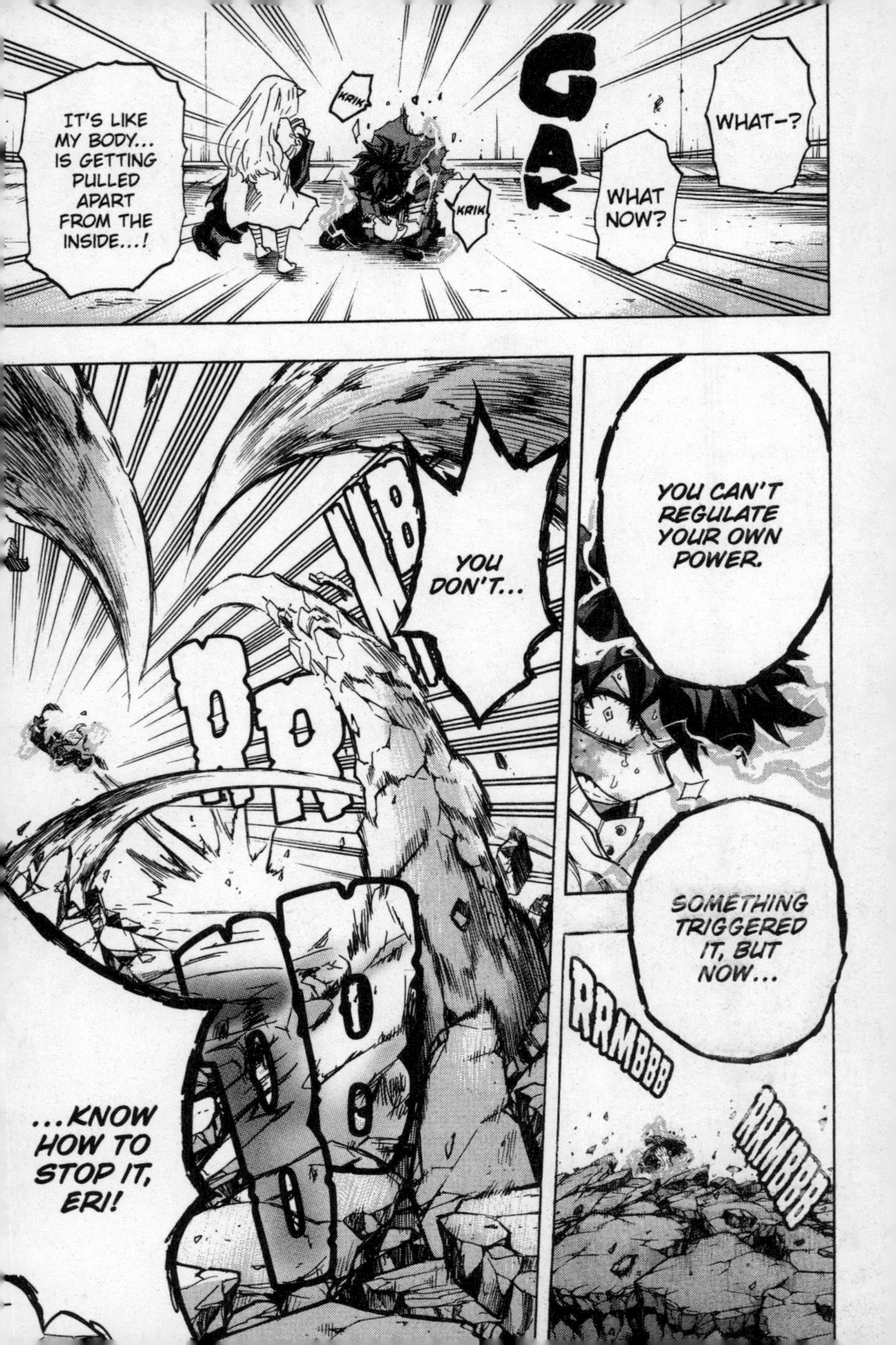
WHAT-?
WHAT NOW?
GAK
KRIK
KRIK
IT'S LIKE MY BODY... IS GETTING PULLED APART FROM THE INSIDE...!
YOU CAN'T REGULATE YOUR OWN POWER.
SOMETHING TRIGGERED IT, BUT NOW...
RRMBBB
RRMBBB
YOU DON'T...
...KNOW HOW TO STOP IT, ERI!

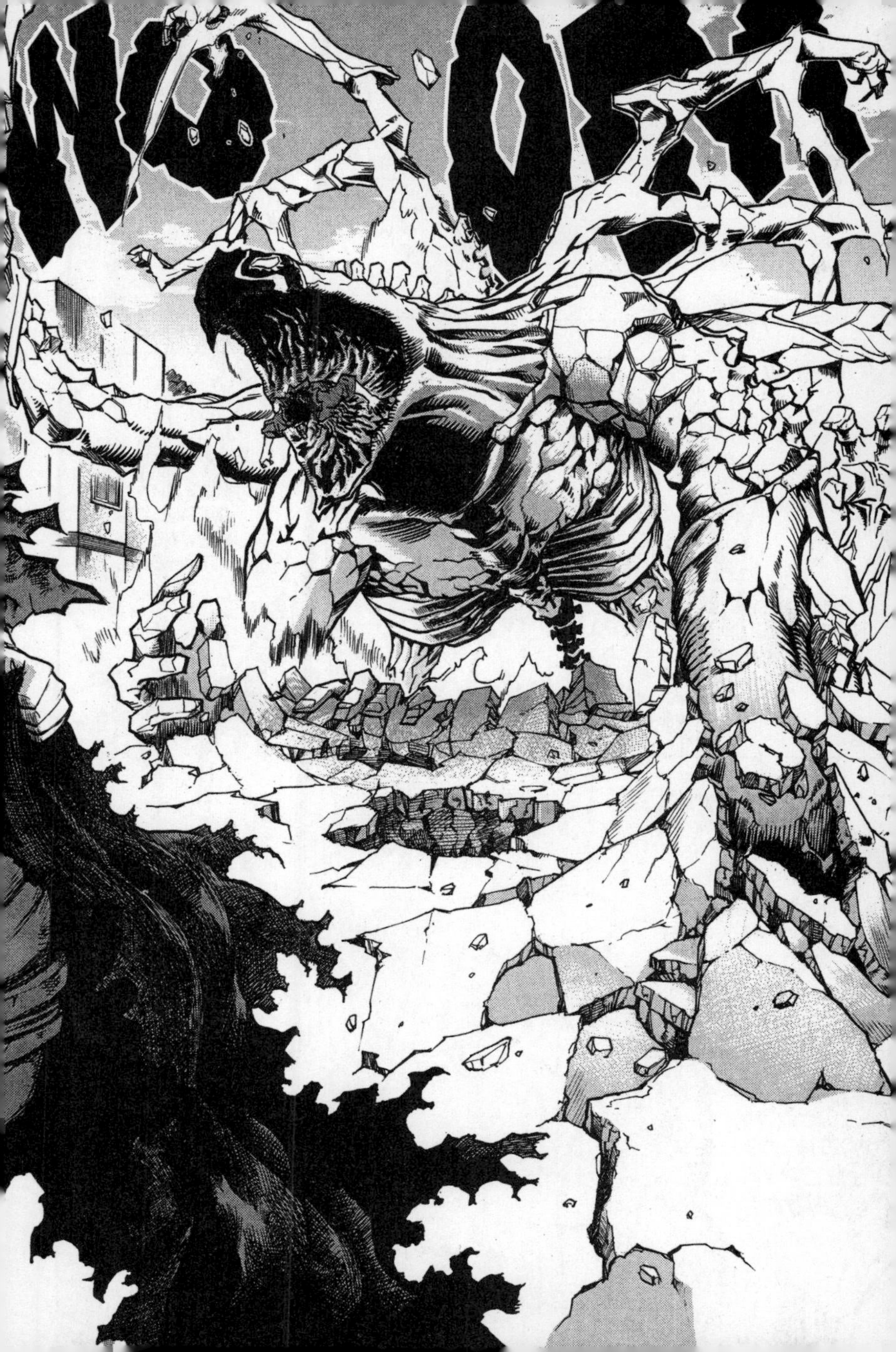

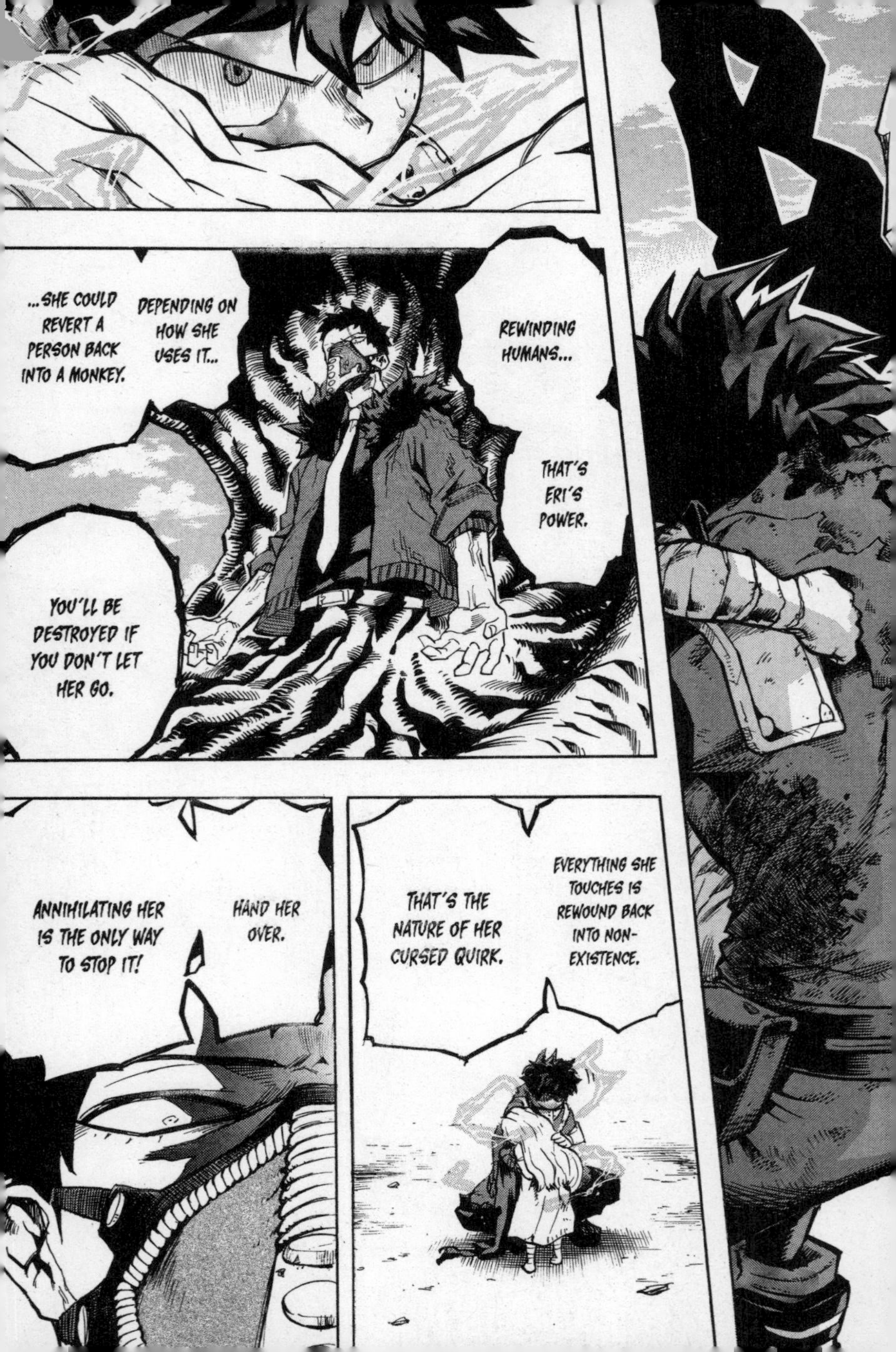
REWINDING HUMANS...
THAT'S ERI'S POWER.
DEPENDING ON HOW SHE USES IT...
...SHE COULD REVERT A PERSON BACK INTO A MONKEY.
YOU'LL BE DESTROYED IF YOU DON'T LET HER GO.
EVERYTHING SHE TOUCHES IS REWOUND BACK INTO NON-EXISTENCE.
THAT'S THE NATURE OF HER CURSED QUIRK.
HAND HER OVER.
ANNIHILATING HER IS THE ONLY WAY TO STOP IT!

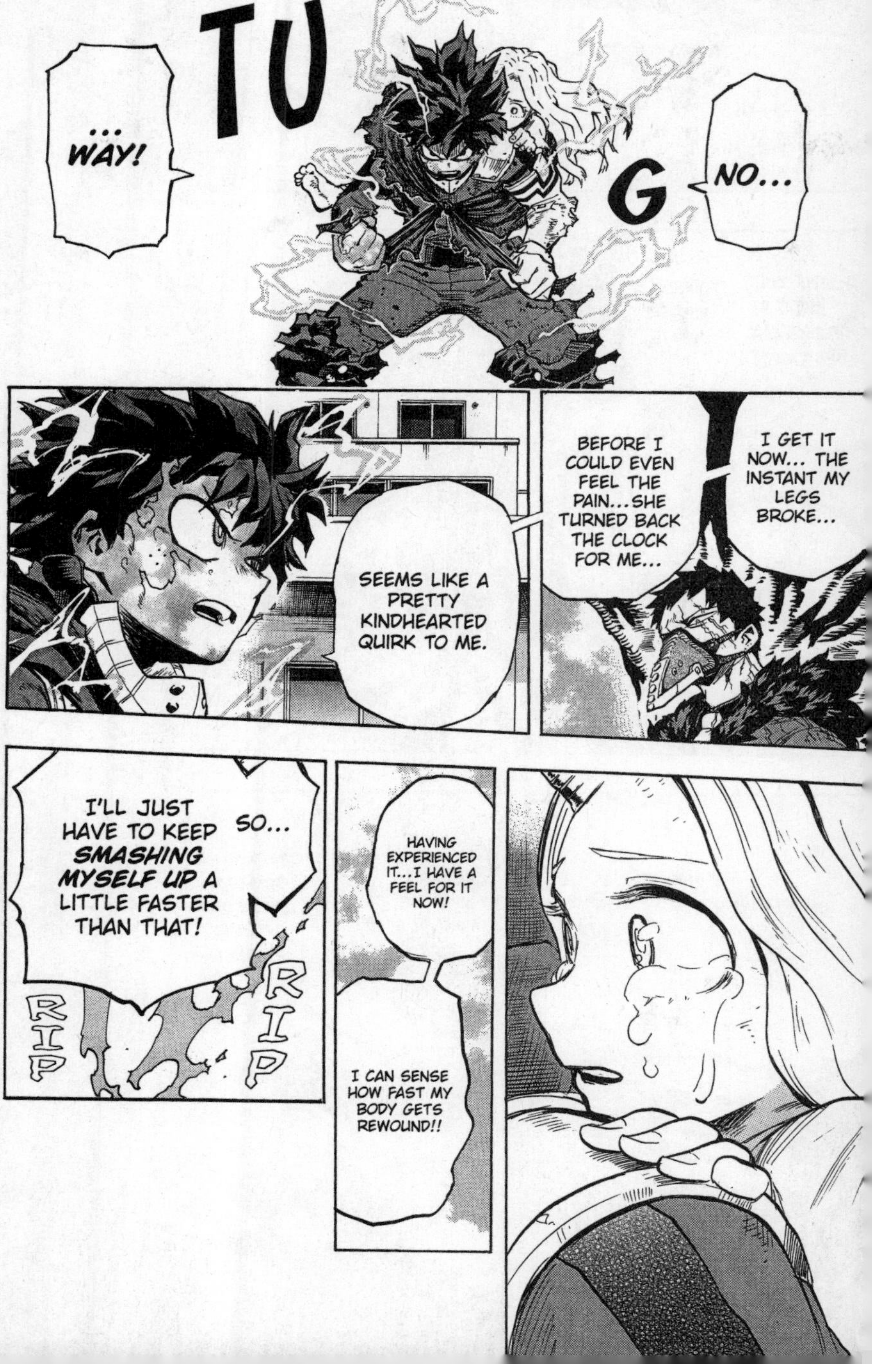

NO...
TU
G
...WAY!
I GET IT NOW... THE INSTANT MY LEGS BROKE...
BEFORE I COULD EVEN FEEL THE PAIN...SHE TURNED BACK THE CLOCK FOR ME...
SEEMS LIKE A PRETTY KINDHEARTED QUIRK TO ME.
HAVING EXPERIENCED IT...I HAVE A FEEL FOR IT NOW!
I CAN SENSE HOW FAST MY BODY GETS REWOUND!!
SO...
I'LL JUST HAVE TO KEEP SMASHING MYSELF UP A LITTLE FASTER THAN THAT!
RIP RIP
RIP RIP

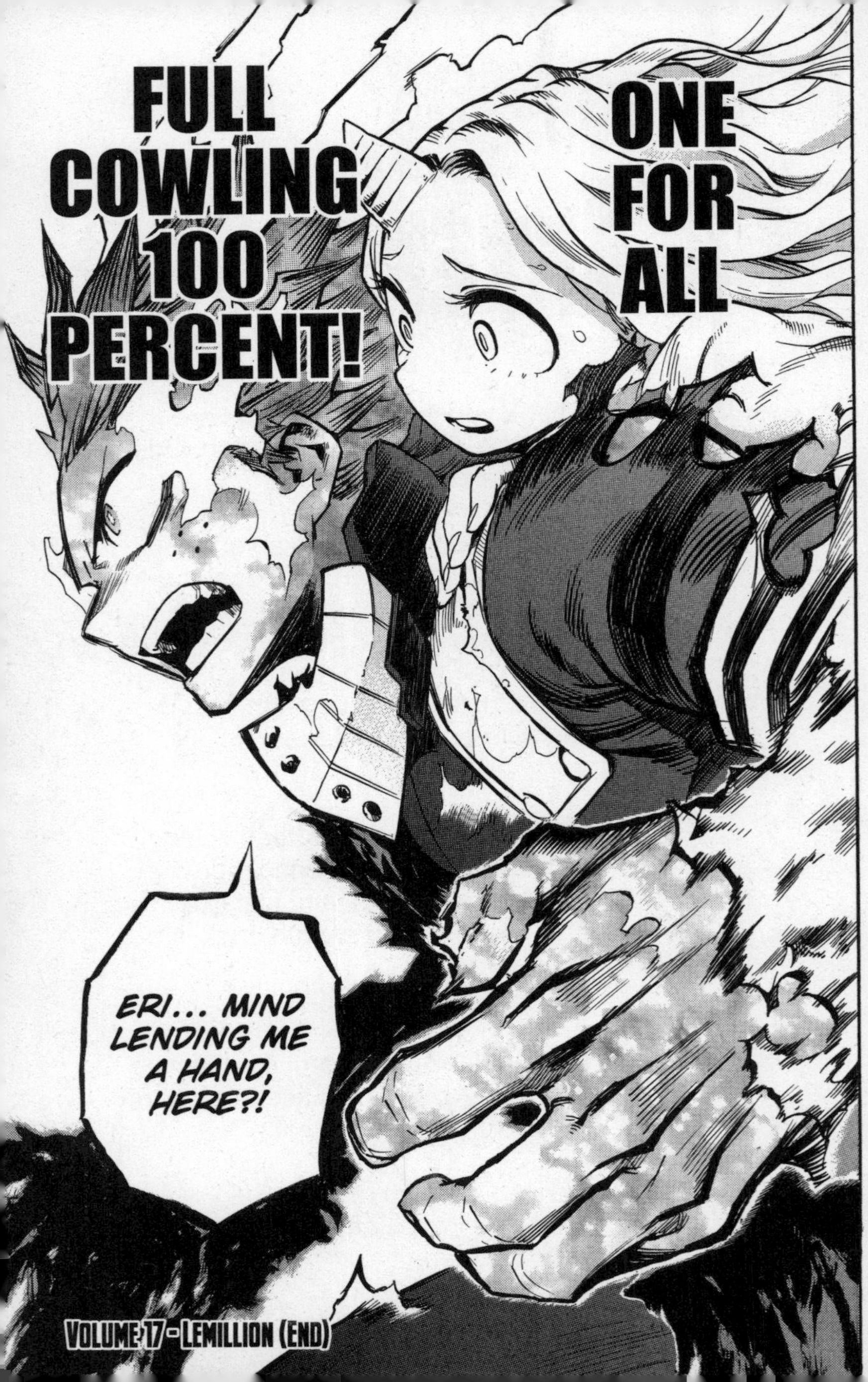
ONE FOR ALL
FULL COWLING 100 PERCENT!
ERI... MIND LENDING ME A HAND, HERE?!
VOLUME 17 - LEMILLION (END)

THE AFTERWORD!

Thank you for reading!! This arc sure is a long one, but it'll conclude in the next volume.

Also, I want to thank everyone for all the fan letters! They're just the thing to cheer me up, so I appreciate them. There isn't enough time in the world to reply to all of them. Instead, I'm using this space to express my gratitude!

When I'm dead tired after finishing up a draft, my editor brings me a stack of fan letters, and just like that, I've got my strength back. No exaggeration.

Energy drinks don't feel so effective to me lately, so now I use fan letters instead.

I'll keep drawing, and I hope everyone keeps enjoying the series! Until next time!!

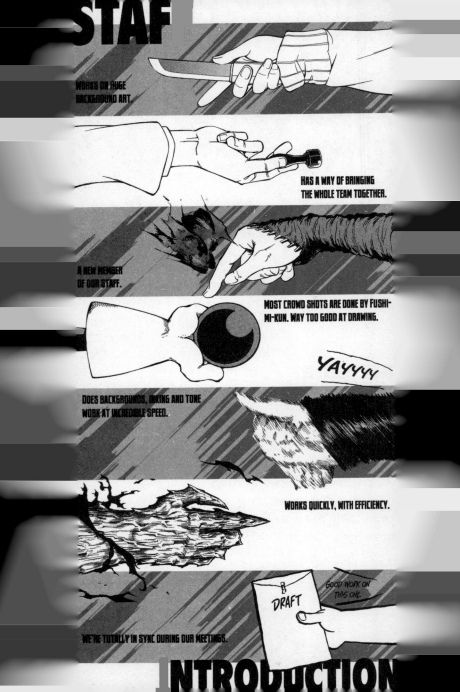

WORKS ON HUGE
BACKGROUND ART.

HAS A WAY OF BRINGING
THE WHOLE TEAM TOGETHER.

A NEW MEMBER
OF OUR STAFF.

MOST CROWD SHOTS ARE DONE BY FUSHI-
MI-KUN. WAY TOO GOOD AT DRAWING.

YAYYYY

DOES BACKGROUNDS, INKING AND TONE
WORK AT INCREDIBLE SPEED.

WORKS QUICKLY, WITH EFFICIENCY.

DRAFT

GOOD WORK ON
THIS ONE.

WE'RE TOTALLY IN SYNC DURING OUR MEETINGS.

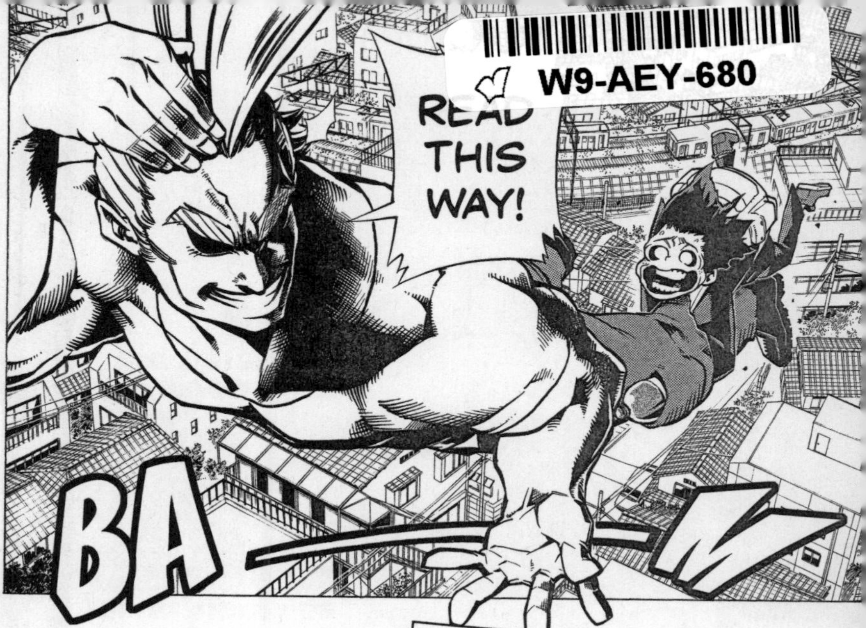
READ THIS WAY!
BA M

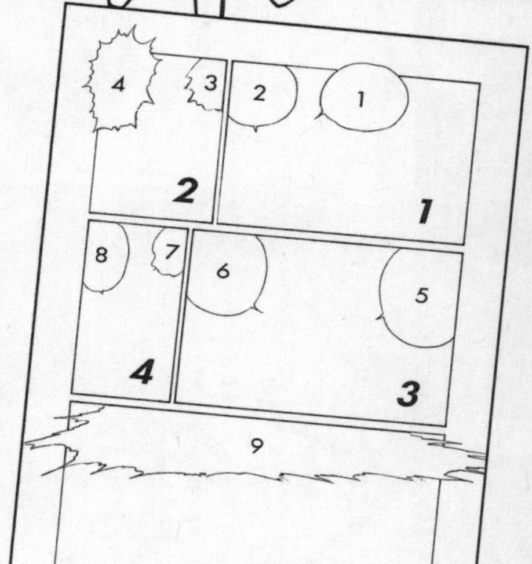
1
1
2
3
2
4
5
3
6
7
4
8
9
5
142

MY HERO ACADEMIA

reads from right to left, starting in the upper-right corner. Japanese is read from right to left, meaning that action, sound effects and word-balloon order are completely reversed from English order.

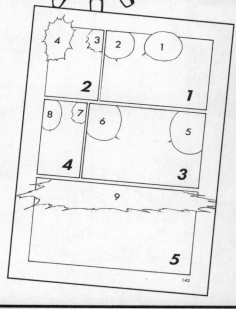